MW00784069

INTEGRATING ANALYSES IN MIXED METHODS RESEARCH

Sara Miller McCune founded SAGE Publishing in 1965 to support the dissemination of usable knowledge and educate a global community. SAGE publishes more than 1000 journals and over 800 new books each year, spanning a wide range of subject areas. Our growing selection of library products includes archives, data, case studies and video. SAGE remains majority owned by our founder and after her lifetime will become owned by a charitable trust that secures the company's continued independence.

Los Angeles | London | New Delhi | Singapore | Washington DC | Melbourne

INTEGRATING ANALYSES IN MIXED METHODS RESEARCH

PAT BAZELEY

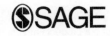

Los Angeles | London | New Delhi
Singapore | Washington DC | Melbourne

Los Angeles | London | New Delhi
Singapore | Washington DC | Melbourne

SAGE Publications Ltd
1 Oliver's Yard
55 City Road
London EC1Y 1SP

SAGE Publications Inc.
2455 Teller Road
Thousand Oaks, California 91320

SAGE Publications India Pvt Ltd
B 1/I 1 Mohan Cooperative Industrial Area
Mathura Road
New Delhi 110 044

SAGE Publications Asia-Pacific Pte Ltd
3 Church Street
#10-04 Samsung Hub
Singapore 049483

Editor: Jai Seaman
Assistant Editor: Alysha Owen
Production editor: Tom Bedford
Marketing manager: Susheel Gokarakonda
Cover design: Shaun Mercier
Typeset by: C&M Digitals (P) Ltd, Chennai, India
Printed by: CPI Group (UK) Ltd, Croydon, CR0 4YY

© Patricia Bazeley 2018

First published 2018

Apart from any fair dealing for the purposes of research or
private study, or criticism or review, as permitted under the
Copyright, Designs and Patents Act, 1988, this publication
may be reproduced, stored or transmitted in any form, or
by any means, only with the prior permission in writing of
the publishers, or in the case of reprographic reproduction,
in accordance with the terms of licences issued by
the Copyright Licensing Agency. Enquiries concerning
reproduction outside those terms should be sent to the
publishers.

Library of Congress Control Number: 2017936758

British Library Cataloguing in Publication data

A catalogue record for this book is available from
the British Library

ISBN 978-1-4129-6185-1
ISBN 978-1-4129-6186-8 (pbk)

At SAGE we take sustainability seriously. Most of our products are printed in the UK using FSC papers and boards.
When we print overseas we ensure sustainable papers are used as measured by the PREPS grading system.
We undertake an annual audit to monitor our sustainability.

CONTENTS

LIST OF FIGURES,
TABLES AND BOXES

Figures

Tables

Boxes

PREFACE: A FOCUS ON ANALYSIS

With the popularisation of mixed methods has come realisation that there are many ways to think about and practise the integration of different data sources and analyses well before conclusions are being drawn. Some of these methods are long established, but many are fresh and developing, as researchers capitalise on and share their creative skills, often supported by the capacity of software to provide new (or more accessible) opportunities for data management, analysis, and integration.

In this book I focus on the various ways in which different approaches to data collection and analysis can be integrated during the *analysis* stage of a project. Other resources focus on *designing* for integration of methods, and it is assumed that the reader has some familiarity with these. Similarly, there are multiple resources available covering both basic and advanced strategies for statistical and other forms of quantitative analysis, and for various approaches to qualitative analysis. Again, it is assumed the reader (or members of the team of which the reader is a member) has familiarity with these; they will not be specifically covered in this book.

This book and the strategies described in it are premised on the belief that data analysis in all behavioural and social research, regardless of the method(s) being used, requires a combination of empiricism and interpretation. Further, to deeply understand human experience and human behaviour at any level, whether that be individual, group, or societal, it is beneficial, if not essential, to employ a variety of approaches, components, data, and/or strategies for data collection and analysis. Integration of those elements is then needed to ensure coherence in results, to satisfy the purpose of the study and to answer the questions asked.

The text is set out in three parts:

- Part 1 provides foundations and a framework for understanding and undertaking integrated analyses in mixed methods inquiry.
- Part 2 describes a comprehensive range of strategies for integrating mixed methods sources and analyses and illustrates each of these with specific examples. Mixed methods projects might involve one of these strategies, a combination of several, or an innovative approach that combines parts to make new wholes.

- Part 3 provides suggestions to help readers maximise the potential of their analyses as they seek to develop coherent outcomes that achieve the goals of their research.

Links to additional resources for the mixed methods analyst are available on the companion website for this book. In addition, two databases are provided in various formats, to allow readers to explore and experiment with strategies using mixed sources of data in their preferred software. Several of the examples in this book have been drawn from these databases.

The *Performance* database is derived from a brief questionnaire containing closed and open questions, sent to all academics in three varied universities at a time when Australia was first introducing performance assessment for research into the university system. For each of eight characteristics, the academics were asked to think about and describe a researcher they knew who might have that characteristic. They were also asked to rate the relative importance of each of those characteristics for doing research, and for assessing research. Data are provided as coded text supplemented by variable data in NVivo, MAXQDA, Dedoose, and QDA Miner formats.

The *Wellbeing* database is extracted from a current project looking at what wellbeing means for older women, how that relates to health, and at the role that gender and age specific, community-based activity centres can have in enhancing the health and wellbeing of older women. Data sources include a group discussion, interviews, a report from survey data, some variable data, links to video data, cultural domain data, and literature. An interim report from the project is also included within the NVivo database.

ACKNOWLEDGEMENTS

Given the multiple chapters and articles I had already written on integrating mixed methods analyses, and the number of years I had been experimenting with different approaches to integrating analyses, I innocently believed that writing a book length version of what I had learned would be straightforward. How mistaken I was! Writing this book has been a long, rather lonely, and always demanding enterprise, all too often interrupted by life events. Throughout, I have benefited from the patient encouragement of Jai Seaman, Sage commissioning editor. Anonymous reviewers provided useful feedback, and colleagues provided reassurance that my endeavour was not being undertaken in vain.

I am indebted to the developers of the four qualitative analysis programs covered in the text for their assistance in providing me with access to their software, for permission to use screen displays of their software, including some directly from their websites, and for their helpful responses when I have had questions. Thank you to QSR International (NVivo), Verbi GmbH (MAXQDA), Provalis Research (QDA Miner), and SocioCultural Research Consultants LLC (Dedoose).

Finally, thank you to those scholars whose work has provided me with the many examples I have used throughout this book. It would have been very obscure and boring without these accounts of your research endeavours. Special thanks go to the Older Women's Network of New South Wales, and the many wonderful volunteers and members whose data are included in the *Wellbeing* sample project database.

ONLINE RESOURCES

Integrating Analyses in Mixed Methods Research is supported by a wealth of online resources to aid study and support teaching, which are available at https://study.sagepub.com/bazeley.

- Read **scholarly journal articles** selected to accompany each chapter to deepen your knowledge and reinforce your learning of key topics explained in the book.
- See how an integrated analysis works in action and master your data analysis skills with the **datasets** ready to upload into MAXQDA, NVivo, Dedoose, and QDA Miner.
- Expand your knowledge and follow real-world conversations on integrating analysis and mixed methods research with resources drawn from SAGE Research Methods.
- Download free trials of MAXQDA, NVivo, Dedoose, and QDA Miner via trial weblinks to see which software suits you and your research best.

PERMISSIONS

Permission to use copyrighted material was granted by the following authors and publishers:

Michelle Howell Smith	Table 4.1, from Howell Smith, M. C. (2011). *Factors that facilitate or inhibit interest of domestic students in the engineering PhD: A mixed methods study.* (PhD), University of Nebraska-Lincoln (p. 69, Table 5).
Jannet Pendleton, University of Technology, Sydney	Figure 6.4
Wiley Online Library (John Wiley & Sons)	Figure 6.6, from Kanzaki, H. et al. (2004). Development of web-based qualitative and quantitative data collection systems: study on daily symptoms and coping strategies among Japanese rheumatoid arthritis patients. *Nursing & Health Sciences*, 6(3), 232, Figure 2.
	Figure 6.7, from Wendler, M. C. (2001). Triangulation using a meta-matrix. *Journal of Advanced Nursing*, 35(4), 153, Figure 1.
American Academy of Family Physicians	Figure 6.1, from Crabtree, B. F. et al. (2005). Delivery of clinical preventive services in family medicine offices. *Annals of Family Medicine*, 3(5), 430-435, Supplemental Table 1 (partial).
	Figure 10.3 and Table 10.1, from from Scott, J. G. et al. (2005). Social network analysis as an analytic tool for interaction patterns in primary care practices. *Annals of Family Medicine*. 3(5), 446, Figure 2, and 447, Table 1.
IBM SPSS Statistics	Figures 8.6, 8.8, 9.4, 9.5, 9.7, and 9.10. IBM, the IBM logo, ibm.com, and SPSS are trademarks or registered trademarks of International Business Machines Corporation, registered in many jurisdictions worldwide. Other product and service names might be trademarks of IBM or other companies. A current list of IBM trademarks is available on the Web at "IBM Copyright and trademark information" at www.ibm.com/legal/copytrade.shtml.

PART 1

A FOUNDATION FOR
INTEGRATED ANALYSIS

Mixed methods, as an approach to research, has both a long and a short history. During those histories, researchers across both natural and social sciences have instinctively embraced both numbers and words to understand and communicate their discoveries. They have fought paradigmatic and disciplinary condemnation and wars, there has been marriage and separation. But now a "mixed methods movement" has been birthed, or perhaps "rebirthed", to the critical acclaim of researchers who seek legitimation of what is really an obvious choice – to use whatever combination of approaches and methods best suits their purposes and best answers their questions. This book focuses on the analytic work being done by those researchers who choose to combine methods of data collection and analysis in an approach now commonly referred to as mixed methods research. This first part of the book helps to prepare readers for mixed methods analysis by reviewing the foundations of the mixed methods movement and of mixing methods in research on the one hand, and on the other, by reviewing the preliminary steps to analysis that need to be considered if methods are to be effectively and productively mixed.

Integration of data sources and analyses during the course of undertaking a research project is key to mixed method analysis. Indeed, coherence in pulling together elements of theory, information gained, and insight is critical in any research project. Integration doesn't necessarily just happen, however. Also integral to effective, productive, and integrated mixed methods research is thoughtful planning ahead by the researcher, while he or she also remains open and flexible about a design that might need to adapt to unexpected circumstances or interim results. Elements of design that impact on analysis are therefore included in this Part 1 review of preliminary steps to analysis.

Part 1 then concludes with consideration being given to the interpretive nature of analysis and the analytic process. Regardless of the specific methods used, thoughtful judgement must be exercised in assessing the meaning and significance attached to data, to what is learned through manipulating data, and in determining the next step to take in analysis. The claim of those using mixed methods is that by thoughtfully combining methods they will advance a more rounded, more complete, and better developed understanding of the phenomenon being studied than would otherwise occur. It is hoped this will be your experience also.

1

MIXED METHODS IN CONTEXT

CHAPTER OVERVIEW

Why mix methods?

In their report to the Mixed Methods International Research Association (MMIRA) on the future of mixed methods, Mertens et al. (2016a: 12) proposed that researchers live and act in a world that is faced with "wicked problems" and "grand challenges". Wicked problems "involve multiple interacting systems, are replete with social and institutional uncertainties, and [are those] for which there is no certainty about their nature and solutions", while grand challenges arise from multiple environmental, social, and political sources, or combinations of these. This complexity, evident across many fields of action and inquiry, demands methods able to investigate a problem from multiple viewpoints, with flexibility to adapt to changing situations, yet able to produce credible results convincing to diverse audiences.

Social and behavioural researchers employing mixed methods ask complex questions and engage with complex, real-world environments in a socially responsive and responsible way. They go beyond laboratory-based experimentation in which single variables are manipulated under tightly controlled conditions, or studies that observe and describe some small facet of life or practice. Rather, they flexibly employ a diversity of approaches to embrace the multiple perspectives that behavioural, social, and professional complexities demand. Laurel Richardson's (2000) image of the multifaceted and ever-changing crystal, as a model of what happens when qualitative methods are used, seems even more appropriate for mixed methods approaches. Mertens et al. (2016b: 222) described mixed methods as kaleidoscopic with its "seemingly unpredictable patterns full of rich possibilities for diversity and potential to provide opportunities to see things that have not yet been seen". Mixing methods is purposeful, however, rather than random: a "mixed methods way of thinking [intentionally invites] into the same inquiry space multiple ways of seeing and understanding and [engages] respectfully and dialogically with these multiple ways of knowing toward generative insights and better understanding" (Greene, 2012b).

This chapter briefly reviews the development of mixed methods as a recognised movement and approach to social research, key definitions with implications for the way methods are viewed in this book, and approaches to resolving the ontological and epistemological debates that arose when mixed methods began to be explicitly discussed as an approach to research.

The emergence of a mixed methods movement

The combination of multiple methods has an extended history in evaluation and sociological research, and an even longer one in the natural sciences (Maxwell, 2016). Mixed methods thinking and writing can be traced back at least to the eighteenth-century Enlightenment, while paradigm debates can be traced back to the classical Greek scholars, several hundred years BC (Johnson & Gray, 2010). *The Philadelphia Negro*, by W. E. B. DuBois, a field study published in 1899, may have been the first published report to explicitly integrate qualitative and quantitative methods in an attempt to overcome errors associated with either alone (Maxwell, 2016) – although

DuBois did not use the terms *qualitative* or *quantitative* in describing his methods. The field studies of the Chicago School sociologists and social psychologists that followed in the early to mid-twentieth century freely combined multiple methods, for example, in studies of community life in America. Despite the dominance of experimentation and statistical testing in the mid-twentieth century, mixed methods continued to be used unproblematically by some sociologists as well as those in psychology and organisation studies during this period. In citing the psychological studies of Festinger, Riecken, and Schachter (1956) and Milgram (1974) as illustrative, Maxwell suggested that the work of these researchers has largely been ignored by more recent mixed methodologists. Their authors focused on the content area of the study and did not explicitly identify their studies as employing mixed methods, rather, presenting them more as quantitative studies, conforming to the trend at the time.

The 1970s and 1980s then heralded the construction and promotion of a paradigm incompatibility thesis among social scientists in which differing philosophical positions concerning the nature of reality and of knowledge construction became linked with methodologies and methods. This was prompted by Kuhn's (1970) influential writing on the role of paradigmatic shifts in major scientific advances and spurred on by Lincoln and Guba's (1985) promotion of an alternative constructivist paradigm supporting "naturalistic inquiry" using qualitative methods. Irreconcilable conflict was then presumed to exist between qualitative (inductive, observational, interpretive) and quantitative (deductive, experimental, statistical) approaches to social research. The ensuing debates, often referred to as the "paradigm wars", drew attention to the practice of combining multiple methods within a single project, but they also had the effect of complicating and setting back the adoption of mixed methods in the social sciences and the professional disciplines, especially in the United States. While most mixed methods researchers have since worked out a satisfactory resolution of these issues that allows them to progress their own work, remnants of these debates still exist in subtle ways that continue to impede integration of methods for many. For example, the creation of a sharply drawn division between qualitative and quantitative methods, with rules built around this division, continues to limit researcher initiative in thinking about problem-focused sources of data and methods of analysis. Limited communication between communities of practice among mixed methods researchers across geographic continents and in different discipline areas, for example between those in management and organisation studies and those in health and education, also impeded shared development of strategies for integrating methods.

Thus, the practice of mixing methods is not at all recent, but the recognition of mixed methods as a third major approach to social science research, or as a methodological movement in addition to qualitative and quantitative approaches, is relatively recent, dating from the later decades of the twentieth century. The consequent burgeoning of theoretical literature and published research studies in handbooks, texts and new journals has both fed and been fed by increasing popularisation of mixed methods as an approach to the broad domain of research in the social and behavioural sciences and in education and health in particular. As mixed methods move into the mainstream, the danger is that some of the "creativity, inventiveness, and risk taking" characteristic of it as a "methodological innovation" will be lost (Fielding, 2012: 125).

Defining the mixed methods territory

Studies are infinitely variable in the way methods are used and combined. To clearly define and set boundaries for mixed methods as an approach to research is difficult if not impossible, and any attempt to do so is bound to be disputed. Johnson, Onwuegbuzie, and Turner (2007) listed and reviewed 19 definitions of mixed methods contributed by then leaders in the field in an attempt to arrive at a composite definition:

> Mixed methods research is the type of research in which a researcher or team of researchers combines elements of qualitative and quantitative research approaches (e.g., use of qualitative and quantitative viewpoints, data collection, analysis, inference techniques) for the purposes of breadth and depth of understanding and corroboration. (Johnson et al., 2007: 123)

This definition covers *what* is being combined and the *purpose* of combination, yet agreement is not universal even with this limited formulation. The majority of researchers consulted by Johnson et al. considered that mixed methods necessarily involves a combination of both qualitative and quantitative approaches, but not all did so. Researchers can (and do) include mixes of methods without predefining each as qualitative or quantitative. Others deliberately include reference to combinations that would generally be considered as belonging to the same overall approach (e.g., grounded theory with ethnography or phenomenology; interviews with document analysis, an experiment combined with a questionnaire). Similarly, "combines" is very differently interpreted and practised by different researchers. There is general agreement that the combination of methods in a mixed methods study is designed to contribute insights and understanding beyond that derived from the component parts. Opinions differ, however, as to whether those components are able to make independent contributions as well as contribute to a mixed outcome (Creswell & Tashakkori, 2007), or if defining a study as mixed carries an inherent assumption that at least one of the components will be subservient to and incomplete without the other (Morse & Niehaus, 2009). Yin (2006) argued that for methods to be genuinely integrated rather than parallel, comparability and mixing is needed at all points in a study, from question setting, through design, sampling, and instrumentation, to analytic strategies.

Recently I reviewed a series of articles to evaluate trends in adoption of mixed methods among management researchers (Bazeley, 2015a). The boundary issues become very apparent when one attempts a task such as this. How much qualitative data and how much analysis and reporting of that data are necessary in a predominantly quantitative study to warrant classification as mixed method? Does inclusion of some numeric data and/or reports of counts (e.g., of themes) in a qualitative article make it mixed? When do studies that draw on different sources and types of data (possibly including coded text) to create variables used in a variety of statistical analyses cross the boundary into mixed methods? What about those that draw on varied sources and types of qualitative data using varied approaches to analysis to eventually build an integrated narrative account and/or model of an experience or process? When I had to make a decision about these, a critical consideration was not whether there were sources that could be defined somehow as qualitative and quantitative, but rather, whether a "conversation" between the different sources and/or methods used was evident within the analysis, continuing into the presentation of results and discussion of those results.

Do definitions and boundaries matter? Even the boundary between qualitative and quantitative methods lacks clear delineation. As long as we have a shared idea of the core of what is being discussed, then boundary issues are important only for methodological comparative reviews and for determining where to publish methodological (rather than substantive) articles. Paul Vogt (2008) regards these debates as a distraction from the more important issues of determining what methods will best answer the questions being asked, and of focusing on the phenomenon to be studied. He points to pain as an example of a *subjective* experience often measured with a *scale*, which might then be used in answering a *categorical* question (surgery or not?). "We believe that the quantitative-qualitative argument is essentially unproductive ... quantitative and qualitative methods are 'inextricably intertwined', not only at the level of specific data sets but also at the levels of study design and analysis" (Miles & Huberman, 1994: 41).

Integration as a core component

If boundaries are porous, and quantitative plus qualitative is both disputed and inadequate as a distinguishing feature, is it possible to define a study as using mixed methods? Teddlie and Tashakkori (2012: 775) proposed nine characteristics based on common practice, but several of these are characteristics of quality research of any type. I propose just one core characteristic to distinguish mixed methods from other approaches to research. I treat *mixed methods* as a generic term to include any research that involves multiple sources and types of data and/or multiple approaches to analysis of those data, in which *integration* of data and analyses occurs prior to drawing final conclusions about the topic of the investigation. A study in which integration occurs only as conclusions are being drawn from separate substudies would be better described as multimethod than mixed method (although the boundary here is porous as well).

Integration asks about the relatedness, or degree of "mutual illumination" (Bryman, 2007: 8) occurring between the different components of a mixed methods study. I define integration, therefore, in terms of the relationship between methods in reaching a common theoretical or research goal (Bazeley, 2010a: 432): *purposeful interdependence* between the different sources, methods, or approaches used is the critical characteristic that distinguishes integrated mixed methods from a monomethod or even a multimethod approach to research. Interdependence speaks to a "conversation or debate" between findings, leading to a "negotiated account" (Bryman, 2007: 21), a meaningful two-way exchange of information and inferences between varied types of sources gathered and/or analytic strategies employed during the design and analysis processes of a study, without which the component parts cannot fully function in meeting the overall study purpose. Sources and strategies might be predominantly quantitative, predominantly qualitative, or a hybrid mix of these. This has implications for setting boundaries, but more importantly, it points to the core of what makes methods mixed without being restrictive in defining how that interdependence is to be achieved.

Ultimately what matters for research is not whether a study meets some abstract criterion, but whether the methods chosen and the strategies used, be those single or multiple, independent or interdependent, serve the *purpose* of the research.

Terminology

As with definitions, so also many terms associated with mixing methods have been proposed and debated since combined methods of data collection have been specifically discussed. Some methodologists have been concerned that what was being mixed were not necessarily methods, while others considered "mixed" as inappropriate. Max Bergman concluded:

> Disputes about an appropriate terminology are part of any discipline. ... diverging from an established terminology also leads to confusion, rather than clarification, even though the initial aim may have been clarification. Until there are good reasons to abandon the now well-established term mixed, I suggest acquiescing to this terminology. (Bergman, 2011: 271)

Similarly, although we might not be particularly happy with the terms qualitative and quantitative when referring, for example, to text or numeric data types and related hermeneutic or statistical analysis strategies, or to the broadly defined approaches that employ these different data and strategies, it is less confusing to use these generally recognised terms as "shorthand" (Small, 2011) than to try to create or establish alternatives that are inevitably no more successful in defining territory. Describing the terms qualitative and quantitative as the "straw men" of research, Bergman (2008a: 14) suggested, rather, that qualitative and quantitative methods "represent large and heterogeneous families of methods under convenient headings", families so internally varied that most characteristics overlap and few are unique to one or the other.

Qualitative and quantitative: dimensions of difference

Phenomena, material or immaterial, intrinsically have both qualities *and* quantities. It is quite natural to describe an object or an event, or even an idea, using both qualifying words and numbers indicating magnitude or count or time – often in the same sentence: "The infection I acquired last Sunday was serious enough to give me a splitting headache and keep me in bed for four days." Quantities (time, sizes, even numbers themselves) have quality – their meaning is theory based (Gorard, 2010b) and relative to their context; qualities have quantity – they can be evaluated and counted. Different authors have attempted to distinguish qualitative and quantitative approaches to research in a variety of ways, most often on the basis of the type of data employed, or the form of their analysis. Others have added distinctions based on purpose and questions (e.g., exploratory or confirmatory); philosophical underpinning and approach (e.g., postpositivist or constructivist); design and methods (e.g., structured or unstructured); and data treatment, analysis, and interpretation (e.g., variable or process oriented).

Our inability to clearly specify a distinction that all of us generally sense is indicative of the lack of a clear and defining difference (Small, 2011). Examples of the presumed distinguishing features for one approach can be found also in research purporting to be of the supposed opposite approach (Pearce, 2015). Rather, what we are talking about is a continuum with multiple dimensions (or axes) along which any particular research investigation may be placed, with any one study rarely being entirely at one end or the other for all dimensions (think gender – see Box 1.1). If one uses numbers, interpretation is still involved (by both participant and researcher). If one's data are texts, counting and even statistical manipulation may still be appropriate for revealing trends and associations. Numeric data and statistical analyses might be used in an inductive, exploratory study; observational data and interviews in a deductive, confirmatory study. Variables do not necessarily have clear-cut meanings (with meanings as understood by researcher and participants often differing); processes can be revealed through numeric analyses as well as through narrative; and so on. Because there is no essential congruence between positions along the different dimensions of the quantitative–qualitative continuum within any one study, the terms quantitative and qualitative are most useful either for giving a sense of overall direction in a study (hence I prefer to refer to these as *approaches*), or simply as broad descriptors of the type of data or analyses being used. More specific terms or descriptions of any data or analysis components are likely to be more useful. Definitions of mixed methods, multimethod research, integration, and qualitative and quantitative, insofar as these terms are used in this book, are listed in Box 1.2.

BOX 1.1

A gender analogy

One might compare defining differences between qualitative and quantitative with defining differences between males and females. The characteristics of data and the research process override distinctions between qualitative and quantitative much as that which makes us human overrides the distinctions between male and female. Nevertheless, we do draw multiple distinctions between quantitative and qualitative, just as we draw multiple distinctions between being male or female. And similarly to studies identified as using quantitative or qualitative methods, each person demonstrates more or less of the various qualities that are associated with masculinity or femininity, although any one person can usually be identified as one or the other.

BOX 1.2

Defining core elements of the mixed methods territory for this book

In *mixed methods* research, varied approaches, sources of data, methods of data collection, and/or strategies for analysis are integrated during the process of achieving the purpose of the research. Multimethod research also uses varied strategies of data collection or analysis, but without integrating these prior to drawing final conclusions.

Integration occurs to the extent that different data elements and/or varied strategies for analysis of those elements are combined in such a way as to become interdependent (a two-way process) in reaching a common theoretical or research goal.

Quantitative approaches to research are those that focus on measuring or estimating the quantities of things, while *qualitative* approaches focus on describing and interpreting their qualities. These terms define the poles of a multidimensional continuum in which many descriptors are used to delineate the dimensions of this difference, with any piece of research being located at varying points along each of these multiple dimensions.

The challenge of integration

Integration presents challenges that are "undertheorized and understudied" (Greene, 2007: 125), and yet these designs constitute the heart of integrative mixed methods inquiry. Many mixed methods researchers experience difficulty in "bringing together the analysis and interpretation of the quantitative and the qualitative data and writing a narrative that link[s] the analyses and interpretations" (Bryman, 2007: 10). In their early review of mixed methods evaluation articles, Greene, Caracelli, and Graham (1989) found 44 per cent of studies conducted analyses entirely independently, and just five of the 57 studies integrated data and analyses prior to final interpretation and conclusions. This could be seen as a particular problem of evaluation studies, in that the different contributing components are likely to be answering different questions related to process or outcome. Nevertheless, in his review of 232 mixed methods projects across a range of social science disciplines, Bryman (2006) also identified relatively few studies that demonstrated integration of different data forms or analytic procedures in the analysis phase. Katrin Niglas (2004) reviewed 1156 articles from 15 educational journals and classified 145 as using a combined approach, although some were included on the basis only that frequencies of themes were counted. She concluded "that substantial integration of qualitative and quantitative data during the analysis was exercised very rarely" (2004: 98).

The challenge of integration becomes most evident when results from studies purporting to use mixed methods are reported separately, or when separately developed components are reported sequentially within a dissertation, report or article. Even when specific findings derived from different components of a study are reported in parallel, it can appear as if the task of integrating them is the responsibility of the reader. When they examined reports and publications from a sample of 48 mixed methods projects funded by the UK Department of Health, O'Cathain, Murphy, and Nicholl (2007) found only 21 per cent exploited their potential for integration, with even less resulting in a mixed methods article being published from their study; 28 per cent were partially integrated; and in 51 per cent of the studies no attempt was made to integrate data sources in written reports or publications.

Challenges to integration experienced in social, behavioural, and health sciences arise from paradigmatic differences in philosophical orientation and disciplinary traditions associated with different methods, personal predispositions and preferences of researchers, the training and skills of researchers, and conflicts within mixed-background teams. Pressure from funding agencies for particular styles of research limits opportunities. Journal preferences and restrictions on word limits further contribute to difficulties in reporting and publishing results from an integrated study; researchers also lack templates for writing and experience difficulties in structuring articles. These challenges will be explored further through the text and examples that follow in this book, with strategies suggested for overcoming them.

What does mixing contribute?

If all phenomena inherently have both quality and quantity, it necessarily follows that research approaches that capture both of these aspects and the connections between them must be applied if one is to properly investigate, describe, and understand any particular phenomenon or group of phenomena. "Social experience and lived realities are multi-dimensional and ... our understandings are impoverished and may be inadequate if we view these phenomena only along a single dimension" (Mason, 2006a). Mason adds "social (and multi-dimensional) lives are lived, experienced and enacted simultaneously on macro and micro scales". The need to link or mesh study methods across those macro and micro strata of social experience necessarily involves the use of different sources and kinds of evidence (Irwin, 2008).

> In our mixed methods study of what it meant to be an early career researcher, I and my colleagues considered dimensions of opportunity (at local and national levels, in public and private spheres), training, experience (past and current), aspiration, support (personal, departmental, institutional) and productivity (qualification, publications, and grants) as well as age and gender. Data from all of these dimensions, at their various levels, were integrated to inform a definition of early career and recommendations relating to the funding support of early career researchers (Bazeley, 2003b; Bazeley et al., 1996).

The foundation for much of our thinking about the various contributions made by mixing methods was established in a landmark study when Greene et al. (1989) developed a classification of purposes served by mixing methods, based on an analysis of 57 evaluation studies. They saw mixed methods as contributing to building better understanding and stronger inferences through:

- increasing confidence in results that are supported by multiple sources of evidence
- designing better instruments and samples
- increasing the depth or breadth of a study
- providing a more complete or comprehensive understanding of the topic
- initiating fresh insights through contradiction and paradox.

The most commonly stated justification for mixing methods is that the different data converge to complement or extend each other, allowing the analyst to develop a richer, more analytically dense, more complete, and confidently argued response to their research question(s) (Bryman, 2006; Fetters, Curry, & Creswell, 2013; Fielding, 2012). The belief that integration allows researchers to build stronger inferences than is possible using a single method is often based on the assumption that the strengths of one approach compensate for the weaknesses of the other (e.g., Johnson & Onwuegbuzie, 2004), but as Sandelowski (2003: 328–329) pointed out, methods are only strong or weak *in relation to particular purposes* – they are not inherently so; it is more appropriate to view different methods in terms of the different facets each contributes to the solution of a research problem. For example:

> The careful measurement, generalisable samples, experimental control, and statistical tools of good quantitative studies are precious assets. When they are combined with the up-close, deep, credible understanding of complex real-world contexts that characterise good qualitative studies, we have a very powerful mix. (Miles, Huberman, & Saldaña, 2014: 43)

In the domain of applied research, analysis of multiple data sources extends understanding of the processes leading to effectiveness (or otherwise) of an intervention. In evaluation studies and experimental trials involving an intervention, understanding *how* the intervention might be contributing to an outcome can be integrated with knowledge of *what* that outcome is. Process information contributes to explaining causal pathways and contributes capacity for more effective implementation on a wider scale. Studies of causal processes, more generally, are enhanced by mixing methods, as regularities are assessed through statistical analyses and contexts and mechanisms are identified and described through qualitative means (Maxwell, 2004a, 2012b).

Data from different sources might complement each other, but they do not always converge. Unexpected or conflicting insights from different sources can lead the researcher along unintended paths (Caracelli & Greene, 1993; Rossman & Wilson, 1985). Provocation, contradiction, and paradox are welcomed, however, as "it is in the tension that the boundaries of what is known are most generatively challenged and stretched" (Greene & Caracelli, 1997: 12). "Creative and at times even playful meshing" serves "to encourage serendipity and openness to new ideas" (Brewer & Hunter, 2006: 69). This iterative movement between methods is strongly associated with an abductive logic: ideas based on previous experience and knowledge are challenged, leading to further exploration, development, theorising, and testing; and to switching between subjectivity and objectivity in a back and forth movement between inductive and deductive processes (Morgan, 2007).

Failure to integrate

When opportunities to exploit multiple data components are *not* taken up during analysis, this works to the detriment of the study's conclusions. Focus group data used to generate survey questions are all too often ignored once the statistical data are in, primary qualitative sources are not considered in relation to available demographic and other case data, results from different components are separately presented, and so on. Without integration, questions are left unanswered and possibilities for deeper insights unexplored. Worse, inappropriate conclusions might be drawn.

In a chapter focusing on criteria for quality in mixed methods studies, Alicia O'Cathain (2010) reflected on her experience of a lost opportunity to fully exploit mixed data. A series of leaflets promoting informed choices about aspects of care during pregnancy and birth were prepared for women having babies and the health professionals caring for them. Parallel experimental and ethnographic studies were conducted within the same health care settings to evaluate the effectiveness of the leaflets. Each study was conducted independently and to a high standard, with results of each published side by side in the same journal. Results of the experimental trial showed the leaflets were not effective in promoting informed choice. The inference from the ethnographic studies was that the staff in each setting operated a culture of "informed compliance", in which they "steered" women to preferred decisions, rather than allowing informed choice. The study lacked an integrative question, however, and so there was a lack of attention to meta-inferences. O'Cathain noted that even a simple meta-inference from the studies, that "leaflets were not effective in maternity units with a culture of informed compliance" would have added to the utility of the study beyond the sum of the parts (2010: 549).

Philosophical foundations for integration in mixed methods analysis

Whether we think about it or not, each of us has an implicit understanding of the nature of the world around us – what is real, what is changeable, and where we fit within that – shaped by our cultural context and social relationships. Additionally, as naturally curious beings, we explore the world in ways that are increasingly refined through learning from others and from our experience of acting in (or on) the world. Ontology is the term that describes our understanding of reality. This might range from seeing the world around us to exist as an independent entity governed by unchanging natural laws, through various intermediate positions, to an extreme relativist view which views all phenomena as mental constructions of the individual knowers, such that there is no absolute truth or validity. Epistemology describes the processes by which we come to know or understand the world around us, again ranging from a view that we can only know what we can observe and measure, to recognition of the validity (for each of us at least) of our subjective knowing. Historically, the term *paradigm* has been used in various ways (Morgan, 2007); in the mixed methods context it is usually seen as incorporating a "package" of ontological and epistemological understandings, with epistemology in particular having potential implications for methodology. Paradigms are themselves social constructions that cannot be researched or proven, generating debates which cannot be resolved (Krantz, 1995). "It is not that people first acquire epistemological and ontological assumptions and then decide how they are going to investigate the social world. Rather, they acquire particular [investigative] practices and various methodological and philosophical assumptions, consciously and unconsciously, more or less simultaneously; and each subsequently shapes the other" (Hammersley, 2008: 167).

Paradigms and mixed methods

Debates about tensions created by combining methods presumed to have conflicting paradigmatic (ontological and epistemological) bases dominated the early mixed methods theoretical literature (in the 1980s and 1990s), especially that originating in the United States. Quantitative methods were typically associated with positivist or post-positivist thinking and deductive processes, while qualitative methods were associated with interpretivist or constructivist thinking and inductive processes. Rapprochement was facilitated by the widespread recognition that a purist positivist position (which seeks verification of truth, rather than falsification of hypotheses) was untenable, and that the theories, background, knowledge, and values of the researcher influence what is observed. Nevertheless, a post-positivist position that seeks objective truth through a process of conjectures and refutations (Popper, [1963] 2002) is still seen to stand in contrast, for example, to a constructivist position that insists social phenomena do not exist independently of the knower and can only be understood through appreciating the discursive processes by which they are created.

Much was written about the way in which these two approaches to understanding reality and associated methods for investigating that understanding were incommensurable (e.g., Smith & Heshusius, 1986) until arguments supporting commensurability were developed and overtook and outweighed those against (e.g., Howe, 1988). These epistemological arguments sharpened our thinking about issues related to mixing methodologies, particularly for those of us "brought up" as researchers before Kuhn (1970) and others (e.g., Lincoln & Guba, 1985) brought attention to the ways these assumptions could impact on research. Their lingering legacy, however, has been to slow the progress of integration of methods as researchers became nervous about interweaving or merging the various strands of their research before they reached the point of drawing final conclusions.

In the current mixed methods context, readers might consider the alternative ways they can similarly approach debates about paradigmatic perspectives insofar as they impact on integration when designing, conducting, and reporting mixed methods projects. For specific applications, when a paradigmatic position is put forward in the written account of a project, there is a need to then ensure that the kinds of questions asked, methods of data collection, and interpretations of data are all in harmony with the stated approach.

Five approaches to managing paradigm issues

Five alternative strategies are offered to the mixed methods data analyst with regard to resolving issues raised by the possibility that the different approaches they are taking may be based on conflicting paradigmatic (ontological and epistemological) assumptions. The intention here is not to provide extensive reviews of specific paradigms; sources for those interested in pursuing these are provided at the end of the chapter.

Be unaware of, or dismiss the issue

Despite the high level of attention given to the issue of paradigm commensurability in the US literature, just one of the 20 British mixed methods researchers interviewed by Alan Bryman (2007) raised conflicting ontology as an issue in integrating data derived from different methods. A researcher might adopt practices before they recognise and reflect on any philosophical and methodological assumptions that might underlie those practices and thus say nothing about the philosophical basis for their work. Whether it is an issue that needs to be addressed appears to depend on the culture of the nation, the times, the discipline, and the particular journal.

Seeing paradigmatic issues as not important to real world practice was referred to by Teddlie and Tashakkori (2010) as an a-paradigmatic stance. For Miles and Huberman (1994), the question to ask was not *if* different methods should be combined, but when, how, and why to do so. Nor did Seale (2004: 411) "think social researchers wanting to produce good-quality work need to be over-concerned with the problem of philosophical foundations, or the lack of them, since the practical task of doing a research project does not require these things to be resolved at the philosophical level". The most common argument people present for taking an a-paradigmatic position is to recognise the primacy of the research question in choosing what methods to use in research, rather than paradigms, although Mertens (2015) suggests that in doing so they adopt an implicit pragmatism or subtle realism.

Maintain separation

When the different methodological components contributing to a mixed method study are seen as being tied to incompatible ontological and epistemological bases, it is then logically necessary to keep data gathering and analyses for each component separate. One cannot simultaneously work from the assumption that reality is universal and absolute and that we can empirically observe and measure it, and a view that reality is a construction of the observer and includes the unobservable. Thus, whereas most would see a study considering *burnout* from different angles as a study of a single phenomenon that could involve use of mixed methods, Sale, Lohfield, and Brazil (2002) argue, for example, that a "measure of burnout" and "lived experience of burnout" are different phenomena requiring different and independently executed methods. Even if the results generated by the different methods are discussed together in the conclusion of the study, which Sale et al. consider as a possibility, such a study would best be described as one adopting a multimethod approach rather than mixed methods. If methods used are seen as being based on incompatible assumptions, however, then logically the information derived through them would also be incompatible and therefore not able to be combined as a follow-on to the presentation of the separate results (Moran-Ellis et al., 2006). Maintaining separation does not provide a viable solution for the mixed methods researcher.

When Greenhalgh et al. (2009) attempted to synthesise a diverse literature on electronic patient records (EPR) that was based on heterogeneous philosophical assumptions and historical roots, they were unable to simply aggregate the findings of studies in which even the EPR itself, its users, and the clinical work it was designed to assist were differently understood. They therefore "compared and contrasted the different meta-narratives and exposed tensions and paradoxes; and [they] sought explanations for these in terms of how researchers had conceptualized the world and chosen to explore it" (2009: 5).

Apply a common paradigmatic (interpretive) framework

A paradigmatic framework that recognises and draws on both qualitative and quantitative approaches to investigating the social world provides the most straightforward resolution to the problem of apparent conflict. The widespread adoption of a (US-derived) pragmatic paradigm by mixed methods researchers heralded a way forward from the quagmire of purist debates (also largely of American origin). The pragmatist arguments that (a) learning is built on experience, and (b) the truth or value of an idea or result is tested by whether it works in action, support a mixed methods approach because, as attested from long experience, mixing methods "works" (Johnson & Onwuegbuzie, 2004). Others have drawn on a (British-derived) critical realist approach, viewing mixing methods as a way of providing a more complete and contextualised understanding of social processes and causal mechanisms. Critical realists see a need to consider both regularities that are assessed through empirical observation of patterns of association and the context-driven mechanisms behind those patterns, the latter being identified primarily through understanding people's constructions of their experience and of the processes involved (Maxwell, 2004a, 2012b; Pawson, 2006). Both of these philosophical approaches recognise the existence of an underlying reality (more complexly described by critical realists than pragmatists) but also emphasise the tentativeness of our observations, and both typically draw on abductive logic that characterises an iterative movement between inductive and deductive methods.

Take a dialectical approach

Alternatively (or as well), one might deliberately employ a combination of varying paradigms (mental models), as a way to initiate fresh ideas and knowledge (Greene, 2007, 2012a; Johnson, 2017; Schultz & Hatch, 1996). A dialectical approach celebrates the tensions and uncertainty created through the use of different approaches and methods as a means "to meaningfully engage with the differences that matter in today's troubled world, seeking not so much convergence and consensus as opportunities for respectful listening and understanding" (Greene, 2008: 20). Similarly, Schultz and Hatch's (1996) paradigm interplay is about finding contrasts and finding connections (interdependencies) to create a new form of (postmodernist) understanding, without being concerned about or attempting to resolve contradictions. Multiple views are held in tension as the researcher moves back and forth between permeable paradigm boundaries, allowing for cross-fertilisation between them.

Burke Johnson (2017) has drawn on dialectical thinking through the ages to extend, complement, and formalise Greene's dialectical approach in mixed methods by proposing dialectical pluralism as a metaparadigm for mixed methods research. He claims:

> Dialectical pluralism provides a way for researchers, practitioners, clients, policy makers, and other stakeholders to work together and produce new workable "wholes" while, concurrently, thriving on differences and intellectual tensions.

Johnson emphasises the importance of having multiple and different groups participating reflexively in research, bringing to it multiple mental models, using multiple sources of evidence, and working through tensions to democratically and collaboratively produce "warranted, provisional truths and working knowledge" that satisfy multiple standards for validity. Benefit accrues in the form of new ways of thinking and *practical theory* that incorporates abstract theory *and* local values and contexts.

Apply an overriding theoretical or ideological position

This is not so much an alternative paradigmatic position as an additional perspective to justify a mixed approach to research. When a project has a strong theoretical basis that brings coherence to the work, as is displayed for example in a project evaluating a theory of change or built on a logic model, then that substantive theory, rather than a particular paradigm, will become the guide for design and analysis and reporting of the project. "The importance of this stance for a mixed methods argument is that methods are subservient to concepts in theories. In particular, data are not analysed and aggregated by method; rather, data analysis [also presentation of results] is framed and organized by concept or theory" (Greene, 2007: 74).

Donna Mertens (2007: 212–213) has actively promoted a "transformative paradigm" as "a framework for examining assumptions that explicitly address power issues, social justice, and cultural complexity throughout the research process". Those occupying different places within social structures are likely to have different understandings of reality, making it necessary both to be explicit about these contextual influences on perceptions and values, to actively incorporate members of the researched community in the research process, and to draw on different methods in doing so. Feminists and other standpoint theorists also observe that "all knowledge is knowledge from where a person stands" (Ezzy, 2002: 20). Transformative and standpoint approaches reach out to more broadly challenge the way research is done through asking whether there are particular ways of knowing, and whether knowledge produced by one group about themselves differs from that produced by those in an alternative power position. Biddle and Schafft (2015) link a transformative approach to pragmatism, suggesting that it provides the axiological (values) component that is largely missing in pragmatist writing.

Seeing common ground

Some of these approaches address the issue of potentially conflicting paradigms more directly than others. Those that effectively support integrating methods recognise the following areas of "basic agreement" between contrasting positions (Johnson & Onwuegbuzie, 2004: 16).

- what appears reasonable is relative, i.e., it can vary across persons
- the theory-ladenness of facts – what we notice and observe is affected by our background knowledge, theories, and experiences
- it is possible for more than one theory to fit a single set of empirical data
- a hypothesis cannot be fully tested in isolation, testing involves making various assumptions that mean alternative explanations will continue to exist
- recognition that we only obtain probabilistic evidence, not final proof in empirical research
- the social nature of the research enterprise – researchers are embedded in and are affected by the attitudes, values, and beliefs of their research communities
- the value-ladenness of inquiry, affecting what we choose to investigate, what we see, and how we interpret what we see.

As Miles and Huberman (1994: 4–5) observed: "In epistemological debates it is tempting to operate at the poles. But in the actual practice of empirical research, we believe that all of us … are closer to the center, with multiple overlaps".

Researchers' responses to one further (rarely discussed) question will surely impact on their resolution of these issues. Is a philosophical paradigm something that can be switched on and off, or around, to suit an immediate purpose, or is one's world view and associated mental models a relatively enduring characteristic of the person (while still being subject to development and considered change)? While many researchers write of "adopting" a paradigm (or paradigms) as the need or wish arises, in my personal experience and understanding the latter position is more tenable. This does not mean, however, that one cannot appreciate and understand an alternative position taken by another.

Concluding remarks

In this foundational chapter, attention has been given to delineating the field of mixed methods and its core components. Particular emphasis has been placed on the importance of integration in mixed methods analysis, with integration being seen as the creation of *purposeful interdependence* between methods and/or their associated analyses.

The development of a mixed method movement, with the desire of some to mark out the distinctiveness of a mixed methods approach to research, created a "paradigm shift" in the social science community. Approaches to resolving the philosophical issues raised in the acrimonious debates that followed have been outlined, in order to allow researchers to move forward with "doing what comes naturally", given that all phenomena are multifaceted, are able to be represented in multiple ways, and can be investigated using multiple tools.

Further reading

History and overall approaches to mixed methods

Teddlie and Tashakkori (2009) comprehensively cover of the field of mixed methods research, including its history, development, paradigms, and practice.

Greene (2007) includes a historical account of the development of mixed methods and of the paradigm wars from the perspective of her personal experience of the period within a more general text covering the practice of mixing methods.

Brewer and Hunter (2006) and Rallis and Rossman (2003) review the history of mixed methods in social and evaluation research (respectively).

Maxwell (2016) argues that integrated mixed methods have been practised unproblematically for at least the last two centuries – well before the currently claimed dawn of mixed methods. He draws lessons about strategies for integration from examples of studies in disciplines as diverse as geology, ethology, and social science.

Small (2011) reviews mixed methods studies in sociology, and in doing so, considers issues of definition and styles of mixing.

Bergman (2008b) has edited a collection that covers issues of definition, practice, and validity in mixed methods research.

Johnson and Gray (2010) trace mixed methods thinking back to the ancient Greeks and then forward through the ages.

Gürtler and Huber (2006) describe the ambiguous use of language in qualitative and quantitative publications, explore the criteria presumed to divide these two approaches, and conclude that one cannot be achieved without the other.

Philosophical foundations

Crotty (1998) explains a range of ontologies and epistemologies in straightforward language. This has been a foundational text for social scientists for two decades, although it is dated with respect to newer developments relevant to mixed methods (it doesn't cover pragmatism or critical realism, for example).

Schwandt (2000) discusses interpretivism, philosophical hermeneutics, and constructionism within the context of epistemological, ethical, and political issues, with a focus on qualitative enquiry.

For specific approaches:

Pragmatism: Biesta (2010); Feilzer (2010); Johnson and Onwuegbuzie (2004); Morgan (2007).

Symbolic interactionism: Charon (2009).

Constructivism: Lincoln and Guba (2013).

Realism/critical realism: Bergene (2007); Danermark, Ekström, Jakobsen, and Karlsson (2002); Danermark and Gellerstedt (2004); Maxwell (2004a, 2012b); Pawson (2006, Chapter 2); Sayer (2000).

Dialectical pluralism: Johnson (2017); see also Greene (2007) for a dialectical approach.

Feminist approach: Hesse-Biber (2010).

Transformative approach: Mertens (2007, 2009, 2015).

2
PLANNING FOR ANALYSIS

CHAPTER OVERVIEW

Approaches to design for mixed methods research

Designing for analysis

Research purposes, research questions and analysis

Defining cases and case structure to facilitate data management and integration

Sampling when methods are mixed

Data flexibility and scope

The point(s) of interface

Visualising design elements

Mapping and modelling to identify project elements and linkages

Tables and visuals to summarise links between theory, data, and analysis

Design diagrams to show the flow and exchange between methods

Describing design

Using software for analysis

General purpose programs

Word processors

Analysis software

Specialised analytic tools

Skills and teamwork in mixed methods research

Working in teams

Concluding remarks

Further reading

Preparation is important for any research endeavour, and perhaps even more so for mixed methods research, with its inherent complexity in both data collection and analysis phases. This chapter focuses on some key aspects of planning for a mixed methods project from the point of view of how choices made in the planning and early project development stages might benefit or constrain analysis and integration of analyses. It is *not* intended to provide a comprehensive overview of design and related matters for mixed methods projects (suggestions for where to find such are provided at the end of the chapter). The aspects considered, each in relation to mixed methods and integrated analysis, are:

- research purposes and questions
- design, and visualisation of design, in mixed methods research
- understanding cases and sampling options in mixed methods research
- data sources and software options that support integration
- skills and teamwork in mixed methods research.

Approaches to design for mixed methods research

As procedures for carrying out mixed methods studies were developed, several methodologists developed theoretically and/or empirically derived typologies of design – classification systems that set out diverse ways in which mixed methods projects might be conducted. These were based on different ways of combining elements that were predefined as quantitative or qualitative, using two primary dimensions of priority of methods (whether quantitative or qualitative was dominant, or both were equal status) and sequencing of methods (concurrent/parallel or sequential, and if sequential, which came first). Some also gave consideration to the purpose of the study (e.g., exploratory or explanatory), whether the methods are independent or interactive (i.e., the stage at which they were integrated), and to the theoretical drive underpinning the study (deductive, inductive). These design options were accompanied by a notation system that uses capital and lower-case letters (QUAL, qual, QUAN, quan) to indicate priority of method, and plus (+) and arrow (→) symbols to represent the way in which the primary elements of a design fitted together, with parentheses used to indicate combinations within phases (Morse, 1991). Typologies and the dimensions on which they are based are helpful as conceptual and teaching tools, especially for novice researchers, while the notation system has been widely adopted and promoted as a diagrammatic way of communicating an outline of a design. One of the earliest typologies was that developed by Greene, Caracelli, and Graham (1989), which focused on the study purpose (triangulation, complementarity, development, expansion or initiation) rather than methods used. One of the most widely promoted methods-oriented typologies is that of Creswell and Plano Clark (2011), which comprises four basic designs:

- a convergent parallel design, in which quantitative and qualitative data and analyses are collected and conducted separately, with results then compared or related, leading to interpretation

- an explanatory sequential design, in which quantitative data collection and analysis is followed up with a qualitative component to assist in interpretation of the quantitative results
- an exploratory sequential design in which qualitative data collection and analysis contributes to the design of a more extensive quantitative study, and
- an embedded design where, for example, a qualitative component is conducted in association with a quantitative trial.

Emphasis is given to analysing the separate datasets before considering integration in each of these designs. These four are supplemented by a version of any of these that is conducted within a transformative (or other) framework, and by a multiphase design in which basic designs are combined and connected in a more extended project. Variations are possible (indeed, likely). When a particular project is being described, procedures and purposes are added to a diagram depicting the design. Typologies are intended to be comprehensive but not exhaustive, as designs evolve according to circumstances and purposes (Teddlie & Tashakkori, 2009).

Typologies, and typological thinking, can be limiting, however. The primary criticism is that they, and their associated diagrams, encourage binary (quantitative–qualitative) thinking, ignore the contribution of new technologies (such as georeferencing and network analysis), and they do not adequately represent complex projects (Gorard, 2010b; Song et al., 2010; Weine, 2015). Lack of predictability in multi-strategy research becomes problematic for those committed to a particular design (Bryman, 2006). They focus on "whole of study design" when studies often embrace multiple design types with a degree of variability that defies easy categorisation (Guest, 2013). Neither do they really capture what happens in a reality where phenomena inherently have both quality and quantity, where serving a research purpose is more important than whether data are quantitative or qualitative or whether a particular design is utilised, and where a need to combine strategies and to modify methods at multiple points during a project is far more common than can be adequately represented in a typological classification system. As a design tool, there is a danger that pre-existing design frameworks might be applied as "cognitive shortcuts, that substitute for more effortful thought" (Mark, 2015: 29). Similarly, there is a danger that labels are substituted, often inappropriately, for adequate description of what has been, or will be, actually done, often evident in research proposals and articles (Bryman, 2006).

Flexibility in both the design and conduct of mixed methods research is required. "Most research progresses as a combination of some preplanning coupled with judicious emergent decision-making as the research is carried out" and design is "discerned in post hoc pattern recognition of what has been an unfolding, evolutionary, pragmatic adaptation in the research process" (Hunter & Brewer, 2015: 186). This is "design for serendipity", when contexts change, data become unavailable, results are contradictory, or time and costs impose limits on research teams, and the researcher has to be prepared for any contingency (2015: 187). "Research design is not a stage, it is a process" (Fielding & Fielding, 2008: 558), and that process is neither fixed nor linear, but rather a reflexive, interactive process iteratively evolving throughout a project (Hammersley & Atkinson, 2007; Maxwell, 2013).

Focusing therefore on the *process* of design rather than on design *types*, Maxwell (2013; Maxwell & Loomis, 2003) described design as interaction between research purposes, conceptual frameworks, research questions, methods (sampling, data collection, and analysis), and the need to ensure validity. Attention is focused on developing coherence between these five primary elements, and between these elements and the larger environment where contextual factors, researcher experience and skills, and ethical constraints play a part. Focusing on interactive design elements allows for creativity and flexibility in design, thus allowing for changes in the relationship among components as a study develops (Maxwell, Chmiel, & Rogers, 2015). "Design research" (Huysmans & De Bruyn, 2013; Mertens et al., 2016a) is a further development relevant to mixed methods design that models a cyclical process for solving design tasks in complex projects. In design research, different methods or a combination of methods are used to develop, test, and refine solutions at each stage in the design process.

The detailed case studies of mixed methods projects described by Burch and Heinrich (2016) demonstrate the iterative flexibility required of mixed methods researchers working in policy and programme areas as they respond to contextual opportunities and challenges, including evolving policy developments and purposes for the research results. Similarly, from their experience of working in a complex longitudinal project, Weiss et al. (2005: 61) reported:

> We learned to impose structure on our mixed-methods process but also to be pragmatic and tolerate complexities ... we learned that mixed-methods approaches could only be rough guides and that intentional designs might have to give way to real-world problems of data availability and deadlines. Accordingly we developed a sense of our mixed-methods work as a dynamic hands-on process, guided only very generally by mixed-methods analytic models.

Release from predetermined design constraints fostered added creativity and flexibility in Weiss et al.'s analysis, and yielded valuable contributions for developing policies relevant to the overall project goals.

Designing for analysis

Options for choosing *analysis* strategies are guided by research purposes and how they will be achieved, by questions and how they will be answered. They are constrained by design decisions about the structure, number, and selection of the cases to be analysed, and the types of data that will become available for analysis. Filtering through all of these considerations are the frameworks and mental models adopted by those doing the planning and the analyses. Giving consideration to how the planned-for data might be integrated and used from an early design stage of a project helps to ensure that data are collected in a way that facilitates analysis, to anticipate the kinds of analysis strategies needed, and to be aware of the skills required to carry out those analyses.

Research purposes, research questions and analysis

Clarifying the overall purpose and goals for research is essential for setting and retaining direction and focus throughout any project. Researchers' *purposes* derive from one or more of satisfying a personal need or curiosity, wanting to influence or evaluate practice, or seeking to contribute to knowledge (Maxwell, 2013). The choices made are influenced by personal experience, current situation, implicit or explicit world view (or mental models), values, and intended audience.

Refined by a conceptual framework derived from previous research and/or the literature, purposes and goals give rise to questions the research will be designed to answer. Purposes and questions will then drive major dimensions of design, such as whether the research is exploratory or explanatory, retrospective or prospective, cross-sectional or longitudinal. Or indeed, it is possible that a particular preference for certain methods or a desire to experiment with a newly discovered method might lead a researcher to design questions to suit their methods choice (Mertens et al., 2016a). Either way, methods of data collection and analysis are selected to provide data that will answer the questions, provide warrants for those answers, and satisfy the goals of the study.

There are typical or preferred methods for answering particular types of questions, yet any question can potentially be answered using one or more of several different methods and with different data sources (Gorard, 2010b). Decisions will be guided by the kind of data needed and whether they are available and accessible. A critical question is how these data will be managed and used and what they can reveal, given the proposed methods of analysis. Setting this out in the form of a table or diagram as a planning strategy (as described later in this chapter) provides useful clarification.

Defining cases and case structure to facilitate data management and integration

Cases are understood differently in different disciplines. Because most analysis strategies described in this book are organised around cases, it is necessary to clarify how this term is being used in this social science oriented, mixed methods context.

A case is a single entity or a coherent set or group of entities from a human, other living, or non-living population, or it is an instance of a concept (Abbott, 1992). A single case might be the focus of a complex analysis, with this type of research usually being referred to as a *case study*, for example of a person with dementia, or a business unit. Alternatively a single case might be just one of a large number of cases on which data to be analysed are focused, for example, young people involved in Scouts, or letters written by soldiers. Cases, therefore, are often referred to as "units of analysis", although where cases are groups, such as organisations, there might also be additional units of analysis embedded within cases. Cases of one type will be apparent as belonging to or being representative of one phenomenon, yet each case will have its own distinct features. They will be distinguishable in one or more ways from cases of another type (Bazeley, 2013: 5–7). Thus, for example, cases of dogs vary in their features, but they remain distinct from cases of cats. Both are cases of animals.

Defining who or what are cases for a mixed methods study facilitates data management, with selection and definition of cases being continuously guided by the research question. Each case holds data from different sources and of different types together, thus cases provide the lynchpin for integration of data. The application of case-based logic in managing and linking data is elaborated in some detail in Chapters 5 and 6 respectively.

Sampling when methods are mixed

Sampling is the process of selecting a number of cases to illustrate or represent a larger population, usually employed because it is not feasible to research and report data about the whole population. Selecting a sample involves (a) deciding whom or what to sample (i.e., identifying the cases), (b) determining how many cases to sample, and (c) determining a strategy for selecting cases. Sample design is related to the goals of analysis more than it is to the type of data involved: the way a sample is selected will impact on the type and the validity of the conclusions that can be reached and the wider population to which they might apply. For some types of generalisation, primarily in the sciences, an illustrative case is all that is needed: one test is sufficient to show that gravity applies equally to light and heavy objects, or that water is comprised of hydrogen and oxygen. In the social sciences, results and inferences to a population are rarely so clear-cut and a sample larger than a single case is almost always required. On the one hand, large, randomly drawn representative samples are considered necessary where the goal is to generalise to a broader population. On the other hand, exploratory, experimental, descriptive, and theory-development studies might use moderately sized matched or deliberately contrasting samples, or smaller, purposively selected samples, allowing for case-to-case transfer or analytic generalisation (Firestone, 1993).

Combining methods that require different sampling strategies and typically draw on different sample sizes further complicates matters. Collins, Onwuegbuzie, and Jiao (2007) identified four primary ways in which component samples in mixed methods studies might be combined to facilitate integration of results: identical, parallel, nested, and multilevel.

- identical designs collect different types of data from the same sample
- parallel designs draw different samples from the same or comparable populations
- nested designs draw a smaller sample for one form of data collection (usually qualitative) from within a larger sample from which different (usually quantitative) data are being collected

- multilevel samples include participants drawn from two or more populations at different levels of investigation, such as children in a class, and their teachers and parents or community members.

Disturbingly, when Collins et al. reviewed 121 mixed methods studies from across nine fields, they found over half drew inferences, primarily statistical generalisations, that were not consistent with the sampling design used. Difficulties arise when inferential statistics are applied to variables obtained from purposive samples, and there is a temptation to over-interpret small numbers (frequency or crosstabulated data) generated from coded texts.

Different strategies for sampling and the purposes for which they were being employed are demonstrated in the following illustrations:

Example 1

Nickel et al. (1995) used a brief quantitative survey as the basis for qualitative sampling of a difficult to identify group of young people engaging in high-risk sexual behaviours. They first used cluster analysis to identify their target population, selected the most typical case for each cluster of relevance to the study, and then randomly sampled within each cluster from the remaining "fitting" cases. Their purpose was to explore factors in youth sexual behaviour that increased risk of exposure to HIV-infection or unintended pregnancy.

Example 2

After a period of ethnographic involvement in the online game, World of Warcraft, Williams et al. (2006) used bots (automated characters) to collect data on measurable behaviour of players logged into the game over a one-month period, including their social networks. From this census of characters, the extent of their playing, the guilds they belonged to, and the groups they formed, they were able to design a stratified sample of those who were part of guilds (the focus of their study), based on their faction (Horde or Alliance), the size of their guild, their centrality within it, and their server type (player versus player, role-playing, player versus environment). Forty-eight participants were selected randomly from within strata to provide a representative (nested) sample. Online semistructured interviews allowed the researchers to construct a typology of guilds and to examine leadership and player practices and attitudes within guilds. By combining interview data with the original sampling data, they were also able to explore the extent and type of social capital in relation to the social structure of guilds and participants' positions within those structures.

Example 3

Sharp et al. (2012) employed an elaborate four-step mixed methods sampling strategy for their multisite case study of an education policy initiative. They needed to select a manageable sample of eight cases (high schools), from a pool of more than 150, that was theoretically justified in that it provided maximum variation on six facets of policy implementation of relevance to the outcomes for their study, while controlling for a range of contextual variables. They began with chi-squared analysis to select industrially diverse regions with different levels of workforce investment; next came hierarchical cluster analysis to select school clusters (four were identified) that varied across regions but were similar within regions, based on a range of local economic resources; in Stage 3 they ranked each of the remaining 31 schools on 41 indicators of their level of implementation of the target programme, within each of the four clusters. Ten schools willing to participate were selected to represent high and low scores within each cluster. Finally, in Stage 4, site visits with interviews and observations were conducted to validate the scoring of the previous stages, with the final sample of eight schools varying in level of programme implementation, poverty, urbanicity, and industry characteristics.

Data flexibility and scope

Any phenomenon has both qualities and quantities, *each of which* might be described both objectively and subjectively. Quantitative data do not necessarily require a deductive logic, nor should it be assumed that qualitative data have no place in an experimental study, or that information involving variables can't be inductively explored. There are alternative frameworks for categorising data, with the degree of control the researcher exercises when collecting them being an important consideration (Gorard, 2013; Sánchez-Algarra & Anguera, 2013). Mixed methods researchers can be open to thinking simply in terms of what kind of data they need in order to answer their questions and to provide warrant for the kinds of findings they wish to generate, how to gather those data, and how they will fit together for analysis, rather than whether they are fulfilling arbitrary requirements to have a quantitative and a qualitative source.

Creativity in thinking about data sources (and methods of combining them) is encouraged in mixed methods research. Reviews suggest that the majority of mixed methods studies combine interviews with survey methods (57.3% in Bryman's 2006 study), with additional studies combining surveys with focus groups. While there is no doubt that these combinations are often appropriate, it is worth considering just some of the alternatives that are available, and how they might be used in integrated analyses:

- Observational data are inherently mixed, and can be separately or coincidentally recorded using numbers, words, and pictures from either a participant perspective or a disinterested observer's perspective, to provide counts, measures, description, narrative, and/or journaled field notes and reflections.

- Documentary sources ranging from historical archives, to organisational or company records, to clinical notes also provide data in numeric and textual form, with measures extracted and text coded for hermeneutic and/or statistical analysis. Similarly, letters, books, photo libraries, memorabilia, and other artefacts provide data that can be used for separate or combined textual, visual, and statistical analyses.

- National social science data archives existing in some countries make quantitative, mixed, and qualitative datasets available for secondary analysis (Corti, 2012). Researchers can access these sources and integrate them by combining or comparing them with each other or with their own data.

- Social media in its various guises is becoming increasingly accessible as a source of data for analysis, with a selection of tools available for "scraping" large volumes of posts and their accompanying metadata from corporate through to individual sites (Hogan, 2017). Analysis is likely to require some form of autoprocessing because of the volumes involved. Because social media implies linkages, it is attractive to those working with social network analysis.

- Big data shares some similarities with (and may include) data from social media. It is largely coincidentally recorded data, such as locational data from mobile phones, purchasing trends from credit card or loyalty programme records, or all the words appearing in books about the French Revolution. Or, data recorded for another, usually administrative purpose, such as birth records, high school graduation records, or club memberships might be analysed to determine trends in, say, the size of babies being born, or the racial composition of high school graduates. The defining feature of big data is the size of the datasets involved, which have necessitated new forms of data management and new techniques for analysis that depend on machine learning (Kitchin, 2014).

- Locational references within interviews or news stories or other qualitative sources might be mapped, for example, to facilitate identification of places visited (Christensen et al., 2011) and/or calculation of distances travelled (Skinner, Matthews, & Burton, 2005). "From geography, social science can gain better sensitivity to scale, place, context, and flows. From social science, geography can gain better practices for documenting processes and cultural variation, systematic code-based data management, and formal analytic strategies" (Fielding & Cisneros-Puebla, 2009: 353).

- Mixed methods researchers are typically open, also, to making use of "opportunistic data", such as incidental comments and observations that are more usually regarded as noise and discarded. On an Oxford Public Opinion Survey, 27 per cent of respondents added marginal comments, with many of these being substantive comments querying the validity of the questions, adding to or qualifying answers, and revealing, for example, contrasting rationales for giving the same answer to a 4-point scale to rate the effectiveness of prison sentences (Feilzer, 2010). Such opportunities would be lost in a web survey, unless a comments box is provided with each question.

Further options for gathering and making use of more specialised types of data, including hybrid forms, will become apparent as analysis strategies are being reviewed in Part 2 of this book.

The point(s) of interface

A key element in a mixed methods research design is the question of when, where, and how the different components will come together, at "the point of interface" (Morse & Niehaus, 2009). Planned strategies for integration need to be considered during the design stage of a study, so that its importance is established early and it remains in focus as an issue. Schoonenboom and Johnson (in press) suggested "points of addition" should be noted also. These were defined as the point at which a further method is added to the mix. Points of addition do not necessarily become points of interface.

Although integration is now commonly referred to as occurring at *the* point of interface, having multiple points at which different components will come together in an integrated mixed methods project is quite possible. It is also likely that once a critical point of interface has been reached, integrative processes will more or less continue from that point on until the conclusion of the study. Some projects will be characterised by continuous iterative exchange of information and ideas across methods, and to some extent, unless there is a reason to take deliberate steps to avoid it, some "bleeding" of ideas from one method to another throughout a study will (fruitfully) occur anyway. Researchers are advised also to include planned stopping or decision points at which they intentionally look for ways in which one analysis could inform another, throughout a study (Greene, 2007: 144).

Visualising design elements

Visualising links between questions asked, data sources, and knowledge gained provides helpful clarification about how different strands of the research relate to each other, both for the researchers involved, and for other stakeholders. They facilitate analysis by pointing both to the entities (nodes in a diagram) for which data are needed and to the potential links between them, to be tested during the analysis.

Three types of visual strategies clarify the connections between primary research questions and design elements in a mixed methods project:

- Various versions of modelling a project, including concept mapping, mapping a conceptual framework or theory of change, and logic modelling help the researcher to identify those specific elements and potential linkages that need to be considered for data gathering and analysis.
- Tabular displays summarise the connections between, for example, specific research questions and their theoretical base, samples and data that will contribute to answering them, and proposed forms of analysis.
- Design diagrams show the flow of data gathering and analysis steps to indicate how different strategies might interact to produce the final outcome.

Because of the complexity of most mixed methods projects, models and tables become almost essential tools to assist in designing a project and in communicating that design. Key concepts, actions, people, and the links between them are identified as foci of attention, and pathways between purposes, background theory, questions, data sources, and methods of analysis are made plain.

Mapping and modelling to identify project elements and linkages

With maps and models, the substantive and theoretical basis for a project is laid out in diagrammatic form, with linkages and anticipated outcomes. The process of creating them forces clarity of thinking about assumptions, known and unknown items, variables, people and/or processes, and their relationships. They provide a focused framework for data collection and analysis. When modelling is approached as a team task involving everyone with a stake in the project, it helps to build a shared vision of the project.

Concept mapping adds to the clarity (and theoretical development) of key concepts involved in a project. It helps with thinking about how to structure the elements that might be involved, and the linkage between them. A concept map will be progressively refined in the process of reading and building knowledge and growing understanding through project experience. Keywords and/or coding categories from notes, discussion with colleagues, literature, and participants in the research contribute ideas for items in the map. As new elements are added to the map, links are used to show connections between them (e.g., Figure 2.1; this concept map is part of the ongoing *Wellbeing* project and is therefore still in development).

Theory of change diagrams and/or logic models provide "a snapshot of an individual's or group's current thinking about how their idea or program might work" (Knowlton & Phillips, 2013: 4). A theory of change diagram details the processes through which change is thought likely to occur (e.g., Figure 2.2). Alternatively, a conceptual framework maps the theoretical links between entities in a project.

The steps in a *logic model* work as a series of if–then operational sequences showing a causal pathway, including necessary resources and outcomes, based on a theoretical model of change (e.g., Figure 2.3). Each form of modelling asks what conditions or circumstances need to be in place for changes to take effect. The model points to the elements for which evidence will need to be gathered for each identified step along the way, to allow the researcher to draw formative conclusions, to change the programme of research if necessary, and during the research to make interim summative statements about what effect the activities undertaken are having on whom. These principles for setting up intermediate observation points are not limited to evaluation studies – they can be applied to a range of process-oriented studies. Models such as these also form the initial basis for process tracing, a strategy that will be reviewed in Chapter 12.

Tables and visuals to summarise links between theory, data, and analysis

A table, such as Table 2.1, directly links each *research question* with the data sources that will allow it to be answered and the analyses that will be developed from those data. Alternatively, a table (e.g., Collins & Dressler, 2008: 369, Table 1)

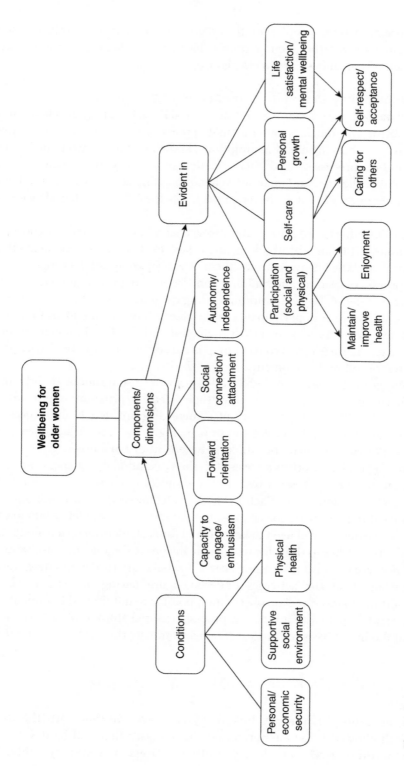

Figure 2.1 Concept map of wellbeing for older women

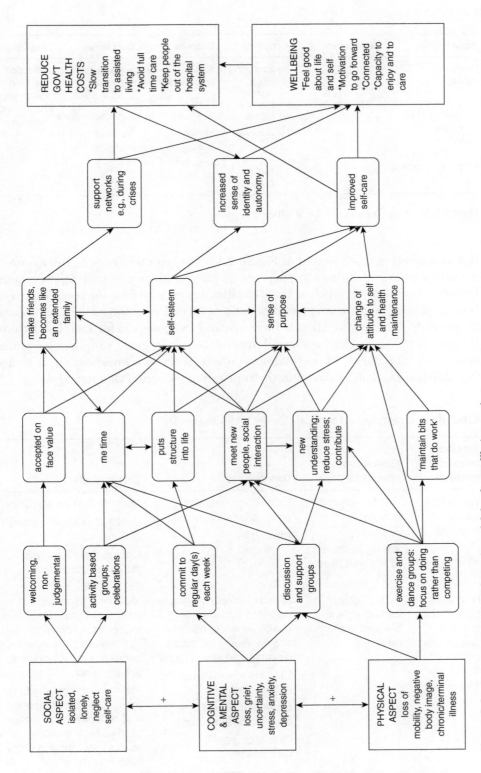

Figure 2.2 Process (theory of change) model for the Wellbeing project

Inputs	Resources	Activities	Outputs	Outcomes	Impacts
Women experiencing: – social isolation – grief and loss – depression – lack of confidence – physical decline	Coordinator Activity leaders Physical space Volunteer helpers	Regular group activities – physical – discussion Occasional activities – social – outings	Social connection Physical fitness Self-esteem Self-care Purpose for living (and staying well)	Social support networks Self-efficacy Self-maintenance Sense of wellbeing	Reduced demand on government health and care services

Figure 2.3   Logic model for the Wellbeing project

or a visualisation (such as that in Figure 2.4 below) can take each *source of data* as a starting point, with links to purposes or the questions each will answer. Doing tables and/or diagrams such as these clarifies design issues for the researcher; even though details might change as the study is carried out, the exercise of creating them ensures that preparation is thorough and the potential for road blocks along the way is reduced. They are useful also to include in grant proposals or journal articles as summaries of methodology where space for presentation is limited (a published example is shown in the concluding section of Chapter 5).

Table 2.1   Questions and methods for the Wellbeing project

Specific research questions	Theoretical/ conceptual basis	Data sources	Data analysis
What does wellbeing mean for older women?	Goertz – theorising concepts Capability – agency approach to life well lived	Free-listing, pile-sorts, photo elicitation, drawings Interviews	Cultural domain statistics Concept analysis – identify dimensions Critical realist analysis – attributes, structure, environment, agency
How does participation in OWN programmes impact on health and wellbeing?	Active ageing/ healthy ageing theories and research	Annual (linked) surveys – variables include use of health services, health and wellbeing indicators, physical and social activity QL comments on aspects of participation Observations and attendance statistics Case studies of participants	Statistical analyses: descriptive stats, repeated measures, comparison with national data, relationships between age, attendance, activity levels and outcomes MM – relate comments to indicators of participation and outcomes; build case profiles from multiple sources. Within and cross-case analysis

Specific research questions	Theoretical/ conceptual basis	Data sources	Data analysis
What motivates and maintains attendance?	Social connection as motivator for physical activity	Longevity/regularity/ attrition in attendance stats; classes selected Annual surveys (QT + QL)	Descriptive statistics Connect attendance stats and survey responses with reasons for coming and stated benefits of coming
What is the relationship between physical health and general wellbeing?	Adaptability Life satisfaction set-point theory Self-determination theory	Surveys Interviews – aspects of health and wellbeing, incl. agency, autonomy, competence	Statistical – relationships between H and WB variables Theorising relationship (grounded theory; CR – identifying mechanisms in relationship)

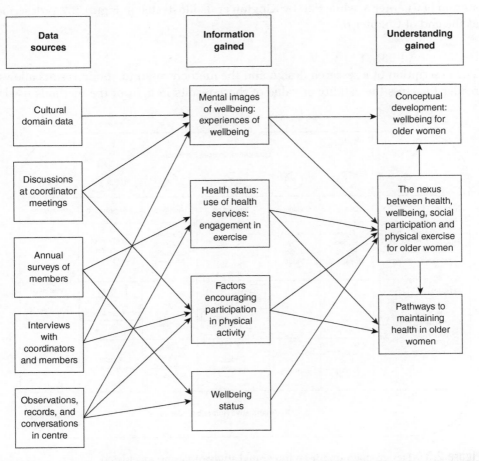

Figure 2.4   Visual model of research inputs and contributions to knowledge about the health and wellbeing of older women

Design diagrams to show the flow and exchange between methods

Because of the relative complexity of the steps in most mixed methods projects, Creswell and Plano Clark (2011) and others have strongly recommended the use of diagrams to clearly and economically convey that complexity, in full or in part. Figures 2.5 and 2.6 provide examples. Figure 2.7 incorporates additional detail of procedures and products within the diagram, as recommended by Creswell and Plano Clark. Design diagrams are of value to the researchers in that the process of diagramming encourages clarity and thoroughness in thinking through the implementation steps for their project. They are also of value for efficiently communicating complex design at the research proposal stage (Saint Arnault & Fetters, 2011), and again in reporting from the project (Hunter & Brewer, 2015) as a means of clearly demonstrating what was actually done. Examples can be found in the majority of empirical articles reported in the *Journal of Mixed Methods Research*. (Partial results from the study by Castro et al., illustrated in Figure 2.5, are shown in Table 6.2. The study by Woolley, illustrated in Figure 2.6, is described in detail in the concluding section of Chapter 5, while that by Kington et al., illustrated in Figure 2.7, is described at the end of Chapter 6.)

Describing design

The description of a research design and the methods used to obtain results allows a reader to assess the validity or value of those results in light of the methods used to

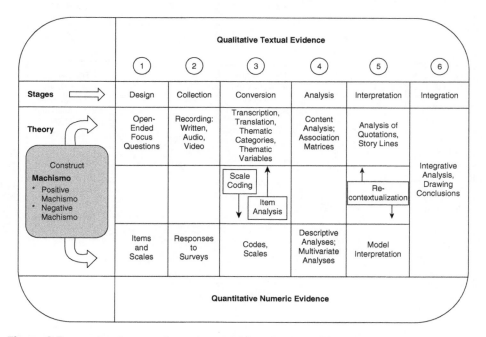

Figure 2.5   Design diagram for an integrated study of Latino machismo

Source: Castro et al., 2010: 345, Figure 1

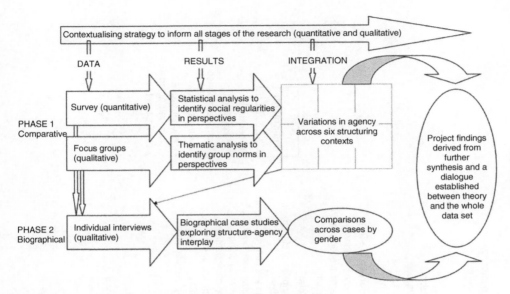

Figure 2.6   Design diagram for a study of youth agency

Source: Woolley, 2009: 12, Figure 2

obtain them. It also allows another researcher to replicate the study, should they choose to do so. Many research reports fall short on these functions, omitting critical details, relying on labels rather than explaining designs, methodological approaches, and the actual methods used. Song et al. (2010: 730–731) found terms like qualitative and quantitative uninformative, suggesting that "they reify a view of the world of inquiry as divided into two". They then described the mixed methods literature as a "terminological morass ... whereby distracting labels for designs substitute for clear explanations of what is planned or was done in a study and why". With so much variation and confusion in the way researchers use labels for terms, designs and methodologies, explicit description of what was done, perhaps supplemented by tables and diagrams, is far more effective.

Using software for analysis

Use of statistical software for the analysis of numeric data has been widely accepted since the beginning of the digital era, reflecting the long established and widespread acceptance of statistical procedures for analysis of data, and the relative ease of converting these to numeric code. Acceptance and use of qualitative approaches to data analysis among social scientists developed more recently, and so also the development of qualitative data analysis software (QDAS) and acceptance of its legitimacy as a tool for analysis has been more recent. The first programs emerged publically in the 1980s; they underwent considerable development in the decade that followed, while QDAS as we know it today is a product of the twenty-first century. Pockets of resistance to its adoption

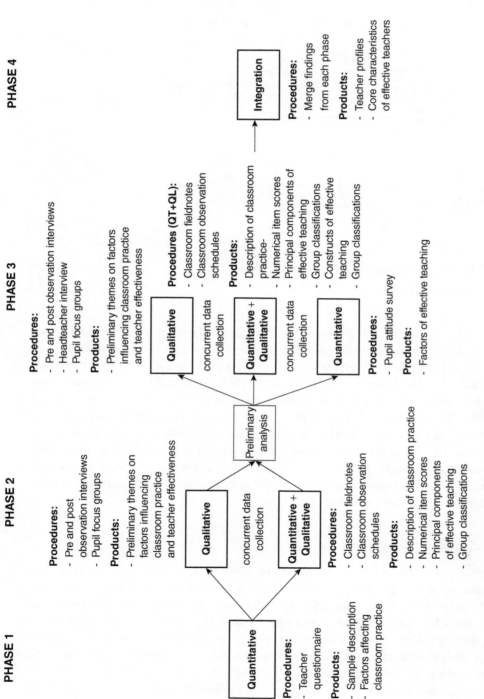

Figure 2.7 Procedural diagram for a study of effective and typical teachers

Source: Kington etal., 2011: 108, Figure 2.

remain, in a way not seen with respect to statistical programs, among those who are concerned about the way its use might impact on the way they conduct their analyses (Woods et al., 2016). The "learning curve" associated with effective use of qualitative programs, which necessarily have to be flexible enough to deal with diverse methodologies (and therefore can present as complex to use), also inhibits adoption by some. Nevertheless, whereas 10 years ago it was comparatively rare to see authors of qualitative or mixed methods articles reporting that they had used QDAS, now it is commonplace.

What software does is provide tools to *assist* in analysis of data, from simple to complex. Both statistical and QDAS programs are designed to be flexible; neither type prescribes a methodology. Nor will they interpret data; rather they facilitate the processing of data, under the direction of the researcher, so that the products of that processing can be used by the researcher(s) to help interpret whatever their data are saying. Software (both quantitative and qualitative) assists the general processes of analysis, interpretation, and reporting by:

- reducing limitations on computational capacity and the time needed to complete complex computations
- helping researchers to see data in new ways, thus contributing to building deeper and/or more insightful understanding
- promoting greater depth to analyses through comprehensive data querying systems
- ensuring more systematic and transparent analytic processes, as evidence for conclusions can be traced
- providing tools with which to visualise data.

Each of these features has the potential to add to researchers' inference-drawing capacity and quality, but not necessarily to the *integration* of mixed methods data.

As mixed methods approaches to research have become more acceptable and more widely adopted, software developers traditionally offering either quantitative *or* qualitative analysis tools have responded with new features to import and combine different types of data, to merge differently structured datasets, and to facilitate the translation of data from one form to another, thus serving integrative purposes. Additionally, new forms of digital technology offer new resources for data collection and analysis to support methodological integration (Fielding & Cisneros-Puebla, 2009: 349). Those who work with more specialised and hybridised forms of data and analysis have also developed software to facilitate those processes. Many of the analysis strategies outlined in Part 2 of this book would simply be not feasible without the assistance of both qualitative and quantitative software.

Software options for mixed methods researchers fall into three broad categories: (1) using well-established, broadly purposed, statistical and qualitative analysis software; (2) making use of general purpose software for particular mixed methods purposes; and (3) employing special purpose programs which are designed to support particular types of analyses. Statistical, and especially qualitative analysis, software offer a much more comprehensive and useful range of tools than are available in general purpose programs.

General purpose programs

Word processors and spreadsheets are the two primary types of programs being considered here in terms of their potentially having a role in integrating mixed methods analyses. Although a spreadsheet can be a tool of first choice, these programs are used primarily where more specialised software is not available.

Word processors

The primary benefit offered by word processor software, such as Word, Open Office, or Scrivener, is to facilitate gathering of pieces of information from various sources under headings created within the program, without needing to code those pieces beforehand. Use of heading styles within a word processor allows the user to view a

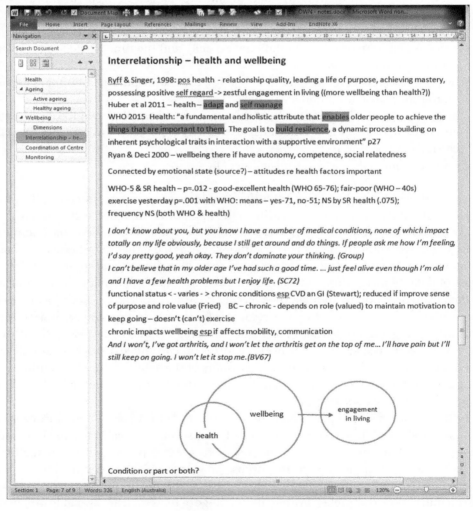

Figure 2.8 Diverse types of information gathered under headings in Word

"map" of the topics for which they have information (using the navigation or summary pane from the View menu). Hyperlinks in the map are used to directly navigate to the selected section within the document whenever there is a new piece of information to add. Information might come directly from raw data, or from analyses being conducted in other statistical and/or qualitative software. In a sense, incoming information is coded "on the go". It can be supplemented with reflective or interpretive comment, and a reference to where the information came from is added (Figure 2.8). Once sufficient information has been gathered, the notes can be turned into descriptive and interpretive prose, and the sections sorted to create a structured report.

The primary integrative role served by word processors then is to facilitate analyses serving a complementary purpose. A secondary integrative role can be served if word processor tables are used to set out comparative analyses, for example, showing information from different sources (in columns) that relates to particular themes or topics (in rows).

Spreadsheets and databases

Excel, Filemaker, and other table-based software, which along with word processors are available on almost every computer, also serve both complementary and comparative functions with respect to integrating data and analyses. Additionally, as a simple-to-use data entry or transfer tool, they support other statistical and qualitative data analysis programs. Excel is used also for statistical analyses in some disciplines (more often in business studies and by economists than by other social scientists).

Brief notes, summary text, or short quotes for each case entered into spreadsheets and databases alongside numeric data, make possible analyses that integrate these different sources. Usually, columns are defined by content and rows are defined by cases, with cells containing the specific information for each case for each defined topic area (Figure 2.9). As with a word processor, that information does not necessarily need to have been "preprocessed" before it is entered, making spreadsheets a tool of choice for rapid analyses. As data entry and analysis proceeds, additional columns can be added if necessary, either for new kinds of information that become apparent, or to recode and perhaps categorise information already entered so that it can be used for sorting tasks. This gives the spreadsheet valuable flexibility for data entry.

Two kinds of integrative analyses can follow. Table-based software brings together information from disparate sources for consideration by the analyst, to support complementary and pattern analyses. These are assisted by being able to hide columns or split the screen so that information held in selected columns can be easily brought side by side for consideration as part of the analysis process. Secondly, columns containing categorical or scaled variable data can be used as a means of sorting rows (Figure 2.9). This brings together all the data on any (column-based) topic for subgroups of (row-based) cases, sorted according to those categorical variables, thus facilitating cross-case comparative analyses. Those familiar with Framework Analysis, or the kinds of matrices advocated by Miles et al. (2014) will see a direct parallel in this process.

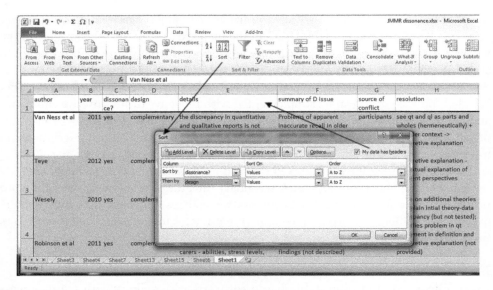

Figure 2.9   Data in Microsoft Excel, sorted using categorical values

Analysis software

Two major types of broad-function analytic programs are those designed primarily for statistical analysis and those for analysis of qualitative data. Each has functions that support integrative mixed analyses, to a greater or lesser extent.

Statistical software

Statistical programs have developed limited features that support integrative aspects of mixed methods analysis to add to their extensive array of options for pure descriptive, inferential, and exploratory statistical analyses. For example, using the add-on SPSS text analysis module (www.spss.com), open-ended survey responses are automatically categorised using natural language processing and sentiment analysis, with fine tuning of the categories by the researcher possible. The new categories are then incorporated with other data for statistical and exploratory analyses. All statistical programs additionally provide output in visual form as charts, graphs, and models, with some programs being more user-controlled and interactive than others.

WordStat (www.provalisresearch.com) sits somewhere between statistical software and qualitative analysis software, and comes as part of a fully integrated suite that includes QDA Miner for qualitative analyses and SimStat for statistical analyses. Exploratory text mining in WordStat allows the user to extract information automatically from text, for use in topic modelling or co-occurrence displays. Using WordStat's content analysis features, long passages of text as well as short answer responses can be coded into categories. Coding might be based on existing categorisation models. Alternatively, based on an initial understanding of the topic and content analysis of

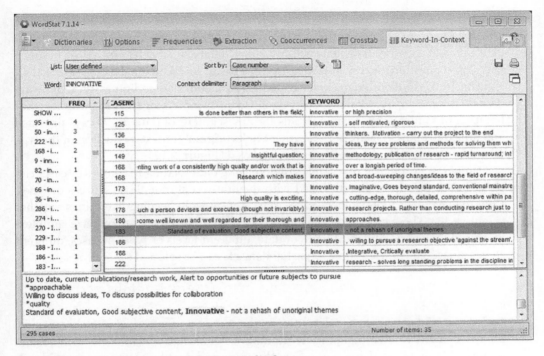

Figure 2.10   WordStat: keyword in context display

words and phrases in the text, the user can create their own dictionaries consisting of words, word patterns, phrases, or rules for categorising both current and future sets of data (Figure 2.10). Resulting variables are then combined using user-defined algorithms to locate text data fitting the user's queries (e.g., find A when it co-occurs with B but not C or D), or they are combined with other categorical or scaled data, with results shown using statistics, charts, and multidimensional displays.

Qualitative data analysis software (QDAS)

Developments in QDAS have made the most noteworthy contributions to *integration* of mixed data sources and analyses. Qualitative software assists integration through facilitating management of varied non-numerical data sources, through combination or comparison of different qualitative and quantitative data types in an analysis, and in converting qualitative data into formats that allow for transfer to other modules or other types of software for further analyses. Four programs stand out as being most useful for combining quantitative with qualitative methods of analysis (in alphabetic order): Dedoose, MAXQDA, NVivo, and QDA Miner. Each has particular strengths and weaknesses. A fifth program, Atlas.ti, is less useful for general mixed methods analysis work, but has good multimedia and georeferencing capability for those wanting to combine those with text analysis.

In terms of data management

QDAS allows for the importation, annotation, and coding of textual, video, audio, and image data in a variety of formats within a single database, as well as mixed-form (open and closed question) survey data and, in some cases, social media data (Figure 2.11).

Data from different sources are coded using a common coding system, allowing data relating to any particular code or theme to be displayed together to facilitate combination or comparison. Source details for any segment of data are always provided and linked to allow viewing of the segment in its original context, regardless of the type of source or where in the program it is displayed (Figure 2.12).

Demographic, quantitative, and georeferencing data relating to sources or cases can be added to or imported and linked with qualitative data for those sources or cases. Data management tools (folders, cases, sets, etc.) assist in keeping like things together (Figure 2.13). These tools allow the data to be cut in multiple ways to manage complexity within and across different types of data, different levels or types of cases, different stages, phases, or times. Whole or partial datasets can be selected for analyses.

For combining and comparing data from different groups and or source types

Coded material can be compared within cases and across cases, including across subgroups defined by demographic, locational, or quantitative variables, with results presented in matrices giving access to both counts and qualitative content for each cell in the matrix (Figure 2.14).

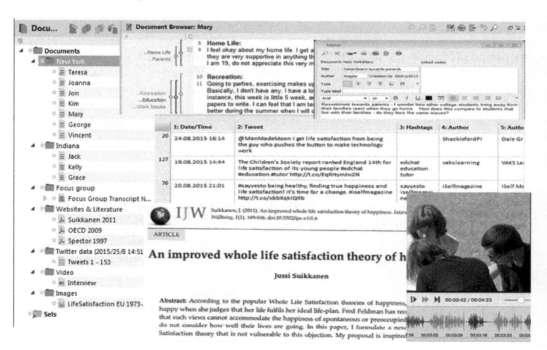

Figure 2.11   Document system in MAXQDA

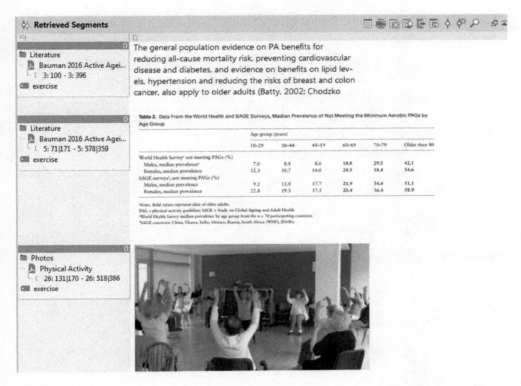

Figure 2.12   Data coded "exercise" retrieved from varied sources in MAXQDA

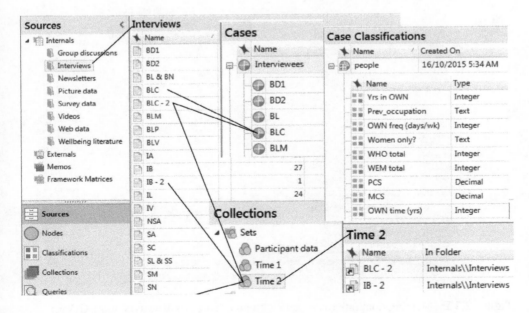

Figure 2.13   Data management tools in NVivo

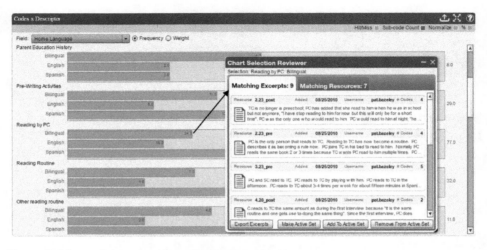

Figure 2.14   Codes by descriptor display in Dedoose

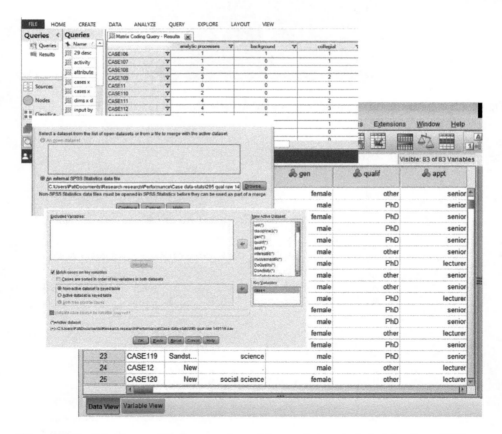

Figure 2.15   Merging qualitative case data with an existing statistical database (NVivo to SPSS)

Comparative analyses are similarly conducted within cases or across groups of cases based on organisational variables such as phase or site of data collection, or type of data. Thus, for example, changes over time in experience of anxiety (or any other category of interest) for different individuals or groups can be examined; or individual responses reflecting on the impact of climate change can be compared with those coming from focus groups, twitter feeds, media reports, or the scientific literature.

For conversion and linking

Qualitative coding can be counted in various ways for each source or case and reported in the form of a case (or variable) by variable table to allow for statistical analysis. Varying types and levels of analysis can be carried out within the program or an associated module, or the data can be easily exported in tabular form. It can then be used separately or in combination with other data in visual displays (e.g., graphs or charts) or for further statistical analyses (Figure 2.15).

Georeferenced qualitative data allows visual modelling within the qualitative software, or links with other geographical (GPS, GIS) data to assist location-based analyses (see Figure 6.3 and Figure 10.2 in later chapters).

Data visualisation tools

Options for visualising qualitative data in charts, models, maps, networks, and a variety of other mixed data forms are designed to assist analysis by helping users to "see" their data (Figure 2.16). These are available to varying degrees and in varying forms within different programs. Elements in visual displays that represent project items, such as codes or sources, always link directly to the underlying data held in those items, for deeper analysis.

Detailed information about the range of tools provided by different QDAS programs and links to developers' websites, where more information is available and trial versions can be downloaded, are available on the University of Surrey's CAQDAS resources page: www.surrey.ac.uk/sociology/research/researchcentres/caqdas/resources/

Specialised analytic tools

Information about tools designed to facilitate integration using specialised types of data and analyses such as social network analysis, qualitative comparative analysis, geospatial data, repertory grid analyses, Q-sort analyses, and others are provided along with details of how those analyses are conducted, primarily in Chapter 10.

Technology will continue to develop, prompted especially by new forms of data, but also because of the economic imperatives driving software development companies. Nevertheless, "the role of the researcher remains paramount in deciding issues relating to the meaning of codes, the appropriateness of samples, the choice of techniques for manipulating data and methods of analysis, and the interpretation of the data tables and displays produced using the computer" (Bazeley, 2003a: 418–419).

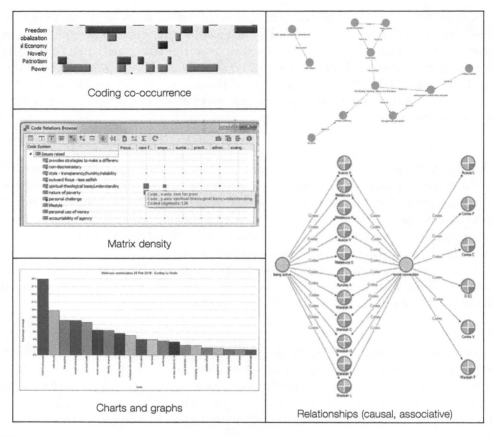

Figure 2.16 Examples of visual tools available in qualitative software

Skills and teamwork in mixed methods research

Basic skills in analysing both statistical and qualitative data are necessary for undertaking a mixed methods analysis. These skills are assumed in this book, as the focus here is on the *integration* of analyses. Those wanting additional resources in either statistical or qualitative analysis might check references listed in the Further Reading section of Chapter 3, or browse the many readily available internet resources, including short instructional videos for particular analysis techniques.

The breadth of skills required for mixed methods research is often listed as one of the constraints on conducting a mixed methods study. Some researchers do combine skills in different types of statistical and qualitative analyses, and yet even then, they are regularly confronted with new methodological developments requiring different areas of expertise and questions best answered by analyses not previously encountered. Breadth of background is, however, a definite advantage in that it makes new skills easier to learn, or when it is necessary to draw on the skills of a specialist, it is possible to understand (and appropriately guide) what the specialist is doing with those data. Similarly, the broad-based generalist has a valuable role within a mixed methods team in assisting people with different skills to work together harmoniously.

In larger projects where multiple researchers are involved or in projects where individual investigators do not have the range of skills required, it becomes necessary to create and build a team of people, each of whom contributes some of the necessary skills. Building an inventory of skills required during the conceptualisation and design phase of a project will help to ensure that a person, persons, or team is available to cover all of these.

Working in teams

Mixed methods project teams typically involve members from different disciplines, as those members bring the different skills required to contribute to the research design and conduct the research. Projects are both enriched and challenged as people with these different backgrounds and skills are brought together in a working relationship, designed to achieve a common purpose.

Mixed methods teams involving members with different disciplinary backgrounds are usually described as *multi*disciplinary, *inter*disciplinary, or *trans*disciplinary. In a multidisciplinary team, members work in parallel or in sequence, each contributing knowledge and skills in their area of expertise. Members of an interdisciplinary team work more collaboratively, with each engaging in all components, sharing knowledge and learning skills from each other (O'Cathain, Murphy, & Nicholl, 2008; Simons, 2007). Transdisciplinary teams work similarly, but with perhaps even greater emphasis on producing an integrated outcome that includes also perspectives from outside the academy (Szostak, 2015). The consensus of opinion, supported by data from a review of projects by O'Cathain et al., is that interdisciplinary approaches to mixed methods team functioning are more productive of integrated outcomes than multidisciplinary approaches.

Benefits and challenges

Mixed methods research requires integration of usually diverse types of data and findings generated through different analyses to produce unique insights. For a team to achieve this, it is necessary for each member to be free to make their particular contribution and to be able to present a case for a preferred way of doing things, but also for members to be open to different perspectives and respectful of others' contributions – prepared to accept, if not learn, new approaches and practices from others. The "sparking of ideas" that can result contributes directly in adding value to the experience and to the outcome. As one of the participants in O'Cathain et al.'s research observed:

> I think that's been wonderful here because it's the tensions between the different things that spark ideas, and spark off thoughts, and spark off discussions. And we've had some wonderful discussions in the team, quite often related to the qualitative type, research type, field and objectives and thinking and the hard

numbers and where they collide, and whether they can expand and explain each other. And as researchers that's what made it a joy, the discussions and arguments if you like that spark out of that. (O'Cathain et al., 2008: 1580)

Sparking, however, can light a fire. Bringing researchers from different disciplines together in a project team accentuates epistemological, methodological, methods, and language differences. For example: Is the person living in a nursing home a resident, patient, client, or consumer? Those from particular disciplines often lack understanding of research processes associated with alternative disciplines, including sampling, analysis strategies, and interpretation. They have different understandings of what counts as evidence and what counts as quality, with different audiences, timelines, and publishing goals. These differences increase the potential for power games resulting in disagreement and delay. The "dysfunctional" team, with unresolved differences, will usually produce separate reports of project components and/or reduced overall output.

Creating success

Teams that work effectively in producing integrated mixed methods reports and articles:

- pre-establish agreement as to the purpose of the project and/or develop a common vision through early communication
- communicate across disciplines and methodological divides throughout the project in regular team meetings and through email or other means; this is facilitated by having someone in a designated coordination and liaison role
- exhibit mutual respect and accommodation of differences in approaches to design and analysis
- ensure that both qualitative and quantitative components get sufficient attention and resources
- enjoy working together.

(See Further Reading for articles and chapters providing more details of these and the following strategies.)

Facilitative leadership from a principal investigator who values integration and the contribution of all members is critical in ensuring that teams develop these necessary qualities. Harmonious working and coordination of effort in a situation where some conflict is inevitable is aided by having at least one key team member who is methodologically bilingual. Coordination of effort and integration of methods is supported when qualitative and quantitative components are designed concurrently, and/or when team members blend roles and collaboratively work together to design data collection tools. And finally, mutual understanding and respect between team members is fostered through reading and discussing each other's previous articles, sharing knowledge and resources, learning from each other through structured analytic exercises, and participating with researchers of other traditions in their data collection activities. Some teams have found it useful to engage in these activities prior to embarking on their joint project.

BOX 2.1

Fostering project integration in an interdisciplinary team

Rick Szostak (2015) described four project-related techniques specifically designed to help foster harmony and integration in situations where conflict-resolution is needed in an interdisciplinary team of researchers:

- redefine concepts to achieve a common meaning
- extend a theory (or its assumptions) to be more inclusive of elements identified by others
- organise different insights and theories in a map, to see them within an overarching framework
- transform opposites into dimensions, so conflicts become differences in degree rather than absolute.

Concluding remarks

The emphasis throughout this chapter has been on ensuring that preparation for a research project is thorough in terms of preliminary conceptualisation and in planning for data, as each of these will help to ensure fruitful analysis and enhanced capacity to contribute to knowledge and practice in the wider world. Realistically, there is often a measure of initial "fluffing around" during the early days of developing a project as the parameters and the dynamics of what one is dealing with are clarified. Mixed methods projects are inherently complex, and so this can be thought of as a necessary phase in the conceptualisation and planning stage of a project. In the final analysis, the particular types of data employed are not nearly so critical as sampling choices, whether the variables or concepts and processes considered are relevant to the issues raised by the study's questions and framework, the attention given to context, and of course, the depth of analysis that is applied to those data sources. Use of visual strategies (models, tables) as an aid to design and to communication of design have been a feature of this chapter, as has the use of software to support and facilitate both separate and mixed analyses.

Having laid the groundwork of design, it is to analysis, and specifically integration of analyses, that our attention now turns.

Further reading

Because this chapter provides just a brief, analysis-focused introduction to design, researchers without a strong background in mixed methods research are encouraged to look into other resources on more general design principles and other aspects of data preparation and management. The list below provides some starting points, as well as references for those who wish to extend their knowledge in particular areas.

Design

All general texts on mixed methods research carry chapters on designing a mixed methods study.

A typology of purposes served by research designs developed by Greene et al. (1989), which has been highly influential for most mixed methodologists' approaches ever since, is described in detail by Caracelli and Greene (1997).

Typologies of design are provided in: Creswell and Plano Clark (2011), Morgan (1998), Morse and Niehaus (2009), and Tashakkori and Teddlie (2010).

Maxwell (2013; Maxwell & Loomis, 2003) presents a (preferred) interactive approach to design as an alternative to more linear typological designs.

Gorard (2010b) explains necessary design features for a mixed methods project that apply regardless of the specific methods of data collection being used. Gorard (2013) provides a more comprehensive general text on design features that contribute to building warranted conclusions.

Guest (2013) critiques typological approaches and recommends focusing on where the point or points of interface will occur in designing a study, as an alternative for complex projects.

Saint Arnault and Fetters (2011) describe and illustrate elements of a good mixed methods funding proposal, including the value of having a theoretical framework and pretested methods.

Wisdom and Fetters (2015) provide guidance regarding all the ancillary elements of project design, including locating sources of funding, timelines, budgeting, and awareness of the review process for funded projects.

Ivankova (2014) describes the quality criteria applied in designing a sequential study of student engagement in online research training in which she purposively selected a sample of survey participants for qualitative follow up.

Cases

Ragin and Becker (1992) is a classic text with contributions from authors with differing perspectives on what is a case.

The concept of cases and their role in qualitative methods is discussed in some detail (with relevance to mixed methods research) in Chapter 1 of Bazeley (2013).

Sampling

Collins et al. (2007) comprehensively list variations on both random and purposive sampling strategies and provide guidelines regarding minimum sample size requirements for different methodological approaches.

Patton (2002: 243–244) lists and explains an extensive range of purposive sampling options.

Teddlie and Yu (2007) list, discuss, and illustrate mixed methods sampling options that combine random with purposive sampling.

Small (2009) reviews the issues of and potential solutions to sampling problems (choice and size) faced by ethnographers (and others) using mixed methods who are seeking analytic rather than population generalisation in fields dominated by demographers and other quantitative researchers.

Modelling and visualisation

Knowlton and Phillips (2013) explain and illustrate logic modelling as part of project design and execution of projects involving implementation of change.

Dyson and Todd (2010) explain the value of a theory of change modelling process in projects "where initiatives are complex, indeterminate, and set in complex contexts" (2010: 124).

Plano Clark and Sanders (2015) explain the role of visual displays in mixed methods research and point to a range of examples, the majority of which focus on design.

Mixed methods teams

Multiple references provide detailed analyses of team-related issues and suggestions about strategies for managing mixed methods teams (Bowers et al., 2013; Brock, 2005; Burch & Heinrich, 2016; Curry & Nunez-Smith, 2015; Curry et al., 2012; Szostak, 2015).

Lunde, Heggen, and Strand (2013) detail the experience of a team that could not reconcile their discipline-based epistemological differences.

As well as discussing a variety of benefits and challenges of interdisciplinary teamwork, the article by O'Cathain et al. (2008) is an exemplar of how to write up methods and analysis strategies, as used in their examination of teamwork in a number of health care policy studies.

Using software

Methodological texts and references for qualitative analysis can be found at the conclusion of Chapter 3, and for statistical analysis at the conclusion of Chapter 8. Those listed below focus on the use of software, although they do so with reference to methods.

Field (2018) shows how to use SPSS for analysis of quantitative data, with clear explanations of how and why the various types of analyses are conducted. Parallel versions are available for R and SAS.

The Stata website (www.stata.com) lists an extensive range of books published by their own press as well as others, covering every aspect of using Stata, for all levels of users. Videos are also available.

Silver (2015) reviews QDA Miner (with SimStat and WordStat) as a tool for mixed methods research.

Silver and Lewins (2014) provide an overview of the issues in and practice of using a range of QDAS programs for qualitative (primarily) and mixed methods analysis. The companion website (https://study.sagepub.com/using-software-in-qualitative-research) contains three sample projects illustrating different types of studies, including a mixed methods study. It also provides step-by-step guides to basic use of a wide selection of QDAS, including Atlas.ti, Dedoose, HyperRESEARCH, MAXQDA, NVivo, QDA Miner, and Transana.

Silver and Woolf (2015) introduce readers to their Five-Level QDA® method for learning and teaching qualitative software, based on extensive experience of teaching and research in this field. It lays the groundwork for three books by Woolf and Silver on qualitative analysis using the Five-Level QDA method for each of Atlas.ti, MAXQDA, and NVivo, to be published by Routledge in 2017.

Bazeley and Jackson (2013) guide the researcher through using NVivo, explaining how and when to use the various strategies available in the software.

Kuckartz (2014) explains the theory and practice of qualitative text analysis, with a chapter included on using MAXQDA software (which he was instrumental in developing).

Corbin and Strauss (2015) illustrate the use of MAXQDA in developing a grounded theory.

Friese (2014) describes the use of Atlas.ti in the context of a notice-collect-think model of analysis.

All developer websites for qualitative analysis programs provide links to video and other resources for learning to use the software (see www.surrey.ac.uk/sociology/research/research centres/caqdas/resources/ for further links and information about different programs).

3
INTERPRETING DATA

CHAPTER OVERVIEW

The task of data analysis

An interpretive orientation to data and analysis

Interpreting statistical and non-numeric data sources – some cautionary notes

    Cautions in interpreting numeric data and statistical tests

    Interpreting text: beyond descriptive accounts

    Keeping track of research decisions, activities and reflections

A framework for mixed methods analysis

    Typological and dimensional frameworks for integrated analysis

A process-oriented logic model for integrated analysis

    Starting points (resources) for mixed methods analysis

    First level processes

    Second level processes

    Interpretive outcomes and applications

Concluding remarks

Further reading

Interpreting data and drawing inferences from data is never a straightforward, cut and dried activity, but rather is subject to the vagaries of design decisions, administrative choices, procedural fashions, and contextual influences. Capacity for data analysis involves being able to view the world from the position of another, combined with skills in critical thinking that are applied to the interrogation and interpretation of data. Inferences drawn should make sense to those who contributed the data, to other researchers working with that or similar data, and in the light of what is already known – to which they should, hopefully, add further insights.

Specific strategies for working with, analysing, and integrating mixed methods data are the subject of Part 2 of this book. The topic of generating and supporting conclusions built from mixed methods data is covered in Part 3. My primary purpose in this chapter is to provide a conceptual and practical framing for interpretation of data. It presents a perspective that sees all forms of analysis, whether statistical, qualitative, or mixed, as being essentially interpretive. The chapter concludes by introducing a model describing mixed methods analysis.

The task of data analysis

Regardless of what type of data has been gathered and the broad approach to analysis that is taken (quantitative, qualitative, or mixed), tasks involved in data analysis follow a similar pattern, as outlined below. The way these are carried out and the period allocated to each step will vary for different types of data and different approaches to analysis, however. Although there is a pattern to these steps and they appear to be describing a linear process, it is not prescriptive; there is considerable overlap in both time and content between stages. Analysis involves frequent stepping back to move forward; it is an iterative process of querying data and challenging hunches until a warranted conclusion is developed.

1   Prepare data, to be ready for analysis.

- Numeric data are entered under named categories to create variables for statistical analysis. Audio data are transcribed and the transcripts checked. Documentary data, field notes, and other non-text sources are labelled and organised.

2   Explore the data, to see what is there.

- Initial descriptive statistics provide an introductory overview of the "shape" of the variable data. This also facilitates "data cleaning", in which gaps and coding errors are revealed for correction. Text, images, and related non-numeric data are explored through reading, imagining, and reflecting in annotations and memos, with perhaps some initial codes developed to identify key ideas to pursue in further data collection and analysis. Ideas flowing from one set of data prompt exploration in or with another, to foster the conversation between methods.

3   Manage, reduce, sort and code data to identify relevant concepts and themes.

- Codes are used to connect, represent, and maintain links to the content of textual and other qualitative data. These might be informed by literature or other data, or they might be "emergent" from the data themselves. Additionally, storylines will be identified and context noted – seeing things from a participant's perspective.

4   Describe what is being revealed by the data.

- Frequencies and/or descriptive statistics are recorded for variable data; content of coded categories for qualitative data are reviewed and summarised. Higher order variables, conceptual codes, and/or thematic categories are developed. Conversations between sources will be about identifying common concepts and themes, comparing and potentially synthesising data sources based on those.

5   Undertake comparative analyses that answer research questions about differences and/or help to discern deeper meaning.

- Patterns of open responses are compared across subgroups defined by numerically based variables or text-based coding categories, or across different contexts or situations to refine descriptions and to see the data in new ways. Continue the conversation between methods by using quantitative variables as a basis for comparisons within qualitative data.

6   Investigate patterns of association.

- Relationships between variables are explored or tested to provide more explanatory detail on differences revealed through comparative analyses. Similarly, patterns of association between coding categories are explored, in a search for and assessment of connections across them. The goal is to build towards interrelated thematic or explanatory/predictive statements based on variables and/or codes, keeping in mind the purpose and questions of the research. Alternative explanations are explored and tested.

7   Report results, inferences, interpretations.

- Sequenced statements of results are prepared, supported by data displays (models, tables) and by source evidence that has been built up during the analysis process. These are then reviewed for publication or other forms of reporting.

An interpretive orientation to data and analysis

Interpretation is the lynchpin of decisions made and processes used at *every* stage of the research process, by both researcher and participants. All scientific observation and analysis involves "acts of interpretation by researchers", all investigation is theory laden (Howe & Eisenhardt, 1990). "Ultimately all methods of data collection are analysed 'qualitatively,' in so far as the act of analysis is an interpretation, and therefore of necessity a selective rendering, of the 'sense' of the available data" (Fielding & Fielding, 1986: 12). When preparatory work is carried out using focus groups or interviews, inductive qualitative understanding drives the design, and therefore the eventual interpretation, of surveys and other forms of statistical data collection, even when these are considered to be the major quantitative component of the research (Morse, 2015). When Jick (1979: 609) needed to piece together elements of evidence from different sources and resolve a problem of dissonance between them, he referred to "qualitative data and analysis" as the "glue that cements the interpretation of multimethod results".

Statistics have been located within a paradigm of post-positivist empiricism as a means of discovering information about our world as it really is. In association with randomised trial methodologies, they are still viewed this way by practitioners across many disciplines. Yet even those who once promoted it are increasingly challenging this perspective. Donald Campbell (1974: 30), well known for his experimental and statistical writing, reflected in his later years: "If we are to be truly scientific, we must re-establish the qualitative grounding of the quantitative." David Howell (2014: xi), author of one of the most popular statistical texts for psychology students, observed: "Statistics is not really about numbers; it is about understanding our world." As with a piece of beautiful music, statistical data can be analysed, appreciated, and admired, but they also must be interpreted. *How* they are interpreted determines their ultimate value and usefulness.

Take the design and analysis of a survey or questionnaire, for example: frequently used in mixed methods research, and usually classified as a post-positivist quantitative tool, I prefer to describe these as hybrid tools that happen to use numbers rather than words to capture participants' responses to questions about themselves and their experience, usually for the convenience of the researcher (Box 3.1). The intention here is not to downplay the value of statistical tools and quantitative approaches to research, but to recognise the role played by interpretation in those approaches as well as in specifically qualitative approaches. There are assumptions and choices made in the way we handle all kinds of data that moderate the claims we can make from data.

BOX 3.1

Survey/questionnaire design and analysis: measuring or interpreting reality?

Good survey research and questionnaire writing always has, as a preparatory stage, a thorough (interpretive) review of the literature on the topic to be studied, to examine the various ways it has been seen before. Some preliminary interviewing or discussions with those in, or involved with, the participant group will be undertaken in order to understand how they view the issues to be investigated and how they express those thoughts. This is in the hope that the resulting structured

(Continued)

(Continued)

questions are meaningful to them and sit somewhere within *their* reality. The items are then gathered and made into a series of questions or scales, designed according to the best judgement of the researcher. Questions might be designed to deductively test a hypothesis, or to inductively explore experience or build a theoretical model. Those responding interpret the intent of each question or scale item. They then record their answers using numbers to represent their response, or their response is converted from words to numbers by an interviewer or coder in the process of data entry.

The researcher interprets the statistics generated from the items and the interrelationships between them, or uses factor analysis to create scales from the items, choosing a solution that "best fits" the data. The choice of how many constructs (factors) there are in the data, what to call them, and what they mean are all matters of interpretive judgement by the researcher-analyst. The scales are then refined for use and scores are generated to give an indication of the level to which each factor/dimension/construct matters for each of the respondents. The term *construct* itself implies something that is made rather than found. The final numerically based report is presumed to provide a reflection of respondents' states of being, usually with little recognition of the degree to which both participant and researcher – and indeed, the final reader – have interpretively constructed the data and the findings generated from them *at each step in their production*.

Interpreting statistical and non-numeric data sources – some cautionary notes

Many researchers believe that it is necessary to first analyse separate qualitative and quantitative component studies before the results from those studies are drawn together and interpreted as mixed methods data. While preliminary processing of particular data sources, of whatever type, is usually necessary, the analytical extent of that will vary depending on the purpose of the study and the way the various sources are intended to be used. Whatever analytic pathway is selected, integration must remain front and centre of attention, so that a conversation continues throughout between different sources, between different methods of data collection, and between different approaches to analysis. While there are times when a particular data source shines a spotlight on an area of interest that is worthy of publication, the danger of focusing on separate analyses is that the study will disintegrate into its separate components. When these are published as separate studies, the added benefits of integration as a mixed methods study are lost.

Readers are assumed to have existing knowledge of the separate quantitative and qualitative procedures that are of relevance to their work (further reading is suggested for those seeking more depth in one or other area). Because mixed methods analysis incorporates principles and practices of both statistical and qualitative analyses, however, some cautionary notes are suggested, to be kept lurking in the background as analysis proceeds.

Cautions in interpreting numeric data and statistical tests

Statistics are used to describe, to discern, to explain, and to predict, based on counted or measured variables, each of which represents specified qualities of situations, things, or people. They are incredibly useful for telling us if a measure or index varies across time or differs across people or groups or organisations to a degree that is worth noting. Statistics are also useful for indicating if some kind of relationship exists between variables such that when one varies, a proportional variation in the related variable is also likely to occur.

Interpretive issues arise from the inherent qualities of numbers as representations of phenomena and from the way statistics are applied. Numbers, and the statistics that are derived from them, provide a degree of precision that is valued by researchers and attractive to policymakers, but they can also be "precisely inaccurate". It is important therefore for mixed methods researchers to understand how statistical results are generated and to be aware that they need to apply their interpretive skills, including a healthy scepticism, to statistical results as much as they do to other types of observations.

Errors in judgement can arise when employing and interpreting statistics that derive from both their inherent qualities and the way they are applied, as seen in:

- inferences derived from samples that are too small, too large, or that do not reflect the population from which they are drawn, including when non-response creates bias in statistically calculated estimates
- application of inferential statistics (i.e., statistical procedures intended for creating population estimates) to complete populations where actual numbers are available
- use of averages across potentially diverse cases or subsamples, masking sometimes marked differences, e.g., in effect of a treatment
- reliance on null hypothesis testing, significance testing, and p values as an arbiter for valid conclusions
- application of measures and scales without regard for the specifics of context.

These and other more specific issues will emerge in later discussions, and alternatives to standard inferential statistics will be suggested where appropriate.

Interpreting text: beyond descriptive accounts

Textual, visual, and other sensory data (assume *textual* to include all these) are a source of rich insights into experience, behaviour, participant attitudes and beliefs, and the contexts that affect these. Whereas the researcher can appear to be somewhat absent during statistical processing of numeric data, the researcher is very much present and influential during the entire qualitative data analysis process. Qualitative analysis seeks understanding of the complexities of individual, social, and institutional worlds from the perspectives of those who are impacted by them. Interpretation is influenced by research purposes, an underlying conceptual framework, the context in which the data were obtained, choice of methodology, and the awareness, sensitivity, and reflexivity of the researcher. The inductive, comparative methods and iterative movement between data and analysis commonly associated with qualitative approaches have the potential to reveal a level of detail and depth of understanding of experiences and processes not available through statistical methods. Difficulties can arise, however, through absence of the kind of standardised procedures that give quantitative methods an appearance of greater rigour.

When "authors give no demonstrable recognition that qualitative research itself encompasses a diverse range of methodological approaches suitable for different purposes", then qualitative methods are essentialised (Song et al., 2010: 729). "Grounded", "thematic analysis" of textual data is ubiquitous, and all too often undertaken in a way that comprises little more than identifying, coding to, and describing a few key "emergent" categories or ideas. This is particularly evident in supplementary qualitative components of mixed methods studies in the professional disciplines (health, education, management). Thematic analysis, when fully developed as a qualitative approach, might begin with some coding to categories, but it goes well beyond that to generating inter-related analytical, conceptually grounded thematic statements that model and perhaps begin to theorise the main findings from the data.

Beyond (or building on) thematic analysis, there is a rich array of methods and methodological choices available to inform analysis of textual and other qualitative data that help to capture the richness and potential of that data (see Further Reading for guidance). These different methods are based on different epistemologies and principles, and serve different purposes. Mixed methods researchers therefore need to (a) become aware of the choices available to them regarding different ways of approaching and handling textual and other qualitative data, and then (b) select for use, from the different approaches, those elements or methods that best serve the purpose of their research and directly contribute to answering their research questions.

Figure 3.1   Recording research decisions, activities and reflections

Keeping track of research decisions, activities and reflections

Keeping a regularly maintained description, an audit trail, to document decisions made about ways of working both with and between different kinds of data is an invaluable resource, regardless of the type of data and analysis process being adopted (Figure 3.1). An audit trail becomes part of the analysis process as it includes reflective writing about assumptions brought to a project, the way the project proceeded "on the ground", how results were obtained, and how conclusions were reached. Pointers or links to data that prompted or support those reflections and insights should be included. The process of writing itself clarifies and enhances the writer-researcher's development of ideas and understanding.

Recording reflections, accompanied by or linked to evidentiary data, lays a foundation for later reporting as well. Whether or not a named methodology is used as a basis for interpretation of numeric or textual data, this kind of record facilitates writing in a way that allows a reader to understand the researcher's processes for working with data, interpreting them, and drawing conclusions from them. Documentation of options considered, decisions made, actions taken, and their consequences all help when it comes time to build a case for the trustworthiness of the conclusions reached.

Marian Carcary (2009) explains how she found it useful to keep both an "intellectual" (reflective) and a "physical" (action based) research audit trail as she employed a multiple case study/grounded theory approach to evaluate the ICT investment process for student records in Irish Institutes of Technology.

A framework for mixed methods analysis

The process of mixed methods analysis is best viewed as the continuation of a conversation between methods that began as the foundations of the study were laid, but which gains in intensity once data become available and formal analysis is begun. People intentionally engaging in focused conversation exchange and develop ideas at varying levels of intensity, sometimes supporting and sometimes disagreeing with each other's statements, drawing ever closer towards a common position, or to a "negotiated" understanding (Bryman, 2007) and perhaps acceptance of another's alternative perspectives.

Methods of working with data in a mixed methods study are drawn from a range of methodological traditions, each with established conventions for "proper" conduct of research. When methods are combined in a mixed methods project, adaptations are often necessary that risk corruption of the methodology from which they are drawn. The time given to an ethnographic component might be less than desirable, samples incomplete, values for variables missing, or in a study designed to develop a grounded theory, theoretical sampling might not always be possible. Shortcuts are taken in order to cope with the greater time commitment required in a mixed methods study.

A balance needs to be struck between adherence to the techniques, perspectives, and values associated with each of the traditional methods used and the ability to draw useful strategies for the current situation from those traditions. Critical to this process is a recognition of the ways in which a methodology has been adapted and the methodological implications of doing so, so that an assessment can be made of implications for the results obtained in the mixed methods study.

Typological and dimensional frameworks for integrated analysis

Typological models of integrated analysis generally assume independent sources of qualitative and quantitative data that have undergone separate qualitative and quantitative analyses (respectively) prior to combination and drawing meta-inferences. Additionally, the typology of analysis methods presented by particular authors typically follows their (or others') particular typologies of design.

- Creswell and Plano Clark (2011: 215–220) discussed four basic integrative processes: (1) merging the results of analyses of the quantitative and qualitative datasets to compare results; (2) merging analyses through data transformation; (3) connecting from the analysis of quantitative data to the collection of qualitative data which is then used to explain the previous findings; and (4) connecting from the analysis of qualitative data to the collection of quantitative data which is then used to build on (and hopefully generalise) the previous findings. Additional design types within their typology use various combinations of these four processes.
- Teddlie and Tashakkori (2009) proposed five broad data analysis strategies, with some internal variations based on the order or priority of components. They classified their five approaches as parallel, conversion, sequential, multilevel, and fully integrated forms of mixed data analysis; with application of analytical techniques from one tradition to data from the other proposed as a sixth strategy – sometimes referred to as a cross-over strategy. Fully integrated designs are defined as occurring when the mixing of analyses "may be characterised as iterative, reciprocal, and interdependent" (2009: 280), although they additionally observe that the analysis of separate strands can inform other strands well before the development of meta-inferences in some of their other designs.

Caracelli and Greene (1993) identified four specific integrative strategies from a subsample of their earlier (1989) sample of evaluation studies, these being data transformation, typology development, extreme case analysis, and data consolidation/merging. Several other authors have adopted these in combination with their original five-category classification of purposes (triangulation, complementarity, expansion, development, and initiation) as the basis for their own approaches to analysis (e.g., Brannen & O'Connell, 2015).

Onwuegbuzie and Combs (2010) identified thirteen dimensions used by different authors in creating analysis typologies (Box 3.2). Guided by their three analysis orientations (variable oriented, case oriented, and process/experience oriented), they listed an extensive range of qualitative and quantitative analyses that could be used "in an almost unlimited number of combinations" (2010: 420). They then developed a meta-framework of mixed analysis designs that incorporated all thirteen dimensions, in an attempt to outline the choices available, presented as a diagram so complex as to be more confusing than helpful (Figure 3.2).

BOX 3.2

Onwuegbuzie and Combs' dimensions for building mixed methods analysis typologies

1. Rationale/purpose for conducting the mixed analysis
2. Philosophy underpinning the mixed analysis
3. Number of data types that will be analysed
4. Number of data analysis types that will be used
5. Time sequence of the mixed analysis
6. Level of interaction between quantitative and qualitative analyses
7. Priority of analytical components
8. Number of analytical phases
9. Link to other design components
10. Phase of the research process when all analysis decisions are made
11. Type of generalisation
12. Analysis orientation
13. Cross-over nature of analysis. (Onwuegbuzie & Combs, 2010: 411)

As with the development of design typologies, analysis typologies and identification of dimensions have the benefit of setting out a range of options for ways of combining data and analysis methods that can serve to extend the possibilities considered by less experienced or less confident researchers. The implication of Onwuegbuzie's attempt to create a meta-framework capturing an "unlimited" number of combinations of methods, however, is that any attempt to codify or proscribe a set of mixed methods analysis strategies is doomed to failure. Additionally, typologies fail conceptually in that they essentialise quantitative and qualitative analyses as unitary approaches despite, as Onwuegbuzie and Combs (2010: 411) point out, there being many, many different ways of working with both numeric and non-numeric data. As noted in Chapter 1, the differences within these two families of methods, the blurred boundaries between them, and now the emergence of alternative forms of data, can be considered too great for them to be seen as separate and coherent primary elements in typological models.

Typological models of analysis, like their design counterparts, become a problem when they constrain researchers' choices, or when they focus the researcher's attention

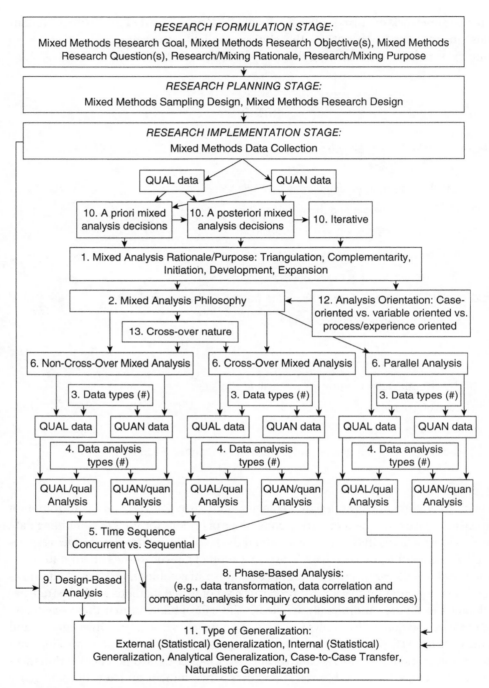

Figure 3.2 Meta-framework of mixed analysis strategies

Source: Onwuegbuzie and Combs, 2010: 424, Figure 17.6

on concerns in analysis that are not especially relevant to their current situation. There are additional dangers. By focusing on the necessity for prior separate analyses of the quantitative and/or qualitative data before considering (or allowing for) mixing they create a tendency to not consider (or encourage) the possibility of iterative exchange before the defined point of interface, rendering the mixed analysis less effective. Alternatively, they do give recognition to the likely occurrence of iterative exchange before the nominated point of interface, rendering the mixed analysis less transparent. In too many cases, no formal attempt to combine insights from different methods is made before final interpretation of the obtained results and evidence of interrelationship is not recorded until the discussion section of an article. A further danger is that typologies encourage segregated (binary) thinking right through to the writing up stage, rather than a focus on the question to be answered, what data are available (or accessible) with which to answer it, and what analysis processes can best be used to maximise the benefit of combining the different sources and types of data.

A process-oriented logic model for integrated analysis

Logic models operationalise a theory of change (Knowlton & Phillips, 2013). The theory of change behind mixed methods analysis is very simple. It is that (a) effectively combining more than one source or type of data and/or more than one approach to analysis will deliver a gain over using a single source, type of data, or approach to analysis, and (b) effective integration of sources and analyses will also deliver a gain over separate analyses of different sources. An adapted logic model to describe processes of mixed methods analysis is proposed in Figure 3.3.

Starting points (resources) for mixed methods analysis

From the point of view of analysis (which is the focus of this book) integrative analytic processes are shown as starting from any of four points in a project: (a) directly from the various sources of data in their more or less raw form, as elements from them ("data items" and insights) are brought together without prior processing; (b) from "preprocessed" data, that is, using data that have undergone some preliminary processing and descriptive analyses, usually involving some form of coding or indexing; (c) during the analysis process, where different styles of analysis are worked interactively side by side and together; and (d) during the writing process, where a focus on writing about the substantive issues covered means integration will develop further as the writing proceeds. Most integrative analysis strategies described in the literature (and in Part 2) focus on categories (b) and (c). Once integrative processes are engaged at any stage, they will naturally embrace later stages; for example, integration of the products of preliminary processing (b) will necessarily involve further integration as analysis proceeds (c) and during writing (d).

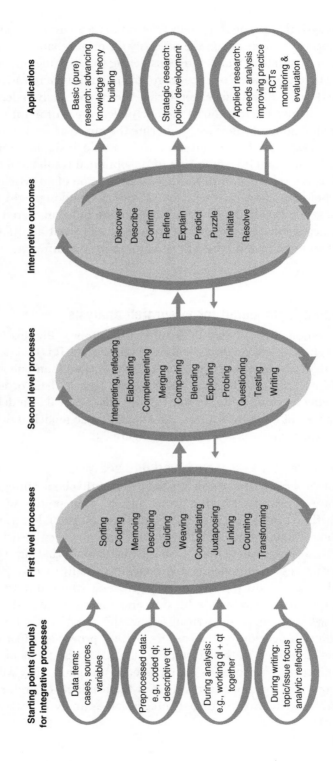

Figure 3.3 Operationalising mixed methods integration

First level processes

First level processes are operational procedures that are applied directly to the data or analyses specified as the starting point for integration, and serve as the basis for more advanced (secondary level) processes. For example, sorting and coding are most likely to be used with raw data, but might also be needed to facilitate integration of previously coded data where previous coding has not allowed for merging across common categories. Preliminary processing of data might be all that is necessary to guide development of the next stage of the research, or to allow for weaving or juxtaposing of different elements of data as the basis for more advanced complementary or comparative processes. Weaving and juxtaposing of relatively unprocessed data elements might also be possible. Counting and transforming could be applied directly to unprocessed or preprocessed data, or alternatively during the process of analysis, leading to further secondary level processing. First level processes are often applied in combination.

Second level processes

Second level processes take integration further, requiring more interpretive skill and reflection as part of their application than first level processes. Working iteratively between first and second level processes is common, but analysis and integration progressively moves forward to focus more on these higher-level processes. They rarely are applied in isolation, but work interactively with each other, always with a focus on achieving the goals of the project. Exploring, testing, and questioning possibilities in the data will push analysis further, while beginning writing will also prompt ideas for further analysis as unresolved problems are revealed and pursued using other second-level processes.

Interpretive outcomes and applications

Interpretive outcomes are a consequence of successful secondary analyses and integrative processes. Again, as outcomes are being developed, there will be frequent backwards and forwards movement between these developments and the analyses and integrative strategies that lead to them. There might be more than one type of outcome from any particular project. Outcomes will vary, depending on the intended application of the results of the project.

Specific first and second level processes (strategies) outlined in the model are described and illustrated in Part 2 of this book with their interpretive counterparts, while those processes that bring the products of those strategies together in developing a cohesive outcome are presented in Part 3.

Concluding remarks

The interpretive foundations for analysis have been the focus of this chapter. Data analysis for all types of sources follows a basic pattern, but not a routine procedure: interpretation is involved at every step as decisions are made and inferences drawn, whatever data analysis tools and strategies are used. After considering currently available models, an alternative framework for mixed methods analysis was proposed, one that focuses on the integrative processes seen as an essential aspect of mixed methods studies. Different starting points, from raw data to partially or fully completed statistical or qualitative analyses, provide the basis for first level integrative processes that work directly with those data or interim results. These perhaps produce direct outcomes, but they are more likely to be combining, comparing, or transforming the data (or all three) in ways that will allow for deeper analysis. Second level processes take the integration of sources and methods further as data continue to be interwoven and explored, compared, probed, interrelated, and challenged, in order to generate interpretive outcomes with application to knowledge or practice. Reflection and writing were seen as critical components facilitating interpretation and integration throughout the process.

Further reading

Interpreting numeric data

Interpreting counts and using statistical analyses are covered in some detail (including further reading) in Chapters 7 and 8 respectively.

On the question of constructing, interpreting, analysing, and integrating survey data as a hybrid mixed method, see Feilzer (2010) and Schrauf (2016).

Qualitative methods and analysis

Bazeley (2013) provides detailed, comprehensive, action-based steps one can take in undertaking analysis of qualitative data at a very practical level. Many of these strategies apply not only to the qualitative components of a mixed methods study, but are also relevant to analysis and synthesis of mixed methods data. Bazeley (2009) is an accessible, article-length introduction to the analytic approach described in the more detailed book-length version.

Braun and Clarke (2006) is a much-cited article describing thematic analysis of qualitative data.

Tracy (2013) provides a clear and comprehensive overview of qualitative methods from initial conceptualisation through proposal writing, fieldwork and analysis, to publishing and exiting the field.

Hesse-Biber (2017) covers the design and conduct of several types of qualitative studies. Topics include paradigmatic approaches, ethical issues, researching mass media, and analysis, interpretation, and representation of qualitative data.

Saldaña (2015a) describes and illustrates an extensive array of strategies for coding and beyond.

Saldaña (2015b) offers 60 different modes of thinking to extend the value of qualitative data.

Richards (2014) has written a user-friendly guide to getting one's hands dirty with qualitative data, and growing insightfully from there.

Miles et al. (2014) updates the authors' legendary approach to qualitative data analysis with its emphasis on visual and matrix-driven approaches.

The authors contributing to Wertz et al. (2011) introduce qualitative research in psychology, then each writes in detail to present one of five approaches to qualitative analysis: phenomenology, grounded theory, discourse analysis, narrative analysis, and intuitive inquiry. Each is illustrated by drawing on the same written story and follow-up interview transcript containing a detailed description of trauma experienced and resilience shown.

PART 2

INTEGRATIVE ANALYSIS
STRATEGIES

Data analysis in mixed methods research involves a complex interplay of interdependent strategies. The process is inherently messy and often exploratory, untried, and emergent. There is no definitive list of mixed methods approaches to inquiry or analysis. In reading the mixed methods literature one is continually stimulated by observing innovative new ways of combining methods to work with data. Being flexible and pragmatic about design, open to data, and having a touch of inventiveness in approach to analysis are invaluable assets for the mixed methods researcher.

My goal is that researchers will fully exploit the integrative potential of their data, as they seek to answer the questions they have posed. This involves making a point of stopping at various points during analysis to write, and to look for ways that one method might inform another. At the same time, one needs to be aware of the challenges to data integrity that can arise as data are merged, modified, transformed, or synthesised. The strategies outlined here are designed as a pool to select from, to use, modify, and combine as needed, given current purposes, data, and audience.

In this part I start by describing sequential strategies in which the analyses and results from one method guide the development or analysis of another, followed by complementary methods that involve the interweaving, merging, or juxtaposition of data sources involving different types of data. These methods are relatively straightforward, conceptually and computationally, but because so much of the exchange between the different data is occurring in the mind of the researcher, they are difficult to describe as a discrete series of strategies and steps. Integrative strategies that involve applying a mix of analytic approaches to one or more sources follow. These are somewhat easier to describe because they involve application of a series of specific analytic tools and steps, although, again, it is the interpretive processing by the researcher that is essentially driving the integrative process. Strategies can prompt, aid, and support the researcher's thinking processes, but they cannot substitute for them.

Throughout this process of working with data, keeping a research diary or journal for recording inferences that can be drawn from these analyses, the evidence that supports each, and reflections about each is strongly recommended. This will prove invaluable when it is time for writing reports, articles, or theses.

4

SEQUENTIAL INTEGRATION: ANALYSIS GUIDING DESIGN AND FURTHER ANALYSIS

CHAPTER OVERVIEW

Methodological purposes

    Mapping sequential integration

Developmentally inform design

    Inform design of surveys, scale items, or questionnaires

    To check, locate, contextualise, or create variables for statistical analysis

Elaborate and extend understanding

Sequential confirmation, generalisation, or validation

    Generalise findings from qualitative data

    Confirm theory built from qualitative data

    Assess tool validity through multiple phases of development

Typology development to inform analysis

    Use a quantitative framework to guide coding of qualitative data

    Apply a common framework based on qualitative data

Iterative cross-fertilisation between methods

Using software in sequential and iterative studies

Writing sequential methods

Concluding remarks

Further reading

Researchers have always drawn on literature, informal sources, focus groups, or interviews to design a survey or questionnaire, but they have not usually regarded themselves as carrying out a mixed methods project by doing so. Indeed, often these preliminary activities are mentioned only in passing and data gleaned from them are neglected once they have served their purpose of informing the design of either questions or variables for the primary data collection and analysis. When insights from one approach to data gathering and analysis are used as a tool to guide the development of another, integration occurs along the way as the design of the second method is contingent on and enriched by the analysis of data from the first method. In the context of mixed methods, where integration and interdependence of methods are to be considered, researchers using these approaches will find added benefit from drawing on their earlier data and results as they work through analysis and reporting for the subsequent phase of the study.

Three terms – *development*, *expansion*, and *iterative exchange* – are commonly used to describe the design structure of mixed methods studies in which different methods are used sequentially within the ambit of a single project, where analyses from one phase of the study inform the methods choices and detailed design of the next phase. In some cases, the later stage might serve a *confirmatory* purpose, in a form of sequential triangulation. Less commonly, analysis from one component of a study will inform the way in which *analysis* is approached in another component – often sequentially, but sometimes concurrently.

In this chapter, sequential, developmental methods are viewed in terms of the analysis and results from a first or supplementary phase of data collection:

- being a preparatory step to design of a primary data collection tool
- informing and guiding design of a second phase of data collection and analysis to test or elaborate the results from the first phase
- guiding the analysis of further data
- becoming the first of several phases of data design, collection, and iterative analyses.

Methodological purposes

These approaches to integrating methods are used by researchers who wish to:

- design and refine instruments (scale, survey, or questionnaire items)
- develop a sampling strategy
- guide analysis strategy
- extend or elaborate information already obtained
- investigate anomalies/obscurities
- develop and test theory
- test the application of initial results across a wider population.

Mapping sequential integration

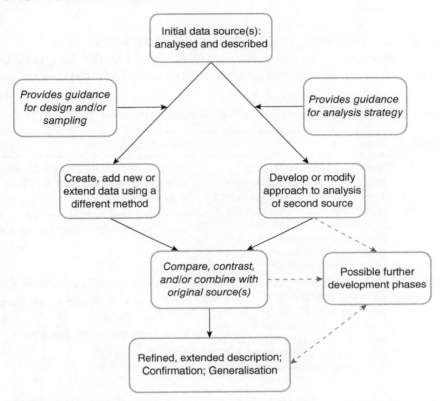

Developmentally inform design

In sequential mixed methods studies with a developmental design, analysis of the preliminary data informs and/or initiates the development of a subsequent phase of data collection. Without the preliminary work, the main phase of the research would either not be possible, or would be less fit for purpose.

How might the use of mixed methods be enhanced in these studies in which the first phase is often undervalued and underutilised? Researchers will benefit, for example, from returning to their first phase data during or following analysis of the second phase data to aid interpretation in that analysis. Presentation of results for their various audiences will be enhanced when illustrated by examples from the first phase. Although primarily intended to support the development of a second phase instrument, there can be occasions in which first phase data warrant early publication. Similarly, the instrument developed in the second phase often becomes divorced from its first phase foundations, especially if it becomes more widely adopted. Data from both phases cover the same topic areas, however, and so from an integrative point of view, the initial (usually qualitative) material is best integrated with the main results and interpretations from the developmental study, rather than being reported separately.

Inform design of surveys, scale items, or questionnaires

Sequential development is most commonly used to describe the design of a mixed methods study in which a limited number of focus groups or interviews are used in

Table 4.1 Development of questionnaire items from qualitative data

Sub-theme	Quote	Scale Items
Balance of Work, School, and Family Life	Most PhD programs are not structured for people that work. They just aren't. And that makes it extremely difficult to pursue it. If you're someone that has a family and has a job, and things go along with that like a house. It's extremely difficult.	Family responsibilities would make it difficult for me to pursue a PhD in engineering. Balancing school, work and family time would be a factor in considering a PhD.
Confidence & Self-efficacy	I could work full-time while earning a PhD part-time. And when you think that it's unreachable or unattainable or you couldn't—you know, it seems too hard or I'm not smart enough or something like—even though you're doing fine.	I am smart enough to complete a PhD. My GPA is good enough to get admitted to a PhD program. I feel confident in my academic abilities.
...	...	...
PhD-Level Engineering Work	I guess, um, they could make it more interesting to me if they could show a reason, a difference between being a, just a PE, or being a PE and having a PhD. Like I can't see, I don't know what difference there is adding your PhD, they pretty much can do the same thing.	A Professional Engineering license is more valued by industry than a PhD. I understand the kind of work that engineers with PhDs do. I think people with a PhD in engineering are overqualified for most engineering jobs. I can do the same kind of work with a bachelor's degree that an engineer with a PhD can do.
Professors/ Mentors	I think the teachers themselves are the best, uh, advocates for continuing to get a PhD... I think, if they talk more about it, you guys get your PhD, your doctor's, even more students would be interested in it.	No one at my undergraduate program ever talked about earning a PhD as a possibility. Professors have described the importance of the PhD in the engineering field. Professors have discussed earning a PhD as an option in one or more of my classes. Professors in my undergraduate program encouraged me to pursue a PhD in engineering.

Source: Howell Smith, 2011: 69, Table 5 (partial)

the first phase of the study to develop survey instruments or questions. The survey or questionnaire is then administered and analysed as the second-phase, primary dataset. At times further qualitative work is needed to clarify inconsistencies within the quantitative results. Data from the first phase are not usually intended to stand alone, but nor should they be neglected after the survey or other instruments have been designed: if understanding gained from inductive qualitative work has guided the design of quantitative instruments, it will also necessarily guide the interpretation of data from those instruments, even if the second data collection is the larger component of the study and statistical reporting is dominant (Morse, 2015). Table 4.1, from a doctoral study by Michelle Howell Smith (2011), illustrates this process of moving from a grounded theory approach to understanding the issues involved in the topic (factors influencing local students enrolling in an engineering PhD) to developing questionnaire items (the Exploring Engineering Interest Inventory). The inventory was then tested for its psychometric properties before being administered to undergraduate engineering students. Results from that administration were then integrated with the original interview material, for reporting in the dissertation.

Theoretical and research literature provide a conceptual framework and an understanding of theoretical issues for the study. Local knowledge gained through exploratory qualitative methods is needed also to ensure that those issues are both understood and framed in a way that is relevant to the local population. This will ensure questions designed to assess the theoretical concepts use language and a form of understanding that is meaningful and culturally sensitive (Dowson & McInerney, 2003) – a beneficial step for all survey and scale design, *even in ostensibly familiar environments* (e.g., Bradley, Curry, et al., 2012; Curry et al., 2011). In a cross-cultural context, sound ethnographic understanding is essential for both designing and interpreting survey data (Fricke, 2005). For example, Luyt (2012) described a situation in which a scale designed to measure traditional norms of masculinity was interpreted by men in South Africa as being a scale assessing attitudes to homosexuality; interpretation of specific items differed depending on the racial grouping and socioeconomic status of the participants providing feedback. Similarly, Guest (2000) clearly illustrated how having sound ethnographic knowledge was essential to making judgements about the inclusion or exclusion of items in developing a reliable Guttman scale.

Durham, Tan, and White (2011) wanted to develop a questionnaire and index based on a recognised sustainable livelihoods framework that could be used to assess community recovery after removal of ordinances (e.g., land mines) following a period of conflict in a country subject to high levels of poverty (Lao PDR, in their case). They reviewed tools already available, but none covered all relevant dimensions of the livelihoods approach. Two reference groups were

(Continued)

(Continued)

established, one of international mine experts, and the other of local people involved in mine action. A locally employed co-researcher helped with translation. Focus groups and interviews were conducted with local people who had benefited from mine clearance. These contributed multiple items for each of the five asset groups covered in the framework, with quotes being used to write items in appropriate language. Relevant mediating items (income, gender, type of land use, etc.) were also identified, with appropriate questions for assessment of these. The scales were translated and back-translated, then checked again by locals for interpretability. They were then pretested with a sample of 30 respondents, further modified, tested again with a sample of 50 households, modified again, and finally pretested in a further 20 households, with a repeat 10 days later. At each of these stages, psychometric assessment was matched with feedback and explanation from local people. Thus, for example, they found that the size of rice harvests needed to be given in bags rather than weights, even though bags were a less reliable measure; "how afraid" had to be changed to "how much do you worry"; "optimistic" to "confident"; "toilet" to "place to shit"; and examples were added to some items for additional clarification. Despite this preparatory work, the authors recognised the limitations of using scaled items to develop indices and recommended that when implemented, their tool should be supplemented by stories and vignettes recorded for a subset of the sample as they responded to the scaled questions.

Cognitive interviewing using think-aloud protocols with a small sample representative of a target population is another strategy that has been used to test question design for self-report questionnaires and web-based surveys. As respondents answer each question, they are asked what they were thinking about as they did so. These thoughts, combined with analysis of their responses, alert the survey researcher to problems of comprehension or relevance, allowing for improvements in question design. Coast et al. (2008) demonstrated a particularly thorough approach to scale development, with cognitive interviewing comprising just one of several steps in the process. Latcheva (2011) used cognitive interviewing as one of two methods to check on the validity of questions used to assess nationalism in the International Social Survey Program (ISSP) in Austria. She particularly focused on reasons for giving a "can't say" response, as this was far too common, and she found that problems with terms used in the questions (such as "proud of", and "influence") were affecting the validity of the scales.

Joanna Coast and her colleagues (2008) needed to develop a measure of well-being for older people that might help with allocation of health and social care services in the UK. They discussed activities, relationships, health, wealth, and surroundings as inputs to quality of life (QoL) with a sample of 40 purposively selected older people. From these discussions they identified attachment, role, enjoyment, security, and control as five factors important to the wellbeing or QoL of older people. Based on their discussions, they argued that poor health, limited wealth, etc. were not so important in themselves; they were important only insofar as they impacted on the capacity of the older people to achieve these five attributes in their lives. They then cognitively tested the wording of items in a prototype scale focusing on capability (rather than functioning) for these five attributes with a new sample. Security was particularly difficult to capture as words like "vulnerability" were misinterpreted; their eventual choice for this item was "I can think about the future without concern". Their final step was to engage in a best–worst scaling exercise with a further sample to determine specific values for each of the four possible choices for the five items in the scale in a way that allowed for each item to have different intervals between scale points.

To check, locate, contextualise, or create variables for statistical analysis

Initial ethnographic work or document analysis might be used to identify new variables and/or to check the relevance of variables available through administrative and other data sources, so that they can be tabulated and used in statistical analyses. This strategy is quite common in management studies and sociology, but its full potential is rarely capitalised on in an integrated mixed methods sense as these researchers typically neglect the initial data once they complete their regressions or other statistical analyses.

Sine, Haveman, and Tolbert (2005) studied the adoption of technology by new firms in the independent power sector in the United States. They used variables derived from mixed sources of data, analysed statistically, to show that different types of institutional (e.g., regulatory, financial) forces operating at different times or in different environments impacted on the proportion adopting risky versus established technologies. Data for the study included a government database providing descriptive details for the firms, 52 interviews within firms, and 20 with a wider sample of diverse stakeholders that grounded understanding of the sector and guided choice of measures. The authors also drew on multiple qualitative and quantitative sources to classify technologies used by firms, to assess heterogeneity of firms, and to index the regulatory, cognitive, and normative effects of regulatory and other institutions. Many of the variables involved complex operationalisation of information gained from categorised qualitative or computed quantitative sources. While some contextual description derived from these extensive and varied data sources was provided in the introductory and methods sections of the report, the results presented and then taken into the discussion were entirely statistical. Methodologists would have different opinions about whether or not such a study would be described as mixed method or quantitative.

Elaborate and extend understanding

In these studies further data of a different kind is obtained to explore, explain, or extend results from the first. Data are usually gathered sequentially, with design and/ or analysis of the second phase being dependent on analysis of the first. Data from both phases will mutually (interactively) inform the results of the study.

In the most common form of expansion study, researchers follow up a number of their survey or questionnaire respondents in order to further explore issues that were not adequately addressed through the initial data collection, or that are revealed through initial analyses as being of particular interest for the investigation. Analysis of the first set of data feeds directly into the design of the (usually purposively selected) sample. It feeds also into the framing of questions or topics for the follow-up interviews (or observations or other form of data collection), with the intention that responses to the latter will either clarify or add detail to the results already obtained (Ivankova, 2014). In these studies, the first phase will usually be dominant, although both phases could become of equal weight in contributing to the overall study. While it is not essential, if data obtained in the second phase can be matched for individual cases with that from the first phase, additional analysis options become possible (as outlined in Chapter 6).

At times these studies are written up as a sequential narrative, in the form of an unfolding mystery. Rather than assuming a sequential ordering of results, however, consider how new information from the second set of data might be integrated with that from the first, topic by topic (or point by point) to produce a coordinated and elaborated set of results for the study as a whole. For example, from a study examining which academics win prestigious research grants:

> Applicants who had recent ARC or NHMRC funding[1] were significantly more likely to gain funding for their current project (at 26.0%) (particularly if it was for a related project) although it was by no means a guarantee of continuing support, while those who had "other external funding" in the absence of ARC or NHMRC funding had a reduced probability of success (at just 3.8%) ($\chi^2 = 24.51$, $df = 7$, $p = .001$). When chairs of the discipline panels were asked about this latter apparent anomaly, they suggested that much of what is funded by other external sources might be regarded as "consultancy" or "development", rather than "research", indicating that it is therefore questionable that it constitutes a legitimate research activity resulting in the advancement of knowledge rather than merely the application of that knowledge. For track-record recognition to be gained (within the ARC network) from research undertaken with non-ARC funding, publications emanating from that research must include a basic research component and be widely disseminated or, preferably, be presented as peer-reviewed scholarly publications which will contribute to the development of the discipline. (Bazeley, 1998: 444)

[1] In Australia, the Australian Research Council (ARC) and the National Health and Medical Research Council (NHMRC) are considered the premier funding bodies for research. Primary data were derived from an analysis of biographical and track record data, extracted from ARC proposals.

These forms of sequential integration are not looking to generalise or confirm findings with a broader or different sample, but rather to *expand* understanding gained through an initial phase of data collection. Designs in which method 1 is expanded by method 2 are not limited to survey-interview combinations, nor are the samples or data sources necessarily from the same population.

Anna Krohwinkel (2015) used a sequential combination of survival analysis and qualitative comparative analysis (QCA) to challenge the literature on project performance by showing that internal administrative activities were a major source of delays (with delays being used as a key indicator of performance), in contrast to the assumption that delays are more often related to tasks at the implementation level. She used survival analysis (Cox's proportional hazards model) with the entire population of projects managed by the Swedish International Development Agency within an eight year period (N = 3632) to identify variables that might be significantly related to delay, focusing especially on indicators of priority within the agency. In the second phase, QCA (employing Boolean algebra, as described in Chapter 10) was applied to identify how priority indicators identified as significant in the first phase clustered in producing delay in a subsample of 107 delayed projects from the final year studied. Reasons given for the delays – classified as implementation-related, contractual, and/or administrative – were coded from project documentation. Then, the relative predictive value of four priority configurations that had been shown to be associated with an outcome of delay was assessed against reasons given for delay to produce the surprise result about the impact of administrative delay, with added detail as to the circumstances under which this was most likely to occur.

Sequential expansion is not always planned: researchers faced with unexpected or inexplicable findings can find they need to extend their study, or to abandon their research.

When a friend provided them with a video database of over 11,000 clerk–shopper interactions from 585 convenience stores, Sutton and Rafaeli (1988) thought they had come upon an easy path to writing a career-enhancing article in which they could present data supporting their theories on emotional work in organisations. The focus of this analysis was on displays of positive emotion by store staff ("control moves"), which, it was hypothesised, would increase sales. But no matter what they did with their carefully coded data, the regressions they ran returned negative results, showing that expressed positive emotion was consistently associated with lower sales.

(Continued)

(Continued)

A chance comment by a colleague about crowds and grumpiness in Manhattan sparked an insight into what might be happening in the stores, and so they took a fresh look at their data and confirmed that long lines of customers were also associated with a lack of smiles. Their first instinct (and the advice they received) was to rewrite the hypotheses to suit the data, but the lack of a theoretical underpinning for doing so left them stranded. So, based on what they had learned, they extended their study by interviewing a sample of store executives, by observing behaviour in stores, and with one of the authors working for a day as a clerk. This took their attention away from their focus on the suppression of emotion to understanding the circumstances that invited clerks to be friendly. They observed that when conditions were slow, customers became a source of entertainment and counteracted boredom, hence more displays of positive emotion when sales were down.

The expanded study, with its use of an alternative method of data gathering and analysis, had provided an understanding of the mechanisms operating to create the unexpected statistical associations they had found at first. This was confirmed by reanalysis of the original statistical data. Nevertheless, Sutton and Rafaeli found the path to publication for their article, with its now unconventional structure, was still far from smooth (Frost & Stablein, 1992). Over the course of rejection and multiple reviews, almost every sentence and every paragraph was refined. Persistence paid off, however: the paper was eventually published in the prestigious Academy of Management Journal, and was awarded Best Paper for 1988.

Sequential confirmation, generalisation, or validation

Analysis from an initial method might inform the design and analysis of data from a second method with the intention not so much to expand on the understanding gained from the first, as to test and confirm the applicability of those findings in a different setting, with a different group, or across a broader population. This second phase may or may not have been planned from the start, and its implementation depends on the effectiveness of the first phase in generating results worthy of further exploration or application.

Generalise findings from qualitative data

Data from small, intensively studied samples are valued for their capacity to reveal fresh insights into people's experiences, their behaviour, and the way they think about aspects of their lives. These insights are of value in themselves, and the study might be published as a standalone article. The question always remains, however, of how characteristic those experiences or patterns of thought are of a wider population.

Mixed methodologists often seek to add value to their results and conclusions from studies such as these by taking their investigations to another stage. They will use their initial findings to inform a further study, often a population-based survey, designed to assess the prevalence of the phenomenon they found in their qualitative data, or to see if the results from the first study are confirmed and/or if they have broader application than for just the initial sample. Items for questionnaires and/or propositions for testing are generated by drawing on the first phase experience and results. The initial findings will be confirmed, rejected, or modified on the basis of the analysis in the second phase, with modification likely to require a further round of testing.

Molina-Azorín et al. (2015) developed a series of propositions about the relationships between quality management, environmental management, and competitive advantage in the hotel industry based on a series of long interviews with 13 personnel occupying a variety of senior positions in Spanish hotels. They then tested the ideas they had developed by surveying a sample drawn from across the entire population of Spanish hotels (N = 355). They first checked that the respondents were representative of the population as a whole, then analysed the questionnaire data using a combination of principal components and path analysis, with bootstrapping using 500 subsamples to determine the significance level of their results. These analyses supported the findings they had developed from their qualitative analysis.

Confirm theory built from qualitative data

A similar question of "fit" in a broader population arises also in relation to inductive theory developed through case study, ethnography, grounded theory, or other hybrid or qualitative methodologies. Grant, Berg, and Cable (2014) tested qualitatively derived theory in a quasi-experiment with a sample drawn from a related but different population. Scaled and survey measures supplemented by reflective interviews for the intervention group were used to assess the outcome.

Employees at the Make-A-Wish Foundation (MAW) are always interacting with terminally ill children and their families, hence they experience a high degree of stress and burnout. Grant et al. (2014) were exploring organisational changes initiated by a chapter of the association. Designed to help create magical experiences for sick children, the MAW office was redecorated, new values were fostered, and people created fun titles for themselves. For example, the CEO designated herself as "fairy godmother of wishes"; others chose "minister of dollars and sense", "goddess of greetings", "magic messenger".

(Continued)

(Continued)

These self-reflective titles were added to formal titles on business cards, to email signatures, and to the local branch website. The researchers investigated the meaning, uses, and consequences of the ways in which organisational changes such as these reduced stress and burnout.

Phase 1 involved an inductive study drawing on interviews, field observations, and archival documents. The problem of emotional exhaustion came up spontaneously in all conversations the employees had with the researchers, while the introduction of self-reflective job titles was the most prominent of the initiatives introduced and their use the most "potent" and "salient" in coping with stress. The researchers observed that "identity expression" was prominent across the aggregated codes developed from the data, and through a process of further reduction and discussion they identified three identity-related mechanisms to explain the relation between self-reflective titles and reduction in emotional exhaustion: self-verification (identity affirmation by others), psychological safety (freedom to express identity in the work environment), and external rapport (identity utilisation in fostering external relations).

Because MAW was an extreme environment, in Phase 2, the researchers tested their model in a more regular health service setting using a field-based, quasi-experiment with one experimental group encouraged to create self-reflective titles and two control groups (no intervention; alternative intervention). Standardised scales and other survey measures were used pre- and post-intervention to assess the three mediating variables and the outcome. These were supplemented by post-intervention, open-ended questions for the self-reflective titles group. Using repeated measures analysis of variance, hierarchical regression analysis, and bootstrapping they confirmed an overall benefit from use of the titles, and support for the first two of the three theorised mechanisms.

From a methodological point of view, this study was exemplary in its design, in the thoroughness with which both phases of the investigation and analyses were conducted, and in the methodological detail provided in the written report.

Assess tool validity through multiple phases of development

Tool or scale development generally follows a multi-phase pattern. Initial design using preliminary qualitative data is followed by limited testing and refinement, including item analysis. More extensive testing is then carried out during one or more phases of development using techniques such as exploratory and confirmatory factor analyses or Rasch modelling to assess the structure of the tool or scale. Parallel qualitative data are collected to assess content validity. Each phase depends on, and extends, the former phase.

Long-term care facilities tend to have high turnover of staff, particularly of certified nursing assistants (CNA), their lowest level of staff. On-site observations of a long-term care facility followed by interviews with staff allowed Hemmings, Kennerly, Yap, Beckett and others to build a model of the way in which six (theory-derived) dimensions of occupational subcultures – behaviours, expectations, teamwork, communication, satisfaction, and professional commitment – impacted on various aspects of worker performance, client care and worker retention (Hemmings et al., 2013; Kennerly et al., 2012). The team used this information to develop a Nursing Culture Assessment Tool (NCAT) that could be used to assess workers' perceptions of nursing cultures. The tool was then checked for content validity and relevance across different settings by a panel of experts, and trialled across a range of inpatient and out-patient settings. Data from the trial were assessed using exploratory and confirmatory factor analyses and measures of internal consistency. Additionally, a table was constructed to compare results from separately analysed qualitative and quantitative data for each of the NCAT's six subscales. These measures confirmed the NCAT's usefulness as a basis for assessing and reshaping nursing occupational cultures in positive ways, but also pointed to needed areas of research to further refine and validate the tool.

Maintaining close contact with original theory and qualitative data (gathered initially, if not throughout) is essential in helping to avoid conceptual drift and to ensure continuing relevance of a measurement tool as it is developed through successive statistical testing.

Typology development to inform analysis

Guiding the *analysis* of a set of data using the framework or results from an earlier or alternative approach was also identified as an integrative strategy by Caracelli and Greene (1993), who referred to it as "typology development". Doing so will facilitate direct combination or comparison of results across methods, for example through the application of a common coding system or development of a matrix in which parallel results are placed side by side.

Use a quantitative framework to guide coding of qualitative data

Hildebrandt and Kelber (2005) used a combination of concurrent responses to the General Well Being scale (GWB) and interview data to evaluate the positive and negative impacts of work-based programmes for women on welfare. They

(Continued)

(Continued)

coded the interview data using the same six constructs as are present in the GWB and also categorised the direction of change evident in the interviews for each construct as positive or negative, so that they could directly compare the scaled scores with the direction of the text responses in reviewing their results. In reporting their results they brought information together from both sources, including numeric data and illustrative text examples, in relation to each construct.

The authors used their combined results to provide data that would influence social policy, and so "the rationale for using the GWB tool was to give additional dimension to the dependability and scientific adequacy of the qualitative data and enhance in-depth understanding of both qualitative and quantitative datasets" (Eugenie Hildebrandt, personal communication, 6 May 2007).

Where quantitatively based categories are not pre-existing, factor or cluster analysis might be used to create them. These are then used to guide coding of qualitative data.

An eight-category typology of parents', teachers', and children's perceptions about starting school initially identified through focus groups by Dockett and Perry (2004) was developed into items for a large-scale survey and confirmed using factor analysis. This typology was then used as a basis for coding children's interviews in a further study, as well as data from an open-ended survey question asking parents and teachers to "List the first five things that come into your mind when you think about a/your child starting school". Frequency and content of responses for the eight different categories were found to differ for the three different response groups. By using the opportunity to draw comparisons across varied data from different subgroups, Dockett and Perry hoped to build comparative awareness of the different ways in which different stakeholders experienced a child's transition to school. "Promoting a successful start to school for children requires that educators focus on the perspectives, experiences and expectations of all involved in the process" (2004: 187).

Apply a common framework based on qualitative data

Alternatively, and perhaps more controversially, researchers have found that the framework developed during the process of analysing their qualitative data has usefully informed their approach to analysing quantitative variable data.

Jang, McDougall, Pollon, Herbert, and Russell (2008) set out to understand factors associated with school success for 20 purposively selected elementary schools facing challenging circumstances. They concurrently interviewed and surveyed teachers and principals and conducted focus groups with students. Data were initially analysed separately: survey data were factor analysed, resulting in nine factors, all with high internal consistency; qualitative data generated 11 themes associated with school improvement. Their problem was that statistical factors suggested little variation in staff perceptions about school improvement across the 20 schools, yet the qualitative data showed considerable variability in practices across the schools.

To further understand their data, the authors innovatively combined results to create redefined variables. Survey items were reviewed and regrouped to match eight of the 11 qualitative themes; three qualitative themes and 12 survey items that had no parallel in the alternative data were dropped from further analysis. Some of the new scales with low item numbers were less internally consistent, but scores for the eight newly blended "thematic factors" better reflected the multi-perspective qualitative accounts in capturing the dynamics of the interplay between community factors and school success. Analysis of a second set of survey data from a further large sample of school staff confirmed the blended scales detected more differentiated responses than did the original factors. They were also better able to expose differences across the schools, and understanding of the interrelationships between the qualitative themes was deepened. These analyses allowed the researchers to select schools with strongly contrasting values for further detailed case analysis, and to draw conclusions about strategies associated with school improvement.

Others have used their qualitatively derived thematic framework to sort, understand, and coordinate their quantitative (and qualitative) data.

Harden and Thomas (2005) conducted a systematic review of studies on barriers to and facilitators of fruit and vegetable intake among children aged 4 to 10 years. An initial meta-analysis of effect sizes from trials data on this topic did not show any clear results relating interventions to outcomes. They used NVivo to aggregate findings across qualitative "views" studies in a secondary analysis of the 13 descriptive categories generated from these. This resulted in their identifying six analytic themes contributing to understanding the children's perspectives on what helped or hindered them from eating fruit and vegetables.

(Continued)

(Continued)

These six themes were then used to define rows of a matrix as a mechanism for combining the findings of the trials data with the qualitative data. The matrix facilitated a constant comparative analysis that moved between the views data and narrative descriptions of interventions described in the reports from trials. The authors noted that "the use of children's views to structure the final synthesis challenges traditional notions of who experts are and what constitutes expert opinion" (2005: 264). They have since successfully applied this approach of using views data to structure synthesised data in a number of other systematic reviews.

Iterative cross-fertilisation between methods

Iterative design is "characterised by a dynamic and ongoing interplay over time between the different methodologies … [it] enables a progressive reconfiguration of substantive findings and interpretations in a pattern of increasing insight and sophistication" (Caracelli & Greene, 1997: 23). Weiss et al. (2005: 56) described the "interactive, back-and-forth exchanges and turn-taking" of their quantitative and qualitative methodologies as they pursued their inquiry into family involvement during children's early years of schooling, as part of a longitudinal study of transition to school. For Weiss et al. this involved, for example, modification of questions for later rounds of surveys to take account of the innovative ways in which working parents participated in their children's educational development, based on the additional information they had gained from case study interviews that had followed earlier surveys.

Iterative movement back and forth between types of data and methods of analysis is often a feature of larger or longitudinal projects, during which time, as each element of the research draws from and in turn informs another, the boundaries between the tasks addressed by different methods become increasingly clouded. Such was the experience of Burch and Heinrich (2016) in their use of "fully integrated mixed methods" as they pursued both outcome and process evaluation data in several multisite social projects.

One of the projects in which Carolyn Heinrich was involved was an evaluation of the Child Support Grant programme, designed to reduce child poverty in South Africa (Burch & Heinrich, 2016). Questions were asked about the difference made by early enrolment, and the impact of the programme on adolescents. Although the terms of reference suggested quite separate quantitative and qualitative evaluations, the international evaluation team implemented a tightly linked design with a set of guiding principles requiring

close alignment between these different components. The first task undertaken by the team was to develop a theory of change for the programme.
Then, constructs and measures specified in the theory of change were tabulated with lists of relevant quantitative and qualitative indicators, and during
the course of the project, an evolving evaluation design matrix linked these
to the research questions and increasingly specific measures of programme
impacts. The qualitative work was fundamental to the design of quantitative
instruments and to modelling of decisions that explained non-random selection of families into the programme. Meanwhile those developing quantitative
instruments provided feedback on the kinds of questions being asked in the
field by the qualitative team to ensure greater relevance of their input to
further quantitative design. A member of the quantitative team participated
in the qualitative work and when initial focus group data were being reviewed
to provide input to questionnaire design, team members worked in qualitative plus quantitative pairs on each of the major subsections of the data,
with an interim report of the whole to provide context. The teams also drew
on other documentary information when designing questions. Multiple drafts
were reviewed by both teams. Team members and other stakeholders came
together (online and in person) at critical stages throughout the process for
joint decision-making workshops that were supported by detailed documentation. The process, therefore, was "interactive and iterative" throughout the
project, with benefits in complementary coverage of issues, reduced redun-
dancy, improved sensitivity regarding complex issues, improved sampling
designs for quantitative work, appropriate model specification for statistical
analyses, nuanced interpretation of findings, stakeholder understanding of
and confidence in the findings, and wider academic and policymaker interest in the results of the evaluation.

Using software in sequential and iterative studies

Initial data sources and analyses in the kinds of sequential studies described in this
chapter are usually method-specific, and consequently researchers can make use of
qualitative or statistical (or other) software in usual ways to separately analyse
these component (text and numeric) data. Information can occasionally be help-
fully transferred directly from one kind of software to another as part of the
process of using one method to inform the design or analysis of another, or software can be used to facilitate amalgamation of insights from all methods used as a
further or final step in analysis. The latter is most easily achieved using Excel,
which allows for joint displays of text and numeric data based, for example, on the
common themes addressed by those different data types. Alternatively, summaries
of statistical results can be combined, coded, and queried along with other data in
QDA software. Use of statistical software for integration requires conversion of
text data to variable format.

David Byrne (2009) described an iterative process wherein he (1) used SPSS in a statistical analysis to generate clusters (a typology) within a large existing dataset, then (2) used qualitative comparative analysis (QCA) to establish causal pathways for each of those types, accompanied by (3) use of NVivo to explore contradictory cases revealed by the initial runs of QCA – a process he described as something like "a tool-based version of the hermeneutic circle" (2009: 261). For the qualitative phase using NVivo, as well as coding data, he noted the possibility of attaching attribute-style measures generated through the process of engagement with the data to the cases he was analysing. In qualitative software tools, attributes of cases do not have to be predetermined and fixed, but can be created "on the fly" as their relevance becomes apparent. These can then be fed back into the QCA (or SPSS) as new or refined variables for causal analyses.

Writing sequential methods

When Sampson, O'Cathain, and Goodacre (2010) undertook a mixed methods study to understand patient and carer satisfaction with a new primary angioplasty service, they interviewed users of the new service and their carers and then developed a questionnaire to survey the satisfaction of 595 patients (and 418 of their carers) receiving either the new service or usual care. Finally, 17 of the patients who expressed dissatisfaction with aftercare and rehabilitation were followed up to explore this further in semistructured interviews. Even though they had been gathered sequentially, rather than reporting the findings from the interviews, survey, and follow-up interviews separately, they considered the common meta-themes of speed and efficiency, convenience of care, discharge and after care. For each of these themes they presented the statistical results from comparing angioplasty with usual care in conjunction with one or two quotes from the open-ended survey data or interviews as evidence of the *pattern of* qualitative comments to support and explain the significance of the statistical results. For example (Sampson et al., 2010: 5–6):

Patients were very satisfied with the time they waited for treatment, and the efficiency with which they were treated, with significantly higher satisfaction levels at intervention than control sites for both aspects of care [reference to tabulated data]. Again, these high levels of satisfaction were reflected in the open comments on the questionnaire and in the qualitative interviews. During the interviews at intervention sites, patients and carers expressed amazement at the short time period between contacting the emergency services to the completion of treatment. They perceived an efficiency and 'smoothness' in the care provided, and were impressed at the teamwork involved, often describing how the team were awaiting their arrival.

This for me was the NHS working at its very best. From the 999 call to coming out of surgery took 3.5 h (patient 307, survey).

The speed / efficiency of (transfer hospital) sending me to the (intervention hospital) who, in turn, dealt with me with such speed that I was in the door, up the lift and straight into theatre – brilliant! (patient 242, survey).

Although initial work carried out to design a more extensive form of data collection (typically qualitative work to inform design of quantitative instruments) is foundational to not only the design but also the interpretation of the second set of data, all too often it is either ignored or compartmentalised in the write-up of the results from the study. For most studies, in order to recognise and benefit from all components contributing to the outcome, insights from both sets of data are best presented and discussed together and organised, as did Sampson et al., according to the key issues or subtopics associated with the overall purpose and questions for the study (Bazeley, 2015b).

Concluding remarks

Mixed methods studies frequently involve sequential application of different methods of data collection and analysis. Transfer of information and insights at the switch point from one method to the next is one component of sequential integration. Using the analysis of one set of data to enhance the interpretation of another is a further component, while including insights from all methods and stages in a final report is a final integrative step. Sequential studies can look forward, when one method is used to design content or sampling or analysis strategies for another, or backward as a second method is added to expand or test conclusions from a first. Thus purposes for integrating methods sequentially vary, with the consequence that designs, data sources, and methods of analysis will also vary.

Insofar as they deal primarily with the combination of survey and interview (or similar) data, the methods described in this chapter represent quite traditional approaches to having one form of data sequentially inform another. Yet, as Byrne (2009), Grant etal. (2014), Jang etal. (2008), Krohwinkel (2015), and others reported in this chapter have demonstrated with their innovative use of different data sources or analysis tools, the types of data that can be used and the styles of analyses applied to those data are not limited to those traditional sources or approaches to analysis. Visual data, documentary sources, social network analyses, or geographic data or modelling are just some among the many additional methods that might be considered for inclusion in one or another phase of a study.

When the additional step is taken of integrating the results from component parts in sequential studies so that they mutually inform the written report, those studies develop some of the characteristics of complementary studies (to be considered next).

Further reading

Examples mentioned in the text, and:

Creswell and Plano Clark (2011: 246–247) list joint displays that can be used to convey results in sequential (and complementary) designs serving a variety of purposes.

Ivankova (2014) describes in detail the methodological and analysis process engaged in to ensure quality for her sequential study of student engagement with online learning.

Burch and Heinrich (2016) draw on their experience with complex, iteratively designed and conducted studies to illustrate in detail the strategies they developed for integrating methods.

Moorkens (2015) uses interviews with translation experts in an explanatory sequential design to follow up an initial analysis of translation inconsistencies resulting from use of translation memory software.

Hayden and Chiu (2015) explore preservice teachers' reflective practices from notes gathered over time spent in a reading clinic, then use quantitative analysis based on codes created from the qualitative data to confirm patterns in the way recurring challenges were resolved.

Obstfeld (2005) provides an example of an iterative study using diverse and evolving methods, exploring the role of weak and strong bonds in fostering creativity, innovation, and implementation of innovations in an engineering firm.

Kramer (2011), Houghton et al. (2015), and Stewart-Brown et al. (2009) each provide examples of the use of Rasch analysis in scale development, with Kramer's study using a mixed methods design and analysis.

5

COMPLEMENTARY ANALYSIS OF VARIED DATA SOURCES

One of the more common justifications given by authors for using mixed methods is that combining different data components contributes to better supported outcomes and stronger inferences than using one method alone, especially where the evidence from each of those components, independently, is inadequate in answering the research questions. Data from different sources and of different types, each with different strengths, beneficially come together in a complementary way. Each contributes unique aspects and differing perspectives on a subject to produce a more refined and more rounded understanding, thus giving a better sense of the whole.

Complementary analysis begins when information and ideas garnered from different methods are pieced or merged together such that each reinforces another to create a more complete, more comprehensive whole. Complementary strategies develop from descriptive through comparative analyses to more complex iterative approaches. In these, insights arising from different data are bounced back and forward, data merge to "jointly constitute" the subject of study, and description potentially moves into confirmation or theory-building. This is an area where metaphors for both the processes and the outcomes of mixing methods abound – where weaving, meshing, merging, or triangulating produces sprinkles, mosaics, completed puzzles, collages, and perhaps even an archipelago.

Mapping complementary analysis

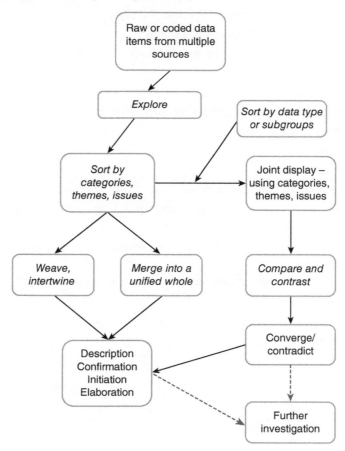

Strategies and methodological purposes

In this chapter, complementary methods are described that take either elements of raw data or initial descriptive results of preliminary analyses as their starting point. Strategies and purposes for bringing these elements together during analysis include:

- using one data source to provide illustrative or contextual material to enhance analysis from another source
- creating a coherent picture or account built of elements from a variety of data sources
- merging or juxtaposing sources to create an elaborated description
- comparing and contrasting complementary sources to verify and/or elaborate interpretation of data
- using different sources to gain a complementary understanding of both process and outcome in intervention studies.

Enhance analysis (and reporting) with supplementary data

In its simplest form, an integrated mixed methods analysis using either concurrent or sequentially gathered data can involve using elements of data of one type to supplement and enhance the analysis and reporting of another type or source. Enhancement might take the form of using the alternative data for illustrative purposes, or to contribute to an explanation, or to contextualise information arising in the primary source. In this situation, the primary component provides the paradigmatic and theoretical drive for the project, with the secondary component complementing or supplementing results from the primary analysis. A primary method will be adequate but potentially limited without the additional data, whereas the latter is unlikely to be adequate to independently generate useful results.

Use data bites to assist in interpreting survey statistics

Qualitative comments from supplementary open-ended questions in a questionnaire assist the analyst to understand ways in which survey respondents interpreted the questions asked and what they might have been thinking about when they selected their categorical or scaled responses. They also help in illuminating fixed responses, or by revealing issues of which the survey designer was unaware (O'Cathain & Thomas, 2004). Sometimes just words or phrases used by participants (identified with quotation marks but not participant source) can be usefully woven into the statistical report, in addition to an occasional fuller illustrative quote. Quotes can often be selected directly from the qualitative data, because the comments are effectively coded by their position in the questionnaire, although attention has to be given to ensuring the selected quotes are representative of a broader pattern.

In a similar way, comments from preliminary or parallel interviews or other data that were used to design questions in a survey or target the same issues enhance a statistical analysis through adding interpretive understanding. When comments are used as illustrative quotes or are combined with statistical data to create vignettes in a report they help to communicate results for readers who struggle to interpret statistical output.

McKeon, Fogarty, and Hegney (2006) used survey data to build a path model showing how organisational variables additively combined with the level of nurses' knowledge in contributing to potentially unsafe medication administration in rural practice in Queensland, Australia. Qualitative comments sought in the questionnaire supported conclusions drawn from the quantitatively derived model by providing illustrative examples of how the variables assessed by the model were evidenced in practice. The comments additionally clarified the impact of practising in rural settings where doctors were less available and nurses were therefore "expected" to sidestep drug administration regulations. This pointed to the need for nurses to be trained and licenced for a higher level of practice in rural settings.

Comments given in free text during or at the end of a survey are less reliable than the main survey data as a source of data, not least because of a potential for bias in who will add them (Garcia, Evans, & Reshaw, 2004). David Karp (quoted in Hesse-Biber, 2010: 23) disparagingly referred to the scattering of quotes through a statistical report as "sprinkling ... like going to the ice cream store and throwing a few M&Ms onto the top of the ice cream to make it look pretty, and it might taste a little bit better". In similar vein, Greene et al. (1989: 269) observed that in many of the evaluations they reviewed "there was a paramedic quality to the qualitative component ... qualitative data often appeared in the emergency room of report writing as a life-saving device to resuscitate what was either a failed program or a failed evaluation". In using this strategy, therefore, it is necessary to ensure the selected data bites add flavour (i.e., meaning) to the argument being developed or presented (rather than simply repeating it, for example), and that they are undergirded by a broader base of data, such as a pattern evident across the sample more generally.

Use statistics to place qualitative data in context

Qualitative methods are regarded as strong on providing contextual detail, but they can be limited by being based on small samples. As well as adding to the analytic understanding of the researcher when interpreting observational or interview data, reporting is enhanced by provision of some basic statistical data relating sampled groups to the broader context and the larger population from which they were drawn.

Elliott (2005) reported a study by Duncan and Edwards (1999) in which the researchers interviewed lone mothers living in two very different settings, a low-income London borough and an "average" coastal community. The researchers supplemented their description of these settings with census data covering the type of housing, proportion of families headed by a lone parent, car ownership, and employment rates, to orient the narratives captured by their qualitative interviews.

In studies with small samples, contextual data for participants might be recorded also on an individual basis. Reporting functional level or hours of care required for persons with a disability using standardised scales, for example, helps the reader to better understand the experience of that person and their carers, as revealed through interviews. Key variable data can be included with (or within) the pseudonym used to identify sources of illustrative quotes included in the report. A summary table of variable data describing the sample might be provided in the methods section of the report, but care needs to be taken that doing so does not reveal identities.

Compose a coherent picture from complementary data

A study in which one method is used simply to enhance the reporting of another would be classed as "MM lite" by most methodologists, if they consider it to be mixing methods at all. Consolidating complementary sources and analyses to build a coherent composite picture with both breadth and depth involves a deeper, potentially more complex process of integration. To continue the metaphor: this can range from carefully adding elements by placing or weaving them together to create a picture that is comprehensive and complete, through to (perhaps experimentally) merging or juxtaposing the diverse media and/or varied colours that are available. The process is likely to include having to manage clashing colours. It will inevitably involve iteratively reworking parts of the picture as clarity is gradually brought to the scene through a mutually enriching variety of elements and creative strategies. Analysis becomes "a creative and at times even playful meshing of data-collecting methods to encourage serendipity and openness to new ideas" (Brewer & Hunter, 2006: 69). Working in this way recognises the multidimensionality of phenomena, and that different methods are better at tapping into those different dimensions before they are brought together to compose the whole.

The actual strategies for bringing different data components together in a complementary way vary depending on the purpose of the study, and on the timing and sequencing of the methods used. A picture is not always composed in one sitting, but rather, evolves and develops increasing clarity over time as more data become available or more cases are added to the analysis. Data from particular components usually (but not essentially) undergo some preliminary analysis, using regular text analysis, statistical analysis, or alternative methods, before being combined with other components. Information from already analysed sources, and indeed, insights from published or grey literature, are likely also to become part of the mix.

Joseph Teye (2012) utilised a concurrent, complementary, mixed methods analysis to examine forest policy formulation and implementation in Ghana. In an article demonstrating the value of this approach for his work he reported thus on his methods and analyses:

(Continued)

(Continued)

The use of both quantitative and qualitative methods was useful for showing intensity of cases while at the same time unraveling different dimensions of forest management in Ghana. Quantifiable data from the questionnaire survey were useful in areas where rates, percentages, and charts were necessary for showing frequencies of responses. For instance, rates were computed to explain the incidence of corruption within the Forest Services Division. Again, by performing chi-square test of independence, it was possible to examine the relationship between forestry officials' respective positions and their satisfaction with conditions of service. Chi-square tests were also performed to examine the association between land ownership status of farmers and their willingness to plant trees on their farms. On the other hand, the qualitative interviews and focus group discussions were useful for understanding the underlying reasons for the observed patterns. During the questionnaire survey, for instance, a significant proportion of forest guards indicated that they sometimes accepted bribes from chainsaw operators. The factors that accounted for such a high incidence of bribe taking were not fully understood from the questionnaire data. However, detailed accounts by some guards, during in-depth interviews, show that guards were forced to connive with local resource users because of poor conditions of services and their perception that their managers are also corrupt:

They [managers] use all our vehicles for their private activities ... like sending their children to school and attending funerals, but we do not even have bicycles to work with. They also take bribes from timber contractors, but expect us to report chainsaw operators to them so that they can get more bribes. (Fuseni, Forest Guard, June 28, 2006).

Narratives of some forest guards also demonstrate how their dependency on people in the forest communities for survival made them powerless when it comes to enforcing forest laws:

It is easy to talk about complete restriction if you don't live here, but this is difficult for those of us here. You know I have friends among them, I eat with some of them on the same table, and they are the people I go to when I need to borrow money. How can I arrest them for harvesting wood from the forest? (Lagmatey, Forest Guard, May 11, 2006).

It is obvious that the questionnaire survey alone could not have unraveled these interesting motivations for the development of informal associations between forest guards and local resource users. Teye (2012: 383)

Because his analyses had been conducted concurrently and the data complemented each other in explaining the situation he found in the forest environment, Teye found (despite advice to the contrary) he needed to write his entire dissertation in an integrated way, paying particular attention to the integration of qualitative and quantitative data throughout the results as well as the discussion.

The researcher as bricoleur

The bricoleur, in the context of qualitative work (and mixed methods), is one who pieces together emergent solutions to a puzzle (Denzin & Lincoln, 1994). The term "bricolage" was used by Lynch (1993: 150) when he wrote of "the *bricolage* of laboratory shop practice" and drew on the works of Schutz and Derrida to describe the scientist as *bricoleur*, that is, as "a jack-of-all-trades who adapts 'the means at hand' – a collection of tools, scraps of material and heterogeneous skills – in trial-and-error fashion to contend with the contingencies arising in an open series of applications". Stepping back a bit further, Lévi-Strauss used the term to describe the artisan process of taking items that were once parts of a whole, and repurposing them in creating a new whole (Crotty, 1998). *Montage* and *collage* similarly describe the outcomes of working in this way and, like bricolage, suggest something quite creative and less organised than, for example, a deliberately planned and carefully composed mosaic or portrait.

Engaging in creating a bricolage might be deliberate choice, especially for an ongoing project not constrained by funding and performance schedules. It is not always possible to plan ahead for the research demands and contingencies one might face in doing so, however. A valuable researcher attribute for this task, therefore, is to have a store of knowledge that gives capability and flexibility to see and take advantage of alternative possibilities and to be able to design or redesign ways of drawing on available sources as needed and as opportunity arises. In community work, for example, unexpected opportunities for data gathering can arise, or surprise developments could mean one might need to set up a hastily constructed evaluation process without having pre-designed targeted measures. Similarly, unexpected discoveries or developments during the course of a project necessitate rapid reconsideration of how the project should run, and what methods and data might be relevant. Shifts in circumstances provide unexpected opportunities, available to those with the resources and skills needed to take advantage of them – or the time to experiment and be creative.

Alan Meyer (1982: 517) referred to his data as "hodgepodges of eclectic data" and his study of responses to "environmental jolts" as a "series of accidents, choices, and surprises overlaid with a combination of phenomenological, theoretical, and verificatory logic". He tells the story of being in the final stages of a PhD study involving a field study of 19 hospitals in the San Francisco area when physicians called a strike in response to a sudden and significant increase in malpractice insurance (Meyer, 1992). On the advice of colleagues, he dropped his initial idea of surveying the 19 hospital CEOs in a natural experiment, and opted to do an intensive case study of three hospitals as they weathered what became a month long strike – but the hospitals' "paradoxical" and "counterintuitive" yet "impeccably logical" responses directly contradicted his predictions. His interest captured, he pursued a conceptual framework and publication based on qualitative data to present an

(Continued)

(Continued)

interpretation of the hospitals' responses. His efforts were heavily critiqued, first by colleagues, then by journal reviewers, leading to multiple revisions. A conversation with the journal editor provided another "jolt" and he revised his approach yet again, this time incorporating a shift in conceptual orientation and a much broader spread of mixed methods data.

> Accepting this conceptual reorientation was hard, but the benefits are immediate and unmistakable: ideas jell, the writing flows, solutions to logical dilemmas present themselves, and new data sources materialize. The work I'm doing now is rapidly shifting the paper's methodological fulcrum from mostly qualitative case analyses to a balanced triangulation between qualitative and quantitative data. I'm collecting new survey and archival data, using them to anchor the three focal hospitals in the context of a larger sample and to conduct regression analyses that verify and extend the qualitative analyses. In short, I'm finally executing my five-year-old idea of presenting the study as a natural experiment. (Meyer, 1992: 93–94)

Meyer presented his revised paper to a conference, extended the qualitative analyses in response to fresh epistemological perspectives, and reorganised the article yet again. Finally, after further minor modifications, the seventh revision of his study, with its bricolage of data and analyses supporting significant conceptual development, was accepted for publication – to critical acclaim.

In composing a bricolage, researchers who employ "a mixed methods way of thinking" consider their varied data sources not so much in terms of whether they are qualitative or quantitative, but rather, in terms of whether the information they provide adds depth or breadth to the picture. The investigator as bricoleur gathers any relevant information that might become available (or be created) from sources of any type, and pieces it together to present an artisan-researcher's interpretation of its subject matter. Data (planned and unplanned; raw or pre-analysed) might be obtained, for example, from single or multiple survey instruments with closed and open questions, from questionnaires or other quantitative sources, interviews or casual conversations, visual images, documentary, archival, and administrative data, geographic, web-based, or observational data, or any combination of these.

To evaluate usage and impact of a teacher stress management training kit developed by an educational agency, I began from a source perspective. The kit had been distributed through regional resource centres, with 10 copies sent to each, and so I started by calling (multiple!) staff in each of these to trace what had become of the kits and how they had been used. As this was generating little in the way of positive responses in terms of evaluation outcomes, I added an end-user perspective by surveying the Principals of a stratified sample of 100 schools, to check levels of awareness and usage of the kit across the system. Discussions were held also with staff involved in the development of the kit and with those who were responsible for the professional development and welfare of teachers at the time it was released.

A cohesive picture emerged: the proposed public launch for the kit had been cancelled, as it was considered embarrassing to admit publicly that teacher stress was a problem. The resource centres were largely staffed by teachers posted for just one year, and so most of the distributed kits had disappeared with teachers returning to schools. Few Principals had any knowledge of the kit, and only one of the 100 contacted was aware of a course having been run. Thus, information gathered from these diverse perspectives together contributed to a picture of ineffective implementation of a well-designed and potentially useful resource.

While selection of data sources contributing to a bricolage can shift and turn unexpectedly, working with those data retains purpose and direction. Keeping a clear sense of the overall goal of the process, even if the detail is unclear and evolving, and developing an effective system for organising records are both vital. Keeping track of reflections in memos or a journal is also essential to the whole endeavour. In some ways, the process of generating a report from this kind of data is like writing a term paper in which all available information is sifted and sorted and evidence dredged, in order to create a picture that is both insightful and convincing about the topic at hand. In his analysis of the National Front in the UK, Nigel Fielding determined to "provide text that was an adequate description based on all the data available to me [news reports, official party reports, own observation], while recognizing that I could not avoid mediating such description, if only by evaluating the quality of items of information from different sources" (Fielding & Fielding, 1986: 64). Inevitably, the artisan nature of the work will colour the research outcome.

Strategic integration of complementary sources

If the image presented above of a process of piecing together complementary data sources through a series of emergent analyses seems altogether too random, then be assured that a more strategic process of working with complementary data not only is quite possible, but is more usual (or is presented as such in publications). Compare the construction of a patterned mosaic or a jigsaw with that of the bricolage. Being more strategic starts at the planning phase for the project; it requires foreknowledge of the types of sources available and the kinds of data they will provide. Documents will be sourced, surveys planned, observations made, interviews held, each designed to contribute specific data and additional insights in answer to the questions being asked about the subject of the research.

Before they are collected, thought will be given to when and how they are to be combined – and again as they are being collected and again as preliminary analyses are being carried out (although, even with the best plans, modification is likely to occur along the way). That combination might be designed such that different sources contribute data relating to complementary parts of an overall puzzle (as in Joseph Teye's study, described earlier), or it can be designed such that each source contributes information in parallel on each of the major issues being investigated (or both). In the case of parallel information, analysis is likely to resemble those described later in this chapter as juxtaposed or jointly constituted, where data from different sources are directly compared and contrasted.

When I investigated the mental health needs and resources of a disadvantaged community in the 1970s as the first phase of my mixed methods, action research PhD project, I modelled my approach on methodologies used in classic early- and mid-twentieth-century US and UK sociological community studies (Bazeley, 1977). Extensive ethnographic observations and interactions with members of the community, census and agency based social indicator statistics, and key informant interviews were combined with a face to face household survey comprising scaled items as well as open and closed questions. Results for each subtopic were framed within the context of theoretical and empirical literature related to psychological wellbeing and mental health. Together these sources built a picture of a community experiencing economic, social, recreational, educational, and psychological disadvantage. Many were caught in a cycle of poverty, having limited skills with which to respond to life's challenges and few, if any, readily available resources to call upon.

Two decades later, I led a team in taking a similar complementary approach to determining the status and funding needs of early career researchers (Bazeley, 2003b; Bazeley et al., 1996). Results from two major surveys of early career academics and a cohort of PhD graduates were combined with reviews of university-based and national granting schemes; analysis of the characteristics of successful grant applicants; interviews with heads of departments, successful researchers and university grants administrators; submissions from recent graduates in response to a newspaper advertisement; case studies of two contrasting university departments; published reports; and literature. A comprehensive report resulted, setting out stages in the career development of academic researchers, with their funding experiences and needs. Based on this background, evidence was presented to support a definition of early career that could be applied across disciplines in making funding decisions. Elements of data from varied sources were drawn on and reported together, as needed, to present each aspect of the study's results.

Lawrenz and Huffman (2002) used the evocative image of an archipelago as a metaphor to describe studies in which integration of information from multiple separate sources of data pointed to a greater level of knowledge or understanding than that which could be obtained by simply reporting from each source. An archipelago is a set of islands connected underwater to form a group, such that the separate yet connected islands that show above the surface are just the tips that evidence the presence of a much larger underwater structure. Some evidence is in plain view, but much remains more or less hidden and can be difficult to reveal. Each island in the archipelago appears on the surface as a separate entity; not all are of the same size. Some islands are outliers; some others may not in fact be part of the archipelago but exist in their own right. Islands emerging as a result of continuing undersea volcanic activity will develop later than others and shift position slightly over time. Interrelationships between the islands, with their multiple dimensions, provide the framework for integration across the archipelago. Such a model points to the multidimensionality, but also the interconnection, of knowledge gained through multiple sources of data and approaches to working with them.

Those writing about their use of complementary methods make frequent use of the words "nuance" and "balance" in describing the results of their analyses. Often, they have had to resolve issues raised by dissonant data, yet it is this that often directly contributes to refinement of their understanding of their research participants and topics.

Berger and Paul (2014) analysed data from 56 women who had experienced the trauma of infertility using a scaled Social Support Questionnaire, the Posttraumatic Growth Inventory, a demographic survey and responses to an open-ended question in which they described their infertility experience. Quantitative data suggested moderately high levels of satisfaction with family support, but descriptions of their experiences as they encountered medical, financial, logistic, and socio-cultural challenges were far more negative. In the more nuanced picture developed from integrating their data, they were able to see that these experiences create a loneliness in which family support becomes "lost in transit" so that "for those struggling with infertility, the non-supportive attitude of medical and financial systems may have superseded support from other informal systems, muting their potential positive effects" (2014: #9). The idea that vulnerability results in denying need for and receipt of support, defined in the literature as invisible support, was also helpful in explaining why the women might give higher scores to mask their more negative experiences.

Draw on theory to harmonise integration of complementary data

Conflict in sources, such as that experienced by Berger and Paul (2014), is a not uncommon problem faced by those working with supposedly complementary mixed methods data. Drawing on theory to provide a common conceptual framework to planning and to analysis of results from varied data sources can be a way of guiding their more harmonious integration (Evans, Coon, & Ume, 2011). For example, Beringer, Fletcher, and Taket (2006) applied Giddens' structuration theory to their study of coordination of caregiving in children's wards, using its three main concepts (allocative resources, authoritative resources, and rules) to synchronise results from multiple data sources. From this, they developed a model "depicting how the instantiated rules and resources in the coordination of children's inpatient health care promote inconsistency and diversity in practice" (2006: 332). Few studies were found to take advantage of this approach, however.

A theoretical framework influences the particular perspective taken on a phenomenon; it consequently shapes observations that are made and interpretations of what is observed (Cooper, 2008). Mixed methods researchers are advised to develop an explicit conceptual or theoretical framework as part of the research design process (Maxwell & Loomis, 2003). Doing so improves coherence across all elements of the study. A framework assists in identifying gaps in the literature, in providing a basis for communicating significance and innovation to funding bodies, in foreshadowing potential outcomes from the study, and in the realm of practice, in planning for interventions (Evans et al., 2011).

Evans, Coon, and Ume (2011) used the theoretical constructs associated with a life course perspective (adapted from sociology, with an emphasis on temporality) to guide collection of narrative interview data and appropriate demographic and scaled data in their longitudinal study of caregiving in Mexican American families. Variable data were used to identify broad patterns across cases and guide selection of 110 caregiver–recipient pairs forming three groups at varying stages along a trajectory of caregiving. Caregiving trajectories, transitions, turning points, timing, strategies, and family influences were mapped together across life course timelines over 15 months in a case-oriented approach. The focus provided by the theoretical life course perspective facilitated management and analysis of the large and complex dataset, allowing them to present a detailed picture of the complexity of caregiving over time. Their data both supported the existing literature on life course perspective, and added new concepts of collective caregiving and of sons providing personal care to mothers to the literature on caregiving, especially as it related to Mexican American families.

Application of a particular theoretical framework that is blind to variations in perspectives and experience might also limit or close options (Dowson & McInerney, 2003). Flexibility is needed, for example, when *a priori* codes don't fit the data. An early surprise and complication for data collection for Evans et al. was the discovery of households with multiple caregivers and multiple recipients, the phenomenon they termed "collective caregiving". In such situations, pragmatists and critical realists alike advocate an abductive approach that allows for back and forth movement between theory and data as new understanding is developed. There is benefit, too, in applying more than one framework and assessing the relative utility of each in developing explanations, for example, when contradictions are encountered in new data (Wesely, 2010). A theoretical framework that provides a guiding structure should not preclude discovery.

Complementary analysis in practice

What practical strategies can be employed to assist the process of meshing, weaving, or piecing elements together to create a cohesive whole? As with a bricolage, and complementary data more generally, effective data management systems, systems for coding or sorting data, and for recording conceptual links across data and reflections on data are all necessary to an effective process.

In my largely pre-computer PhD days, for the analysis stage of the community study described earlier, this meant having a notebook with pages set aside for each topic and subtopic being covered. As results were generated or observations or interpretations made from any data source, they were noted under the appropriate topic heading, thus facilitating the development of integrated understanding about each topic. This level of integration was evident, then, in the chapter reporting that community study.

A similar but more effective process can be constructed using a word processor (as illustrated earlier, in Figure 2.8). Use heading styles to identify topics and subtopics, the document map shown in the navigation or summary pane at the side of the screen to allow immediate (hyperlinked) access to any topic, and outline view to rearrange topics as needed. Once sufficient information has been gathered under a particular heading, that section is turned into (draft) prose, pending review when all are done and the sections are reordered.

Now even greater efficiency is possible with the ready availability of software programs for qualitative and mixed methods data analysis. When data from all sources have been imported into a single project structure and a common coding system is applied, then simple code retrieval will bring data from all available sources together for each aspect of the topic while still referencing the particular source for any data segment (Figure 5.1, see also Figure 2.12). Memoing systems allow for recording ongoing reflections on the material, and linking tools connect source material or results from queries to ideas that emanate from them. Complementary analyses don't usually require sophisticated use of software query tools, but they will be enriched by checking where particular ideas have come from and from noticing connections between different facets of the emerging picture. When it comes to writing up, coded material and ideas from memos are drawn together in a word processor, as above.

Creating visual models (such as Figures 2.1 and 2.2 in Chapter 2) and using the software's visualisation tools while working are also helpful as integrating strategies, as visualisations clarify what concepts are in use and how they interconnect. They can be of additional benefit in reports, as a way of communicating ideas to an audience.

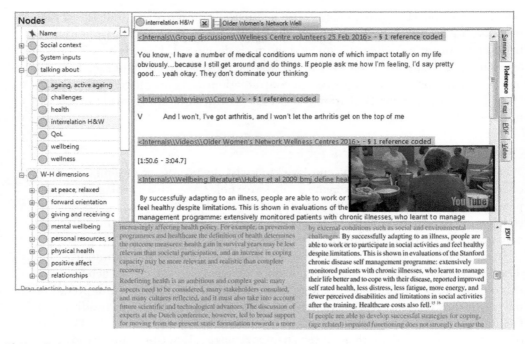

Figure 5.1 Coding retrievals from varied sources in NVivo

Juxtapose complementary sources

When different data sources provide information about the same range of topics and subtopics, interpretive and integrative value is added by juxtaposing information relating to particular categories, themes, or issues. This makes it possible to deliberately compare and contrast contributions from the different sources, point by point, as in a study by Classen et al. (2007).

Classen et al. (2007) combined data from a national crash dataset with stakeholder perspectives on the causes of older drivers' crashes in order to plan appropriate socio-ecological interventions. Results were clearly set out in an expanded coverage for each of 11 overarching themes identified in the two substudies. They employed a standard layout for each theme covered: topic area; quantitative data; qualitative data; comparison or integration; discussion; and implications (for intervention planning and/or further research needed). This way of considering and presenting evidence provided particularly strong support for conclusions from the study.

How analysis will be handled depends on the degree to which preliminary analysis of the separate sources has been undertaken and on the extent to which different sources speak to the same issues. Processing of the data almost always involves coding all sources using a common coding system, but purposes can shift from coordination of complementary data to confirmation or validation using parallel sources.

Juxtapose in joint displays

Juxtaposition of data is most effectively achieved using joint displays in which thematically sorted or case-based data of different types or from different sources is placed side by side, facilitating exploration of both commonalities and differences across those data types or sources. Timothy Guetterman and colleagues (Guetterman, Creswell, & Kuckartz, 2015; Guetterman, Fetters, & Creswell, 2015) developed a classification scheme for joint displays of data and used it to review the displays presented in a sample of 19 articles found in a selection of health and methodological journals over an extended period. Their typology included side by side, comparing results, statistics by themes, instrument development, cross-case comparison, adding qualitative data into an experiment, and adding a theoretical lens displays. Some displays combined types. The type of display varied according to the overall design and purpose of the study, but they nevertheless served similar integrative and analytic purposes in helping the researchers to identify patterns across the data, and to compare, contrast, and perhaps merge results from different sources. Displays such as the one in Table 5.1 that combine qualitative insights with statistics were the most common type used in their sample. These are found primarily in convergent (complementary) designs involving a merging approach to integration.

In her study of teachers' experience of providing instrumental music education in an urban context, Kate Fitzpatrick (2016) used an integrated display to explore the alignment of focus group, survey, and case study data. To assist in integration and interpretation of data for each aspect of the teachers' experience for which she had mixed sources, she added a "data convergence label" indicating whether the results confirmed or contradicted each other, were mixed, or simply enhanced understanding. Tables 5.1 and 5.2 provide extracts that illustrate both extended and condensed forms of integrated display as used by Fitzpatrick. Through her analysis, she found that teaching in an urban context required knowledge of context, special skills, and modified pedagogy, and was challenging but also satisfying and rewarding. Her innovative use of data convergence labels assisted her in the process of identifying relationships across data types, and in succinctly summarising complex relationships.

Table 5.1   Extract from full data matrix

Research Question 3: What attitudes and beliefs do teachers hold towards teaching instrumental music in urban schools?

Associated survey theme	Quantitative data	Qualitative data examples	Associated qualitative code	Data convergence label
Beliefs: About programs	Moderate agreement with the statement "My program provides a haven from the problems in the rest of the school" (M = 3.52, SD = 1.06). Moderate agreement with the statement "My program provides a haven from the problems of the neighborhood" (M = 3.71, SD = 1.04).	Students "hang out" in Ms. Sanders' room: "I think they just have fun in here, where they can't anywhere else in the building" (interview, May 22, 2007). Mr. Michaels: "Oh, yeah, they hang out. We have to kick them out oftentimes" (interview, May 30, 2007). Mr. Sims: "A lot of them would rather be here than at home" (interview, May 25, 2007).	The program as a haven	Confirm

Source: Fitzpatrick, 2016: 284, Table 2

Table 5.2   Extract from condensed data convergence matrix

What attitudes and beliefs do teachers hold towards teaching instrumental music in urban schools?

Quantitative Survey Theme	Qualitative Code	Label
Beliefs: About themselves	Commitment to improving student lives; Personal investment	Enhance
Beliefs: About students	Belief in students	Confirm
Beliefs: About programs	The program as a haven	Confirm
Beliefs: About programs	Focus on the traditional	Contradict
Beliefs: Definitions of success	Definitions of success	Mixed
Attitudes: Rationale for taking positions	Reasons for becoming a teacher	Enhance
Job satisfaction	The balance of frustration and reward	Enhance

Source: Fitzpatrick, 2016: 283, Table 1

Juxtapose to "jointly constitute" different data

Holger von der Lippe (2010) drew on a longitudinal dataset using event history analysis (a statistical method described in Chapter 9) and combined this data with open-coded interviews to model the transition of young men into first-time parenthood within the (former) East German cultural milieu. By using these complementary methods, he was able to capture individual differences in both intentional (conscious) and nonconscious aspects of their goal setting and motivations, and selectivity regarding partners. After preliminary analysis of each dataset, von der Lippe juxtaposed his results, observing:

> We posit that the rationale of our approach of juxtaposition and full analysis of correspondence of qualitative and quantitative findings has been one of *joint constitution of the research object*. ... we subjected every result from the one approach to the scrutiny of the respective other approach [rather than selectively combining to illuminate or support]. ... In doing so, each method was used to provide a thorough and instructive review and specification of what the respective other method suggested. (2010: 216–217, emphasis in original)

"Joint constitution of the research object", then, is a particularly thorough and deliberate process of comparing data point by point, with the potential to develop a *merged* rather than additive result.

Comparing and contrasting source data across coded concepts or themes is a strong starting point for the process of complementary integration, but further integrative work informs deeper understanding. For von der Lippe, each concept or theme was considered also in relation to the narrative profiles of the individual cases, to place them in that broader perspective.

Triangulation – a shifting metaphor for comparing and combining parallel data

Triangulation is a much used and abused metaphor applied to mixing methods generally, to validation or convergence of results within and across methods, and to combining methods to widen and deepen understanding of a subject. Use of the concept in the methodological literature is usually traced to Campbell and Fiske's landmark article in 1959, in which they argued for the value of a multitrait–multimethod (correlation) matrix to evaluate both convergent and discriminant validity, using multiple different measures to assess multiple traits associated with personality. Embedded within the reflected matrix generated by their procedure was a series of triangles separated by validity diagonals and a reliability diagonal. Although they did not specifically use the term triangulation, the foundation for using multiple methods for validation was established in that (purely quantitative) article. The term was first used a few years later by Webb, Campbell, Schwartz, and Sechrest (1966, note Donald Campbell's common authorship) in the context of a discussion about operational definitions and multiple measurements for social concepts. Referring to Campbell and Fiske's article, Webb et al. argued that "once a proposition has been confirmed by two or more independent measurement processes, the uncertainty of its interpretation is greatly reduced. The most persuasive evidence comes through a *triangulation of measurement processes*" (1966: 3, emphasis added).

The term triangulation was popularised and extended by Denzin (1978), primarily in the context of qualitative research, to cover four strategies designed to strengthen confirmation: use of multiple methods, varied data sources, different theoretical perspectives, and multiple investigators. Denzin distinguished between *within method* triangulation, in which use of multiple scales for a quantitative study or multiple groups in a qualitative study involves cross-checking for internal consistency or reliability, and *between method* triangulation, in which external validity is assessed by comparing and contrasting the *results* of separate substudies. Historically, then, triangulation was seen as a tool for ensuring reliability in results, or validation of conclusions through having more than one method produce the same result. It continues to be referred to as a tool of validation in the mixed methods context by Greene (2007) and others, but because "the triangulation term has accumulated so many renderings" Fielding and Fielding (2008: 556) suggest "it is now clearer to use the terms 'convergence' or 'confirmation' when seeking cross-validation between methods". They suggest also "the value of triangulation lies more in 'quality control' than any guarantee of 'validity'" (2008: 557).

When methodological triangulation is being employed specifically to test convergence of results in order to corroborate or validate conclusions, ideally both data gathering and initial analyses for each of at least two methods are conducted separately, but close enough in time (usually concurrently) that the phenomenon being studied does not change. It is only after the analyses for each method have been completed that an assessment is made regarding the level of convergence in the results, with conclusions drawn based on parallel results from all sets of data.

Pager and Quillian (2005) telephoned employers to inquire about the acceptability of potential applicants of different races with a history of drug use for their advertised jobs. They compared their responses with observations of the way those employers responded to job seekers who matched the description given in the phone conversation. Race had no impact on likely success when employers were interviewed, yet white applicants were much more likely to be called back following an actual application than were black applicants.

In more complex studies, this ideal of complete separation of data sources until finalised results are being compared is less commonly achieved in practice, however (as with Floyd et al.'s 1994 study below), and at least some of the different data sources are likely to reveal different aspects of the phenomenon being studied, rather than confirmation of the same phenomenon (Erzberger & Prein, 1997). When research involves human subjects, the process of measurement itself creates change, affecting any further data collection (Fielding & Fielding, 1986; Sanford, 1970). Researchers who point to the conceptual and empirical difficulty of obtaining confirmatory results from methods with contrasting epistemological bases argue that different theories and methods arising from different traditions, when combined, are able to give a fuller, more complete, or enhanced picture with greater analytic density, but not necessarily a more valid one (Fielding, 2012; Flick, 1992; Meetoo & Temple, 2003).

Using a structured questionnaire with scaled items followed by two open-ended questions, Floyd, Schroeder, and Finn (1994) investigated the issue of order in authorship with 146 authors of articles in three leading management journals. Open-ended questions asked for positive and negative experiences of collaboration. Closed questions covered motives for collaboration, activities that contribute to authorship, protocols for determining author order, and background items such as gender, rank, and tenure status. Qualitative coding was undertaken before analysis of the closed questions. Three common themes cut across the positive and negative categories: 1) focus on task elements, schedules, and division of work; 2) focus on friendship, trust, and flexibility; and 3) power differences. Participants who were motivated by a desire to increase productivity focused on equity in authorship, while those who were motivated by collaborative social relationships focused on equality. These themes were found to link with existing distributive justice theory. They then explored the validity of their framework through principal components analysis of the variable data from the questionnaire. Four motivational factors (productivity, social relationship, learning, and helping), four criteria for inclusion in authorship (providing support, collecting or analysing data, having the core idea, doing the writing), and three factors describing different bases for determining order (equity based on contribution, egalitarian based arbitrary order, power based on prestige) were identified, providing a good match to the qualitative data. Relationships between these factors and tenure were further explored, and a typological model of four different approaches to collaboration and authorship (each with the potential to generate different forms of conflict) was developed, with associated propositions, based on concordance across both sets of data.

The term triangulation has, in general, become more widely used to include the practice of seeking data from two or more sources with complementary strengths and non-overlapping limitations, such that data from one source complements or extends the other (Erzberger & Kelle, 2003; Moran-Ellis et al., 2006; Sandelowski, 1995). Studies that set out to use triangulation to confirm or validate results often evolve into dialectic or complementary analyses, when it is found that the different components provide data that are not able to be used for convergent cross-validation as originally intended – a circumstance which speaks to the great difficulty of using methods based on different assumptions and different theoretical frameworks to address exactly the same points. Even when triangulation results in dissonance, this too is a step forward (through falsifying assumptions, leading to the formulation of new hypotheses) in the process of validating theories.

The health and health service usage of homeless youth in Germany was investigated by Uwe Flick (2010) using three methods: observation, interviews with youth, and planned interviews with experts. Each of the methods involved different samples, gathered using different methods. Flick described his study as one employing triangulation, initially seeking validation, but he found instead the different methods worked in a complementary way to generate a picture of the conditions under which medical care for homeless youth became difficult to be claimed or supported when the issue of housing was ignored, despite there being universal health insurance available to the young people. In his conclusion Flick described each of these methods used in the study as having an additive benefit in building a more complete picture of health issues for homeless youth.

The metaphor that has become more strongly associated with this broader idea of triangulation is derived from surveyors' use of that term. The surveyor fixes the location of an observable point by using the baseline between the two known points and the angles made at each end of the baseline when the distant third point is in view, to construct the sides of a triangle. The sidelines will meet, fixing the location of the distant point. This metaphor reinforces the idea of an approach involving a *complementary* use of two different types of equal-status data (the lines and angles of the triangle) to elaborate on something partially known, or to construct new knowledge. If validation rather than complementarity is the goal:

A better analogy ... would be the drawing of an accurately measured line. To ensure that a line is correctly placed, say, when doing carpentry, the distance from the baseline is measured in at least three places as a check. In describing validation, this analogy points to the need for three separate sources of information, as two are insufficient to ensure accuracy. Seeking three concurring sources overcomes the problem that lies in using just two: with two, both may be wrong in the same way, or if one is wrong, the conclusion drawn may be skewed. With three, if there is a discrepancy, then a fourth measurement (i.e., data source) or a careful check of the discrepant source, or both, will usually be necessary to determine which of the three was misplaced. (Bazeley & Kemp, 2012: 70)

Triangulation in practice

Beyond metaphors and labels, what practical steps might one actually take to triangulate complementary data? The following guidelines were adapted from a protocol Farmer et al. (2006) developed in response to those who advocate triangulation but don't explain how they actually do it. They are also informed by von der Lippe's (2010) idea of jointly constituting data and share some of the characteristics of the approach Fitzpatrick (2016) developed, described earlier.

Using data from different sources or gained using different methodologies:

1. Create a list of shared concepts or themes related to the research question using both sets of data. Ensure that the concepts used are grounded in an understanding of the individual cases that make up the sample.
2. Juxtapose sources using a matrix with frequencies and quotes to compare for meaning for each concept or theme, the frequency of each within each type of data (transform if needed), and similarity of examples.
3. Assess convergence (the triangulation goal). Identify where coded or thematic data are a) in full agreement, b) in partial agreement, c) silenced when covered in one set of results but not the other, or d) dissonant, when results differ on meaning and prominence. Are differences related to the nature and/or focus of the datasets, to the conditions under which the results were obtained, or do they represent legitimate differences in findings?
4. Assess completeness. Compare nature and scope of unique topic areas for each type of data; identify key differences in scope and/or coverage. Does an omission in one set of data stem from the nature of the data (its type, coverage, or depth), or is its absence more meaningful? Does this complement other data from the same or other sources?
5. Where multiple researchers are involved: compare assessments of convergence and completeness. Plan for managing disagreements.
6. Develop a unified description and interpretation of each concept or theme, merging the information in the light of the whole, to constitute the research subject.

> Given that no method, dataset, or analysis process is without flaws, it is important for [mixed methods] researchers to be up front in their acknowledgement and recognition of limitations of the sets of findings that they use as inputs into a triangulation process. In addition, given that the purpose and content of particular datasets will vary, researchers should be clear on how they have chosen to use the datasets and if they have weighted a particular dataset within the triangulation process. (Farmer et al., 2006: 391)

Tonkin-Crine et al. (2016) demonstrated an application of Farmer's triangulation protocol in a retrospective analysis of data from a randomised control trial. Four groups (including a control) were established to assess the usefulness of

(Continued)

(Continued)

training in communication skills for GPs combined with a patient booklet explaining alternative care and/or a C-reactive protein (CRP) point-of-care test for discouraging prescription of antibiotics to a patient with acute cough. Data sources comprised survey and interview data with both GPs and patients, across six European countries. Key findings from each of the four datasets were presented as statements. Each was then compared with every other key finding (in pairs), with redundancies eliminated, using a matrix set up in Excel (Table 5.3). Relationships were then marked as silence, dissonance, agreement, partial agreement, or not applicable (not present in either), according to Farmer et al.'s criteria. Instances of dissonance were of most interest, one in particular where doctors and patients compared the two interventions, with opinions differing regarding the value of the CRP test. In findings where there was agreement, the interview data often helped to illustrate the survey findings. Overall, the authors found the protocol easy to apply, and resulted in a key new finding, "that GPs perceive that the CRP test is useful in persuading patients to agree to a non-antibiotic approach, but patient data suggested this was unnecessary if a full explanation about the disease and non-antibiotic management was given" (Tonkin-Crine et al., 2012: 6).

Table 5.3   Examples of key findings set out in Excel to enable comparisons

Key Finding	GP Quantitative	PT Quantitative	GP Qualitative	PT Qualitative
8	GPs in the CS & CM groups increased confidence in reducing prescribing whilst those in the CRP group decreased in confidence.	Silence	1. Booklet increases confidence in not prescribing; 2. CRP decreases uncertainty; 3. CRP has barriers to use.	1. Some patients felt the booklet supported the GPs decision; 2. Patients talked about the CRP test as a tool for the GP.
10	Silence	Most patients (84%) in CS & CM reported having received the booklet and having used it (78%).	Booklet can be used in everyday consultations.	1. Some patients reported that the booklet contained new information about their illness which was valuable; 2. Most patients were happy to receive the booklet; 3. Not all patients took the booklet.

Key Finding	GP Quantitative	PT Quantitative	GP Qualitative	PT Qualitative
14	Silence	Only a third (38%) of patients in the CRP & CM groups received the CRP test.	1. Booklet can be used in everyday consult CRP only in a few; 2. CRP has barriers to use.	Patients were happy to have the CRP test carried out.

Source: Tonkin-Crine et al., 2016, supplementary data, partial table only

Notes: CS – communication skills training and booklet; CRP – diagnostic test only; CM – combined skills and test; C – control group; AB – antibiotic

Constructing an integrated (joint) display, as described earlier, is a visual way of juxtaposing information and interpretations of key concepts or themes (and/or literature) from different sources. The display facilitates determination of points of concordance (agreement) and points of discordance (dissonance, or conflict). Farmer et al. added frequency counts to the rows of their matrix. Fitzpatrick added a data convergence label. Creativity that adds interpretive value to the use of display tables is encouraged!

As with complementary data more generally, the process of managing different data sources and of bringing different data together around particular issues or topics is facilitated by use of computer software. Options include: (1) using sections marked by heading styles in Word to organise material (as in Figure 2.8); (2) juxtaposing summary data, statistics, or critical quotes from different sources using columns in a Word table or in Excel, with rows defined by thematic content (as in Table 5.1); or (3) using coding systems and comparative matrices in software designed for qualitative data analysis (Figure 5.2).

Exploring process and outcome: integrating complementary sources in analysing the effectiveness of interventions

Using qualitative and quantitative data in a complementary way has a practical application in experiments, trials, and intervention studies as both outcomes and the processes that brought about those particular outcomes are assessed, along with the potential for wider implementation of the intervention. The advantages to be gained by introducing qualitative data in association with experimental or other quantitative data in these studies is even further enhanced when those data are linked on a case by case basis (as described in the next chapter).

Combining methods in randomised control trials and experimental studies

The pure double-blind randomised control trial (RCT) is still considered by many to be the "gold standard" for testing drugs and other interventions, with its use of

	Document group = Literature	Document group = Survey reports	Document group = Interviews
exercise	c) How active are older adults in the UK? While they have the most to gain, older UK adults have the lowest levels of physical activity compared to other age groups and fall well below the levels of physical activity recommended for healthy ageing [15]. Self-reported activity data from the Health Survey for England show that less than 30% of 65–74 year-olds and less than 15% of adults aged 75 and over reported any exercise or sport lasting at least ten minutes during the previous four weeks. Fewer than 10% of men and 5% of women aged over 75 met current physical activity recommendations [16]. Also it appears that older adults are not getting much activity in their daily routines. In Project OPAL, physical activity and physical function was objectively measured in a diverse sample of 240 adults [1]. The 70–75 year-old participants averaged 5500 and those over 85 years only 2000 steps per day (minimal daily movement usually produces 3000 steps). Almost all (98.7%) of those over 70 years did not meet recommended amounts of activity. This mirrors national statistics using accelerometry suggesting that less than 5% of men and women aged 65 and above achieve recommended levels of physical activity. Literature\Stathi et al. AVONet 2014: 12: 888 - 12: 2475 (0)	Half of the women have participated in exercise/ physical activity classes elsewhere as well as at OWN during the past year. Involvement in other organised physical activities or classes outside OWN Wellness was not associated with age or length of attendance at OWN. It was also not associated with higher WHO scores. Those who reported poor general mood ('yes' on the MGMQ) were less likely than others to not participate in extra classes or activities. Survey reports\2016 SWSLHD report: 61 - 61 (0) Most (32; 76%) exercise for 20 minutes or more several times each week with 9 of those doing so daily. More than half (28; 64%) did so 'yesterday'. Neither was associated with age or length of attendance at OWN. Those who exercised yesterday had significantly better general wellbeing than those who did not (WHO 71:51; p=.001) and tended to experience better general mood (MGMQ) Survey reports\2016 SWSLHD report: 62 - 63 (0) Aus: Q25b How often: physical activity Aus Frequency Aus Percent B_OWN Freq B_OWN %	L: Because I go to aqua aerobics on a Tuesday and then I do a bit of walking myself during the other days. Interviews\SL & SS: 101 - 101 (0) S: Well, yes but I add (?) that with the exercises for me because I had the osteoporosis and arthritis, the flexibility, the exercises, um, Tai Chi is good for me as well. Interviews\SL & SS: 160 - 160 (0) and I love to come here to Wellness and do the international dancing for an hour, and then the gentle, gentle exercise – that's enough for me. And I ah, play a little bit of tennis on a Tuesday with friends who I played comp tennis with many years ago. So I'm socialising, exercising, and out in the fresh air. Interviews\IV: 4 - 4 (0) V: Yes, well, with my arthritis sometimes I hit the ball and my racquet goes too, but reflexes are still quite good for my age, but my grip, with the osteoarthritis and that, but on the whole, um, I've really tried to you know, stay as active and as interested in things. Interviews\IV: 12 - 12 (0)

Figure 5.2   Juxtaposing data from different sources in MAXQDA's quote matrix (Wellbeing data)

placebos, random assignment of participants to treatment and control groups, and both givers and recipients of the treatments being blind to their group assignment. Experimental and trial researchers have traditionally focused on manipulation and measurement of a key variable in an intervention, without concern for contextual influences as these are considered to be eliminated from the process through randomisation of sample groups. Analysis tends to be a straightforward assessment of post-trial differences between groups, with theory providing the rationale for causal processes assumed to explain those differences.

Assessment of interventions in health, education, and international development have drawn on the standards and ideology of the scientific method that undergirds the RCT, but the dominance of this model for assessing interventions in and beyond drug trials increasingly is being questioned. Researchers face issues in fidelity to trial protocols, with challenges in field settings where randomisation is ethically or practically difficult. The complexity of factors involved and consequent variability of individual responses to any social, educational, or health service intervention, with the inevitable influence of context on participant responses, add further challenges to design and analysis assessing intervention effects (Drabble & O'Cathain, 2015). Additionally, researchers, methodologists, and practitioners have questioned the value of assessment that relies on a measure of change that is either disinterested in or presumes an understanding of the processes and mechanisms involved in creating the observed changes (Maxwell, 2004b).

More advanced statistical models and methods have been developed for trial and evaluation research, in an attempt to consider the contribution of various initial and intermediate factors to the outcome. These include using multiple regression to identify the additive contribution of the treatment over all other known (and measured) variables, and path analysis and structural equation modelling to identify the direct and indirect contribution of each variable to an outcome where one variable cannot be effectively isolated for experimentation. These methods, however, do not satisfy the need to understand the deep-seated mechanisms and contexts that allow intended changes and unintended variations to create the outcomes, nor do they necessarily convey what the outcomes might actually mean for the people experiencing them. These aspects are seen as being more appropriately met using qualitative or mixed methods.

A qualitative element might be included within the design of a trial or services intervention:

- to clarify conceptual issues and inform the design of the intervention, including improving recruitment and involvement in the study, for example, through a feasibility study
- to understand the role of intermediary and contextual factors ("validity threats") in producing the outcome
- to improve understanding and utility of an intervention, for example, by helping to interpret and explain results
- to enhance understanding about research participants who drop out or are non-compliant

- to assess the fidelity of implementation, particularly as it is translated from its original setting to a more natural setting (Drabble & O'Cathain, 2015; O'Cathain et al., 2014).

Additionally, in health-related research, patient preferences for treatment might be assessed prior to randomisation and then taken into account when considering results, or a parallel trial might be conducted alongside a larger RCT where patients choose their preferred treatment, and results are compared with those from the randomised groups (Sedgwick, 2013; Torgerson & Sibbald, 1998).

Since 2000 there has been increasing use of qualitative methods to complement the experimental and statistical work of trials, particularly for those involving a health services or community-based intervention (O'Cathain et al., 2014) and those involving dementia patients and their carers (Gibson et al., 2004). When the trials are extended to health services interventions (rather than drugs alone), the complexity of the environment within which the intervention is being applied means that compromises in trial design often become necessary. As well as strategic and ethical difficulties in randomising assignment to experimental and control groups, it is almost impossible to blind those providing, managing, or receiving interventions to group assignment (Song et al., 2010). More particularly, social and community interventions are inevitably fuzzy and multivariable in their nature, and understanding process is critical to assessing the value of the intervention. It is not useful, for example, to know that something makes a significant difference overall, if half of those in the intervention group show no benefit (as in the following example). One needs to know who is likely to benefit, and why the intervention works for some but not others.

Outcome data for a trial of individualised nurse coaching and support for cancer pain management demonstrated a significant improvement in pain control overall for trial participants, but detailed analysis revealed that half of the intervention group was still actively engaged in problem solving at the end of the six week trial period and needed more time to show effective change (Plano Clark et al., 2013). Audiotapes of coaching sessions, primarily designed for auditing of intervention fidelity, provided a "rich source of data about patients' and family caregivers' experiences with pain management" (Schumacher et al., 2005: 269). As well as outcome data and surveys, additional naturally occurring data were available from field notes and pain management diaries. The multiple research strategy employed to capitalise on this data included a qualitative content analysis of the audiotapes to explore problem solving during the patient coaching sessions, categorisation and statistical analysis of open entries in diaries to assess the usefulness of tools used, and a focused content analysis of data from 11 patients for whom the intervention did not work at all. From these analyses the researchers were able to suggest revisions to the coaching protocols, to the pain management diary, and alternative strategies for those who were particularly resistant to using opioid pain management. Insights from the combined analyses were incorporated into a second, 10-week trial, with the assessment of that trial also including a qualitative component situated within the context of the primary questions (Plano Clark et al., 2013).

In order for the different methods to be integrated effectively, a trial or evaluation team needs to see inclusion of the qualitative component as of equal priority and working in tandem with the quantitative assessments (O'Cathain et al., 2014; Spillane, 2010). Qualitative aims and methods need to be valued and incorporated from the start. This is preferably achieved through the qualitative researcher having a senior position on the team, supported by open communication between different members of the team. Additionally, enough time and funding must be dedicated to the qualitative component to ensure quality research and time for analysis, rather than its being done on the side by trial managers. Even where the goal is to have the methods mutually informing each other, circumstances can intervene, as when one set of results is ready well before the other and so there is pressure to publish data about outcomes before process data are available (Simons, 2007). This common tendency in clinical trials to publish different components of the results separately also serves to inhibit their eventual integration (O'Cathain, 2010).

Analysis strategies that integrate process with outcomes in trials are rarely achieved beyond their being mutually informing but separate, as using mixed methods in trials is still considered to be an innovative practice. If different methods are complementary in that they are contributing different elements, the design, testing, and perhaps further development of a process model or a theoretical model that included intermediate as well as final outcomes (as described in Chapter 2) would be beneficial to achieving a more integrated analysis (e.g., Brady & O'Regan, 2009). If different methods are covering some or all of the same issues, then application of the triangulation protocol described earlier, or a similar form of joint display, could be used (e.g., Tonkin-Crine et al., 2016). Where different types of data are available for the same cases, some of the linking strategies described in the next chapter become appropriate. Integration of analyses during a trial extends possibilities for adaptation of the trial protocol, a practice that can facilitate the process of identifying effective or ineffective treatments (Meurer et al., 2012). Thus, while the baseline is to apply complementary methods, greater levels of integration are both possible and desirable.

Evaluation research

Unlike those conducting medical trials, researchers engaged in programme evaluation have a long history of using multiple methods to assess effectiveness in reaching target groups, in implementing intended strategies, and for understanding the nature of the intermediate processes as well as participant response to the intervention and outcomes from it (Rallis & Rossman, 2003). Even so, specific methods are still commonly seen as contributing to different elements of the evaluation – quantitative measures for summative (outcome) evaluation, and qualitative insights for formative (process) evaluation, making integration and added value from integration more difficult to achieve.

Social interventions are inevitably complex, and occur in complex environments. In evaluation research, theory of change and logic models are frequently used to inform the design of both the intervention and the research into its effectiveness (Connell et al., 1995; Dyson & Todd, 2010; Knowlton & Phillips, 2013). As explained in Chapter 2, these set out hypothesised steps from change to outcome, as a basis for designing intermediate observations and measurements that will assist with understanding the causal processes involved in the intervention, the influence of context, and in identifying point(s) at which practice does or does not concur with theory.

Arbitrary distinctions between quantitative and qualitative methods are best ignored when choosing methods to use in evaluation of social, educational, and health service interventions. Choices will be impacted by the availability of data sources, time, skills, and financial resources. An effective mixed methods approach integrates these different sources and methods throughout the implementation and evaluative process, including for summative assessment, where that is required (Weisner, 2005; Yin, 2006). For example, Yin suggests asking questions covering both quantity and quality for both process and outcome aspects of the evaluation; defining units of analysis for each method that "reach into the realm of the other" to facilitate integration rather than isolation; nesting samples for different methods within each other; using different data sources and methodological tools to cover some of the same variables; and use of "counterpart" analyses. Examples of the latter include building regression models to mimic logic models; assessing whether the different methods "tell the same story"; and whether they offer common typologies (such as might be reflected in coding systems) for the subject being studied. Evaluators using multiple methods frequently report gaining unexpected insights from one method that can then be incorporated into the (re)design of other methods, to enrich the study (Burch & Heinrich, 2016).

Because projects are frequently modified during implementation and implementation might occur differently in different locations, an advantage of employing integrated methods and including a focus on process and context as well as outcome is improved capacity to determine whether lack of evident change is a consequence of design failure or implementation failure (Bamberger, Rao, & Woolcock, 2010). Contextual and process analyses are usually iterative, with initial qualitative assessments often converted to ratings for inclusion in statistical analyses, to be followed by a return to qualitative data to explain why and how contextual and process factors are operating. Using multiple sources of data for process analysis, where data from different sources can be compared, helps to overcome problems in particular reporting systems.

The multiple, complementary sources and methods used in an evaluation contribute to a report that *describes*, providing details of the programme and its implementation;

compares internally across programme elements, methods or sites; *compares* externally, to show how this programme is different from others and to assess the relative benefits (which might be different for different subgroups); and *predicts* for future implementation, recommending improvements and providing guidance on wider implementation (Rallis & Rossman, 2003). Process and outcome are clearly interactive, so although the descriptions of each might initially be separated, they must then be brought together in a cohesive integrated explanation showing just how, and under what circumstances, which process led to what outcomes. Only then can the analysis successfully contribute to the goal of predicting for future, wider implementation.

Transformational approaches to mixed methods evaluations pose a further challenge to traditional evaluation methods. Mertens (2007, 2015) points to the necessity of engaging the users' viewpoints and perspectives in planning for both an intervention *and* its evaluation. An intervention that assumes rather than investigates reasons for a problem is bound to be ineffective. Evaluators, therefore, are ideally involved with the programme to be evaluated and with those who will be affected by it, from its planning phase. Flexibility in design, including approaches to analysis, is then required to allow the opportunity to follow up programme changes, unexpected observations, and new leads.

Ramon Flecha (2014) describes how communicative methodology (CM) was used over five years to study the impact of the INCLUD-ED programme[1] at La Paz elementary school, in one of Spain's most underprivileged neighbourhoods. This mixed method approach is designed to create opportunities for active participation throughout the research by those "at the grassroots", who are most directly affected by it. Also evaluated, therefore, was the transformational impact of the research process itself.

La Paz school was created on INCLUDE-ED principles through community action. It was a replacement for an existing but dysfunctional school that had further disadvantaged an already marginalised group (the Roma) in a conflict-ridden community. As part of a longitudinal case study, mixed forms of data were collected concurrently in four rounds, with results and experience from each informing the next. Vulnerable but active people in the local community participated in an Advisory Council. Members were involved in monitoring both the research and the school's progress, and as the project progressed, they and others through open meetings had input into the kinds of information gathered each year. New items were added to questionnaires, interview protocols were

(Continued)

---

[1] INCLUD-ED Project: Strategies for inclusion and social cohesion in Europe from education, 2006–2011. 6th Framework Programme. Citizens and Governance in a Knowledge-based Society.

(Continued)

adjusted, new people were included. For example, as community members shared how involvement had changed their lives, researchers brought evidence of this from other places. Consequently, the fourth round of the study gathered information on how community involvement in the school had influenced aspects of wider society, such as health and employment.

Specific data sources included student and family questionnaires distributed collaboratively by Roma and the research team; interviews with community activists, school administrators, and professionals; daily life stories from family members and students that were conversational and reflective; naturally constituted focus groups engaging in intersubjective reflection; and communicative observation in which researchers compare information with those they are observing. Public contributions to the project of information, insights, and direct involvement in data collection and analysis increased over the period of study. This collaborative involvement of community members with researchers ensured that results from all methods were considered together, to create a validated picture of progress to date and input for further data collection – and community action.

Complementary analyses: a caution and a final example

Recognising that different methods often embrace different conceptions of reality, but also seeing opportunities for "harnessing creative tensions" and "thinking outside the box" by using them in a complementary way, Jennifer Mason cautions:

This kind of approach is hugely challenging because by definition it pushes at the boundaries of social science philosophy, knowledge and practice. The approach is at risk of fracturing into a parallel logic, or organising itself too neatly into an integrated one. "Creative tensions" are not easy to achieve, and researchers need to feel they are sharing ideas and differences in a "safe environment", where they can take intellectual risks and be interested in alternative approaches without fear of immediate reprisal (for having sold out), contradiction (by those who favour alternative approaches) or annihilation. It requires considerable skill and commitment from researchers and teams, who need to have the capacity and inclination to see beyond disciplinary, epistemological and ontological distinctions, without simply wishing to critique all others from the perspective of only one, or to subsume all others into one. Yet it requires that the distinctive nature of different approaches is respected and allowed to flourish, rather than reducing all to a bland lowest common denominator which is assumed to be "interdisciplinarity". In this sense, it also contains within its own assumptions a particular theory or philosophy of social science, which in turn provides a model for how methods can be mixed. (Mason, 2006b: 10)

Complementary analyses are, indeed, especially prone to conflict arising from different perspectives, disciplines, data sources, or participants. Mutual respect in an interdisciplinary team has to be cultivated (as noted in Part 1), but, as Mason notes, this should not be designed to produce an homogenised result of little interest or import. Rather, the different facets of the crystal exposed by interdisciplinary or dialectical "creative tensions" in mixing methods reveal the multidimensionality of phenomena, and their contextual association.

A final example

Claire Woolley (2009), informed by a theoretical framework, studied the interplay of social structures (gender and three institutional settings) and personal agency (scope to shape one's own life, indicated in confidence, independence, proactivity) in young people's transitions towards adulthood. Her choice and execution of a complementary mixed methods approach, with an emphasis on integration of findings, exemplifies many of the points that have been made throughout this chapter, and so it is presented in some detail here.

The study was conducted in two phases (illustrated earlier in Figure 2.6). In Phase 1, variations in types and levels of agency across six structuring contexts defined by setting and gender were explored using a survey combined with equal status group interviews. These data were collected close together in time, and group participants were drawn from the survey sample. In Phase 2, biographical case studies were created using interview data combined with survey and interview data from Phase 1. Contextualising (documentary, statistical, and interview) data were also recorded. Analysis began as soon as data were available, and continued throughout, with early analyses informing later data collection and analyses, for example, specific empirical questions were shaped by results of factor analyses of the survey data. Specific source information available to answer each question were mapped, to provide a guide for managing and analysing a complex array of data (Table 5.4).

Woolley described her approach to analysis and writing thus:

> The findings from the survey and focus group interviews were reported together, rather than in parallel. ... The analysis progressed in conjunction with writing about the results. The different types of data were juxtaposed in addressing each question in turn. Headings and subheadings were specified, but not considered fixed, at the beginning and provided a framework that directed and organized the analyses. The headings were chosen to reflect the four empirical research questions and accompanying table as well as the project's overall aim of investigating agency as a socially and temporally embedded process through consideration of young people's perspectives on their past, present, and future lives. By addressing each of the questions and their associated subheadings in turn, the analyses and writing proceeded in tandem; writing in an integrated way was an aid to analyzing in an integrated way. The final version developed

Table 5.4   Plan for combining quantitative and qualitative data

| | | Young People's Perspectives | | | |
| | | Individual Agency | | | |
Data Type	Perceptions of Opportunities and Constraints	Work-Related	Personal Life	Collective Agency	Views on Their Future Prospects
Factors (Quantitative)	Opportunities open to all (C3) Ability not rewarded (C6) Achievement barriers (S5) Blame own weaknesses (C4)	Fulfilled at work (C2, S4) Active career seeking (A2) Planning, not chance (C5) Frustrating situation S6	Fulfilled personal life (C1, S3) General self-confidence (S1) Social self-confidence (S2)	Political activity (A3)	Unlikely to move (F1, A1) Negative view of future (F2)
Questions (Quantitative)	Barriers to achievement (Q11) Influence of where you live on getting a job (Q23) Influences on opportunities (Q24) Getting a job depends on... ? (Q25) Economic locus of control (Q31)	Influence on present situation (Q16) Experiences at work (Q17) Career search methods (Q19) Main attribution for present situation (Q21) Changed expectations since school (Q22)	Leaving home (Q13) Independence (Q14) Experiences in personal life (Q17) Equipped? (Q26) Self-image scale (Q36)	Work-related values (Q32) Participation in group activities (Q33) Voting behavior (Q34) Interest in politics (Q35)	Get the job you want? (Q27) Have plans? (Q29) Expectations (Q30)
Focus group thematic coding (Qualitative)	Gender Ethnicity Money Family background Social class Qualifications Area Talent to the top	Opener—how did you come to be in? Influences Pressures Work and free-time balance Confidence Control	Live with parents Independence	Politics Community involvement Free-time activities	Optimism
Focus group concept-driven coding (Qualitative)	Positive aspects Negative aspects Success depends on...	Presence and absence of agency		Collective agency	Optimism

Source: Woolley, 2009: 17, Table 1

from a process of drafting and redrafting as findings were tested against each other and as a more elaborated understanding emerged and was incorporated into the presentation of results. (2009: 16, 18)

The biographical case studies were used to further test the earlier findings, and to explore *how* individuals experience the interplay of the processes that had been identified. Parts of her data sources were linked for individual cases, facilitating analysis in ways that will be explored in detail in the next chapter.

Woolley concluded that her study demonstrated the benefit of complementary use of mixed methods:

The sum was greater than its constituent quantitative and qualitative parts specifically because these parts were linked at all stages of the project; in other words, there was integration of data at the analysis stage, of findings at the interpretive stage, and in the presentation of these at the reporting stage. In this way, it was possible to use parts of the dataset to deepen understanding, to qualify, and to elaborate on findings emerging from other parts of the dataset. (2009: 19)

Detailed descriptions of every stage of the methodology were provided, with the background and justification for all choices made. Similarly, details were provided of analysis strategies used for each element of the data and phase of the study, with samples of results. Woolley concluded her review of her methodology by evaluating it in terms of Yin's (2006) criteria for doing mixed rather than multiple methods studies.

Concluding remarks

Complementary methods are foundational in mixed methods research as they involve the bringing together of data from different sources for conjoint analysis. The strategies discussed in this chapter have traversed from the relatively unstructured approaches of picture-building through somewhat more structured approaches, to eventually arrive at the highly structured strategies involved in juxtaposing and triangulating source data and results of preliminary analyses in order to deepen or verify interim conclusions. Complementary methods find their application in rich descriptions of behavioural and social phenomena. They have always had special relevance, as well, to evaluation research with its focus on both process and outcomes, and increasingly complementary methods are being found relevant in research associated with trials of clinical, social, and educational interventions.

When data are able to be linked on a case by case basis, additional detail and precision can be added to complementary (and especially comparative) analyses, as will be seen in the next chapter. But what's to be done if different data do not come together in a complementary way, as happens quite regularly? Strategies for handling dissonance and divergence are offered in Chapter 11.

Further reading
Complementary methods, including triangulation
Garcia et al. (2004) describe the benefits and limitations of using free-text comments from surveys to expand on or clarify statistical analyses, based on examples from two large-scale National Health Service surveys in the UK.

Mason (2006b) looks at six approaches to integrating data in ways that parallel those described in this chapter.

Maxwell (2016) illustrates complementary integration of analyses and writing with examples drawn widely from across disciplines, including the physical and life sciences, and across time (centuries). He describes and provides links to classic and unusual examples, including a report by Minta, Minta, and Lott on hunting associations between badgers and coyotes, and Jane Goodall's summary of her 25 years of work with chimpanzees.

Plano Clark, Garrett, and Leslie-Pelecky (2010) demonstrate three methods of combining qualitative and quantitative data, using a study of non-traditional graduate education as an example. Combining methods in a discussion most closely parallels the methods described in this chapter; combining using a matrix, and using transformation, are covered in detail in later chapters.

Flick (1992) and Mathison (1988) are both older but valuable discussions on the history, theory, and varied uses of triangulation for validation or completeness.

Flick (2010) and Flick et al. (2012) report ongoing studies of youth homelessness and health in Germany, illustrating complementary triangulation of methods in action.

Latcheva (2011) provides a strong methodological discussion of triangulation for validation, and illustrates this by comparing the use of factor analysis and cognitive interviewing in assessing the validity of items in the Nationalism module of the International Social Survey Program.

Complementary studies
Teye (2012) reports on the issues he faced as a doctoral researcher exploring forest management practices in Ghana, both in terms of conducting the study, and in writing up a complementary study for publication.

Drawing on data from interviews, focus groups, and a survey, Panda et al. (2015) paint a dramatic picture of severe discrimination against people living with HIV-AIDS and their families in rural East Bengal, leading to the design of an "intervention roadmap".

Crooks et al. (2011) use complementary methods, including GIS, to evaluate and potentially further develop a model incorporating community readiness for locating palliative care services in a health region in Canada (models from this study are shown in Chapter 12).

Complementary methods in trials and evaluation
Bamberger et al. (2010) outline principles for conducting programme evaluation in international contexts.

Chatterji (2004) presents an argument for using extended term (i.e., longitudinal) mixed methods designs rather than randomised field trials to demonstrate causality and effectiveness in educational programme evaluation.

Dyson and Todd (2010) discuss using theory of change modelling in educational programme evaluation.

Rossman and Wilson (1985, 1994), in these two seminal articles, describe how corroboration, convergence, expansion, and initiation were used within a large-scale educational evaluation project, to justify and illustrate the combination of text and numbers within a single programme of study.

Rallis and Rossman (2003) specifically address the use of mixed methods in evaluation practice. They review four exemplary evaluations to illustrate the principles they have identified.

Weisner (2005) has edited an excellent and fascinating set of chapters describing diverse mixed methods evaluation studies focusing on children's development.

Weine (2015) critiques standard typological designs for mixed methods. He then provides a strong theoretical and practical basis arguing for using mixed methods in global health research and evaluation. He supports his approach with guidelines for designing intercultural research, built from and evidenced by experience in international field projects.

QUESTS, http://quests.ie/, located in the National University of Ireland at Galway, is a research group focusing on the inclusion of qualitative and mixed methods data within trial methodologies.

6

ANALYSING LINKED DATA: SEEKING PATTERNS AND CONTRASTS

CHAPTER OVERVIEW

When components of complementary data are linked, paired, or matched for each case within the sample, a more nuanced account of how the different data corroborate, illustrate, or elaborate each other is possible. In a trial or experiment, linked data from an embedded sample adds explanatory power to impact results from a larger sample. In sequential studies, linking initial data with follow-up data from the same person gives a two-way benefit through contextualising what is said and deepening understanding of their responses from one or other source.

The embedded or matched sampling procedure that is inherent in a linking process enhances integration of analyses (Yin, 2006). When data are linked, data items from different sources are paired or grouped on the basis of sharing a common characteristic – a particular data point, such as the person to whom they relate, or perhaps the specific time or place where they occur. Data from multiple sources are integrated around each of these individual data points, which effectively become the cases for analysis. As multiple data sources are combined into a common dataset, data from different sources can be compared and contrasted across individual cases or groups of cases. In contrast to looking for similarities and differences across groups or sources within which the sample members are not differentiated, group patterns and differences are more reliably detected because they are based on data that have been matched for sample members. The benefit from linking data on an individual basis in this way is analogous to the increased power to detect similarity and difference between groups when a repeated measures or matched samples t-test is used, compared with an independent samples t-test. As with t-test, being more powerful does not necessarily mean group differences will be greater, but rather, patterns across groups will be more detectable, as will those cases that diverge from overall patterns.

Cases is a term that has multiple meanings in social research. Because the concept of a case as a unit of analysis (rather than as a special focus of study) underpins effective linking of data, this chapter begins with a discussion about using cases in this way as a foundation for the strategies that follow. Attention then shifts to practical strategies for linking case-based data, beginning with those that focus on connections within individual cases. Computer based strategies that are designed to uncover comparative patterns across larger groups of cases follow. Consideration is given also to longitudinal mixed method inquiries, and to the problem of missing data in linked analyses.

Mapping strategies using linked data

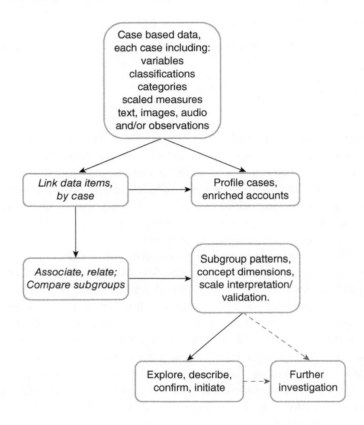

Methodological purposes

Linking or matching different forms of data for individual cases serves one or more additive, comparative, and/or relational (theory-building) purposes in connection with mixing methods. These purposes might coexist in the same project, being served by different aspects of the same data sources.

Additive purposes: adding value to analyses is commonly claimed as a primary purpose of using mixed methods. Thematically linked data enables complementary analyses, where the different sources work together to elaborate or jointly constitute complementary or confirmatory accounts of what has been found (this was given extended treatment in Chapter 5). When thematically linked data are matched also on an individual basis, this may serve to further enrich analysis by providing additional detail derived from understanding how data from each of the sources work together.

Comparative purposes: matching and comparing data within and across cases refines comparative analysis. The assumption being tested through the comparative process is that characteristics associated with a case, such as a person's gender, or age, or role, or the size or age of an object, is relevant to whatever textual, numeric or other data are available for that case. In a simple extension of this principle, responses to precategorised questions (such as yes/no, or often/sometimes/never) or scaled measures (e.g., level of life satisfaction, scores on a measure of social alienation) might also be relevant to interpretive analysis of the qualitative data. Comparison reveals differences in responses across subgroups of the sample, with the potential a) to show whether those grouping variables have relevance to the topic of discussion, b) to reveal patterns (including divergent cases) that might otherwise be obscured by whole group data, and c) to point to further explorations of relationships that might explain why those subgroup differences occurred (e.g., What is it about being in this role that prompts this difference in behaviour?). Additionally, comparison facilitates exploration of dimensionality in data and validation of scaled data.

Relational purposes: linking data across individual cases or groups of cases reveals the way in which one aspect of what is happening for a case is related to or contingent on another. This helps to clarify observed patterns or assists the analyst to see, for example, the conditionality and/or consequences of actions and processes for individuals, or groups of individuals.

Cases as units of analysis when linking data

Any identifiable data point can be used as a basis for linking data from different sources. Usually, these data points will have been defined as cases for the project. Cases in this context are typically individual people, but they could equally well be organisations, or families, places, dates, events, books, films, archaeological sites, grid points, objects, and so on. These are the foci around which multiple types or sources of data are linked, matched, or merged, and they become units of analysis for the project.

While data are gathered and matched for individual cases in this type of project, in most instances the individual cases are not, themselves, the object of study. Rather, in these projects, each case is one among many and the focus is on the issue or issues that these cases together illustrate or for which they provide information. Case study, in which the single case or a small number of cases are the focus of the study, serves different purposes and involves different strategies, and is discussed elsewhere.

More than one case type?

A distinction needs to be made between cases, and attributes of cases. Most of us have no difficulty thinking about people or organisations or even objects as cases for a study, that is, until we have data, for example, about both organisations and the people within them. Then a decision has to be made as to whether the matching of different data sources and the focus of analyses will be based around the people or the organisation. Organisations might be regarded as cases in their own right; alternatively organisational membership might be treated as an attribute of the person, to be used as a basis for comparison with other data such as attitudes to sustainability.

While most projects will involve just one kind, or type, of case, occasionally a project will involve more than one case type, with different attributes for cases of each of those types. The way in which organisations evolve and respond to various events could be studied using their own records, newspaper reports, and interviews with their leaders, while the actions or attitudes of particular members within those organisations are also studied. Data for the organisations (one case type) might then include the data for the members, as a second *embedded* case type. Or, an analysis might involve two *intersecting* case types, such as sites and people, or times and people, or sites and times, without embedding the data from one within the other. When multiple case types are being considered, analyses will be conducted within each case type independently before analyses exploring the intersections between the types are considered.

People as cases for linking data

Social research primarily focuses on, and draws information from, people as individuals or as representative of larger social groups. Data sources to be linked typically include survey responses and interviews. Consider also linking observations, diaries, drawings, and other objects relating to the persons on whom they focus or to whom they belong. If contributions to focus groups, meetings and other group sources can be disaggregated to identify the individuals making the contributions, these also can be linked with other data for those individual participants.

In the Wellbeing pilot study, each interview with an older woman was linked to her individual scores from standardised scales measuring physical and emotional health, depression, and general wellbeing, to contribute to an assessment of the usefulness of each of the scales for evaluating the impact of being part of a community-based group offering a varied and ongoing programme of social, cultural, and exercise classes (Figure 6.1).

Within QDAS, "cases" are created (or coding categories that can function as cases) for bringing varied source or part source data relating to individual persons together for analysis. Demographic and other variable data are then linked to the case codes (where possible), or alternatively, to sources holding each person's data.

Alternatively, create summaries in Excel, using a row for each person and columns to hold summary data from each of the different sources, to enable a within-case view across a row, or a cross-case view by sorting the data on a categorical variable.

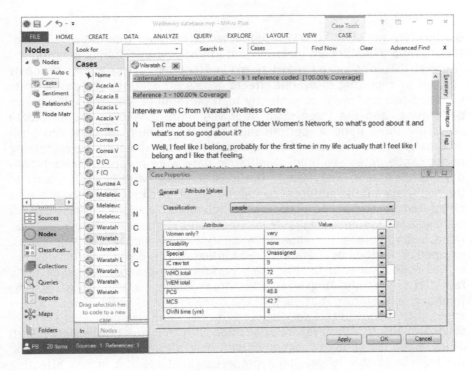

Figure 6.1   Case node linking text with attribute data in NVivo

Organisations or organisational sites as cases for linking data

Research and evaluative studies involving organisations, businesses, or community-based groups focus on things like organisational histories, structures, finances, work practices, development, or interrelations rather than on the lives of individuals within those organisations. Business studies often operate over multiple sites, dealing with variations in sites depending on how independent each is in the way it is structured and operating. Similarly, evaluation studies are often focused on multisite programmes where implementation has varied across organisational sites (e.g., schools or school districts), and those sites then become cases in the evaluation (Burch & Heinrich, 2016; Miles & Huberman, 1994).

Organisations will have their own administrative and historical records, politics, activities, and networks, as well as aggregated data from their members. Examples of data could include annual reports, newsletters, staff records, minutes of meetings, websites, and news reports as well as focus group data or observational data. Integrated studies in which organisations or organisational sites are the units of analysis therefore differ from studies of people who have the attribute of belonging to one or a range of organisations and who might at some stage be compared on the basis of organisational membership.

Bradley, Byam, et al. (2012) conducted a detailed qualitative study of seven primary health care units in rural Ethiopia, drawn from a longitudinal study of 20 units, in an effort to explain sources of variation previously masked by reporting of overall effects across all centres. The seven units included two that were consistently high performing, two consistently low performing, and the three most improved units, based on monthly data assessing three national performance targets in antenatal care and birth attendance over nine months. Improvement was assessed by regressing performance data over time. Qualitative data were obtained through two-day site visits and interviews in the local language with key informants in the health care units and local communities. Site visits and interviews were structured to ensure coverage of key domains including infrastructure, management systems, available services, and challenges. Data were analysed using constant comparative analysis to identify 14 key codes, grouped as six themes. Data were then integrated by comparing the content of the coded material for the three performance groups. All seven units reported similar challenges regarding three themes relating to geography, finances, and culture, but each of the three groups showed marked differences with regard to the way they talked about and demonstrated problem solving at the facility level, relationships with the woreda (district) health office, and community engagement with health issues. From this analysis, the team were able to develop hypotheses about specific factors affecting the performance of the primary health care units, to be tested in further studies across wider geographic and cultural settings.

Again, a spreadsheet or QDAS database can be used to keep track of organisational records and data. In a QDAS database, folders for each different type of source hold similar materials together. Case codes (or sets) hold varied source materials relating to particular organisations or sites together. Variable data are linked to qualitative data in sources or within case codes (as for people).

Social network analysis (Chapter 10, Figure 10.3) allows for exploration of organisational and inter-organisational networks based, for example, on common memberships.

Artefacts as cases for linking data

Artefacts are objects with purposes, descriptive characteristics, and histories that convey information. Obvious physical objects, such as finds from an archaeological dig, books, and vintage cars; more ephemeral objects such as letters and emails; and less tangible objects such as policies, creeds, principles, or plans, are all artefacts about which multiple sources of data might exist, and samples of which might become objects of study in their own right.

Premalatha Karupiah (Universiti Sains Malaysia) is working on a research project that explores how sexual violence is portrayed in Tamil movies. Quantitative content analysis is used to explore the type, severity, and frequency of sexual violence, while qualitative content analysis is used to explore how sexual violence is constructed in the movies. The analysis goes on to explore if and how the portrayals of sexual violence in the movies are related to the meaning of sexual violence in everyday life as understood by Malaysian Indian viewers.

Audio and visual capabilities of QDAS are helpful for managing data that include video material, aural files, photographs, other images of physical artefacts, or related data (Figure 6.2).

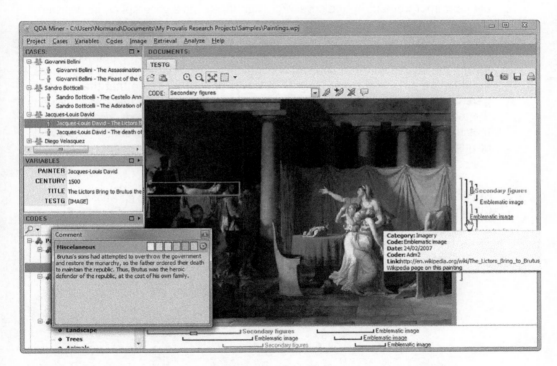

Figure 6.2   Visual artefact, with variable data, coding, link, and memo in QDA Miner

Locations as cases for linking data

When several sources of data all reference particular locations, the locations are the primary connecting points between those data (and the cases for the project) rather than simply being characteristics associated with, say, people or organisations. A study of eco-tourism, for example, might focus on particular locations as cases. The focus is on the place, what it is like and what is happening there, and how that compares with or relates to what is happening in other places. Data, including physical and social characteristics of the place, and perhaps its history, politics, culture, and economy, as well as observational or experiential data from local residents, will all be referenced by the location to which they relate. Spatial referencing of all data through mapping facilitates comparison and connecting of different sources of information for the same site through using a series of maps or by overlaying them on the same map.

Nightingale (2003) explored the changes brought about by the (re)introduction of community forestry in an area of Nepal after a period of degradation under government management. Varied oral histories told by the forest dwellers suggested there had been great improvement with community ownership; interpretation of aerial photographs, supported by a quantitative vegetation inventory, indicated only 3–4 per cent improvement in tree cover. For Nightingale, as a geographer, inconsistencies between the histories and the photos challenged the objective, neutral image produced by the photos; reconciliation demanded recognition that both photos and histories were partial and situated, and that they had to be given equal weight. By linking the stories with the apparently conflicting map and vegetation data across the different sites in the area, Nightingale was able to conclude that the villagers were valuing the most accessible sites, and indeed, it was these that had improved the most. Analysis of the "gaps and spaces" between the methods also suggested that the villagers had political motivation to emphasise improvement – to avoid having the land reclassified and returned to government management.

GIS and/or GPS software, or QDAS with georeferencing capability (e.g., Atlas.ti, MAXQDA, QDAMiner) are used for linking text, quantitative and geographic data (Figure 6.3).

Figure 6.3   Interactive plot of geocoded data points in QDA Miner

Times as cases for linking data

Time of occurrence would most commonly be considered in relation to an event, or when someone lived or engaged in a particular action, or perhaps to whether this was a first or second wave of data collection for these people. In those situations, time is an attribute of events or people, and the events or people might be compared across times, but the event or the person is the focus around which data are matched. Times become the primary units of analysis for the study when data are matched on the basis of when things occurred. Specified or evolving times become the focus of analysis, as for example, in a study of geological, social, or political history, or the unfolding of events and the stories about those events across a campaign. Time can be considered in terms of a point in time, or a timespan. Visual methods, using timelines that facilitate linking different types and sources of information, are popular when linking data on the basis of times.

In their study of caregiving in Mexican American families, described in the previous chapter, Evans et al. (2011) constructed timelines for each family, focusing particularly on "constructed time" – transitions, turning points, and adaptive strategies in the care trajectory. Each of these significant time points identified by caregivers was explored culturally and socially through interviews, while those that occurred within the 15 months covered by the study were linked also with standardised measures for both caregiver and care recipient. Thus times became the connecting point between the different data sources for each family.

Studies which focus on the links across sources in relation to time often also have a secondary (case type) focus on tracing the progress of those times for individuals. Examples include a study of the "metamorphosis" of early career researchers (Laudel & Gläser, 2008); another of the link between pain, mood, and activity scores for sufferers of rheumatoid arthritis (Kanzaki, 2004: see Figure 6.6), and Jannet Pendleton's doctoral study of a public relations (PR) campaign to have a new vaccine added to the (government-funded) childhood immunisation schedule (Figure. 6.4). Timelining has been used as a valuable aid in participant-focused interviewing (Adriansen, 2012; Kolar et al., 2015; Sheridan, Chamberlain & Dupuis, 2011) and while these authors focus on people as cases, the method could be adapted for a study focusing on times as cases.

Qualitative data analysis software, with times employed as attributes or variable data, or created as cases, can be used for storing and coding multi-modal data. These can be analysed to show patterns of coding across time or the connections between sources in relation to time, then displayed using interactive matrices and associated graphs (Figure 6.4). QDA Miner provides a visual timeline created from time-stamps on sources or in interview segments. Items on the timeline hyperlink to the time-stamped sources or coded segments (Figure 6.5).

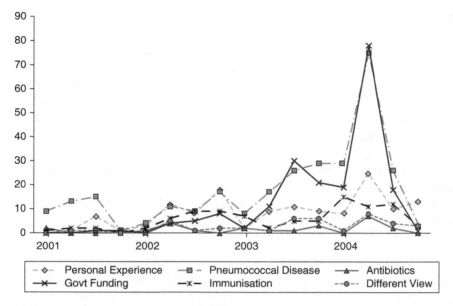

Figure 6.4 Time-based graph showing fluctuations in topics covered by press releases in a PR campaign

Source: Jannet Pendleton, University of Technology, Sydney

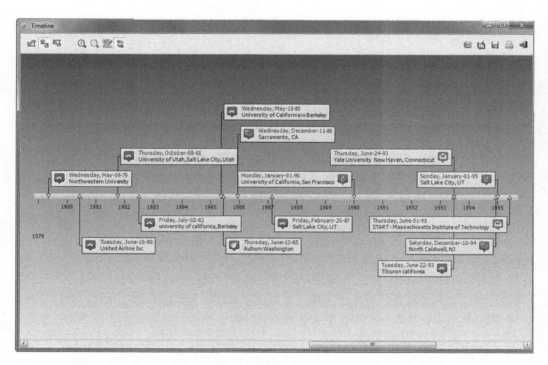

Figure 6.5 Time-based data displayed in QDA Miner

Preliminary processing of data sources

The strategies involved in integrating data through linking typically assume some preliminary processing of the data, especially where these are to be combined in a QDAS matrix.

Preliminary processing of quantitative or survey data might include:

- Calculation of total and relevant subscale (e.g., factor) scores for scales. Individual items comprising a scale are generally not needed for the linked analyses.
- Identification of which survey or other variable data will be most relevant to the combined analyses, given that there are likely to be too many variables for each to be considered in detail. This selection might be based on those that appear, from the statistical analyses, to have most relevance for the issues being addressed by the study.
- Categorisation of continuous variables, to create a manageable number of categories within each for use in framework, spreadsheet or QDAS matrices for relating, sorting, and comparing qualitative data.
- Clustering of variables, to create a typology, either as a basis for coding qualitative data and/or as a basis for comparing qualitative responses for related themes.

Preliminary processing of qualitative data might include:

- Sifting and sorting (i.e., coding) qualitative sources into content-related or thematic categories. Coding might proceed on an emergent basis, or will be directed by the issues and categories raised in or by a prior survey or theory.
- Categorisation or conversion of qualitative coding for inclusion as sorting variables in matrices or to create a case by variable table for combination with a statistical database (as described in Chapter 8).

Strategies for analysing linked data sources

Integration using linked datasets involves *combination* of data through association, comparison, or relational analyses. Even if data are collected sequentially, linked analyses involve working with all datasets together. Most strategies use simple contiguity to explore relations between varied data. Alternatively, there is benefit from developing matrices for managing and visualising linked data to facilitate comparative analyses.

Building knowledge one case at a time

In this first approach, with a relatively small number of cases, a complementary or confirmatory picture is built for each case from the connected data sources, or sources are compared in what they reveal regarding that case. Linkages are established *within* cases rather than across them, retaining close connection to context. Knowledge is built incrementally as new cases, with their integrated data sources, are added. This approach is particularly suited to building associative or relational (rather than comparative) analyses. The danger of this approach is that rather than progressively building an integrated understanding as more cases are added, the study will deteriorate into a simple collection of independent case stories that may not be synthesised as they are gathered.

Benefits for understanding health care issues derived from combining scaled measures with narrative data for individuals were reported by Kanzaki et al. (2004). Using the internet to gather daily data from 12 female rheumatoid arthritis patients over a one-month period, Kanzaki et al. found that by "combining a graphic representation of pain, mood and activity scores with patient narratives", they "could identify the changes in coping and coping strategies in conjunction with changes in symptoms" (2004: 233), see Figure 6.6. Each was analysed independently, with two illustrative cases described in detail, before general conclusions were drawn. Some of the women reported co-existing positive and negative coping, a finding that would not have been apparent through the use of standard coping scales alone.

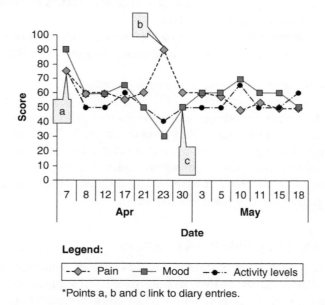

Legend:

-◆-· Pain —■— Mood —●-· Activity levels

*Points a, b and c link to diary entries.

Figure 6.6   Patient data showing relation between pain, mood, and activity level over time

Source: Kanzaki et al., 2004: 232, Figure 2

Analysis in this approach can be similar to that occurring in projects using theory elaboration or analytic induction as a qualitative theory-building technique in which a generalised understanding is developed from the particulars of specific cases (Bazeley, 2013; Hammersley & Atkinson, 2007; Vaughan, 1992; Znaniecki, 1934). Using analytic induction, a preliminary theory is built from the first case examined. Specific requirements are confirmed or dropped as further cases exhibiting the phenomenon of interest are added until the essential factors that make someone or something what it is are identified. Elements retained in the theory fit all cases.

Creating composite case profiles as a basis for further analysis

In a second, related approach, different data are merged into a composite profile of the case. This is written into a consolidated form in which text is interspersed with or complemented by visual, numeric, and/or statistical data. Some preprocessing of raw data (coding, calculations, potentially using software) is likely to have been necessary before the different data or elements drawn from them are woven together. Assuming there are multiple cases in the study, these integrated compilations or narratives then become the basis for further analysis.

Wendler (2001) explored the effectiveness of therapeutic touch in controlling anxiety and pain in people requiring venipuncture. After analysing

VS trends	Subject qual data	Practitioner qual data	Other comments	Reflective response
MBP T1 92 then 86-92-78-88-89 then 98-95-104 HR T1 55 then 53-57-54-53-56 then 58-59-56 AVDS *0/0* PVDS *1/1*	'Relaxing. I felt it was relaxing and a form of distraction from the blood drawing. I really found nothing uncomfortable about the procedure. I believe this would be extremely calming for someone who had a fear of needles'.	'[Subject] felt tense at first but quickly relaxed against my hands. He felt warm through his T-shirt very quickly. He and I synchronized breathing quickly. I found my mind wandering at T4 and had to consciously recenter myself. I felt somehow connected to him as he stared out the window - as if I were drawn in through his skin where I touched him to the out of doors. (It is a beautiful, sunny winter day, very bright.)'	RTM notation, 'Needles' don't bother me any more. When stuck with the needle, stated to RTM, 'You're very good'. Had small meal, had 3-4 cups of coffee, and had venipuncture this past month. Had >5 cigarettes this morning, last tobacco 1-5 hours ago. Is 48 years old.	MBP above 95% CI at T1, within at T2, above at T3, well below at T4, above T5-T7, within at T8, above at T9. HR 95% C.I. at T1-T9, throughout. Note mirroring of the word 'relaxing.' Note the recentering at T4 coupled with significant, transient drop in MBP at T4. Much fluctuation in MBP, reason unknown. Could be many influences – eating – caffeine – nicotine – age. I also wonder – why was his pulse so slow, despite nicotine and caffeine? Was he taking medication he didn't tell RTMs about? Seemed not to have anxiety with procedure.

Figure 6.7 One line of a metamatrix holding case profiles, Tellington Touch study

AVDS = anxiety verbal descriptor scale, before/after; CI = confidence interval; MBP = mean blood pressure; HR = heart rate; qual = qualitative; PVDS = pain verbal descriptor scale, before/after venipuncture; prac = t-touch practitioner; RTM = research team member; VS = vital sign; T1 = baseline; T2-T6 = during visit/t-touch; T7, before venipuncture; T8, after venipuncture; T9, five minutes after venipuncture. Tellington touches used: CL = Clouded Leopard (T2-T4); PL = Python Lift (T5); NM = Noah's March (T6).

Source: Wendler, 2001: 153, Figure 1

(Continued)

(Continued)

quantitative and qualitative data separately, she linked the data for each of her cases, setting out the physiological measures over the period of treatment, patient comments, practitioner comments, other observations, and researcher reflections side by side on a single page for each person. This provided her with "a secondary opportunity to determine if patterning exists that was not captured through compartmentalization into the quantitative or qualitative data analyses. Further, by using the meta-matrix, spontaneous comments and naturalistic events may be captured and considered within the context of the case" (2001: 523), see Figure 6.7. A review of the data in this form revealed several unexpected relationships; for example, participants and therapists often used identical words to describe what happened, mirroring each other's language despite the sessions being largely conducted in silence, and in so doing provided evidence of nonverbal communication.

When the constructed narratives are more extensive and detailed, further analysis often involves applying a qualitative content analysis strategy to the case profile, but narrative analysis strategies can also be useful. For example, storylines focusing on purpose or plot can be constructed, or structural elements in a narrative identified and then linked to show time-based or other functional links between particular segments. Alternatively, contrasts and connections in the narratives will be identified through visually mapping or tabulating their elements to reveal either common patterns or factors implicated in creating difference.

Concerned at high rates of suicide among US military personnel (one per day) Rosenberg, Lewandowski, and Siegel (2015) used an integrated method to test the application of goal disruption theory, as evidenced in military personnel who are prompted to endure more harm than they should in striving to maintain their belief in their goals and their ability to achieve them. The authors created merged profiles for each participant by combining quantitative measures of their need to achieve and their purposive harm endurance (created using regression analysis on responses to scaled items) with thematically coded qualitative responses about their most salient goals. Content analysis of the merged profiles allowed detection of goal disruption (based on indicators of theoretical constructs), as well as identification of the types of goals most associated with need to achieve and endurance of harm.

Developing a combined case data matrix for linked analyses

Setting out data in a matrix to analyse varied case-linked data sources facilitates seeing both connections and contrasts for individual cases, and then across the whole sample, with the goal being to identify patterns across the data. Columns are used to record each element of data gathered, with their content determined by a combination of data type (quantitative, qualitative, visual, etc.), conceptual framework (e.g., providing *a priori* categories for each topic of interest in the project), and/or themes identified from a preliminary analysis of the data. Each row represents a case, with all the numeric, categorical, text summary, text samples, and other information for that case entered in cells across the row for the relevant columns (e.g., Table 6.1). On occasions, either quantitative or qualitative data are categorised rather than being entered in their raw form, as this can make it easier to see patterns of association (Happ et al., 2006).

Crabtree et al. (2005) used a comparative case study design (N=18) to examine the method and frequency with which three types of clinical preventive services were delivered in family general practices. They tabulated information from medical records, observations, and interviews with multiple staff members (Table 6.1). This allowed them to explore patterns within and across cases, allowing them to conclude, for example, that competing demands meant that no practice was excellent in all three areas of preventive services considered, and that focus on prevention was independent of office systems used but benefited from having a champion in the practice.

Table 6.1 Key characteristics of participating practices and approaches to delivering preventive services (2 of 18 cases)

Practice Size and Location	Practice Characteristics[1]	Preventive Service Delivery, %	Defining Characteristics of Approach to Delivering Preventive Services[2]
9. Small urban	PA or NP: Yes System owned: Yes High volume: Yes	Screening: 65 Smoking counseling: 31 Immunization: 31	Prevention is clinician driven with minimal office-level protocols, and staff are not supportive. Charts are well organized, and clinicians rely on a mental protocol to deliver preventive care opportunistically in most visits. Few patients attend HCM visits, and many patients have complex, multiple chronic health problems, so encounters have many competing social and economic constraints that make prevention difficult.

(Continued)

Table 6.1 (Continued)

Practice Size and Location	Practice Characteristics[1]	Preventive Service Delivery, %	Defining Characteristics of Approach to Delivering Preventive Services[2]
12. Small suburban	PA or NP: No System owned: No High volume: No	Screening: 58 Smoking counseling: 69 Immunization: 16	Clinicians often spend a great deal of time with patients in lengthy visits. Preventive care is delivered in all visits. Thorough HCM visits are provided, using comprehensive sex- and age-specific prevention flow sheets. A reminder system is used for female annual examinations. High-quality educational materials are available. Charts are a mess and poorly filed, often unfilled in piles around the floor. Staff are all part-time and not involved in prevention.

Source: Crabtree et al., 2005: Online Supplemental Table 1 (www.annfammed.org/cgi/content/full/3/5/430/DC1)

Notes: [1]PA = physician's assistant, NP = nurse practitioner; [2]HCM = health care maintenance

Matrices of this type were extensively developed and popularised by Miles and Huberman (1984, 1994) who used them as a central tool for compressing and ordering large volumes of data in order to develop coherent, often explanatory, conclusions. In their simplest (and original) form, matrices were hand drawn and filled from data summarised from field notes and related sources. Data might be entered for all content categories being considered, to provide a complete dataset in one table, or as was more usual for Miles and Huberman, data (columns) might be selectively drawn, with cases ordered by time or role or some other variable, to explore or present particular relationships in a one-page display (e.g., Table 6.2).

In their study on the Latino gender-role construct of machismo, Castro et al. (2010) juxtaposed different types of data on a case by case basis, but then compared groups defined by extreme values (Table 6.2). This facilitated the development of integrated storylines.

Using a spreadsheet or database for linked analyses

Categorical, unstructured, and other forms of data can be similarly combined in a spreadsheet or database by defining a set of topics to explore, and entering values or brief summaries for each case in rows under each topic. Additional columns for

Table 6.2 Juxtaposition of responses to compare (within case) and contrast (across cases)

Case Number	Life Satisfaction Score	Quoted Statement About Machismo Self-Identification	Story Lines
Highest on Life Satisfaction			
ID133	2.17	"I care about my family"; "For me it's acting like a gentleman"	*Story Line 1:* Men who value and engage in family caretaking exhibit high levels of caballerismo (positive machismo) in their male gender role identity, are giving and responsible, and they also experience *high* levels of life satisfaction
ID147	1.57	"I'm respectful of women"; "I never bring shame to the family"	
ID164	1.50	"I do my best to take care of my family"	
ID343	1.48	"I treat women with respect and don't beat them"	
ID371	1.42	"I bring home money and make sure there is food on the table"	
Lowest on Life Satisfaction			
ID160	−1.15	"I have my flaws, I'm selfish"; "I hold a grudge forever"; "I'm not afraid to cry in front of others even strangers"	Story Line 2. Men who *do not* value or engage in family caretaking exhibit low levels of caballerismo (positive machismo) in their male gender role identity, are selfish and irresponsible, and they also experience *low* levels of life satisfaction
ID162	−1.21	"I don't identify with working hard or taking care of my family"	
ID149	−1.67	"I never had aspirations to have any children or family responsibility"	
ID399	−2.58	"In prison I acted in ways I didn't want to, and even today I still do"	
ID370	−2.63	"I'm lazy, I'm selfish, I have a short fuse"; "I have low self-esteem."	

Source: Castro et al., 2010: 355, Table 3

emerging topics can be added as needed. This reductionist approach can be especially useful where, for example, transcripts of interviews are not available, as summaries can be entered in relevant columns from notes or while listening to the audio file. It is also useful for entering observational data, with the columns guiding the observer in what features to record. Such summaries facilitate the detection of patterns, as in Figure 6.8 where a pattern of association between parents' level of education and their approaches to thinking about immunisation becomes immediately apparent.

The use of a spreadsheet facilitates and extends the kinds of analyses otherwise done using more manual means. Spreadsheets and databases such as Excel and Filemaker Pro not only allow for the entry of numeric, categorical, and text data within the same database, they also provide tools to facilitate comparison and thus the rapid examination of trends or discernment of patterns through their capacity to instantly sort and re-sort data. All the data for each case are entered in a single matrix, with the cases entered in any order. Data can be sorted one way (based on categories in one of the columns), interpreted, then sorted another way (Figure 6.8, see also Figure 2.9). The emerging patterns across the grouped rows are examined, consistent patterns evident for each group are summarised and interpreted. If, to extend the analysis, entries in a text column need to be used as a basis for sorting against another column, it is a simple matter to add an additional column into an existing table to categorise those. This allows for comparisons based on that categorisation, while retaining the original summary or illustrative text sample. Hide columns and split screen options provide additional assistance for exploring relationships between data across columns,

	A	B	C	D	E
1	Case	Education	Ch age last time (mths)	Mention of needles, pain in account of last immunisation	Main thoughts re immunisation
2	Wendy	some HS	12	child cried	it will hurt and she'll cry
3	Felicity	some HS	12	fear of pain	important, but fear of pain
4	Vivien	some HS	18	mother hates needles	needles, but has to be done
5	Helen	some HS	18	tense, fear of pain	fear of pain
6	Margie	some HS	50+	screams and kicking	upset children, fear of needles
7	Kirstie	some HS	50+	child getting upset	child getting upset
8	Susan	some HS	50+	fear of needle, upset	child getting upset
9	Janice	HS Cert	not imm	no mention	risk of reactions higher than diseases
10	Sandra	HS Cert	1	no mention	prevention of disease
11	Sue	HS Cert	18	no mention	possible reaction
12	Angela	Uni	1	fearful beforehand	protection from disease
13	Barbara	Uni	6	no mention	keep child healthy
14	Peta	Uni	6	no mention	possible side effects

Figure 6.8 Mothers' responses to childhood immunisation: summary case data sorted on education

Source: Bazeley, unpublished data (partial)

while pivot tables and graphs generated from the categorical or scaled data provide a visual display for analysis or presentation.

Use QDAS matrices for comparative analysis using linked data

When qualitative data analysis software (QDAS) is used, once the qualitative data are coded and quantitative data are linked for each case, multiple case-based connections and comparisons across whole subgroups can be quickly generated with a high degree of specificity from these *combined* data.

QDAS routinely allows for assignment or importation of quantitative variable data (demographic, categorical, numeric, date, etc.) for cases, to be matched with any qualitative (text, image, audio, video) data available for those same cases. Any coding applied to the case data will consequently intersect with the variable data, thus linking quantitative and qualitative data on an individual case basis. Output is in the form of a comparative matrix (qualitative crosstabulation), usually arranged with values of an independent variable/attribute defining the columns, and one or more coding categories, such as different experiences recorded, attitudes held, emotions expressed, or dimensions of a concept, defining the content of the rows. Cells in the matrix show counts (or in some cases, percentages) of sources or passages or cases containing qualitative data that are identified at the same time by the code specified

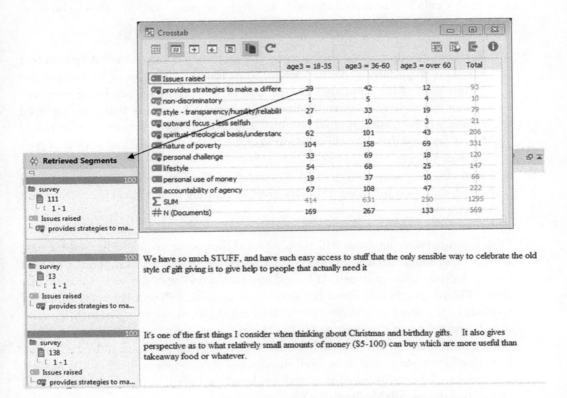

Figure 6.9 Qualitative data sorted for different values of a variable (MAXQDA)

in that row and the value specified for that column. This information can also be shown as a graphic display (e.g., column or line chart) in most QDAS. Double-clicking on any cell (or element in the graphic) will reveal the actual text passages or other data meeting both row and column specifications (Figure 6.9). Reading data for each cell across a row provides a comparison across subgroups.

MAXQDA additionally offers a "quote matrix" which will display text data from a comparative matrix concurrently for up to four columns (exported as an Excel sheet).

Each alternative component of the information provided in a matrix resulting from this type of query (numeric display, found text) adds to the analytic picture, with numeric patterns showing "how many" and comparative texts showing "in what way". Visual displays, such as MAXQDA's Code Matrix Browser, show the relative density of coding across the cells. Depending on which program is used, these tabular displays can be filtered by a row or column variable, exported in Excel format for further statistical analysis (e.g., in SPSS), and/or analysed statistically in a companion program or add-on module, or displayed (and exported) as a chart. While matrix/crosstabulation display outputs from qualitative software are immensely valuable to mixed methods researchers, some caution needs to be exercised in reading them:

- Researchers interpreting the numeric output from a comparative analysis of text based on quantitatively defined groups must remain conscious of the sample size within each of the compared groups, and of what numbers are being reported, especially when results are displayed as charts. The risk is that the displayed results will be misinterpreted because programs do not generally provide charts based on *proportions* of the relevant samples, but rather, use raw counts of passages or sources.
- It is also very easy to over-read the meaning of differences when numbers are small, especially for those who have not had training in statistical procedures and assumptions.

Often, comparative analyses will simply reveal that some groups talk about a particular topic more often than others, or that different groups talk about different topics or raise different issues. At times, however, a review of the sorted text reveals that different groups talk about the same topic in quite different ways, regardless of whether or not there were differences in how many talked about it. These differences may be revealing of dimensions within the concepts being coded or may suggest other conditions that are influencing the theme being examined, extending what can be learned from statistical data. Additionally, instances where individuals go against a trend can be readily identified and explored in detail, using quantitative and qualitative data available for that case.

Maintaining persistence in adherence to treatment recommendations or preventive measures following an educational intervention is often a problem. Casey et al. (2016) conducted a 12-month follow-up study across five sites, with three data collection points, to explore factors involved in self-management after a dietary programme for those with Type 1 diabetes. Both qualitative (interview) and quantitative (clinical and outcome) data were available for a sample of 34 participants, making it possible to explore the relationship between glycaemia control and feeling empowered, over time, in both quantitative (when and how much did they talk about empowerment) and qualitative (how did they talk about empowerment) terms (Figure 6.10). Because data were matched, analyses could be conducted at both group and individual level. Of the three key factors identified from the qualitative data (enduring knowledge, enduring motivation, support), just motivation (including ambitious goal-setting) appeared to influence adherence to the dietary programme, although support may have had a subsidiary role in control for those individuals who started with the poorest control scores.

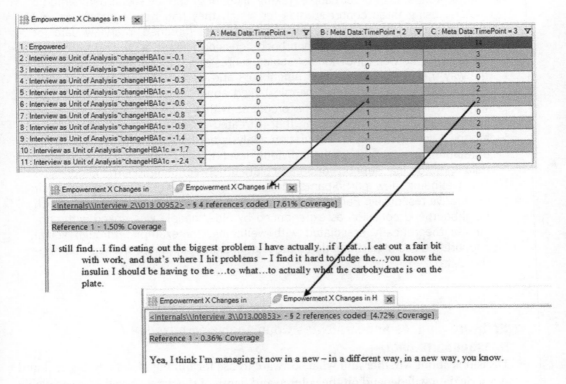

Figure 6.10 Empowerment over time in relation to glycaemia control (NVivo)

Source: Screenshot provided by Casey et al. (2016). The rows of the matrix are defined by the results of a previous matrix, which found only text related to empowerment within each interview.

Linking using QDAS to interpret scaled scores

In this approach, using the same matrix query/crosstabulation approach as described above, scores on scaled items are matched with qualitative data relating to the concept measured by the scale for each case. This would be used as a way of identifying the meaning of each of the scaled scores and of ensuring that that meaning varied in concert with the scaled scores. This strategy is a qualitative parallel for the use of multiple correspondence analysis in assessing the ordinal qualities of a scale (Blasius & Thiessen, 2001) – employing both together would add double value to the assessment of the scale. Similarly, scaled scores can be matched for each case with (quantitative and) qualitative data for a related variable or code, to determine whether a score on the scale is predictive of scores on that second variable in the way that would be expected. Depending on the variables or topic areas chosen, this can help to assess the construct validity of the scale.

Elliott et al. (2014) analysed the link between neighbourhood cohesion and mental wellbeing of older people, taking account of various social-demographic factors, using three cohort studies for which they had both survey data and some biographical interviews. An examination of matched interview data for high and low scorers on neighbourhood cohesion showed a general pattern of consistency between individuals' scaled scores and the sentiment attached to the way they talked about their neighbours and involvement in the neighbourhood, despite that individual people talked about neighbourhood in different ways. Their study revealed some problems with the neighbourhood cohesion scale they had used, however, in that it treated neighbours as a homogeneous group. It was designed for population analysis and did not reflect the diversity of relationships possible at the individual level. Further, while their quantitative data showed clear support for an association between neighbourhood cohesion and wellbeing, few participants made explicit links between these in their qualitative responses. Participants did, however, suggest mechanisms by which neighbourhood cohesion as experienced by older people was linked with constructs theoretically associated with wellbeing, for example, through social support and social participation – associations also supported in their quantitative data.

Software choices and strategies when analysing mixed questionnaire data

Decisions about whether and what software to use for linking and analysing text and numeric data will depend on the volume and depth of the data, as well as on available or preferred programs. Simple comparative sorts of text responses to particular questions according to values on a categorical variable can be achieved in any spreadsheet or database, but researchers will be quickly overcome by large datasets or complex responses if that is their only tool. QDAS has the added advantage of allowing for more detailed coding of responses to questions, perhaps revealing new concepts and ideas that are expressed in common ways across a number of questions. Text at these new codes can then be compared across categorical variables, while keeping track of the questions that prompted them. New categories generated also can be exported as variable data back into the quantitative database for further statistical analysis, using strategies described in Chapter 8.

In her doctoral study of nurses' care of patients who use illicit drugs, Rosemary Ford (2006) used a combination of Stata and NVivo to analyse closed and open-ended responses to a survey instrument. In free-text responses about the interpersonal constraints these patients imposed on their therapeutic nursing role, nurses expressed concerns about patient aggressiveness, manipulation, and irresponsibility, and they reported frustration with the patient, fear in their role, and pessimism about the usefulness of therapeutic interventions. Within each of these more general categories, those from different practice groups expressed unique challenges which required different nursing care and which engendered different attitudes. Midwives dealt with manipulative patients and aggressive partners, but were particularly concerned about and frustrated with mothers' irresponsibility in the context of "putting a baby in the mix". For those working in emergency, attitudes to those seeking care were impacted by the short-term nature of a relationship in which they frequently experienced aggression and manipulation, were angered by irresponsibility towards others harmed by the drug users' actions, and where they did not see any long-term outcomes for the patient from the experience or their care, whereas for those in a medical/surgical practice setting, patients' aggressive and manipulative behaviour over an extended period of time-intensive contact created staffing and care issues.

For questionnaire data from larger samples, text searching, word frequency, or autocoding options provided by either QDAS or statistical software (as described in Chapter 2) can often be used to assist with coding short responses to open-ended questions, as a time-saving strategy. Results link to the source documents for checking and additional coding.

Statistical analyses using linked data

The analytic emphasis in most linked analysis strategies already described is more closely related to qualitative approaches to analysis than quantitative statistical analysis. It is quite possible, however, to transform qualitative data in ways that allow those data to be matched, case by case, with existing quantitative data for further statistical analysis. The kinds of analyses that draw on transformed qualitative data (whether or not combined with existing quantitative data) will be explored in more detail in Chapter 8.

Data linking in longitudinal inquiries

Longitudinal data "tells us about what has happened to a set of research cases over a series of time points" (Elliott, 2005: 61). For such studies, different sources of data gathered over time need to be linked for each sampled case. Van Ness, Fried, and Gill (2011) distinguished between prospective, retrospective, and fully longitudinal studies, based (respectively) on whether qualitative data are collected only at the start, the finish, or at all time points in the study. Longitudinal studies defy such neat categorisation, however (Holder, in press; Plano Clark et al., 2015).

Setting three data collection points as a minimum criterion for selection, Plano Clark et al. (2015) reviewed practices used to integrate methods within longitudinal mixed methods studies indexed by PubMed up to and including 2012. In the 32 studies that met their criteria, they found no standard pattern for how longitudinal mixed methods studies were designed and conducted. Surprisingly, also, the studies lacked explicit discussion of time, of how it was measured and what it meant, especially in their qualitative components. Like longitudinal studies everywhere, many of these studies experienced attrition in samples, missing data, and changes in data collection over time. Reporting of sample details and actual data collected at various time points was often unclear. Qualitative analyses were generally "basic", and integration of qualitative and quantitative data in many was limited. Integrative strategies, when used, included using data from one phase to design the next, comparisons of quantitative and qualitative results, synthesising complementary results, using groups identified in one dataset to examine results from the other dataset, and/or data transformation to allow joint statistical analysis. Few studies in their sample succeeded in combining different types of data and time as a dimension within the same study. Based on their review, Plano Clark et al. (2015: 315) developed six recommendations for those planning a longitudinal mixed methods study, each of which has implications for analysis, integration, and reporting:

- Carefully plan and fully describe the dimensions of correspondence, timing, mixing, level of analysis, and use of time within the study's design. Include expertise in longitudinal quantitative, longitudinal qualitative, and mixed methods on the research team to help negotiate these issues.
- Develop a table or figure that clearly outlines the sample and major quantitative and qualitative data collection for each time point in the study to succinctly and accurately describe the flow of procedures.

- Articulate how time is conceptualised and measured. Resist collapsing longitudinal data into single categories, thereby losing the temporal information.
- When longitudinal qualitative data are collected, incorporate the time dimension into the analysis. At a minimum, note the time point for participant quotes. When appropriate, attend to the development of themes or perspectives within themes across time.
- Be cognizant of missing data and its implications for the quantitative, qualitative, and integrative analyses. Discuss how missing data are handled in the analysis and the implications for the results.
- Think creatively about how to incorporate the longitudinal component when integrating the quantitative and qualitative results. Possibilities include merging the results in terms of quantitative and qualitative patterns over time, developing typologies based on patterns over time, and comparing the different results for each point in time.

The experience of victims of crime as they travel through the justice system varies at each step in relation to the institutions involved, the processes, and the decisions made. Robyn Holder (in press) explored what the idea of justice meant to victims of violence, in context and in real time, at three critical points in their journey through the justice system. Closed and open-ended questions at each time point were both prospective and retrospective, becoming more open and reflective over the course of the three interviews. Holder outlined problems of working longitudinally with a vulnerable population, from accessing a sample, through research conditioning, to sample attrition over an extended period. An additional problem faced in justice research is the variation in time and trajectories between the start and finish of justice processes for different participants. Employing mixed methods over time, however, helped victims "to reflect on, digest, and frame what had happened and what was happening, as well as to give categorical opinion" (Holder, in press: 13).

While most offenders received a guilty verdict, the most common outcome was to place them on a bond to be of good behaviour. Thus, few were sentenced in the way (prospectively) preferred by victims, which was to provide protection of them and rehabilitation of the offender, yet more than half (retrospectively) felt the sentence was "about right". Nevertheless, satisfaction with the justice system declined over the period of victims' involvement. The longitudinal study helped to show how "ideas about justice ripple out from the precipitating incident of violence" (Holder, in press: 13) as people reasoned their way, over time, through the complexity of differences between procedural justice, personal/moral justice, and wider social concerns.

New opportunities for longitudinal analysis of a different kind are opening up with relatively recent developments in digital archiving of historical datasets and the creation of continuously logged real time datasets in which dating of entries is intrinsic to their collection. "Rare events" in the historical chain might be identified and the circumstances surrounding them investigated (Bail, 2015). Institutional and social processes occurring over time that led to significant change, such as the rise of modernity, can be explored using digitised historical datasets from the multiple institutions that played a role in that change (Bearman, 2015). One of the issues arising is the casing of time through identification of turning points, to allow linking of information and understanding across datasets. When digitised historical archives or real time streaming data are combined with the strategies of data scientists, these kinds of studies of social processes can be studied within a fraction of the work time previously required using manual methods (if they were possible at all). They change our conception of what it might mean to undertake both a longitudinal analysis and a historical analysis.

Missing data in linked data sources

When one or another of the data sources to be linked is incomplete for any participants in a study, constraints are imposed on integrating that data with those from other sources. Biases can result from self-selection in surveys, and in longitudinal studies, cases are lost through attrition. In multimethod, multisite studies, the complexity of data collection can mean that data items vary across sites. Variation in what data are collected can vary as well when questions or sources are modified to adjust for unforeseen or changing circumstances, or refined in response to ongoing analyses.

Within data sources, people can skip items, with intent being the critical factor in this. Was it because the data didn't exist, or were missed or ignored at the time of collection? Did someone refuse or block access, or avoid responding to particular questions or talking about some topics? Or was it that they didn't know, didn't care, didn't notice, or weren't sure?

Strategies can be adopted to reduce the incidence of missing data, but these have to be thought through *before* conducting the first data collection. Whenever the problem of missing data is present, its implications for interpreting results has to be examined, particularly where these are to be generalised to a broader population.

Matching data sources when cases are people

Being able to link different data sources, of course, implies either that the different sources or types of data are obtained together (as with a mixed form survey), or a common identifier has been recorded for each. Permission to match data gathered at different times is growing as an issue as a result of human ethics committees' requirements for preservation of anonymity. When data are being collected with a smaller sample, a volunteered pseudonym or allocated code can sometimes be used for matching, rather than a real name. Given that an offer of anonymity is usually required for those answering questionnaires, one way to facilitate planned follow-up of a purposefully selected sample is to ask respondents who are prepared to participate in further interviews to voluntarily provide their name and contact details at the time of completing the original survey. The downside of this approach is that those whose experience was particularly good or particularly bad are more likely to respond to such an invitation.

Checking the representativeness of cases providing additional qualitative responses

Check the representativeness of the cases for whom additional qualitative data are available (e.g., in a survey) by comparing them with those for whom data are not complete on descriptive (demographic) and other variables relevant to the study's purposes and research questions. When the discrepancies on quantitative variables between those cases for which data are complete or not complete are significant, interpretation of the data or any subset of it must take into account how those differences arose and how they might influence what was recorded and thus the results being reported. People who volunteer to be interviewed or who respond to open-ended questions often differ from others in important ways, for example, by expressing more troubled experiences or more negative opinions (as assessed by the quantitative data) than those who do not.

As part of the analysis of her survey of nurses providing care to patients who use illicit drugs, Ford (2006) compared responses on all quantitative questions for the 1028 respondents (64% of the total) who provided qualitative data with those of the 577 who did not. Few differences were found, and all were small in absolute terms: those in the qualitative subsample were more likely to be supportive of innovative drug programmes, and were a little more likely to have had university training. They did not differ on personal characteristics, basic role requirements, or in therapeutic capacity.

Comparisons were also made between those who did and did not give qualitative responses for each of the subsections of the survey. With respect to the interpersonal constraints these patients imposed on their therapeutic nursing role (reported earlier), just 311 of the sample recorded free-text responses. Those providing responses were more likely than others to be in high contact (i.e., clinical) areas of practice and reported more episodes of

(Continued)

(Continued)

extended care for patients who were illicit drug users. They were also younger and less experienced than the remainder of the study sample, and while they reported higher levels of role adequacy, they also reported lower motivation and satisfaction. In reporting results for this section, therefore, caution was applied and the situational context of their nursing role was observed.

Missing data in scales and surveys

When survey respondents miss or skip questions that form part of scales, the total scores for those scales cannot be calculated directly. Comparisons of the complete and incomplete subsamples need to be carried out, to see if those for whom data items are missing comprise a biased subsample in terms of their personal characteristics and responses to other questions, and in an attempt to diagnose the cause of the missing responses. Depending on the possible cause, a range of methods have been developed to construct imputed values for missing subscale items, ranging from substitution with average values (for the item or the person) to calculation of a regression score (or other forms of imputation) using values on completed items (de Leeuw, Hox, & Huisman, 2003). Each method carries its own biases in terms of the way it influences the distribution and spread of scores across the sample, but the advantage of using imputed measures is that the linked sample is not reduced. Alternatively, those missing some scores might be dropped from the sample for an analysis involving that measure.

Attrition in longitudinal studies

Attrition of a sample is a particular problem of program evaluation and longitudinal studies as, over an extended data collection period, people move on and become uncontactable or "drop out" for other reasons. To reduce the likelihood of attrition through losing touch with participants, at the time of gaining consent for the study from participants, obtain multiple forms of contact details (home and work phone, email and physical addresses, social media connections). Some but hopefully not all of these are likely to change (depending on the time lapse between data collection periods). In studies in which the data collection periods are years apart, it can be useful to send an annual greeting card from the project as a way of keeping in touch, helping to ensure willingness to continue participating and providing early warning of changed addresses that will need to be investigated. Providing a contact number for the project with the greeting card will encourage notification of new contact details for recent or intended moves.

Data complexity in multisite, multimethod studies

When data are collected across multiple sites, a "trade-off" has to occur between "gathering comparable data across sites ... and preserving the advantage of flexibility in the less standardized component of the study" (Louis, 1982a: 16). Karen Seashore Louis was faced with this problem in leading an evaluation of a Research and Development Utilization Program, an action research project designed to build problem-solving capacity within schools as they pursued school improvement. Sites were added and, as early and continuous analysis of all data sources proceeded, methods were evolving with each site developing in different ways. Multiple but varied sources of data across a large number of sites meant that 80 per cent of sites had incomplete databases, and qualitative data were not readily comparable. A consolidated coding form with 240 variables, each requiring a rating or score, was developed to capture as much of the qualitative evidence as possible. Multiple strategies were used to ensure the reliability and validity of the ratings before they were linked with quantitative survey data to produce average scores for each site. In this way, credible evidence was produced from non-standardised qualitative data despite the unevenness in availability of data within and across sites.

Integration of linked data: a final example

Kington, Sammons, Day, and Regan (2011), explored factors influencing the practices, strategies, and methods used in the classroom by purposively selected samples of effective and typical teachers who represented a variety of life phases and identities, and geographic, class grade, and socioeconomic contexts. The complex design of their project (set out in diagrams and tables, shown in Figure 2.7) encompassed concurrent elements within four sequential phases, beginning with a conceptual framework of effective classroom practice.

Evidence was gathered and linked for each teacher from multiple semistructured interviews, questionnaires, a repertory grid exercise, and descriptive and systematic observations of classroom practice. Supporting data about each teacher and the school environment were obtained through interviews with school leaders and pupil questionnaires and focus groups. Separately conducted preliminary analyses for each source fed into the design of the next phase of data collection and data from each phase elaborated on previous data so that data and analyses were ongoing and intertwined to contribute to a holistic account of the teachers' practices.

Dimensions of effective classroom practice and relative ratings of teachers based on these were developed from factor analyses of pupil questionnaire data, as a means of grouping the teachers. Teachers were also scored on dimensions identified from systematic classroom observations. Field notes and interview data were imported into qualitative software (NVivo) and coded, with the dimensional scores recorded as attributes of the teacher cases, along with demographic and other statistical data.

Summary measures developed from the qualitative data were also recorded as attributes to use both as a means of further exploring other qualitative data and in related statistical analyses. Analytical matrices were then constructed in NVivo, allowing coded qualitative data to be explored in association with the various recorded attributes, particularly those relating to professional identity and professional life phase. Individual narrative profiles integrating data from all sources were created for each teacher, of interest in themselves as integrated reports, but also forming a foundation for further comparative and group analysis, and providing a means of confirming the researchers' interpretations.

Concluding remarks

The advantages to be had in "tightening" the level of integration by linking data from different sources and of different types on a case by case basis, where cases might be persons or organisations or sites or artefacts or time – or any other foci of analysis, have been demonstrated in this chapter. Linking data allows for the use of demographic, categorical, or scaled variables in creating cross-case analyses of qualitative data (as can occur in an equivalent way using crosstabulations in statistical software). These analyses, in turn, are facilitated by the use of software that allows for multiple data types to be managed as a composite entity for each case. The comparative analyses reveal the number of cases within subgroups who have "spoken" on the topic or point of interest, the volume contributed by different subgroups, and especially and uniquely, the comparative content of responses across subgroups of the sample. As well as being of descriptive value, this information leads to deeper understanding of the dimensions of concepts and of the phenomena being studied. Linking data additionally facilitates the building of complex case descriptions, again an end in themselves or useful in turn for further within-case and cross-case analyses. Longitudinal analyses typically also rely on keeping track of linked data over time, and of integrating different sources of data. Finally, suggestions were made for handling missing data, which can become an issue in case-based linked analyses.

Further reading

Bazeley (2013) in Chapter 9 on comparative analyses gives detailed instructions on how to construct, work with, and interpret comparative matrices (tables) using manual techniques, spreadsheets, or QDAS.

Happ et al. (2006) describes the use of a metamatrix in recording and analysing linked data.

Louis (1982b), the second of two articles from the Research and Development Utilization Program referred to earlier in this chapter, is worth reading for insights into data and team management to ensure integration can succeed in circumstances where data sources are varied and variable in content and completeness.

de Leeuw et al. (2003) provide a detailed review of causes, prevention, and treatment options for item non-response in quantitative data collections.

Further examples of studies that integrate linked data

Bryans (2004) used simulated home visits; focused, post-simulation interviews about the simulated visit; and subsequent observation of actual home visits to explore what home nursing visitors (N=15) actually do. Data were analysed and linked using manual methods.

Bryant (2008) used a survey and linked interviews to explore the role of self-regulation in moral awareness and practices of business entrepreneurs. QDAS and Excel were used for analysis of data.

Van Ness et al. (2011) present some contrasting views on what can and can't be done with linked qualitative and statistical data when used within a hermeneutic framework. They also deal with an issue of conflicting data arising in their study of changes in functional ability over time in a sample of elderly persons.

Youngs and Piggot-Irvine (2012) describe the methods used in a longitudinal multi-source project assessing a programme designed to foster the development of future school principals in New Zealand.

7

FROM CODES AND COUNTS TO CONTENT ANALYSIS AND "BIG DATA"

CHAPTER OVERVIEW

Previous chapters considered integration in analysis as a necessary corollary or consequence of having mixed data sources. This chapter marks a shift in emphasis to mixed *analysis strategies* as the primary locus of integration.

Counts and categories are derived from observations recorded in words, sounds, images, or directly as numbers. Counts are essential descriptive data applicable to all data types. The meaning given to counts is source-dependent, method-dependent, and context-bound, and is as much dependent on an interpretive process as is the meaning given to words.

Counts are a major component of descriptive reporting, and they underpin more advanced statistical techniques for analysing data. Applying statistical analyses to qualitative data or incorporating qualitative data within broader statistical analyses begins with their conversion to numeric form. How that conversion is achieved has implications for the kinds of statistical analyses that can be applied. Whatever method of counting is applied, unlike data recorded directly in numeric form, access to the original qualitative data is retained. This makes possible the reintegration of statistical analyses and their results with grounded qualitative analysis. Importantly, it also helps to ensure that the richness of the qualitative data is not lost in the process of its being quantified. With a full cycle of qualitative analysis, transformation, statistical analysis, *and reintegration*, the result is two ways of viewing the same data, enhancing interpretive understanding.

This chapter focuses on the practical steps and issues involved in generating and using counts – from zero to billions – from qualitative data. It ends by considering the revolution that is currently occurring in counting data: the promises, the possibilities, and the pitfalls "big data" presents for mixed methods researchers. The review in this chapter leads directly into the following chapter, which will look more specifically at the kinds of case-based statistical analyses that make use of quantified qualitative data in the context of mixed methods research.

Mapping counting and content analysis

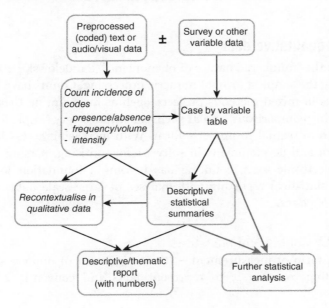

Why count? Methodological purposes

Counts are integral to mixed methods analyses. Counts derived from qualitative data might be used independently of other sources, or to complement those from surveys and other sources. In a mixed methods project, counts and statistical analyses using variables derived from qualitative codes are used to complement the qualitative analyses already undertaken. Assuming clear definition of codes and consistency in coding, using counts from qualitative data can bring a number of benefits for the mixed methods researcher:

- Use of counts communicates more effectively and reliably than does use of vague terms such as "most" or "some" to indicate more or less frequent occurrence of some feature in the text.
- Counts can be viewed as reflecting the importance of various emergent themes and topics, although frequency and importance are not necessarily synonymous.
- Counting summarises patterns in data, such as from comparative and relational matrix analyses, and can allow possible interrelationships to be more easily identified for further exploration.
- Counting helps to maintain analytical integrity by offsetting biased impressions.
- Numbers help to present evidence and can be used in arguing for the strength of a conclusion. They are particularly valuable in persuading policymakers to take action.
- Counts prompt further analysis, e.g., to resolve the puzzle of why some people are not talking about a particular topic when nearly everyone else is.
- Automating counting of the content of text allows for statistical analysis of large volumes of data, for descriptive, comparative, or hypothesis testing purposes. The claim that this lends greater "scientific credibility" to the analysis of text is strongly disputed, however (Bergman, 2010; Krippendorff, 2004).

Counts from qualitative data

Counts reflect the "numbered nature of phenomena" (Sandelowski, 2001: 231), with counting being the simplest form of numeric processing. Counts have been used in a variety of ways in mixed methods projects, such as for counting themes, analysing talk, and making comparisons, and as such, constitute a very simple form of conversion of data from textual to numeric form. With increasing access to text data in electronic form and developments in software for unitising, parsing, and counting contents of electronic texts, counting has become a foundation for increasingly sophisticated statistical reporting and analyses of large-scale datasets, commonly referred to as *big data*.

Understanding counts and measures

Counting is a form of measurement – "the assignment of numerals to objects or events according to rules ... to represent facts and conventions about them"

(Stevens, 1946: 677, 678). Numbers seen and used in quantitative analyses can indicate any of four different types of measures, each of which has different properties. These different properties influence what kinds of statistics and further processes can be applied to the numbers used to represent data.

Nominal measurement is not really measurement at all, but simply the application of numbers for labelling purposes when categorical data are being used for statistical analyses; e.g., Location: UK = 1, US = 2, Australia = 3, etc. The *mode* is the only way of reporting central tendency for these categories: this is the category with the highest frequency of responses. Essentially, nominal measurements are qualitative in nature.

Ordinal measurement is still dealing with categories, but the categories are in rank order to indicate increasing or decreasing levels of the entity being measured. Equal intervals between values cannot be assumed, including in most survey-type scales; e.g., Education: primary = 1, high school = 2, tertiary = 3; Scale: strongly agree = 1, agree = 2, neutral = 3, disagree = 4, strongly disagree = 5. Central tendency is best indicated by the median value of those obtained – the middle score or 50th percentile. The interquartile range is used to indicate the spread of scores. This is the distance between the 75th and 25th percentile values – values that mark where scores of a quarter of the sample are either higher or lower, respectively.

Interval measurement means there is a continuum of values with equal distance between each value, but there is no absolute zero (a point where whatever is being measured ceases to exist). These properties mean that interval measures can be added and subtracted, but not multiplied or divided. Temperatures are an interval scale with an arbitrary origin; dates are another. It is not possible to say that 60° is twice as hot as 30°, but it is possible to say that a rise from 50° to 60° is twice as much as a rise from 35° to 40°. Psychological and social measurement scales (e.g., those based on responses to 5 or 7 point items) are often treated as interval level scales in which units are *assumed* to be equal, although they are likely to not actually be so. Central tendency for interval measures is usually indicated by the mean, or average value, with the spread of scores around the mean being indicated by the standard deviation – a measure based on distances of each score from that mean. The median and interquartile range can also be used.

Ratio measurement, like interval measurement, requires equal distance between each value, but also has a natural zero. This means it is possible to also make comparative statements involving multiplication or division; age and length are examples of ratio measures. Central tendency is usually indicated by the mean and standard deviation. When the distribution of scores is skewed (as with income or house prices, for example, where a few are extremely high), the median and interquartile range might be preferred to the mean and standard deviation.

For statistical analysis purposes, it is primarily important to distinguish between categorical (nominal, ordinal) and continuous (interval, ratio) forms of data. Continuous forms are generally preferred by statisticians as they convey more detail than categorical data, especially when used in analyses where capacity to fine tune differences can impact on outcomes. A greater range of statistical procedures are available for continuous measures, as well.

When analysts do decide to create categories from continuous numbers, such as for income levels, they have to make decisions about where to create the cuts – the artificial boundaries between groups. Sometimes a reasonable solution can be determined mathematically, for example by dividing the measures into four equal groups based on quartiles, or the divisions might be based on some socially meaningful criterion, such as average earnings of those in different strata of employment. But how different, really, is earning $30,000 from earning $30,001? An alternative is to create *fuzzy sets* – ranges of values with overlapping boundaries. Statistics can still be calculated, based on the "setness" of the values – a measure of how definitively a value falls into a set (Smithson & Verkuilen, 2006; Verkuilen, 2005). Fuzzy sets are also used as a way of converting vaguely expressed quantities into measurable variables. Again, this kind of thinking about numbers has particular relevance in social research, where boundaries are rarely clear.

What and how to count: making choices

One's choice of *what to count* – whether that be instances of every code or word, or selected codes or words – will depend on the relevance of those concepts to the research questions being asked. It is not always the case that the most frequently occurring code or theme or word is the most important.

> When Reuben Bolt was a doctoral student at the University of Sydney, he noted that comments about racism appeared often in the stories told by his Aboriginal participants, but he identified other themes (such as pilgrimage, pride, the importance of family) as prime narratives in their stories (Bolt, 2009). He argued that the narrative structure to these themes within their life stories, a structure that was missing from the theme of racism, demonstrated their higher relevance for those individuals.

The *method of counting* that is selected will depend on how the data were obtained and the specific purpose for which the counts are to be used. One can count the incidence or frequency with which an item might be found, the volume of material covered by that item, or the intensity associated with that item. These counts are recorded in or transferred to a spreadsheet or database to calculate descriptive statistics or for further statistical processing.

Counting incidence (frequencies)

One of the first steps in analysing any kind of quantitative data is to count the number of times any option has been selected or used, or any item appears. When counts are derived from qualitative data such as interviews, field notes, or other documents, there are no structured options for responses to questions, but if data are coded, then it is possible to count the frequency with which those codes appear within a given text or texts.

And, whether data are coded or not, the frequency with which different words or phrases are used can be counted.

The things that can be counted in qualitative data vary depending on whether counting is being done manually or using QDAS or a concordance-style software. In general, counts might include the number of times a category, theme, or word appears

- overall
- for each case
- within each different source
- within specific contexts.

Alternatively, counts might reveal the number of

- cases with a particular code, theme, or word
- sources with that code, theme, or word
- passages with that code, theme, or word
- the number of times a code, theme, or word appears in relation to particular contexts
- the number of codes present that contribute to a broader theme.

Qualitative software routinely provides counts of how often particular *codes* occur altogether in terms of the number of sources and the number of separate passages coded. Some qualitative programs will also report word counts, and character counts for each code (Figure 7.1). In most it will be necessary to run a query of cases cross-tabulated with the codes of interest to obtain case counts for those codes, especially if cases include data from part or multiple sources.

Using software for counting carries a range of benefits over manual counting, the most obvious of which are the ease of obtaining counts and the increased accuracy of the counts obtained. Additionally, both specialist word-counting software and most QDAS will provide simple frequency counts of the incidence of *words* within a body

Source Type	Number of Sources	Number of Coding References	Number of Words Coded	Number of Paragraphs Coded	Duration Coded
Nodes\\descriptors\analytic processes					
Document	221	466	5,091	487	
Nodes\\descriptors\analytic processes\analytic, thinker					
Document	151	226	2,683	236	
Nodes\\descriptors\analytic processes\creative, innovative					
Document	138	223	2,314	235	

Figure 7.1 Code counts in NVivo

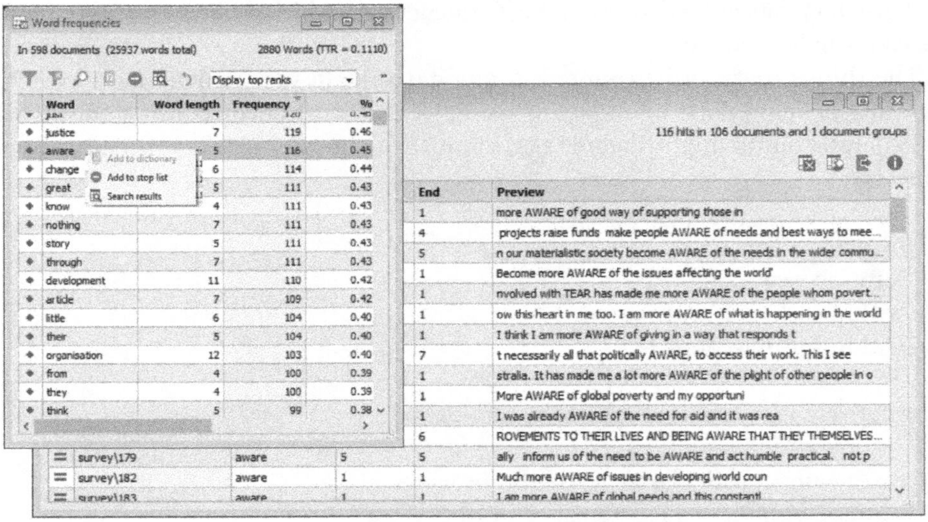

Figure 7.2 Using a word frequency query to generate counts and locate relevant text in MAX Dictio

of text, along with keyword in context (KWIC) information and, importantly for qualitative and mixed methods researchers, the possibility of direct access to more detailed context for any found word (Figure 7.2; see also Figure 2.10).

Counting volume

Within a particular source, case, or context, the *volume* of material coded in a particular way might be shown and recorded as:

- being present or absent, recorded as 0 or 1
- the number of times the code or word appears, recorded as a whole number
- the relative proportion of text (or other data) involved – usually recorded as a percentage of a source rather than case or context
- categorisation of volume, to simplify the measures.

Dichotomous (0/1) counting results in significant loss of information, but may be a more appropriate choice where volume counts are questionable: Does volume signify relative importance in the situation being considered, or is it likely to be a consequence of some incidental variable? The decision to count by presence/absence, frequency, or proportion is influenced by (a) whether all cases had equal opportunity to mention the relevant item, (b) how voluble each participant was, as this makes a difference to the likelihood of the counted item being present and how often it might be present, (c) the use to which the counts are being put, and (d) whether QDAS was used for coding the qualitative data.

> Bryans (2004), when analysing comparable simulated home visits to clients by 15 health visitors, categorised volume to deal with "considerable" variations in the length of discussion of various issues with the clients, by weighting the coded excerpts on a scale of 1 to 3 (representing variation from single statements to lengthy exchanges). This allowed her "to identify dominant and recurring issues within the simulated visits" (2004: 627).

In contrast, use of software made it possible for Holbrook and Bourke (2004) to work with actual volume counts rather than categorised quantities.

> Counts of the number of standard-length lines of text were used by Holbrook and Bourke (2004) in a study of PhD examiners' reports to determine the relative emphasis given in the report to major components of each dissertation (e.g., literature, methods, results, discussion), as well as the relative amounts that comprised summative versus formative evaluation of the work. This first step in their analysis of the PhD examination process was then followed with qualitative analyses of the types of comments made (Holbrook et al. 2004).

Because it was expected that an examiner's report could provide a range of coverage of each of the areas being counted, including zero, the relative proportion (%) of the report given to each area was an appropriate choice in relation to the research question and the type of data being studied.

> The way in which (qualitative) texts are managed in QDAS has implications for generating counts, particularly those reflecting volume. Say, for example, a passage of text is coded, and then the decision is made that the following text reflects the same code. Depending on whether the passages selected for coding are physically connected or not, that coding could be counted as one passage or as two. Similarly, when coding is removed from a passage, sometimes a blank character or line can be left behind, and so a count for that code is still registered. Retrievals for all codes should be checked before counts are used or exported.

Counting intensity

An alternative to assessing volume is to assess the intensity with which the code or theme is conveyed in the segment being coded. This is recorded, usually, as an ordinal rating or interval score attached to the code. In manual methods and in most QDAS, this would require applying a second code to the same passage, to be used in conjunction with the code that captured the thematic content.

In their study of machismo and resilience in the Hispanic community, Castro et al. (2010) developed a set of core thematic categories from initial in vivo coding of responses to two questions about the meaning of machismo. They then assessed the emphasis given to each of these thematic categories for each of their cases in two ways: by counting their frequency of occurrence within each case; and by assessing the intensity of mention on a scale of 0 to 3, from no mention (0), suggestion of the theme (1), clear mention (2), to emphatic mention (3), with the highest intensity rating recorded for the case used in further statistical analysis. Each of these two measures were then treated as variable data for statistical analyses to examine their distributional properties, in factor analysis, and then to explore machismo in relation to life satisfaction and other variables. Finally, they recontextualised their analyses by relating the statistical outcomes to the original context, creating story lines and giving voice to their participants through the use of quotes (illustrated earlier in Table 6.2).

In their concluding statement, Castro et al. (2010) outlined three challenges in using counts and intensity scores: (a) the need for effective data gathering so that responses allow for development of sound thematic categories capable of being counted and rated, (b) a problem of skewness in weak categories caused by too many 0 scores, and (c) while the categories developed had face validity, they did not necessarily have the same reliability and construct validity that are expected in established scales and so, without further research, their level of cross-sample stability and replicability cannot be substantiated.

MAXQDA and Dedoose facilitate intensity coding by providing an option to rate the importance or intensity of any statement or expression being coded as it is being coded, or in a second pass through the data. These ratings can be reported descriptively or visually, they are exportable for use in statistical analyses, and they can be included as a condition in queries within the software.

Limitations in interpreting counts from qualitative data

Counting words or codes is not as straightforward as it might at first seem. Three problem areas in particular present themselves: from a practical perspective, coding that is to be counted needs to be clearly defined and consistent (i.e., "reliable"); from a hermeneutic point of view, there are potential irregularities in categorising natural language; and, the meaning of a zero count can be ambiguous.

Coding reliability

Inter-coder reliability is claimed to add rigour to qualitative analysis, but its value in doing so is contested. Those working in disciplines with a strong quantitative-experimental heritage (health, education, psychology) are often required to show that a second coder will produce a similar result to that already obtained in terms of the codes used and the actual passages coded. Their capacity to do so, however, is dependent on the extent to which the codes were established *a priori*, and how rigorously the coding rules have been set out. These requirements are a problem in many qualitative approaches to coding where choices in what and how to code are influenced by the question being asked, the conceptual framework governing the study, whether a preliminary review has established a set of codes to use for data that are already collected, and whether modifications to the coding systems were allowed as coding proceeded (Seltzer-Kelly, Westwood, & Peña-Guzman, 2012). People asked to code when they are not part of a project team inevitably will bring different assumptions and knowledge to the task, and will find it difficult to undertake the task. If the researcher is working solo, what matters more is whether the codes used can be justified in terms of the purpose, framework, and questions for the study. The usefulness and consistency of the coding that was applied should be evident in the ways it assisted in reaching conclusions from the study and in how effectively those conclusions could be supported with evidence from across the dataset.

The focus here, however, is on how the issue of coding reliability intersects with using qualitative codes to generate counts and variable data for statistical analysis. In quantitative studies, coding is largely predetermined by the structure of the response options provided. When qualitative coding is converted to quantitative variables, there is an assumption that the coding was consistently applied across the entire dataset. This means that (a) the meaning attached to each code is clearly specified, with examples of how it was applied, (b) data sources coded early in the project are reviewed to ensure consistency in the codes selected and in their application to the data, especially if the coding system was allowed to develop during the course of the project, and (c) the text assigned to each code is reviewed, as a further means of checking consistency of application. If these checks are carried out, there should be no additional need for measures of inter-coder reliability for purposes of quantification in a sole researcher project, or even where a small team is working very closely together.

Agreement on what the coding is designed to achieve does become important when people work in teams. If a measure of inter-coder reliability rating is required in that situation, then this is usually evaluated using Cohen's kappa, calculated from the sum of observations in agreement divided by the total observations, corrected for the probability of chance agreement. Alternatively, a rating may be determined by the sum of observations in disagreement divided by the total observations with or without correcting for chance. Most QDAS now provide a means of calculating these measures (e.g., Figure 7.3), but a problem is that these often apply a much too fine level of discrimination, basing counts on coded characters rather than words or meaning units. Thus, if Sue codes the same passages at Code X as David, but tends to include a few more words either side of the passage when doing so, those extra words will reduce their inter-coder reliability scores in a way that does not reflect the essential agreement they shared. When this is the case (as in NVivo, for example), the actual measures calculated by QDAS are often less useful than the visual displays that are also available, showing where discrepancies are occurring (Figure 7.4). In qualitative teamwork,

Node	Source	Kappa	Agreement (%)	A and B (%)	Not A and Not B (%)	Disagreement (%)	A and Not (%)	B and Not A (%)
Habitat	Barbara	0.5743	94.47	4.16	90.31	5.53	0.49	5.04
Habitat	Charles	1	100	0	100	0	0	0
Habitat	Dorothy	0	92.51	0	92.51	7.49	0	7.49

Figure 7.3 Statistical output from a coding comparison query in NVivo

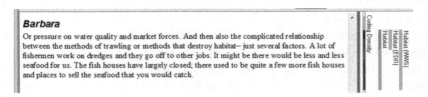

Figure 7.4 Comparing the coding detail for two users in NVivo

these provide an early opportunity for differences in coding to be discussed and resolved, serving an educative role for further coding.

QDA Miner overcomes the constraint of having to have exactly the same segments of text coded by having an option that allows for the level of overlap (agreement) to be relaxed by a user-specified degree. It also allows for a variety of tests, three that are based on different forms of agreement for individual codes in individual sources, and

CODE	AGREE ABSENT	AGREE PRESENT	DISAGREE	PERCENT	FREE MARGINAL
Environment	51	1	0	100.0%	1.000
Ethic	47	3	2	75.0%	0.500
Family	47	4	1	88.9%	0.778
Freedom	50	1	1	66.7%	0.333
Globalization	50	1	1	66.7%	0.333
Local Economy	48	4	0	100.0%	1.000
Novelty	50	1	1	66.7%	0.333
Patriotism	39	11	2	91.7%	0.833
Power	47	3	2	75.0%	0.500
Race/Ethnic relation	47	5	0	100.0%	1.000
Representativeness	39	10	3	87.0%	0.739
Tradition	47	3	2	75.0%	0.500
TOTAL	562	47	15	75.8%	0.516

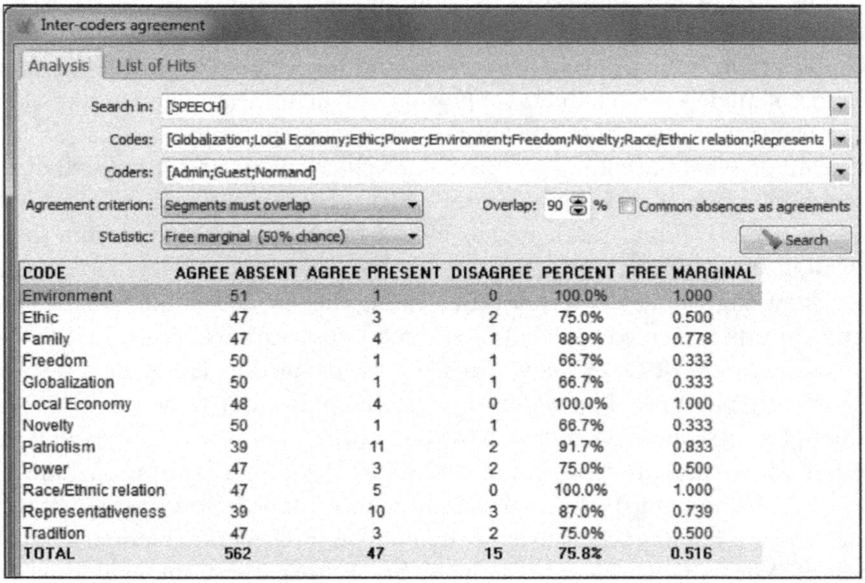

Figure 7.5 Inter-coder agreement set up and statistics in QDA Miner

three statistical tests that are based on the required degree of overlap in specified codes across specified groups of sources (or all), to give a considerably more useful overall measure (Figure 7.5).

Codes applied automatically in larger datasets (e.g., using word search or predictive coding), when designed for transformation to allow statistical analyses, should be sampled for checking to ensure the coding rules are meeting the requirements for the project. Depending on the size of the dataset, there can be some tolerance for inaccurate coding (usually set at 1%). Whether the coding and the variables derived from it are capturing the implicit meaning of autocoded data is another (non-statistical) question entirely.

Words and meanings

Words can assume multiple meanings. Which meaning applies at any given time is judged by the listener or reader in relation to the context of the word (referred to as disambiguation). When words or phrases are counted, they are removed from that context, especially if the counting is being done by a machine. When context-based human judgement is removed, specific parsing rules that take account of the grammatical context need to be established to deal with problems, for example, created by words with the same spelling that have different meanings and by different words that have a similar meaning.

What does zero mean?

Zero (0) as part of a volume or intensity count is only meaningful if it anchors a ratio scale where the difference between 0 and 1 is the same as the difference between 1 and 2, or between 2 and 3, or 0 and –1. Indeed, the meaning of a zero count, itself, needs to be questioned when it is derived from qualitative coding:

> Present and absent may signify different things in transcribed interview data. Present in interview data may, among other options, mean that "it" (a) spontaneously came up in discussion, (b) was directed to come up in discussion, (c) was seen by the analyst between the lines, and (d) truly was a dimension of experience. Absent may, among other options, mean that "it" (a) did not come up; (b) was not seen by the analyst; (c) was forgotten as a factor by the participant; (d) was thought by the participant to be so understood as to not require bringing it up; (e) was a factor, but the participant did not want to bring "it" up; (f) was not brought up because the conversation veered away from "it"; and (g) truly was not a dimension of experience. 1 or 0 may signal a host of such diverse circumstances. (Sandelowski, Voils, & Knafl, 2009: 217)

Whenever possible, therefore, the way in which zero was construed should be recorded and reported with the analysis of the data.

Don't know, as a response to a specific question, can create similar issues. For counting purposes, it will be recorded as absence (0) or as a missing value, but when making *don't know* entries in a manually constructed matrix Miles and Huberman (1994) recommend doing so in three versions: DK1 for when the question was not asked; DK2 for when the question was asked but not answered; or DK3 for an ambiguous or unsure answer.

Interpreting counts from small samples

Tables and other displays involving small numbers are quite common in mixed methods projects. The question is, how best to analyse and interpret the data they contain? Small samples pose a range of problems for statistical analysis. As well as raising questions about sample selection, the large standard errors associated with small samples makes it difficult to reliably reject a null hypothesis (e.g., of no differences between groups) using tests of significance.

- Continuous measures for small samples are often not normally distributed (i.e., evenly distributed around a mean value), and so a non-parametric statistical test is likely to be more appropriate for testing whether a comparative difference or change or relationship is a non-chance result – if, as Gorard (2010a) asks, statistical testing is relevant at all.
- The novice statistician is likely to over-read differences in a comparative table when numbers are small. It helps, as a warning, to think about how many cases would have to move from one column to another to change the interpretation for a particular row – often it is only one or two, which means there really isn't a difference there!
- When reporting proportions from small numbers, use actual numbers (e.g., 3 of the 15 xyz cases). To avoid a distorted view of the numbers involved, use percentages only when the total within each group includes at least 20 cases (statisticians would say, technically, at least 100).
- Sometimes a consistent pattern across a number of measures will be evident that might be worth noting even if some individually are not statistically significant, especially if there is other evidence to support the pattern (issues in significance testing are reviewed in the next chapter).

Reporting counts – some points to watch

Descriptive and comparative counts derived from both qualitative and quantitative data provide a valuable component of the reports from many mixed methods studies, with lists, tables, and graphs often summarising large amounts of data in a clear, communicative and concise manner. When the primary purpose for counting is to provide the foundation for more elaborate statistical analyses, the descriptive reports of data remain necessary to contextualise the interpretive findings from those analyses.

- In using counts as part of a written report in a mixed methods study, avoid relying on numbers to tell the whole story. Provide sufficient context (e.g., based on the qualitative content) to allow the reader to fully interpret the numbers.

- Do not report counts in a way that suggests a representative sample where this did not exist. Statistical generalisations to a population from the kinds of samples used in many mixed methods studies are not valid.
- Before drawing conclusions from counts, it is helpful to have a basic understanding of probability theory in relation to sampling error as a precaution to over-reading or misinterpreting comparative figures.
- Avoid reporting in a form that gives a false sense of precision or rigour. For example, use whole numbers rather than decimals unless the degree of accuracy in measurement really does warrant one or two decimal places. If decimal places are being used, apply them consistently throughout the report (e.g., put in .0 when a whole number is involved).
- Beware reducing evidence to the amount of evidence. Evidence must be placed in the context of an account that reflects what has been learned from interpreting the text, sound, images, observations – perhaps even statistical reports – that provided the counts used in your study.

Content analysis – quantitative or mixed method?

Content analysis extends the idea of counting texts, and gives it a particular purpose. It has been defined as "any technique for making inferences by objectively and systematically identifying specified characteristics of messages" (Holsti, 1969: 14). It was first seen as a strategy for research by Max Weber, who presented it at the first conference of the German Sociological Association in 1910 (Kuckartz, 2014). He presented categorising and counting content as a tool for analysing change over time in component parts of newspapers. Weber understood content analysis as both quantitative and qualitative – starting with measurement, followed up by qualitative analyses.

Content analysis has moved through a number of phases with shifting emphases and degrees of popularity over the century since Weber's work. Classical content analysis developed as a technique used primarily in communication research following the Second World War, where it had been employed as a tool in analysing propaganda. It became viewed as a quantitative method, in line with the general trend to "scientific" research in the social sciences in the mid-1900s. This was exemplified in Berelson's definition of content analysis as "a research technique for the objective, systematic and quantitative description of the manifest content of communication" (1952: 18). In the latter half of the twentieth century, spearheaded by Kracauer, the emphasis gradually shifted back to interpretation of meaning as well as counting of texts (Kuckartz, 2014). Qualitative content analysis re-established as a dominant form from the 1980s with the work of Philipp Mayring (1983). It remains a strong tradition in German sociology and psychology with Mayring (2000) arguing that qualitative content analysis constitutes a form of integrated mixed methods research. Hermeneutic-classificatory content analysis (Roller, Mathes, & Eckert, 1995) similarly uses classic content analysis techniques to find dominant patterns and co-occurrences in text, followed by the use of qualitative retrievals to complete a "fine grained" analysis of frequent and rare responses. In a further modification along a similar theme, Bergman (2010) described a method of hermeneutic content analysis that involves, firstly, qualitative content analysis (i.e., coding), then (statistical) dimensional analyses based on the co-occurrences of codes to reveal patterns not discernible qualitatively, with those patterns then recontextualised within the qualitative data (the application of exploratory dimensional analyses to coded data is discussed in detail in Chapter 9). Hermeneutic forms of content analysis, which require interpretation of text to generate codes, are necessarily limited in terms of the volume of material that can be analysed.

Increasing capacity of computers to handle large-scale and complex processing tasks has allowed a relatively recent expansion in the availability of software for automated coding of language-based materials. Once again, this is dramatically shifting the focus and popularity of content analysis as a method of social science investigation. At its foundation it continues to rely on methods of counting frequencies, volumes, or proportions of words or expressions within a corpus. Where it varies most is in the degree to which interpretive analysis based on the original texts is integrated with the descriptive statistics.

Software for content analysis searches text records for words, phrases, expressions, or statements that are considered by the researchers to reflect the domain of interest of the research question. It then automatically codes or categorises them. Programs vary in terms of their broad approach, including:

- those that descriptively calculate word frequencies within specified texts, such as concordance type software, e.g., WordNet, and most QDAS
- QDAS (and other researcher-developed programs not considered here) that allow the creation of project-specific, user-defined dictionaries to direct the search routines, e.g., WordStat/QDA Miner and MAXDictio
- purpose-built programs that use predefined dictionaries of terms and expressions on larger searchable databases, TABARI being one of the better known examples.

Some programs (including some QDAS) will do predictive coding of additional texts based on preliminary coding of current texts and some incorporate sentiment analysis as an autocoding feature. The more sophisticated programs examine co-occurrences of terms and include complex syntactical rules to determine relationships between the concepts that are embedded within statements. Grimmer and Stewart (2013) reviewed methods of automating content analysis within political science, where much of the development of these techniques has taken place. In pointing to the complexity of language and the impossibility of accurately accounting for the meaning expressed in text, they emphasise the necessity for "careful and close reading of texts" (2013: 268), advocating that automated methods can amplify or augment close reading and thoughtful analysis, but never replace it.

Counts from automated content analysis are analysed statistically to provide descriptive summaries and comparative analyses, for example, to compare media reports of different political events (Schrodt, 2000) or to reveal the psychological states associated with different experiences (Berth & Romppel, 2000). The advantage of programs in which dictionaries have been developed for a particular topic or measure is that coding is very rapid and totally standardised, especially when compared with earlier hand-coding methods. This makes it possible to design projects based on larger volumes of textual material and, together with the standardisation of coding, allows for more relia-ble statistical inference. The disadvantage is also obvious, that such coding cannot readily take account of unusual expressions or latent meaning in the text.

Berth and Romppel (2000) applied standardised psychological scales based on content analysis (using the German-language program CoAn) to compare the levels of dogmatism and anxiety expressed by East and West German newspa-pers around the period of German reunification (1989–90). They found that East German newspapers demonstrated higher levels of both dogmatism and anxiety, reflecting the greater impact of these events on the East than the West. Temporally based graphs were used to associate fluctuations in the two indices in each set of newspapers with the progression of events. The higher levels of dogmatism were interpreted as the journalists' way of attempting to reduce the people's insecurity in those politically turbulent times.

Since 2000, counting from qualitative data has experienced a digital revolution. The expanded availability of electronic texts, moves to digitise administrative records, fur-ther growth in computing capacity, the advent of cloud-based storage, and the exponential expansion of the internet for social and personal as well as commercial and academic purposes, have all contributed to the continuing creation of new opportuni-ties for investigation and analysis. At their heart, however, all these methods rely on a foundation of encoding and counting, and the way that encoding and counting is man-aged is integral to their reliability and validity. The danger is that the counts and resulting statistics will become ever more divorced from the interpretive understanding of the texts and the contexts that provided them.

"Big data" – a scientific revolution in the making?

In 2000, Philip Schrodt reported that, with a dictionary to analyse lead sentences in media reports of political events using natural language processing with sparse parsing techniques, he could achieve automatic coding of up to 3000 events per second com-pared to 40 events per day by human coders. In 2011, he described coding 26 million sentences generated from 8 million stories, involving approximately 30 gigabytes of text, in six minutes – equating to approximately 70,000 stories per second (Schrodt, 2011).

With the advent of cluster computing or use of distributed personal computing environments and cloud-stored data, high speed coding is no longer an issue. Indeed, the revolution that is big data is derived not only from increased computational capac-ity, nor from the exponential growth in data and data storage capacity as not all datasets are large, but also from the algorithms that drive the computer processing of this data. The right algorithm can reduce a multi-million dollar computing task to something that can be achieved in a fraction of the time on a standard laptop (King, 2016). Development of those algorithms is at the heart of analytic activity in data science. But where does the frenzy of quantitative analysis that is big data fit with integrative mixed methods analysis?

To a considerable extent, it is commercial interests that have driven the big data revolution, making use of existing qualitative and quantitative datasets that arise as administrative by-products or otherwise unobtrusively as we go about our everyday activities. Predictive modelling equates to reduced costs and increased profits, for example through locational targeting for warehousing and targeted advertising to consumers. Nevertheless, there are applications also in the public realm that provide motivation for involvement by researchers and academics. Big data is being used increasingly in epidemiological studies and in public health to predict and control outbreaks of infectious disease, by police to predict criminal behaviour and riots, and in health systems to manage demand and supply (Shaw, 2014). Much of the data that are available come through the several billion social media posts occurring every day, purchasing data from credit cards, and they include also the multiple petabytes of spatio-temporal data generated daily from smart phones and GPS systems. These data are used, for example, in transport studies, urban planning, and health care (Lee & Kang, 2015) – and in sociological studies.

King, Pan, and Roberts (2013) analysed social media censorship to explore the typically opaque Chinese Government's interests, intentions, and goals. They developed a system to locate and download social media posts in China before the Government, working through manual censors employed by each of the 1400 internet content providers, was able to remove them (13% of the total were removed, usually within 24 hours of posting). They used computer-assisted text analysis to identify a theoretically and empirically defined stratified sample covering 85 topics over a six-month period, and then to review the content of the posts removed by the censors. A limitation of their method was that it did not include self-censored content, or content removed before initial publication through keyword blocking. From their sample they found, surprisingly, that censorship was not designed to suppress criticism of the State or the Party, but rather to forestall any likelihood of collective action of any kind (supportive or critical). This was achieved by a focused strategy of censoring all posts during volume bursts that discussed events with collective action potential. In all topics considered, whether collective action was involved or not, statements supporting or criticising the state were equally censored. The authors conclude that with respect to freedom of speech through social media "the Chinese people are individually free but collectively in chains" (King et al., 2013: 339). Collective action, in the face of many thousands of "mass incidents" in any year, is of particular concern to a government that is fixated on retaining power and maintaining stability. The authors then discussed the theoretical and methodological implications of their study, including the possibility of being able to predict major political events up to five days ahead of their occurrence.

Data sources used in big data projects range from those that require the development of sophisticated coding routines, through data that requires cleaning routines, such as might be needed for messy administrative records, to data collected entirely automatically through data logging devices – although these too require cleaning before use to remove duplicate and other irrelevant records. Data might include text, numbers, geospatial coordinates, or network links. Central to the emergence of big data as a research tool have been the development of autocoding capacity in software, new ways of linking datasets, innovative statistical methods and novel computer science, and creative approaches to visualising data (including geocoding: Crampton et al., 2012). These work together to allow humans to then see patterns in the data.

A critical change big data brings to social science is the shift from relying on *accounts* of people's actions in the social world to being able to track those actions in real time, using unobtrusive and/or digital methods (Burrows & Savage, 2014). Compared with data obtained through traditional survey methods or with predictions of outcomes made by human experts, big data can prove more accurate in its predictions despite "noise" that might exist in the data. It can also be "precisely inaccurate" as a consequence of enormous samples producing results that are always statistically significant (McFarland & McFarland, 2015). Validation routines are essential, interpretive caution is needed. Numbers cannot always tell the whole story, and data do *not* speak for themselves; for example, correlations can be misleading (Eagle & Greene, 2014), search terms become outdated (McFarland & McFarland, 2015), and web-derived metrics are biased by heavy users (Park & Macy, 2015). Preprocessing based on contextual understanding is needed to sift relevant from irrelevant data (Eagle, Pentland, & Lazer, 2009). Multiple approaches to analysis of a dataset are often warranted, as each approach, each algorithm, deals with problems generated by others and each contributes different elements to the combined understanding (Bail, 2015).

Nathan Eagle (Eagle & Greene, 2014) tells of using mobile phone call data records to predict outbreaks of cholera in Rwanda. These detected decreasing mobility within communities a week in advance of cholera outbreaks. This reduced movement was suspected to be a result of flu-like symptoms, but in fact turned out to be the result of flooding washing out roads – with the flooding being the cause of the cholera outbreaks. The computational model gave a global view that could predict risk of cholera, but this needed a "reality check" to reveal the actual infrastructure problem that the phone records were exposing.

The benefits of big data are yet to be fully realised, but as a research tool, obvious benefits over traditional data include being able to work in real time using unobtrusive and non-reactive measures with large samples or whole populations. Negatives from the data scientist's viewpoint depend on the type of data being used and the degree of preprocessing required to allow statistical calculations, particularly with text data. From the social scientist's viewpoint, what is lost is the capacity to see and understand subtle meanings within text and the more intangible aspects of human life, society, and culture. Further major considerations are the implications for confidentiality and privacy, and concerns regarding the safety of the data.

Counting, content analysis, and big data in the context of integrated mixed methods analyses

An element of qualitative, lived, observed experience lies at the heart of every number. Clearly, counts and categories have a place in mixed methods research as outlined earlier in this chapter (Methodological purposes). Counts generated to add descriptive detail to qualitative narrative, perhaps to be used in combination with other descriptive statistics (e.g., from a census or survey) contribute to integration in ways described in earlier chapters. These are accepted forms of mixed methods analysis. Less accepted are the more automated and statistically oriented forms of content analysis. And yet, researchers working with counts from qualitative data have recourse to the data – the experiences – from which the numbers were derived, the context from which those data were drawn, and the conceptual and theoretical frameworks that have been used in thinking about these data. Returning to and drawing on these and related sources is imperative for integrative analysis when interpreting the counts, relationships, and patterns their numbers have revealed. The statistician or data scientist who chooses to focus only on the characteristics, volume and patterning of numeric data abstracted from records of social experience, without close reading of the data, is at risk of producing data models at odds with the social worlds they describe.

Big data – counting on a megascale – is changing the way we think about data, about reality, the generation of knowledge, and research (Kitchin, 2014). As a "disruptive innovation" it has, in Kuhn's terms, the potential to be a scientific revolution in the making. Rob Kitchin warns that those who come to big data from science, unaware of social science scholarship, produce analyses that are "reductionist, functionalist", and reproductive of "the same kinds of limitations generated by the quantitative/positivist social sciences in the mid-20th century" (2014: 5). He recommends that scientists work with subject matter experts to appreciate the *why* as well as the *what* of data to avoid producing "anaemic or unhelpful" interpretations. Some developments in big data research have occurred through "forensic analysis" of data without guiding questions. Kitchin argues, however, that rather than being atheoretical inductive exploration, data-driven science supports "a hybrid combination of abductive, inductive and deductive approaches to advance the understanding of a phenomenon" (2014: 5). This is a theory-informed but data-grounded inductive mode of hypothesis generation, a "guided knowledge discovery technique" (2014: 6), which is then followed by a selectively applied deductive examination and testing approach. Kitchin, here, is drawing a clear line of demarcation between data science and data mining. Further, he is suggesting that a reconfigured version of the scientific method using this abductive approach and made possible by riches of data will supersede the traditional deductive model of scientific research that was based on scarce data and limited computational capacity. This paradigmatic change is of great significance also for the social science community, given its compatibility with the way in which most social scientists actually prefer to work, although it is more likely to supplement rather than replace current approaches and methods. Kitchin concludes by suggesting that a potential path forward for social scientists is to adopt an epistemology "in which quantitative methods and models are employed within a framework that is reflexive and acknowledges the situatedness, positionality and politics of the social science being conducted, rather than rejecting such an approach out of hand" (2014: 10).

This is an area begging for involvement by mixed methods researchers, and yet discussions about and engagement with big data have been all but absent in that particular community of scholars. The opportunity is ripe for mixed methods scholars to bring their understanding of ways to integrate qualitative with quantitative methods to the big data table. There they might complement their interpretive understanding of meaning and context with contributions from data science or work in synergy with data scientists to build truly innovative, but grounded understanding of topic areas across the disciplines. They could also add a transformative perspective to big data's potential to improve the human condition.

As an ethnographer working together with two data scientists analysing Wikipedia sources, Heather Ford (2014) observed commonalities in their discipline-based approaches, particularly their shared interest in understanding what people actually do rather than what they say, and their immersion over time in the data. She demonstrated the benefit of their complementary approaches for combining depth with breadth, noting incidentally the importance of having each person in the team experience working in both ways with the data, so as to understand the other's approach.

Concluding remarks

This chapter signalled a shift in focus from integration of different data sources and data types to integration of different approaches to analysis, such as becomes possible when one form of data is transformed into another. It lays the foundation for analyses involving transformation of qualitative coding to quantitative data by showing the different ways that qualitative coding (through either interpretive coding or automatic word searches) can be converted to numeric form, to indicate simple counts, volume counts, proportion of source, or intensity of expression.

The growing trend to automation of coding and of counting words and codes in the form of content analysis, and more recently through the big data revolution, was reviewed, and some implications of these developments for mixed methods analyses were observed. In the mixed methods context, the primary utility of generating counts from qualitative data, at all levels, is to provide data for further deductive and inductive statistical analyses, a focus that will be taken up and developed in the following chapters.

Throughout the discussion of transformation of data, emphasis was placed on always maintaining an awareness of the detail behind the counts obtained, as found in the original qualitative sources. This was seen as necessary for both understanding how the counts were generated and for interpreting their meaning and value.

Further reading

Counting qualitative data

Further articles and papers using counts to explore the PhD examination process by Holbrook and Bourke are listed at: www.newcastle.edu.au/research-and-innovation/centre/sorti/publications/research-into-phd-examination

Anderson et al. (2001) and Reznitskaya et al. (2001) describe experiments in which they used counts from qualitative data to assess the impact of intervention (training) on children's cognitive skills.

Onwuegbuzie and Teddlie (2003) include some examples of using counts within a broader discussion of mixed methods analysis strategies.

Sandelowski (2001) and Sandelowski et al. (2009) examine the benefits and cautions relating to the use of counts from qualitative data.

Content analysis

Grimmer and Stewart (2013) discuss different approaches to automated text analysis and explain the basic principles by which language processing software works in reducing the complexity of words to numbers.

Popping (2015) discusses instrumental versus representational coding in the context of analysing open-ended questions in surveys.

Schrodt (2011) describes problems in data access and coding when dealing with archival data sources.

Bergman (2010) covers basic principles of content analysis and argues for hermeneutic content analysis as a form of integrated qualitative and quantitative content analysis (i.e., as a mixed method).

Big data

Kitchin (2014) provides a really clear exposition of the paradigmatic shift that has been prompted by big data and a discussion of the mechanics and paradigmatic implications of having big data intersect with the humanities and social science.

Wagner-Pacifici, Mohr, and Breiger (2015) wrote an editorial for the July–December 2015 issue of *Big Data & Society*, which usefully reviews 18 of the articles comprising the issue. Both the review and the articles they review are worth following up for their mind-expanding insight into the "pitfalls and promises" of big data.

Lee and Kang (2015) write about the role of geospatial data in the big data mix.

Crampton et al. (2012) discuss ways of balancing the perspective that might be gained through geotagged social media data by combining it with more traditional approaches used in human geography.

8

INTEGRATION THROUGH DATA TRANSFORMATION 1: QUALITATIVE DATA TO STATISTICAL VARIABLES

CHAPTER OVERVIEW

Mapping integration through data transformation (qualitative to quantitative)

The left arm of this map of transformative processes includes procedures covered in this chapter; strategies shown in the right arm are described in Chapter 9.

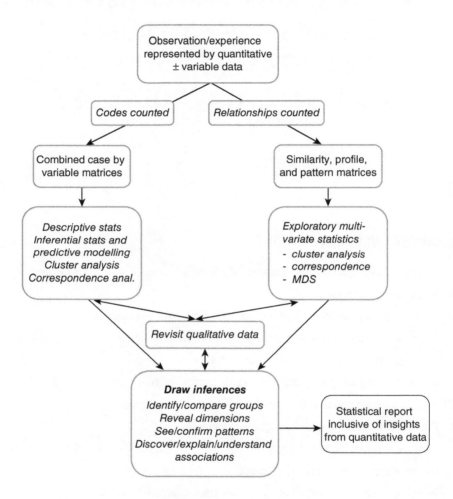

Most mixed methods studies will include quantitative (numerical or other measurement) data as part of a data mix, and most quantitative data will invite statistical analyses. In this chapter, a foundation is laid for understanding and engaging in data transformation as a mixed methods process. I look at the potential for coded qualitative sources that are transformed into variable data to be analysed using descriptive or inferential statistics, and at what those additional analyses might add to an understanding and interpretation of that data. These are the same statistical procedures as are used for many quantitative analyses, especially for survey or questionnaire data. They allow the analyst to describe, compare, relate, and/or predict patterns or outcomes on the basis of numerical patterns and associations in the data.

More exploratory uses of transformed data will be examined in the chapter to follow. The analysis options described in this and the next chapter are not designed to be exhaustive or definitive, but rather to show some of the kinds of things that are possible when using transformed data, either on their own or in combination with other quantitative data. Particular attention is paid to the possibilities and constraints imposed when the data are derived from qualitative sources. The intention of the chapters is that the brief descriptions given for various procedures will inspire readers to explore fresh possibilities for analysis, rather than instruct on the mathematical or statistical details of how to do them. They assume that the reader who wishes to pursue any of the procedures suggested either will already have some competence in statistics, will be working with someone who is, or will be, prepared to seek out opportunities to read, learn, and/or collaborate, in order to make effective use of strategies described.

Methodological purposes

Qualitative data are transformed, or quantified, to facilitate merging and comparison of different data sources or to allow exploratory, explanatory, comparative, predictive, or confirmatory statistical analyses. Integration of analyses using conversion of data bring the power of statistical analysis to an inductive project, particularly in exploring the composition and structure of data, while retaining the freedom and power of the qualitative techniques to provide situated meaning. *Quantification is not intended to replace the detail and depth of qualitative analysis*, but rather, to complement or support it. Transforming data is not an end in itself, but "a means of making available techniques which add power and sensitivity to individual judgment when one attempts to detect and describe patterning in a set of observations" (Weinstein & Tamur, 1978: 140). At the same time, "quantitized data[1] are only as good as the qualitative data gathering and analyses that led to their creation" (Collingridge, 2013: 82).

An additional advantage of using transformed qualitative coding as the basis for statistical analysis, compared with using a survey or questionnaire, is that the researcher does not have to predetermine the categories that will be used for analysis, opening up the possibility of new discoveries. At the same time, there is no guarantee that all participants in the research process will be equally comprehensive in their discussion of the topic. As noted in Chapter 7, this raises the issue of whether absence

---

[1] "Quantitizing" was a term introduced by Tashakkori and Teddlie (1998) to describe the process of transforming data from qualitative to quantitative. I prefer to use the standard English term, quantifying.

of mention of a topic represents lack of importance, deliberate omission, a temporary lapse in attention, or simply that the question wasn't asked.

Quantifying qualitative data for statistical analysis – theoretical aspects

Between the world we observe and experience and having data for analysis there are multiple layers of interpretation and transformation – and then more as data are analysed. Denzin and Lincoln (2011: 3) defined qualitative research as: "A set of interpretive, material practices that make the world visible. These practices *transform* the world. They turn the world into a series of *representations*, including field notes, interviews, conversations, photographs, recordings and memos to self" (emphasis added). One could begin a definition of quantitative research in exactly the same way – numbers are models that *represent* and make visible aspects of the empirical world (Stevens, 1946), and so the difference between forms of data is in the form of representation they employ. Because transformation in one form or another is integral to the process of working with any kind of data, this suggests that epistemologically the process of reading data of different kinds is equivalent: all are to be read as a representation, an interpretation by the producer of that data, rather than absolute or material truth. "Measurement is an intrinsically interpretivist process. ... Personal judgement(s) lie at the heart of all research – in our choice of research questions, samples, questions to participants, and methods of analysis – regardless of the kinds of data to be collected" (Gorard, 2010b: 246).

Transforming qualitative coding for statistical analysis is an extension of counting, portrayed in the previous chapter. Qualitative data are coded or categorised, and those codes or categories are converted to variables with values that are based on choices made between dichotomous, frequency, volume, or intensity counts or measures for each code being converted. The same conditions, cautions, and options apply, therefore, to these initial steps in the transformation process as applied to choosing between different types of counts.

The practice of transforming qualitative data is far from new, in that "there are probably thousands of experiments and quasi-experiments in various substantive literatures in which qualitative data are collected, coded, and analyzed quantitatively" (Mark, 2015: 30). And yet, use of transformed data in statistical analyses has been a largely unexplored, underutilised, and poorly executed area in mixed methods research (Fakis et al., 2014). "A key issue in data transformation is what kind of data is transformed into what other kind of data, at what point in the research process, and by whom" (Louis, 1982a: 9). The critical element that ensures transformation is integrated as part of a *mixed methods* analysis process is that any statistical interpretation is undertaken with full awareness and consideration of the qualitative data sources from which the numeric data were drawn.

Conversion from observations or experience to numeric data might occur:

- as data are collected, by the person whose experiences they are when they fill out a fixed-response questionnaire, by an administrator when they complete a form, or by a field worker when they categorise what they are seeing or hearing (e.g., Edmeades et al., 2010) – these might be further transformed during preliminary processing as counts are converted to broader categories or variables are combined
- during preliminary processing when structured qualitative responses are broadly categorised or autocoded into categories
- after initial qualitative analyses, when qualitatively generated categories and codes are converted to variables (Louis, 1982a).

Richards (2014) draws a distinction between quantitative coding as data reduction, and qualitative coding as data retention. Data transformed to numbers at the point of collection become decontextualised, nuances in expression are lost, and the meanings attached to the numbers by the researcher might differ from those held by the respondents. Transforming coded qualitative data for statistical analysis, particularly when QDAS is used, has a clear advantage over responses categorised as they are recorded in questionnaires or in the field, in that the original data associated with the codes are retained in a readily accessible way. This accessibility assists in interpretation of patterns revealed through statistical analyses and facilitates validation of conclusions through checking findings back against the qualitative data.

Edmeades et al. (2010) melded a narrative-style interview with quantitative survey techniques to understand the circumstances surrounding pregnancy and prevalence of attempted and successful abortions for 2444 married women from Madhya Pradesh, India. The design of the survey was informed by focus groups and interviews and extensively pretested. It was conducted in two parts over two concurrent days, taking an average of 1.75 hours for each woman. The first part explored current circumstances using a standard approach. The second "hybrid" section employed a life-history approach focusing targeted but open questions around key events in women's reproductive history. During the second stage interview, while navigating a fluid path through the questions, locally trained interviewers ticked off detailed response categories to record the narrative. Because of the open questions and level of detail recorded, the researchers were able to reconstruct case studies from the quantitative data to

(Continued)

(Continued)

"illustrate both the complexity of the relationship between women's reproductive desires and outcomes in this context and the effectiveness of the narrative survey approach in capturing its nuances" (2010: 193). They were able also to calculate that abortion rates were approximately five times higher than previously estimated. The authors suggest that "the improved data generated by this approach offer new possibilities for researchers to understand the motivations, constraints, and reproductive needs of women in developing countries and to more effectively contribute to policies and programs" (2010: 195).

Transforming qualitative coding produces, firstly, descriptive statistics, and then any of four "general purpose" types of output, each in table-based format ready for different types of statistical analyses.

- *A case by variable matrix* might be standalone, or can be combined with existing quantitative data or with other data collected at the same time or a future time, providing the records can be linked through individual case identifiers (Figure 8.1).
- *Profile matrices* in which the dimensions or subcategories of a concept or category are crosstabulated with values of a categorical or scaled (usually demographic) attribute (Figure 8.2).
- *Pattern matrices* in which the dimensions or subcategories of one concept or category group are crosstabulated with those of another (Figure 8.3).
- *Similarity matrices* in which the dimensions or subcategories of a concept or category group are crosstabulated with the same dimensions or subcategories to produce a triangular (reflected) matrix (Figure 8.4).

Other kinds of specialised output are possible, for example, to provide raw data for social network analysis or qualitative comparative analysis, discussed in Chapter 10.

An ever-present and fundamental danger for researchers engaged in projects working with data quantified from qualitative data is that they become so engaged with the processes and what can be achieved through them that they forget that they are, for the most part, actually working with a one-sided view of their data. Coding is an excellent way of capturing the *content* of qualitative data, but it is more difficult (and therefore less often seen) for coding to reflect the *connectedness* of what is being conveyed in the data (Maxwell & Miller, 2008). While some of the exploratory methods described in the next chapter create displays showing patterns and links in the data, links in the flow of ideas through and across the data are often more readily understood and conveyed through memos and models. As Maxwell and Miller observe, both coding and connection are necessary.

	analytic, thinker	creative, innovative	strategic	careful, thorough	commitment, persistence
CASE271	1	1	0	0	0
CASE272	1	1	1	1	1
CASE273	1	1	0	0	0
CASE274	1	1	1	1	0
CASE275	0	1	1	1	0
CASE276	1	1	1	0	0
CASE278	0	1	1	1	0
CASE279	1	1	0	1	0
CASE28	0	1	1	1	0
CASE280	0	1	0	1	1

Figure 8.1 Case by variable matrix (case counts; Performance data)

	Case:University = New	Case:University = Green...	Case:University = Sand...
analytic, thinker	42	43	65
creative, innovative	39	42	57
curiosity, open mind	16	16	27
methodologically sound	38	25	32
strategic	28	13	22
substantive knowledge	24	23	39
technical skill	20	6	17

Figure 8.2 Profile matrix (case counts; Performance data)

	creative, innovative	careful, thorough	commitment, persistence	finisher	problem solver
impact	52	13	11	14	18
product	8	1	9	15	5
reputation	4	3	8	7	11

Figure 8.3 Pattern matrix (codes co-occur in response to same question; Performance data)

	commitment...	organised, ...	strategic	methodologi...	technical skill	substantive ...	analytic, thi...
commitment, persist...	133	20	8	7	4	15	27
organised, disciplined	20	74	8	7	4	7	16
strategic	8	8	63	5	4	7	12
methodologically so...	7	7	5	96	12	19	37
technical skill	4	4	4	12	44	6	9
substantive knowled...	15	7	7	19	6	86	33
analytic, thinker	27	16	12	37	9	33	151

Figure 8.4 Similarity matrix (codes co-occur in response to same question; Performance data)

Issues in interpreting variables created from qualitative codes

A number of concerns, additional to those discussed in the previous chapter, arise when qualitative data are converted for further statistical analysis. The manner in which text has been segmented and coding applied is one that has implications for statistical choices as well as researcher interpretation and reader understanding of the results. Qualitative coding can be applied in many and various ways, for example:

- using *a priori*, theoretically informed and/or emergent codes
- using broad or detailed codes, singly or in combinations
- using dimensionalised concepts or directional categories
- to free text ("meaning units"), potentially with overlapping passages, or non-overlapping predetermined segments defined by question structure or of fixed length
- in potentially related or mutually exclusive categories.

In qualitative analysis, multiple codes are often used on the same passage to capture different aspects of what is being said (e.g., for action and response), rather than creating a single code that picks up both aspects in one label. This is particularly so when a structured (taxonomic) system of codes is used in QDAS, for example, where all actions are listed separately from responses, as this facilitates interrogation of the data without creating a "viral" coding system (Bazeley, 2013; Bazeley & Jackson, 2013). The problem this creates for the most common form of transformation (a case by variable table) is that when codes that are applied to multiple passages in a variety of combinations are each transformed into separate quantitative variables, information about those combinations is lost. An alternative is to create a crosstabulation (matrix) of the connections within the qualitative software showing the frequency with which each pair of codes intersects (i.e., codes the same segment of data), and export that as a pattern matrix or as a series of blended variables. Each type of output is specific, however, in the kinds of analyses for which it can be used.

Additionally, codes vary in their specificity and their directionality (Sivesind, 1999). Because variables (codes) are the only medium for communicating information in a statistical dataset, in quantitative work they are necessarily precise in what they are conveying, particularly with regard to whether a category is being expressed in positive or negative terms. Some qualitative codes similarly are quite specific in what they are describing, but others are conceptually based, multidimensional, and multidirectional in that all text pertaining to a particular phenomenon will be assigned the same code, regardless of the way it is expressed (the latter may have been picked up in a second code applied to the same text). For example, all references to a personality trait, whether strong or weak, expressed favourably or unfavourably, might be coded together; or perhaps the issue of the character of a witness was raised in a legal case without identifying whether the judge had a positive or negative impression of that. This kind of coding is used because the analyst is then able to review the concept as a whole before thinking about what its different dimensions might be, or how it links to other aspects of behaviour or experience, or whether it varies depending on context. If the qualitative code is more like this, then the data coded there will usually need to be coded on to more specific codes, such as to reflect a positive or negative assessment, before being converted into quantitative variables (Boyatzis, 1998).

These examples of ways in which qualitative coding differs from coding for statistical purposes point to complexities in transformation that need to be carefully thought through before export, their implications kept in mind as analyses are conducted, and the solutions adopted explained to readers of reports. They also point to the critical importance for meaningful interpretation of the statistical analyses being conducted of retaining access to the qualitative database throughout the analysis and reporting process, and of referring to that database frequently to keep the statistical variables and analyses "grounded". This grounding is central to integration of the analyses when these methods are being employed.

Meeting data assumptions in transformed data

Transformed variables are at risk of not meeting several data-related assumptions for statistical analyses including (a) probability based sampling, (b) interval or ratio scaling of counts, and (c) independence of observations.

Conversion of coding for most statistical analyses (especially case-based inferential statistics) requires (1) a sufficient number of cases to provide statistically sound samples for the procedures being used, (2) cases selected on an equal (random and/or representative) probability basis rather than purposively if they are to represent a larger population in an unbiased way, and (3) preferably, that responses are normally distributed. Meeting these sampling and data assumptions, particularly that for probability-based inclusion, is often an issue for qualitative projects (and increasingly also for quantitative surveys). Use of descriptive and non-parametric statistics, simple visual displays, and techniques such as cluster or correspondence analysis to explore associations in the data rather than predict to wider populations, might therefore be more appropriate with exported coding. In situations where conclusions cannot be generalised to a larger population and must remain tentative, statistical analyses are sometimes useful nevertheless in suggesting leads for further analysis (Bernadi, Keim, & von der Lippe, 2007).

When frequencies (e.g., number of passages coded) rather than dichotomies (presence/absence) are being counted, counts from qualitative data might be better regarded as ordinal rather than interval data unless it can be ascertained that every instance is metrically comparable to every other instance. This issue is not exclusive to counts based on qualitative coding. There is no guarantee that every respondent in a survey, for instance, is interpreting and responding to the same categorical question or scale item in the same way: people respond differently depending on whether a scale goes from −5 to +5 or from 0 to 10, and on how it is set out on the paper or screen; nor are intervals in a scaled item necessarily equidistant, as demonstrated for example by Coast et al. (2008).

Observations (and consequently codes) from qualitative data, generally, are not independent. The person who experiences one emotion is equally likely to experience another, and may do so in relation to the same event. This lack of independence in observations means that statistics such as the chi-squared statistic (χ^2) cannot be used for a series of values in crosstabulated data, unless these were presented to participants as a series of alternatives of which only one could be chosen. Lack of independence in coding can also lead to multicollinearity in regression.

Issues in using and interpreting statistical tests of significance

Inferential statistics are based on probability theory, such that the accuracy with which a description or prediction can be made depends on the size of the sample being used (in absolute terms, rather than in proportion to the population), the degree of variability within the sample, and the likelihood that members of the sample are genuinely representative of the range of members in the population as a whole. Representativeness is usually effected using random selection to ensure that any member of the population has an equal chance of being selected in the sample. The probability theory behind inferential statistics derives from the central limit theorem. This basically states that if multiple random samples are taken from a population, the plotted mean values (averages) from those samples will cluster in a typical bell-shaped pattern around the true mean of the population, to create what is referred to as a "normal distribution". The bigger the sample, the more definitive – or tighter – is the clustering. Depending on the variability and the size of a particular sample, one can then predict with a similarly variable degree of accuracy what the mean of the population might be for the phenomenon being assessed, and whether this sample is likely to come from a (known) population. When one is comparing two groups in relation to a particular variable, the difference in means of the groups is assessed: if that difference in means is large in proportion to the variability within the groups, then the groups are usually assumed to have come from different populations with regard to the variable being measured. Assessing these predictions and assumptions is generally referred to as significance testing.

Significance testing in social research is based on the concept that one can reject a hypothesis of there being *no* difference (e.g., between a measure and what might be expected, between groups, or across time) – the "null hypothesis", but it is difficult or impossible to prove that there *is* a difference between groups or that there *is* an association between variables. The test results in a value (p) expressing the probability that the observed difference or association can be explained by chance alone. When the p-value is less than or equal to 0.05 – that is, there is just a 5% probability that the observed difference is actually due to chance – it is commonly accepted as reasonable to reject the hypothesis of no difference. A p-value higher than 0.05 indicates a higher than 5% probability that the observed difference or association is due to chance alone and the hypothesis of no difference cannot be rejected. Differences obtained and their associated p values will vary from sample to sample, even if the samples are consistent in size and drawn from the same population. This makes them an unreliable measure unless multiple replications of the study are conducted and similar results are obtained (Halsey, 2015; see also: Cumming, G. *Dance of the* p *values*, www.youtube.com/watch?v=5OL1RqHrZQ8 for a visual illustration of this).

A further problem is that researchers usually assume that rejection of the null hypothesis (e.g., that there are no differences between samples) implies that an "alternative hypothesis" suggesting there is a meaningful difference should then be accepted, *but the alternative hypothesis is still unproven*. As well as estimates from single samples being quite unreliable, the *p*-value indicates neither the magnitude nor the meaning of a difference. The *meaning* of a difference will be determined by context. For example, there will be times when a statistically significant difference (or association) between samples (or variables) will be found that is trivial in terms of practice (e.g., De Vito Dabbs et al., 2004), while a potentially meaningful difference will be reported as non-significant if the sample size is small.

De Vito Dabbs et al. (2004) modelled the experience of lung transplant recipients (LTRs) experiencing symptoms of acute rejection, a common complication of the procedure, especially during the first year of recovery. The ability of LTRs to recognise symptoms of rejection facilitates early detection and treatment, ensuring the condition does not become chronic and potentially fatal. The team explored both the physiological signals and the interpretive processes that motivated patients to recognise symptoms and to decide how to respond to them. For one of their analyses, they wanted to see if patient detection of symptoms varied depending on whether they were experiencing acute rejection, pulmonary infection, or no clinically significant rejection problems. On this issue, they concluded that "LTRs with acute rejection reported symptoms at a comparable rate [type and frequency] to LTRs with pulmonary infection and at a significantly higher rate (P < 0.01) than did LTRs without acute rejection, *but the magnitude of difference (2–3 items) was not likely to be clinically significant.*" Additionally, "no symptom or symptoms were found to uniquely characterise acute rejection" (2004: 141, 142, emphasis added).

Rather than using a *p*-value, the *likelihood* of a difference is better demonstrated using confidence intervals for the measures involved (Box 8.1), while the *magnitude* of the difference is better indicated by calculating the *effect size* (Box 8.2). Possible alternatives to standard statistical tests of significance include:

- for large samples, set a higher criterion (e.g., a cut-off for *p* of .01 rather than .05) to determine significance and confidence intervals – but this doesn't solve the problem of making alternative assumptions
- use visual displays such as bar or column graphs, in association with the statistics, to assist in interpreting differences, or scatterplots to visually assess the degree and pattern of relationship in a correlation or regression

- rely on assessing the effect size, rather than statistical significance
- use resampling methods or permutation testing instead (Box 8.3)
- evaluate the practical or clinical significance of the results obtained using other sources (literature or other data) in a mixed methods approach.

A fresh alternative being developed by Gorard and Gorard (2016) is to look for the counterfactual: how different would the data have to be – how many cases with different results would be required – in order to "lose" the finding (see Box 8.4)? They suggest the proposed method "is simple, standardised, and takes into account in one summary figure the sample size, the magnitude of the finding and the level of missing data" (2016: 484).

BOX 8.1

p-values and confidence intervals

Andy Field (2012) provides the following illustration of how the differences between *p*-values and confidence intervals might look (for the same data), and the different conclusions they might lead to. For example, a study with an experimental and a control group is used to look at the effect of a treatment, with 10 repetitions (or there were 10 different outcome variables measured). The statistical test results are shown in Table 8.1. The confidence intervals are shown in Figure 8.5. With just five of the 10 being significant, the *p*-values suggest the treatment is not necessarily helpful, whereas the "forest plot" of the means and confidence intervals confirm the value of the treatment.

Table 8.1 Statistical results from experiment

Study	Difference between Means (E-C)	t	p
Study 1	4.193	3.229	0.002*
Study 2	2.082	1.743	0.086
Study 3	1.546	1.336	0.187
Study 4	1.509	0.890	0.384
Study 5	3.991	2.894	0.006*
Study 6	4.141	3.551	0.001*
Study 7	4.323	3.745	0.000*
Study 8	2.035	1.479	0.155
Study 9	6.246	4.889	0.000*
Study 10	0.863	0.565	0.577

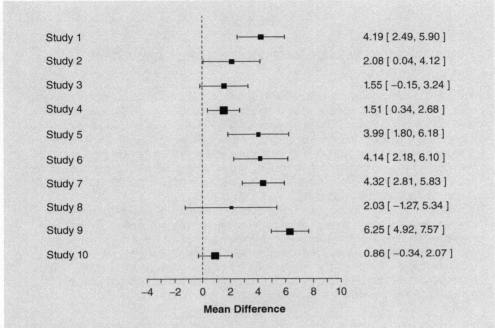

Figure 8.5 Confidence intervals for experiment

BOX 8.2

Calculating effect sizes

The calculation of the effect size is based on standard scores and therefore is not affected by the size of the units in the scale(s) being measured, nor (theoretically) by the size of the sample, although the latter claim was questioned by Gorard and Gorard (2016). The method of calculation of the effect size varies slightly for different situations, but for difference scores, for example, it is generally based on the measure of difference divided by a measure of standard deviation relevant to the statistical test that was used (Hojat & Xu, 2004). Guidelines regarding what are considered small, medium, and large effect sizes, indicating negligible, moderate, or crucial practical importance respectively, are usually based on Cohen's (1987) criteria. Readers are directed to Hojat and Xu for a straightforward guide to effect sizes, giving details of how to calculate effect sizes for different statistical tests. These authors also explain Cohen's criteria, which vary depending on whether it is difference scores or measures of association that are being assessed.

BOX 8.3

Permutation testing as an alternative approach for smaller, non-random samples

When analysing code counts, Dave Collingridge (2013) prefers permutation testing to both conventional and non-parametric statistical tests because of its reliability when used with small samples of the kind commonly generated from qualitative data. He argues that it requires fewer assumptions than parametric tests such as t-tests and analysis of variance, and it has more statistical power than non-parametric tests. Permutation testing is based in resampling theory: it involves taking repeated samples and then comparing the original statistic (e.g., a mean difference) with the distribution of the results from the resampling.

When permutation testing was first proposed theoretically as a distribution-free alternative to the t-test, it was not practical to implement, but modern computing means resampling analyses can be run in a few seconds. Collingridge explains the logic and outlines processes for generating permutation equivalents, including guidance for use of free computer software. He cautions that permutation testing, in the absence of a randomly drawn sample, is subject to the same limitations on generalisation to a population as other statistical methods.

BOX 8.4

Gorard and Gorard's method of assessing difference

General steps for assessing the "number of cases needed to disturb" a finding (NNTD), as devised by Gorard and Gorard (2016: 485), are set out below. They suggest "the number of counterfactual cases needed to disturb the original finding in this way becomes a standardised measure of the robustness of the original 'effect' size. The larger this number is, the safer and more trustworthy is the finding."

- Take the mean and standard deviation (SD) of the group with the most cases.

- If this mean is larger than that of the group with the fewer cases, then add the overall SD to that larger mean. If the mean of the group with the most cases is smaller than that of the group with the fewer cases, then subtract the overall SD from the smaller mean. This forms the standard "counterfactual" score.

- Calculate, by iteration or estimation, how many of these counterfactual cases can be added as cases to the smaller group before the difference between the group means [and the associated effect size] disappears or reverses. This is the "number (of counterfactual cases) needed to disturb" the result (assuming that there is no dropout). (Gorard & Gorard, 2016: 485)

The amount of attention paid to the NNTD depends on the size of the smallest group, the size of the difference between the groups, and the level of missing data. Further details regarding assessment and interpretation of the NNTD, and how to refine the calculation to deal with missing cases, are provided, with illustrative examples, in Gorard and Gorard (2016).

Statistical analysis options for a "qualitative" case by variable matrix

When codes derived from qualitative data are recorded separately for each case in the data (either as presence/absence of each code or as frequency of occurrence), then one has a case by variable matrix, such as that in Figure 8.1. These matrices might be based on counts of *a priori* categories, or on emergent coding categories generated during the process of the qualitative analysis. This type of matrix provides the basic form of data for most forms of statistical analysis, including descriptive reporting, comparative analyses, hypothesis testing, predictive modelling, and some exploratory analyses. It shares the same characteristics as data from a survey or questionnaire, and indeed, will often be combined with survey data for statistical analysis.

While it is conceivable (though unlikely) that counts for a case by variable matrix could be generated manually, using QDAS greatly simplifies the process. A matrix is created by specifying which cases are to be included in the rows (one case per row), while selected codes will define the columns (one code per column). When the intersections of cases and codes are computed by the QDAS to create the matrix, the data shown in the cells can reflect either presence or absence of particular codes (as specified by the columns) for each case, or the number of passages or words coded for each case, or perhaps an intensity score for each case. (Use of intensity scores requires a preliminary calculation or review to find an average or highest score for each code for each case.) The resulting matrix, after initial review, is then exported from the QDAS as a case by variable table, usually in Excel or SPSS format. It can then be opened in Excel and/or imported into a statistical program, or the new variables can be merged with an existing statistical database that includes descriptive demographic data for each case and/or responses to other survey questions or scaled scores, providing there is an identifying field for each case on which the different sources can be matched (even if some cases do not have both sources of data).

Increasingly, QDAS is providing direct access to a range of statistical procedures through either an additional module to the program (e.g., MAXQDA Analytics pro) or in a companion program (e.g., QDA Miner-SimStat)

Preliminary checking and description of variables
The first port of call for any statistician working with case data is to conduct some checks on the variables being used in the analysis, and then to generate descriptive

statistics for each variable included in the dataset, across all cases. This is required, firstly to ensure the data are "clean" (i.e., there are no stray values), and secondly, because knowledge of descriptive characteristics of the data underlies all other statistical analyses.

- For binary (0/1) variables, descriptive statistics are limited to frequency counts for the "1" cases (the number or percentage for whom the code was present).
- If the method of counting or scaling generated ordinal rather than interval measures (i.e., the distances between each pair of adjacent values are not necessarily the same), then descriptive statistics will include median and interquartile range as well as frequency counts.
- For variables based on frequency counts, intensity scores,[2] or scaled scores for which reasonably equal intervals can be assumed, it is useful to produce a graphical display of the distribution of scores for each variable first, as a visual clue to how the scores are distributed. For example, Figure 8.6 compares the distributions of the frequency of coded passages for two variables from the Performance data: note the skew for Ncreativity – a common feature of transformed data. Assuming a reasonably normal distribution, descriptive statistics would include means and standard deviations, but if these scores are skewed it would then be more appropriate to calculate the median and interquartile range for each variable. The normality of a distribution can be tested statistically as well as visually, if needed, using a Shapiro-Wilk test.

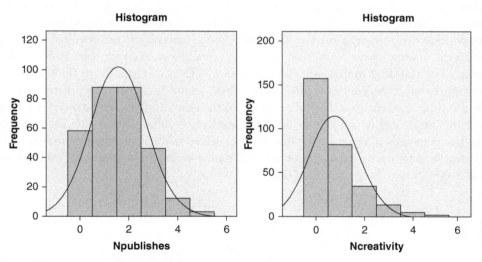

Figure 8.6   Distributions of two transformed variables from the Performance data

---

[2] As intensity scores have similar properties to frequency counts, unless there is a particular reason to differentiate them, I will refer only to frequency counts (the more common of the two) for the remainder of this chapter.

Descriptive statistics are similarly needed for demographic variables, whether these were recorded directly in the statistical database, or exported from the qualitative database. It is also important to look at the interrelationships between different demographic variables, most often using crosstabulations for each pair of variables. Not only does this give a better understanding of the data, but if two demographic variables are related, then this needs to be taken into account when conducting and interpreting further analyses involving one or other of those variables. For example, in the Performance data, level of qualification and seniority were closely related. As seniority was considered to be largely dependent upon level of qualification, and having completing some initial analyses where these produced similar results, attention was therefore focused on level of qualification as a factor in opinions expressed and further consideration of seniority was dropped.

All these preliminary checks on the characteristics of the sample and of the data being analysed are usually done statistically, but it can also be helpful to generate a range of visual displays of the data using either the statistical program or Excel. These might include comparative box plots, column and bar charts, as well as histograms. Visual displays and tables are sometimes helpful when reporting sample characteristics, and for reporting descriptive and comparative data from the main study variables.

Once these basic procedures have been applied and the characteristics of the transformed variables are known, options for further analysis include the usual range of parametric and non-parametric statistical procedures (parametric tests are those that assume the variables being included are normally distributed). Tabular and visual displays will also be useful in exploring relationships between variables, especially for samples that do not meet the assumptions of statistical procedures, as these are better able to make visible any non-conforming cases. Additional caution is required in choice of tests due to the less conventional source of the data, and the need for constant reference back to the qualitative data for interpretive meaning must be emphasised.

Profiling – who talks about what?

These analyses answer very basic questions relating to which kinds of cases provided data that were coded in particular ways. For example: was it healthier or less healthy women who most emphasised aspects of physical health when describing what well-being means in older age? Is age related to expressions of satisfaction with life? Do male and female academics have different views on what is important in research performance? These analyses contribute a global view of the relationships between the qualitatively coded data and demographic or other quantitative factors. They directly complement the analyses described in Chapter 6 where QDAS matrices were used to create comparative analyses using linked thematic and demographic data. Patterns of difference between subgroups revealed through tabular displays and statistical analyses of transformed data will often – *but not always* – reflect (or point to) differences also in the nuances of the matching qualitative data for those subgroups: "how many?" and "in what way?" are separate pieces of the overall puzzle being investigated when using mixed methods.

Crosstab*

			Institution			Total
			New	Greenfield	Sandstone	
Publishes	0	Count	28	9	21	58
		% within institution	27.2%	11.0%	19.1%	19.7%
	1	Count	75	73	89	237
		% within institution	72.8%	89.0%	80.9%	80.3%
Total		Count	103	82	110	295
		% within institution	100.0%	100.0%	100.0%	100.0%

Chi-Square Tests

	Value	df	Asymptotic Significance (2-sided)
Pearson Chi-Square	7.630[a]	2	.022
Likelihood Ratio	7.913	2	.019
Linear-by-Linear Association	2.080	1	.149
N of Valid Cases	295		

a. 0 cells (0.0%) have expected count less than 5. The minimum expected count is 16.12.

*Output from this analysis suggests academics at New University place less emphasis on publishing than those at Greenfield – but is this an element of university culture, or is it because staff at Greenfield include a higher proportion of PhD graduates –or a combination of the two? Contrasts for having a PhD or not are considerably more marked than those for university affiliation.

Figure 8.7 Questions raised in interpreting statistical output

Typical statistical procedures used for profiling include analysis of contingency tables using the chi-squared test of independence (Figure 8.7) or Fisher's exact test for categorical or ordinal variables; t-tests or analysis of variance (ANOVA) when one variable is categorical and the other is continuous; and Pearson product-moment correlations when both variables are continuous. There are non-parametric equivalents for each of the three tests involving continuous variables (Mann Whitney U, Kruskal-Wallis ANOVA, Spearman Rho, respectively) that are especially applicable for smaller samples (e.g., less than 20). When samples are larger, parametric tests provide a reasonable approximation (Norman & Streiner, 1994). This is a good time to be reminding readers that all statistical results, and especially those generated from qualitative data and based on rejection of a hypothesis of no differences, and should be treated as: (a) indicative of relationships that could be interesting to pursue, (b) needing to be interpreted for their meaningfulness in the light of both theory and data, and (c) *not* just a mechanical guide for what should or should not be considered a valid result, given rejection of a null hypothesis does not necessarily mean the alternative hypothesis is true.

The following cautions apply when carrying out these profiling or comparative analyses:

- When constructing contingency tables, it is usual to place the independent variable (i.e., demographic data in this case) in the columns and the dependent variable (values that the independent variable might affect) in the rows. Column percentages help with interpreting the results as it is natural to read, and thus compare, across the rows. The visual display in the table could well be more useful than the statistics that accompany it, especially if just one demographic subgroup stands out markedly from others (this can happen, for example, with over 60s compared to other age groups).
- If values for a variable used in a contingency table need to be combined to satisfy criteria for a minimum expected frequency (>5 in at least 80% of cells), then make sure the combinations can be justified theoretically rather than just being convenient.
- Always ask for *descriptives* (in Options) when using ANOVA, to help with understanding the differences between subgroups and to assess whether the differences really are meaningful.
- When doing correlations, also obtain scatterplots to help visualise the relationships being explored and to see whether a few unusual cases are skewing the results.

When the primary purpose of a study is comparative, then profiling might be all that is required to provide the primary results. This was the case in a study I undertook for a local council to explore the characteristics and experiences of people living in two different types of housing in a new estate. In most research, however, profiling is just one step along the way in analysis. It provides a view of the data that then prompts further, deeper questions that send the researcher back to their data to investigate other relationships between categories (in either or both the qualitative and quantified versions of the data): *How* does satisfaction with life change over the life course? *What is it about being female* that explains why women place more emphasis on the consequent benefits of research than men? Is it because ...?

Interrelatedness of codes within cases

The questions being asked here are about how often pairs of thematic codes (each now converted to variables) *both* appear somewhere within the data for each case. If one is there, does the other appear also? If one is absent, is the other absent also? But, because codes apply only to part of a data source (unlike demographics that are relevant to all the data from a case), the statistics cannot say whether they appeared together in the same context, or if one code necessarily has a meaningful association with the other. A simple co-occurrence for a case could be purely serendipitous. If the statistics reveal an association that might prove interesting, it can be necessary to return to the qualitative data to consider what the actual connection is between the codes (e.g., do they appear in the same contexts, or is one always followed later by the other?), to understand the interpretive significance of this potential relationship.

Statistical procedures and interpretive processes used for these analyses are the same as or similar to those used for profiling, with choices of which procedures to use largely governed by whether the thematic variables for each case were created using binary or frequency counts. Non-parametric tests based on binary or categorical variables set out in a contingency table include the chi-squared test of independence and Fisher's exact test, with assumptions regarding minimum expected values for each cell needing to be met for the chi-squared test. Most tests used for continuous variables (such as t-test and ANOVA) are parametric and assume the values for each variable are normally distributed. Use non-parametric equivalents or permutation testing (Collingridge, 2013) for smaller samples when this is not the case (with the same cautions as noted above).

Building predictive or explanatory models from qualitative coding

When an outcome is known (or supposed), a question arises as to how it came about, and whether future occurrences can be predicted from known factors or events that appeared to occur in association with (and prior to) previous experience of the outcome. Regression statistics provide the basis for these explanatory and predictive analyses, where one or more dichotomous or continuous variables (the independent variables) are assessed for their strength of association with a continuously scaled outcome (the dependent variable). If an association between the independent variables and the dependent variable is found it is often described in terms of the degree to which these variables "explain" the (variability in the) outcome, although it has to be remembered that this explanation is a hypothesis rather than a proof. An event that can help with prediction is not necessarily an explanation, as was shown in the example of the link between phone usage and cholera outbreaks in Rwanda described in the previous chapter (Eagle & Greene, 2014). Integrating these kinds of analyses with contextual and explanatory understanding gained through the original or additional qualitative data can help to further establish causality (Maxwell, 2004a, 2012a, 2012b) and prevent these kinds of misunderstandings built on simple associations. Again, quantitative and qualitative approaches to analysis work in a complementary way as they reveal both regularity or strength of association, and the mechanisms behind that association.

In a mixed methods study using variables created from qualitative data, it is likely that the outcome variable for a regression will be a continuous measure that was available from a quantitative source rather than having been converted from qualitative data. Mixed methods projects involving use of regression and derivatives of it will often use a dataset that combines variables from both quantitative and qualitative sources, or else use a purely quantitative dataset with results from it complemented by qualitative sources. Note that, unlike correlation, regression statistics presume a direction of influence between the variables being considered.

A group of insurance companies were interested in identifying predictors of the amount of compensation awarded by the courts to people injured in motor vehicle accidents, so they had a reasonable basis for negotiating out-of-court settlements and reducing costs for all concerned. Data available were the judgments made in a series of court cases – usually in the form of short documents in which the judge described what he saw as key features of the case and then specified an amount to be awarded to the claimant. Data in each judgment were coded for the "facts" of the accident and the injury (as perceived by the judge), and the judge's perception of other relevant detail such as the character and employability of the claimant, the truthfulness of the various witnesses regarding the nature of the injury, and so on. Coding for the presence or absence of key facts and features (as interpreted through qualitative analysis) could then be used together in a regression with the dollar figure awarded as the dependent variable, to provide guidance to the insurance companies.

In a regression, when there is just one predictor variable, its association with an outcome is best seen (and shown) in a scatterplot that also shows the line of best fit (Figure 8.8). This line is described by a simple equation $\hat{Y} = a + bX$ which allows predictions for new values of Y, based on new values of X, once the starting point (intercept) for the line is known ($a = Y$, when $X = 0$) and the slope or gradient of the line is known (value b, which is the amount by which $\hat{Y}$ increases for every one-unit increase in X).

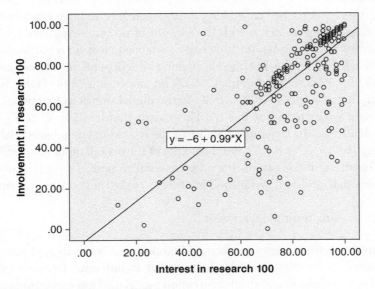

Figure 8.8 Scatterplot with regression line

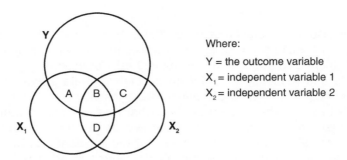

Figure 8.9   Regression modelling illustrated by a Venn diagram

When there are multiple independent variables, the capacity to predict is built on the strength of the combined association between the independent variables being considered and the outcome. It is also possible to determine how much each of those variables independently adds to the overall explanatory power of the regression model, taking into account their interrelationships with other variables in the model, thus helping to manage the complexity inherent in all social situations. In an evaluation design, where primary attention is on one or two key variables, the relative influence of other extraneous or possible moderating factors is partialled out using regression, as a form of statistical control. This can help to support conclusions about the key variable(s), for example where it is not possible to set up a control group.

Multiple regression is often modelled using a Venn diagram such as that in Figure 8.9. (based on Cohen & Cohen, 1975). In this model, the two predictor variables, A and B, together can account for (explain) the amount of variability shown in outcome Y that is included in the areas A + B + C, a figure usually presented as the statistic R^2. Alternatively, variable X_1 can be described as making an independent additive contribution to the model for Y, as shown in area A with the amount of variance explained by X_1 listed in summary tables as β_1 (the standardised regression coefficient for a particular variable). Similarly variable X_2 can be described as making an independent additive contribution to the model for Y, as shown in area C, etc. The model as a whole is described in the general equation: $\hat{Y}=a+b_1X_1+b_2X_2...b_nX_n$. In the model shown in Figure 8.9, X_1 and X_2 are themselves associated (area B + D). This means that if either X_1 or X_2 is removed from the calculation, the separate influence of the related independent variables will be changed (e.g., to A + B, or B + C) and the ability of the overall model to predict the outcome will be affected. Sometimes the additive contribution of a particular variable to the model is small, and so it is removed in order to make the model as parsimonious as possible.

Cautions in using multiple regression:

- Sometimes multiple regression is used inappropriately for an exploratory "fishing expedition" to see what variables best predict an outcome. Decisions about what variables to include in a multiple regression model *and* interpretation of the model obtained *should always* have a sound theoretical basis.

- The sample size required for a multiple regression is based on the number of variables being entered into the regression model: ideally there should be 20 or more cases per variable, and essentially there should be a minimum of 10 cases per variable.

Three or four assessors reviewing each application to the Australian Research Council (ARC) Discovery grants scheme rate both the proposed project and the researcher(s), with researcher(s) assessed primarily on their "track record". Regression coefficients were calculated for 173 solo applicants across five discipline groups to assess the contribution of different aspects of track record to the assessor score for researcher excellence, relative to demographic and other contextual factors. Track record was calculated by counting (separately), for the previous two years, the number of solo or first authored books, articles/chapters, and publications marked as relevant to the topic, and the number of successful applications for ARC and other sources of funding in the previous three years. Track record and demographic variables together explained 26.9% of the variance of mean assessors' scores for the quality of the researcher, with academic status, number of books, and number of relevant publications each making independent contributions. All variables other than these and the appointment type of the investigator could be dropped from the model without loss of explanatory power (Table 8.2). Perhaps surprisingly, the academic status of the researcher (full professor or not) made a major contribution to the variance of the assessors' scores, independently of and in addition to the contribution of the retained measures of publication record.

Table 8.2 Contributions of professional and personal variables to assessor ratings for quality of the researcher (173 solo ARC applicants)

Variable	b	SE	β	t	p(t)
Academic status	7.05	1.29	.39	5.46	<.001
Books	1.85	.71	.18	2.61	.010
Relevant publications	.41	.13	.22	3.30	.001
Research oriented appointment	3.22	1.47	.15	2.18	.031

Source: Bazeley, 1998: 447, Table 3

Note: $R^2 = 25.4$, $F(4,166) = 14.13$, $p < .001$

Logistic regression or variations of it (e.g., probit analysis, survival analysis) follow similar principles. These are used if the dependent variable Y is binary, that is, it has the values of 0 or 1 only, while multinomial logistic regression is used when there are more than two categories of outcome. Logistic regression can be especially useful when treating expression of a theme as a dichotomised outcome variable. Health researchers often convert results of a logistic regression into odds ratios, to describe the likelihood of an outcome given presence of a predictive variable (such as for smoking and lung cancer) while controlling for other factors.

Arnon and Reichel (2009) set out to assess what makes a good teacher in the eyes of the general public in Israel, and to consider the role of gender and cultural differences to those conceptions. Their telephone survey data comprised both open and closed (scaled) questions, but uniformly high positive responses across the set of scaled questions meant they focused their attention on the qualitative responses to the open questions. From these they derived 10 main categories of response, grouped into three core categories describing teaching knowledge, teacher–student relationships, and ethical and moral qualities of a "good teacher". These were converted to binary codes for each person, based on their presence or absence in their qualitative responses, to be used as dependent variables in a model built using logistic regression. Ethnicity was found to impact on the core categories of teacher–student relationships (emphasised more by the Israeli Jews) and ethical person and educator (emphasised more by the Israeli Arabs) – reflecting cultural expectations and values. Neither gender, nor the interaction of gender and ethnicity, made significant contributions to the models for any of the teacher qualities. While their qualitative data suggested that "the Israeli public judges the good teacher less from a professional standpoint and more on an individual and personal basis" (2009: 189), the authors cautioned against seeing this as a general overall conclusion, as the professional qualities of the teacher had been equally valued in the responses given to the scaled questions.

Cases where the actual values diverge markedly from those predicted by the regression line can be identified from plots of the residuals. The mixed methods researcher, with access to original case data, has a particular advantage in being able to explore these in the qualitative data, to gain an understanding of how or why they differ from the pattern shown by the other cases – often providing a vital clue to underlying processes (this strategy will be discussed further in Chapter 11).

Multiple regression provides the theoretical and practical foundation for a whole range of statistical procedures that derive from it (e.g., factor analysis, path analysis, structural equation modelling, multilevel modelling). Explanations of these extend well beyond the scope of this book. When these procedures are used in a mixed methods project, it is typically with quantitatively sourced data, or perhaps with a dataset created from combining sources. The key to integration when that is the case relies not only in referring back to any qualitative sources used but also in sourcing complementary qualitative data that will add to the explanatory value of the regression-based equations and results.

Amabile, Barsade, Mueller, and Staw (2005) explored if and how affect was associated with creativity at work for 222 employees working in 26 innovative project teams in seven companies across three industries. The researchers gathered daily diary records for periods of nine to 38 weeks. These included scaled measures and self-ratings of mood, and two non-directive free-response questions asking for a description of a key event in the day relating to their work, and any other comments. The narratives were coded for affect and broken into separate events (average 5+ in each), with each of the 63,789 events then coded for creative thought and problem solving by trained coders, with high levels of reliability. Fifty-six percent of employees recorded 364 creative events. Lagged analyses were used to predict a given day's creativity from the previous day's affect data, and also to check the relationship between a day's creativity and the following day's affect, controlling for the current day's affect/ creativity and demographic variables. Multilevel modelling assessed unique variance associated with project teams and companies. These analyses showed significant positive links between consistent positive mood on one day to crea- tivity on the next, with the incubation effect lasting up to two days, and no effect from creativity on one day to mood on the next day. Detailed qualitative analyses of the creative events focused especially on those events where emo- tions were described in direct association with the event.

Hypothesis testing and causal explanation

Variables created through transforming qualitative data are sometimes used inde- pendently or combined with quantitative data sources in an experimental design or a design evaluating an intervention. Designs using clearly delineated conditions (e.g., with experimental and control groups) and their associated statistical procedures that test the relationship between these conditions and measured outcomes are gen- erally considered better able to support causal explanations than studies relying on statistical procedures based purely on the covariation of outcome variables with pre- sumed input variables. Regardless of the statistics used, understanding the (theoretical/qualitative) mechanism or process that brings about those demonstrated associations between inputs and apparent consequences remains critical to generating valid conclusions.

Reznitskaya et al. (2001) used transformed qualitative coding combined with an existing quantitative database in an experimental test of the impact of train- ing through classroom discussions involving collaborative reasoning on children's argumentation strategies. Following training, children wrote indi- vidual persuasive essays based on a different problem from that discussed in

(Continued)

(Continued)

training. The essays were coded for the number of idea units that included a formal argument device or use of textual evidence. Analysis of covariance (ANCOVA) was used with a normalised distribution to demonstrate that having an argument schema developed through training enabled students to consider and present more arguments, independently of socioeconomic status or vocabulary skills. Detailed text analyses were then conducted on a purposive sample of essays to examine and illustrate argumentation strategies used by the children, revealing that "collaborative reasoning students are generally more successful [than untrained students] at generating and articulating an argument, considering alternative perspectives, marshalling text information, and effectively utilizing certain formal argument devices" (2001: 171).

Cohen (1968) has presented evidence for the equivalence of analysis of variance and multiple regression using dummy (0/1) variables to represent the experimental and control groups. Using regression allows for partialling out the impact of additional or extraneous variables and gives the considerable advantage of being able to calculate weights (*b*) for each variable to allow for optimal prediction. Ultimately, however, managing threats to validity in the *design* of the study is more important for establishing and warranting causal hypotheses than the statistics chosen for analysing the data (Gorard, 2013).

Other multivariate strategies using case by variable data

A range of other multivariate statistical strategies have been suggested for working with mixed method data that includes variables derived from qualitative coding or mixed qualitative and quantitative sources. Some are briefly described here.

Cluster analysis is an exploratory multivariate strategy that will be explored further in the next chapter. When carried out using a case by variable data table, it is often used for clustering cases, to identify groups within a sample that share characteristics that make them different from other groups. Alternatively it can be run as a way of grouping codes (concepts), to see the patterns of association between them or perhaps to reduce the number of concepts being considered.

Correspondence analysis is also an exploratory multivariate strategy that will be explored further in the next chapter. It is designed to map the relationship between the values of two codes, or two sets of codes (often values of a demographic variable in relation to aspects of beliefs or experiences, etc.) in a low dimensional space.

Principal components analysis (PCA), like cluster analysis, is a data reduction strategy. Unlike cluster analysis, which works with categorical variables, PCA is used with correlated continuous variables to identify a set of components or dimensions that summarise the dataset (with the data set out either in a case by variable matrix, or as a reflected matrix of correlations). Components are identified in order of importance.

Exploratory factor analysis (EFA) also is a data reduction strategy working with correlated continuous variables, but with the goal of identifying a set of latent variables or constructs which explain the observed variables. Interpretation and choice of solution is more reliant on the researcher's theoretical perspective than is the case with PCA.

Latent trait analysis is, effectively, factor analysis for binary variables. *Latent class analysis* classifies binary variables in a similar way to cluster analysis where the number of clusters is known, for example in relating clusters from a range of symptoms to likely diseases.

Curve estimation is an exploratory procedure to identify the best fit of a nonlinear functional relationship between an independent and a dependent variable (usually just one of each). Based on goodness-of-fit measures, a statistical package will select the best performing model from a range of transformation possibilities, and provide a graphical plot. Good understanding of the case(s) being explored is critical for interpretation of the resulting graphs.

Intra-sample statistical analysis (ISSA) is designed to support qualitative conclusions in situations where a large number of observations are available from a small number of cases. Any of a range of statistical techniques might be applied (e.g., to assess the elements in a grounded theory in relation to an outcome), treating the observations rather than the cases as the units of analysis, including the cases as fixed effects, and using variables derived from the qualitative coding of those observations. The major advantage of analysing in this way is that patterns of association can be detected that would be obscured by use of summary statistics for individual cases. Statistical generalisation is limited, however, to the potential population of observations from this sample under the same conditions; analytic generalisation, as with qualitative methods in general, is potentially broader, and with this type of analysis, claims based on qualitative observations are warranted by rigorous statistical analysis (Shaffer & Serlin, 2004).

Rasch analysis is a form of item-response theory used to build unidimensional scales in which each individual item contributes equally and independently, and redundant items are eliminated. The total score can therefore be calculated from a simple sum of item ratings; total scores and scores for individual items form interval scales; and scores for missing items can be more reliably calculated (www.rasch.org/rmt/rmt213d.htm; www.rasch-analysis.com/item-analysis.htm).

In her doctoral study modelling the relationship between whether an organisation's identity orientation was individualistic, relational, or collectivistic and the way in which those organisations related to their internal and external stakeholders, Shelley Brickson (2005) used data primarily drawn from qualitative sources

(Continued)

(Continued)

which were then transformed and used in multilevel modelling. Four qualitative and one quantitative question (each with multiple components) were coded and scored to quantify both external and internal identity orientation for a sample of 1126 individuals from 88 organisations in two diverse industries. Her article provides a very detailed description of the coding process and of the manner in which scores for both external and internal identity orientation were calculated and refined for each individual and each organisation – and then of how the scores were used. In reviewing her use of transformed data, she described it as providing a balance between undertaking intensive case studies and the limited understanding provided by explicit quantitative measures.

Concluding remarks

This chapter has demonstrated ways of conducting two complementary types of analyses using data derived from the same data source(s), made possible by the transformation of data from one type to another. It has pursued the process of transforming qualitative coding into statistical data founded on, but going beyond, the simple generation of counts. The case by variable tables produced from tabulating counts allow for answering additional questions through further statistical analyses. Production of descriptive, comparative, relational, and predictive statistical analyses all become possible. These strategies contribute to analysis of mixed methods data primarily through the clarification, confirmation, or extension of patterns, processes, and trends initially identified through the qualitative analyses. Readers were reminded, as always, to revisit and reconsider the qualitative data from which statistical analyses have been derived as part of the analysis and interpretation of those statistics.

Issues that arise when interpreting results from statistical testing were noted, as were special considerations that need to be attended to when using data that have been converted from a qualitative database. The issue of satisfying the assumptions of inferential statistical tests regarding probability based sampling and normality of distribution of the included variables has been of particular concern – a problem that will be addressed in a different way in the next chapter as attention is turned to more exploratory types of analyses.

Further reading

Using transformed data

Sandelowski et al. (2009) review a range of issues and assumptions involved in quantitising qualitative data to generate counts for use in statistical analyses.

Fakis et al. (2014) review 14 studies using transformed qualitative data.

Schulenberg (2007) describes the technical issues involved in her use of transformed data in association with qualitative data gathered in an observational study that examined the processes involved in police decision making.

Srnka and Köszegi (2007) provide guidelines for rigorous transformation of qualitative data, with an example of using transformed data in an exploratory and theory-testing study of business negotiation processes.

Weaver-Hightower (2014) use transformed data in their study of policy development regarding boys' education in which they compare differences between submissions from informants and the committee's final report to identify influence; they then identify and explore 13 cases that were particularly influential.

Statistical procedures and principles

Howell (2014) offers a readable text covering basics in statistics for those who might think (like students) that statistics is something you consider only when you really have to.

Alternatively: as Howell himself suggests, when you're not sure about a statistical concept or procedures "just google it" and you are likely to find multiple options for further information and investigation.

Field (2018) teaches statistics from beginner to advanced levels in a humorous and user-friendly way through the use of the popular IBM SPSS package. Parallel books are available also for SAS and the R statistics programs. His "Discovering statistics" website (www.discoveringstatistics.com/) carries free handouts, tutorials, extracts from his books, videos and blogs on statistical subjects.

Tabachnick and Fidell (2013) is a comprehensive text covering multivariate statistics, focusing on when, why, and how to do various statistical analyses, for those with a limited knowledge of higher-level mathematics, supplemented by SPSS and SAS syntax and output for each procedure.

Collingridge (2013) provides a clear and detailed description of non-parametric and permutation statistics that can be used for dichotomised qualitative data, including how to run these in R (a free statistical program).

Gorard (2015) challenges standard approaches to hypothesis-driven statistical testing.

9

INTEGRATION THROUGH DATA TRANSFORMATION 2: EXPLORATORY, BLENDED, AND NARRATIVE APPROACHES

CHAPTER OVERVIEW

Transforming qualitative data for exploratory multivariate analyses

Profile, pattern, and similarity matrices from qualitative data

Exploratory multivariate statistical analyses for case and matrix data

Cluster analysis in statistical software

Multidimensional scaling

Correspondence analysis

Use of exploratory multivariate analyses in mixed methods research

Building descriptive and narrative accounts from numeric data

Methodological purposes

Mapping transformation from numeric data to qualitative description and narrative

Profiling individuals, samples, and groups based on quantitative data

Building narrative from quantitative data

Blended analyses and consolidated databases: coding, conversion, and combination working together

Mapping blended and consolidated approaches

Categorising data to create a consolidated database

Creating and using blended variables

Concluding remarks

Further reading

This chapter continues the story of data transformation in the service of mixed methods research, where integration is focused more on blending approaches to analysis than on combining sources. Attention is given first to the potential for using variables created from coded qualitative data, along with other quantitative variable data, in exploratory multivariate analyses, including cluster analysis, multidimensional scaling, and correspondence analysis. These types of analyses are used, broadly speaking, to reveal the associative and dimensional structure of data. In these analyses, visual displays become very important as a guide to interpretation of the statistically generated results.

The next section of the chapter then reverses the process of transformation already described. Event history analysis, cluster analysis, and related quantitative-statistical techniques are used to develop descriptive or narrative text from statistical data. Attention is then turned to strategies for consolidating or blending data drawn from both quantitative and (transformed) qualitative sources to create new variables, often "unlocking" an analysis in the process.

Transforming qualitative data for exploratory multivariate analyses

Matrices (crosstabulations, contingency tables), with their related statistical procedures, have always been a basic tool within statistical software, for use in survey analysis. In that environment, they reveal patterns of relationships between pairs of variables, or allow for comparisons of patterns of response for different subgroups within the sample. In qualitative work, matrix displays can reduce information from complex field notes and interviews into a visual display that similarly provides comparative data, or helps to make evident patterns or regularities in the data.

In the first part of this chapter, the focus shifts to application of profile, pattern, and especially similarity matrices that are built within the qualitative software in exploratory analyses using multivariate techniques. When matrices are built within the qualitative software, a count in a cell represents the number of times the intersecting row and column values coded exactly the same segments of data. This gives a much more precise measure of the connection between those codes than a standard case by variable table, which shows only that codes were each applied somewhere in the data for the case. The QDAS generated matrices therefore provide an ideal basis for cluster analysis, multidimensional scaling, and correspondence analysis – all exploratory strategies that are able to make use of existing matrices. A primary goal of all these exploratory procedures is to reveal the underlying groups or the associative or dimensional structure within the qualitative data. As an integrative strategy, qualitative data are being transformed into a format that will facilitate exploratory and then further statistical analyses in a way that depends on, yet goes well beyond what is possible if working only with the original qualitative database. Insights gained from these statistical analyses of the coded material can be related back to the qualitative database, (a) to verify and strengthen the interpretation of the statistical results, and (b) to extend the qualitative analyses into new directions.

Profile, pattern, and similarity matrices from qualitative data

The reader was introduced briefly to these three types of matrices in the previous chapter. Now it is time to provide more detail on how they are constructed from the coding of the qualitative data and how they will be used for exploratory work.

Profile matrices are those in which a set of topic, conceptual, and/or thematic codes (usually defining the rows of the matrix) are viewed in relation to demographic and/or other quantitative variable data (usually defining the columns), thus providing a profile of which subgroups of the sample provide data concerning particular topics or themes ("who talks about what"), as shown in Figure 9.1. Because attribute (demographic/variable) data are applied to whole cases within QDAS, a profile matrix amounts to a summary of the separate attribute-theme connections that can also be computed from a case by variable matrix. The advantage of starting from a profile matrix is that it immediately shows comparisons across demographic or other categories for a whole set of codes at once, and each cell in the table has easily accessible associated qualitative data that is specific to that particular topic or theme code for the defined subgroup, rather than all the data for the case that includes that code. Profile matrices can be used for correspondence analysis, which shows visually how the topic codes relate to the demographic (or other quantitatively defined) subgroups, usually as a two-dimensional map.

Pattern matrices, similarly, are used to discern patterns of association or difference across a set of codes, by looking at their associations with another set of codes, in order to explore, for example, if certain beliefs are associated with particular actions, or how emotions vary in relation to experience. When a pattern matrix is created in qualitative software, the data in any cell indicates that the code defining the row for that cell *occurred in the same context* (usually specified as intersecting on the exact same data) as the code defining the column. Thus, again, it provides a highly refined view of the relationships between codes. For example, in Figure 9.2, the table is showing how often academics specifically linked each of the column variables (e.g., creativity in research) with research impact, compared to publishing and reputation. Because the "shape" of this matrix is similar to that for a profile matrix, similar kinds of exploratory statistical analyses are possible, but in this case

		Case:University = New ▽	Case:University = Green... ▽	Case:University = Sand... ▽
analytic. thinker	▽	42	43	65
creative, innovative	▽	39	42	57
curiosity. open mind	▽	16	16	27
methodologically sound	▽	38	25	32
strategic	▽	28	13	22
substantive knowledge	▽	24	23	39
technical skill	▽	20	6	17

Figure 9.1   Profile matrix (case counts; Performance data)

	creative, innovative ▽	careful, thorough ▽	commitment, persistence ▽	finisher ▽	problem solver ▽
impact ▽	52	13	11	14	18
product ▽	8	1	9	15	5
reputation ▽	4	3	8	7	11

Figure 9.2 Pattern matrix (codes co-occur in response to same question; Performance data)

they will be helping the analyst to discern and clarify patterns of association between codes based on specific instances of their co-occurrence within the qualitative data.

Similarity matrices created within qualitative software also are based on cell data that indicates the row and column codes occurred in the same context (e.g., were intersecting), while the diagonal on the table will show the total number of finds for each code (Figure 9.3). The difference from other matrices is that the codes defining the rows and columns are the same, and so the data in the lower left triangle of the matrix is reflected in the upper right triangle, rather like a frequency version of a correlation matrix. Similarity tables are ideal for use in multidimensional scaling (MDS), which is especially designed to identify structural dimensions in data. They can also be used in cluster analysis as an alternative to a case by variable table. At times, MDS and cluster analysis are combined.

For pattern and similarity matrices, each cell usually shows either (a) the frequency count of the number of times each pair of row and column variables intersect (i.e., code the same passage) within the data being considered, or (b) a count of the number of cases for which such intersections are found, to give a measure of the proximity or similarity of the two variables. As these intersections of codes usually apply to meaning units (passages) within each qualitative source rather than to whole sources or whole cases, the matrices must be created within the qualitative software where those intersections are recorded. Along with the count of intersections, the qualitative software provides the reader with access to the underlying text behind the numbers showing for the cell. Use this initially to check that the connections are not accidental. Later it will add to the interpretation of meaning.

Intersections (Boolean AND) between codes are the most commonly sought (and most reliable) data for cell content, but alternatives are available for pattern and similarity matrices, for example, locating data in which a pair of codes occur within a

	commitment... ▽	organised, ... ▽	strategic ▽	methodologi... ▽	technical skill ▽	substantive ... ▽	analytic, thi... ▽	creative, inn... ▽
commitment, persist... ▽	133	20	8	7	4	15	27	22
organised, disciplined ▽	20	74	8	7	4	7	16	11
strategic ▽	8	8	63	5	4	7	12	10
methodologically so... ▽	7	7	5	96	12	19	37	27
technical skill ▽	4	4	4	12	44	6	9	8
substantive knowled... ▽	15	7	7	19	6	86	33	15
analytic, thinker ▽	27	16	12	37	9	33	151	43
creative, innovative ▽	22	11	10	27	8	15	43	138

Figure 9.3 Similarity matrix (codes co-occur in response to same question; Performance data)

specified proximity to each other (e.g., NEAR in the same paragraph). Counts based on proximities rather than intersections require extra care in specifying how the counts are constructed; verification of the procedure used through checking the associated text in a sample of cells is strongly advised.

Matrices of all types, once created, are usually exported in Excel format ready for importing into statistical software capable of analysing this type of matrix data. Increasingly, QDAS is making it possible to conduct and create displays from the multivariate analyses within the native software suite (QDA Miner being the most sophisticated in this regard). If analyses are conducted within QDAS, with results shown as a display without showing the matrix on which it is based, extra care needs to be taken to understand the basis on which the program has created the display, as it could be different from that on which a matrix table designed for export would be created (e.g., consult the Help files or other supporting documentation). For example, NVivo provides a choice as to whether the connections between codes are based on shared words in the coded text, or shared coding patterns (common patterns of other codes intersecting with the selected codes). Each can provide interesting results but neither is the same as an exported table showing the frequency of actual intersections of the target codes.

Before putting the qualitative software aside (temporarily) and moving to the statistical analyses, time should be taken to check the finds and ensure that table cells contain the kind of data that are expected to be there. Depending on the nature of the data being dealt with, it can be useful also to interpretively review the text in the cells of the matrix and perhaps also to make summaries of cell content.

Exploratory multivariate statistical analyses for case and matrix data

Exploratory multivariate statistical techniques, including cluster analysis, correspondence analysis, and multidimensional scaling, have been fruitfully applied to quantitative matrices built from coded qualitative data. They go beyond statistics that consider single variables or pairs of variables to consider interrelationships based on the patterning of many variables simultaneously. Results showing these interrelationships are presented in visual displays as well as statistically to reveal otherwise undetected associations, structure, or dimensions in the data, thus adding value to the qualitative analyses. Interpretive results built from the combined evidence are, in turn, reported in the form of descriptive narratives supported by visual or statistical evidence, demonstrating the recursiveness often present in mixed methods analysis and reporting.

Exploratory multivariate techniques are based on investigating and describing patterns of relationships between variables expressed in distance measures, rather than being designed to describe or predict from specific variables to a population or to test hypotheses. As they make fewer assumptions about the data (e.g., regarding linearity, normality, sampling), they are especially appropriate for data drawn from qualitative samples and analyses. Specification of the type of distance or proximity to be calculated by the software for these types of analyses is impacted by the source and derivation of the data being used, however; that is, whether they are binary, nominal, ordinal, or interval measures.

The statistics can be calculated from case by variable tables, as noted earlier, but if the specificity offered by creating matrices within qualitative software is wanted, then pattern or similarity matrices can be used as a starting point for the different statistical procedures. These kinds of analyses are described as exploratory for a reason – not only do they explore structure where there is no prior theory describing that, but the process of generating them is also rather exploratory: it can be acceptable to experiment with the various options available, and see which gives the most interpretable or useful result (Bartholomew et al., 2002).

Cluster analysis in statistical software

Hierarchical cluster analysis is a descriptive classification technique used with a data matrix in which one set of objects (cases or variables) are grouped by comparing the values for each across a set of associated objects, as displayed across the other axis of the matrix. It can organise large amounts of complex quantitative or transformed qualitative data into a manageable number of clusters, to use for profiling or for further statistical analyses, and help to identify outliers in small samples (Dymnicki & Henry, 2012). While groups based on variation in a single variable (such as confidence) across values of another variable (such as education) are straightforward to interpret, those based on multiple interrelated variables are less so. This is where cluster analysis comes to the rescue, by calculating distances (proximity, or degrees of similarity or dissimilarity) between all pairs of variables being considered, to create a similarity matrix. If a case by variable table or profile or pattern matrix is being used as the basis for the clustering, it is necessary to choose which set of variables (row or column) is being clustered. The software then creates a similarity matrix from the case by variable data as step one of the processing. If one starts with a similarity matrix, rows and columns are the same, and the initial set of cell data is predetermined by the method of extraction from the qualitative database. Processing from that point on follows the same principles regardless of source, but case-based data will generate different results from matrix data, because they are based on both codes being present somewhere in the case, whereas matrix data are based on co-occurrences within specific data segments.

Based on this constructed (or imported) similarity matrix, objects with a similar pattern of values are paired again, to create a new (now smaller) similarity matrix, then these pairs are joined again with other similar pairs to make a further reduced matrix, those clusters are then joined with others, and so on until a minimum set of distinctive clusters is reached. The progressive clustering of the objects is recorded in an agglomeration table, with the composition of clusters at each stage in the process shown graphically in an icicle plot (Figure 9.4).

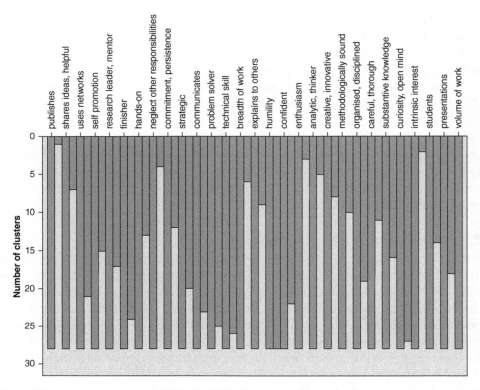

Figure 9.4   Icicle plot showing progressive agglomeration (clustering) of variables (performance data, SPSS output)

Clustering for ordinal variables (such as counts from qualitative data) is commonly based on (a) nearest neighbour/single linkage methods, or (b) furthest neighbour/complete linkage methods. When pairs or clusters are created, nearest neighbour methods use the smallest of their values in determining any further pairing, while furthest neighbour methods use the greatest. Often these methods will give different results in terms of what objects are clustered together, and always in the distances between those clusters. If the distances between the original objects can be treated as scaled (interval) rather than ordinal data, then rather than taking extreme (nearest or furthest) values, average, median, or centroid values for each cluster could be used as the distance measure for further clustering. Another alternative for scaled data, when scores across variables for a pair of objects might differ in absolute terms but have similar profiles, is to use Pearson correlation values as a measure of distance. For binary (0/1) variables, which are common in transformed data, Euclidian distances are created based on the proportion (%) of variables (or cases) on which two objects match, or if only the 1 values are to be considered (because the 0s mean different things for different variables) then Jaccard's coefficient is used. Other more specialised methods of calculating distances are also available (Bartholomew et al., 2002).

Alternative approaches to clustering include hierarchical divisive methods which start with a single cluster and then progressively divide it, based on similar mathematical principles to agglomeration methods (this is used extensively in market segmentation studies); and non-hierarchical methods (e.g., k-means clustering) in which the number of clusters wanted is pre-specified and membership of groups is iteratively constructed to ensure the smallest distance to cluster means, such that variation within each group is less than that between the groups. Sometimes different methods are used together, for example, using a hierarchical method to determine an approximate number of clusters followed by an iterative non-hierarchical method "to improve, refine and, ultimately, optimise the cluster results" (Uprichard, 2009: 137).

Final results of the clustering processes are presented graphically as a dendrogram (e.g., Figure 9.5) with links, in the data being shown, indicating similarities in academics' descriptions of high-performing researchers. A similarity matrix with counts of cases in which codes co-occurred in response to the same question was specified as the input data, and in this case, using the "furthest neighbour" option gave the clearest result. The dendrogram groups the objects being clustered and shows the distances at which they are joined (in SPSS these are rescaled for display purposes). Short distances suggest stronger links, long distances separate clusters. Sometimes clustering is clear, often it is ill-defined. In Figure 9.5, academics describing high performing researchers often used the descriptors *confident* and *humility* in close association, *breadth of work* was associated with *technical skill*, *self-promotion* with *using networks*, being motivated by *intrinsic interest* was associated with being *curious*, and so on. The descriptors, overall, clustered into six main groups (including *publishes* as a solo outlier) that share some similarities with my earlier conceptual analysis of the qualitative data (Bazeley, 2010b), although they are not identical to that.

Clustering objects based on coding of qualitative data is generally best used in an exploratory manner, to provoke ideas, rather than as explanatory evidence of association. Bartholomew et al. (2002: 22), among others, recommend trying different methods, with the usefulness of the method "to be judged by what it produces rather than by the assumptions made along the way". Similar results from different methods give confidence that they are reflecting an aspect of data structure, different results prompt further investigation as to why they differ.

Cluster analysis can be both a useful and a powerful tool, but its use must be tempered with common sense and in-depth knowledge of the raw data. Interpretation is only as good as the procedures that precede it (i.e., code development and application), and applying structure to an unfamiliar data set will have little meaning for even the most seasoned researcher. Used properly and solidly grounded in the data, cluster analysis can help provide meaningful structure to QDA and thematic interpretation. (Guest & McLellan, 2003: 198–199)

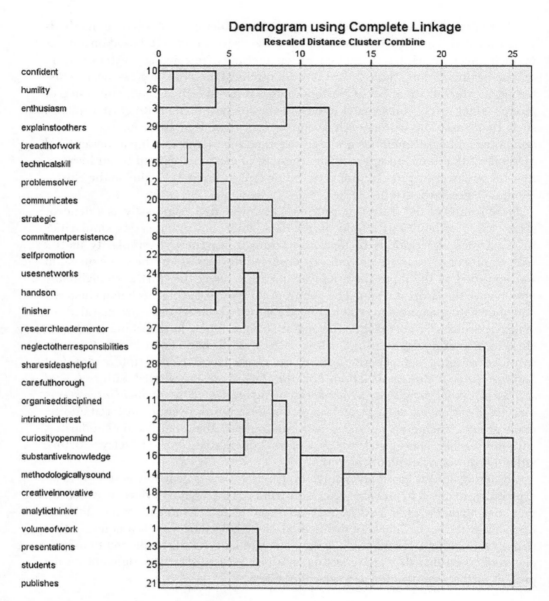

Figure 9.5 Dendrogram showing clustering of descriptors for researchers (Performance data, SPSS output)

> Cluster analysis, based on co-occurring words or codes within sources or codes, can be conducted within Provalis software (QDA Miner and WordStat) and NVivo (Figure 9.6).

Multidimensional scaling

Multidimensional scaling (MDS), like factor analysis, is designed to detect underlying dimensions in data that can account for similarities or distances between objects

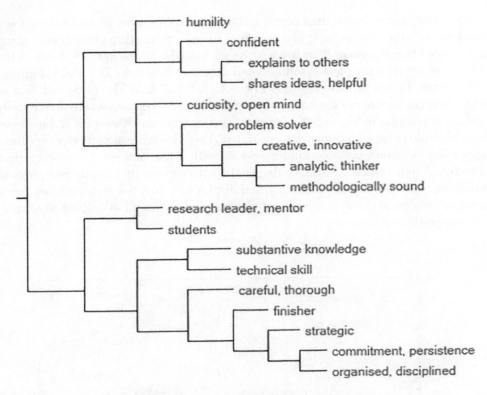

Figure 9.6 Codes clustered by word similarity in NVivo (Performance data)

(cases, codes, variables), but unlike factor analysis, MDS does not require normally distributed, linear variables. Distances derived from a reflected matrix are used to plot objects in multidimensional space. This space is rotated to find a meaningful solution, revealing dimensional axes and possibly also groupings of points that will be of interest.

A similarity matrix derived from coded qualitative data is ideal for analysis using MDS based on counts. The number of times each of the row and column codes intersect or co-occur within a defined context in the qualitative data is recorded in the relevant cells, thus giving a measure of similarity between each pair of codes (as in Figure 9.3). It is also possible to create a similarity matrix based on proximities of codes within cases using the case by variable matrix (as in the first step for clustering). Although they contain "noise", this could be relevant where it is likely to be meaningful that both codes are present regardless of where they appear within the case, but unrealistic to expect those codes to be on exactly the same passages of text. Distance matrices can also be constructed, of course, from actual measures of similarity or distance between pairs of objects (cities are often used as an example) or, say, from participant or researcher ratings of similarity between items (as occurs, for example, in a pile sort exercise).

The statistical software then constructs a requested number of dimensions from the data, with the ideal number of dimensions (usually two to three, ideally two) being determined by *goodness of fit* or *stress* scores generated with the analysis. Stress is the difference between the plotted solution and observed distances. The goal is to minimise stress, ideally to a measure below 0.1 (Kruskal & Wish, 1978), while also restricting the number of dimensions being considered. Dimensions are then usually plotted in pairs (as in Figure 9.7) to facilitate interpretation, although it is sometimes helpful to also plot each dimension separately. Two-dimensional plots can vary from appearing as uninterpretable random clouds with a few outliers, to showing clear directional (horizontal, vertical, or diagonal) patterns with discernible groupings of variables. Software that allows for a visual display in which the 2- or 3-dimensional array of objects can be dynamically rotated is especially useful in helping to identify an interpretable solution.

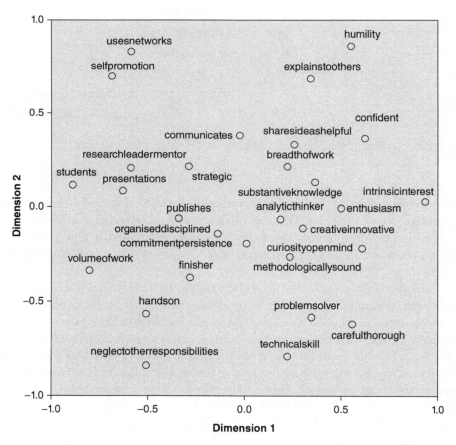

Figure 9.7 Two-dimensional output from MDS of descriptors of researchers using SPSS

Using the same ordinal data showing the frequency of co-occurrences in academics' descriptions of high-performing researchers, Figure 9.7 shows the 2-dimensional matrix resulting from application of MDS, using the PROXSCAL procedure in SPSS. Stress was 0.08, indicating a satisfactory solution from a statistical point of view. One can interpret the display as suggesting researchers are viewed as varying from outward looking to introspective (D1), and technically–practically oriented to socially oriented (D2) – or perhaps, as ranging from doers to talkers! Groupings that make conceptual sense are also evident; these vary in some ways from those shown by the cluster analysis, a probable consequence of limitations of two-dimensional display or use of a different clustering algorithm.

Collins and Dressler (2008) explored whether different groups of human service providers (welfare workers, domestic violence workers, nurses) and the general public shared perspectives on the causes of domestic violence. They began with cultural domain analysis in which participants listed the terms they use to describe the causes of domestic violence. Each group then identified and sorted all the listed terms into groups, recording their comments as they did so. MDS was applied to the similarity matrices resulting from each group. As those from each group were relatively similar, they were then combined into an overall model (Figure 9.8) with the 2-dimensional plot showing controllability (social-personal factors – Dimension 1) and location within victim-perpetrator (Dimension 2) as two perceived causal dimensions for domestic violence. Cluster analysis was used also to identify the boundaries between the groups of items, and analysis of participant commentaries was used to label the common dimensions of meaning for participants. The extent to which individuals were consonant with the shared model was also assessed using quantitative measures, with child welfare workers exhibiting highest levels of agreement within their own group and with the model, and domestic violence workers being most distinctive and most dissonant.

Provalis software (QDA Miner, WordStat) and NVivo both produce interactive 2- and 3-dimensional displays based on multidimensional scaling, using co-occurrences of either codes or words in either sources or codes within the qualitative database.

Correspondence analysis

Correspondence analysis provides a graphical representation of the dimensions in and pattern of association among the values of two categorical variables, or

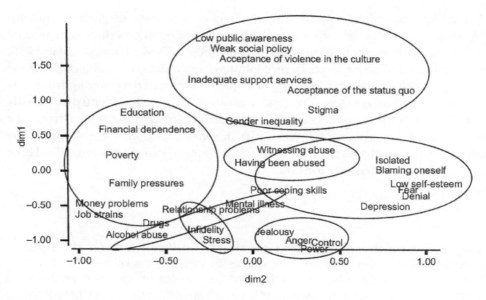

Figure 9.8   Participant-generated causes of domestic violence

Source: Collins and Dressler, 2008: 372, Figure 1

between two sets of variables. Profile or pattern matrices derived from qualitative coding are suitable as input data, assuming there will be some level of correspondence between the two sets of variables defining the rows and columns of the matrix. Thus, for example, the pattern of association between, say, a selected demographic variable and expressed attitudes might be identified; or those dimensions "explaining" the association between expressed attitudes and behavioural choices might be revealed.

Correspondence analysis therefore provides a way of making meaning from a (potentially large) crosstabulation and is an alternative to using a chi-squared or similar statistical analysis, especially where row (or column) variables are not necessarily independent of each other (as frequently occurs with qualitative coding). Initially each set of values or variables is mapped in multidimensional space, to identify the principal axes (dimensions), based on row and column profiles. Distances for the two sets of values or variables (rows and columns) are then rescaled to a common metric around a common origin (the average on each dimension) and each set of values or variables is plotted using identically scaled orthogonal axes, to give a 2-dimensional plot of the distances between members in each set.

To look, for example, at the associations between a selection of 14 descriptors of researchers and three types of research output (an extended version of Figure 9.2) using SPSS, the data needs to be entered in a modified form (Figure 9.9). First, each cell of the table is specified by a line showing the pair of variables that were

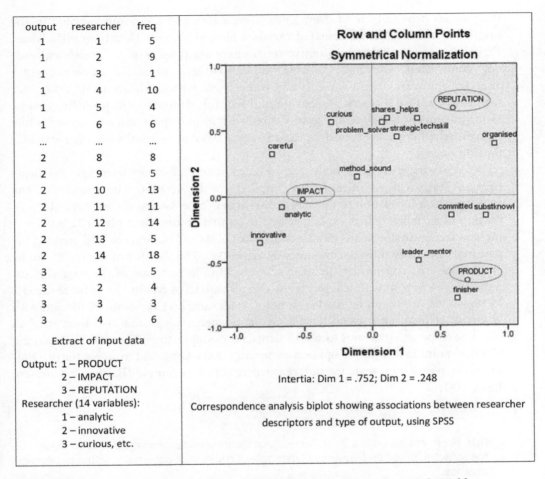

output	researcher	freq
1	1	5
1	2	9
1	3	1
1	4	10
1	5	4
1	6	6
...	...	...
2	8	8
2	9	5
2	10	13
2	11	11
2	12	14
2	13	5
2	14	18
3	1	5
3	2	4
3	3	3
3	4	6

Extract of input data

Output: 1 – PRODUCT
2 – IMPACT
3 – REPUTATION
Researcher (14 variables):
1 – analytic
2 – innovative
3 – curious, etc.

Row and Column Points

Symmetrical Normalization

Intertia: Dim 1 = .752; Dim 2 = .248

Correspondence analysis biplot showing associations between researcher descriptors and type of output, using SPSS

Figure 9.9 Correspondence analysis showing associations between two sets of variables

intersected; these are then weighted by the frequencies (using a check box). Then the associations are shown in a biplot (Figure 9.9).

In interpreting the 2-dimensional plot, one first considers the dimensions represented by the two axes. Points along each axis are examined visually to see what it is that makes the difference as one moves from end to end of the axis. This can also be examined mathematically by calculating the contribution of each point to the inertia on each dimension (sometimes a small frequency of cases for one of the variables might distort its visual placement along an axis). Then, because both rows and columns of the table have been plotted on the same dimensions and the same scale, the proximity of points from each is usually considered to suggest some form of association (Bartholomew et al., 2002). A more stringent test of association than visual proximity is to draw lines from a row and a column variable to the origin (0): the angle for associated variables should be acute (less than 90°). Thus, Figure 9.9 suggests that productive researchers are those who are finishers, leaders, committed, and have substantive knowledge; impactful researchers are analytic, innovative, and careful; and researchers who establish a reputation are technically skilful, organised, sharing and helpful, strategic, and problem solvers. Being curious is associated to some degree with both impact and reputation, while being methodologically sound, at close to zero, is not associated with any particular form of output.

Because correspondence analysis is designed as an exploratory technique, no measures of statistical significance are applied to the results. The quality of the representation in relation to the actual distances is expressed as the inertia – the proportion of variance that is explained by the plotted points (thus higher is better). A higher inertia usually means that the scatter of points will be larger as well, making the plot more interpretable (Bartholomew et al., 2002). The stability of the result can be checked also by re-running the analyses, removing in turn one of the rows (or columns) to see how much each affects the overall pattern of results (Kienstra & van der Heuhden, 2015). It can be used with quite small samples (Maltseva, 2016) and with nominal, ordinal, and scaled data. Correspondence analysis has also been used to examine response structures to survey items, for example, to differentiate the meaning of a mid-point in a scale (no opinion either way, don't care), and to assess the ordinality of the points in a scale for different subgroups in a sample (Blasius & Thiessen, 1998, 2001).

QDA Miner will generate a 2- or 3-dimensional correspondence analysis display within the software, based on frequency of overlapping codes or co-occurrence within a specified distance.

Use of exploratory multivariate analyses in mixed methods research

Three types of exploratory analysis strategies have been described; latent class analysis (a form of factor/cluster analysis for binary variables) is another that can be used. This is an expanding area in statistical analysis, as the capability of computers to manage complex calculations and/or large volumes of data increases. Two characteristics in particular suggest they should be attractive to mixed methods researchers: (a) the ability to use non-normalised transformed data derived from interviews, documents, and other qualitative sources, and (b) the visual displays produced by each of the three methods described, which facilitate interpretation of potentially complex associations in transformed data. Mixed methods researchers then compare these results with their qualitatively derived insights, and/or use them to prompt and guide further statistical or qualitative analyses or to design a further phase of investigation. Their potential as an integrative strategy in mixed methods projects is, as yet, largely untapped by mixed methods researchers.

Building descriptive and narrative accounts from numeric data

Transformation, as a mixed methods strategy, is about converting data into another form, in order to apply a second type of analysis to the same set of data. These are sometimes referred to as crossover analyses, because the type of analysis used is usually associated with an alternative type of data (e.g., by Onwuegbuzie & Hitchcock, 2015). In the previous two chapters and thus far in this chapter, the strategies described have all made use of data from primarily qualitative sources that have been transformed in some way to create numeric data suitable for a variety of complementary statistical analyses. Quantifying qualitative data for statistical analysis in this way is the most common type of transformation practised by mixed methods researchers.

Attention is turned now to transformation in the other direction – to the development of descriptive and narrative accounts from numeric and statistical data. Again a single data source or type of data will be analysed in two different ways. In a sense, transformation of statistical results into a form of narrative occurs whenever a researcher interprets and describes their results and discusses them using prose. Transformation from quantitative (statistical) data to qualitative analysis and reporting as a deliberate analysis strategy is not commonly seen in mixed methods projects, however, suggesting there is untapped potential in this strategy also.

Building a description or narrative account from numeric data might start with using demographic information to profile individuals or sampled groups. The demographic data can be supplemented by comparisons giving average scores or other measures for each individual or group. Cluster or factor analyses assist the process of identifying key characteristics for profiled groups within a population or sample (Teddlie & Tashakkori, 2009). At a more complex level, event histories involving detailed descriptions of sequences and patterns involving individuals and/or groups are built from statistical analysis of data sources with a temporal or longitudinal component (Elliott, 2005, 2011). These include cohort studies, large-scale prospective panel surveys, and retrospective surveys, all of which have narrative potential and the potential to contribute to causal analyses.

Methodological purposes

Strategies to convert quantitative to qualitative data are undertaken primarily as a means of rendering complex datasets in a descriptive or narrative form that can be more readily comprehended and interpreted by readers. Individual cases or groups are profiled from descriptive data, and the storied nature of events embedded in longitudinal data are revealed. Causal models are built when patterns in sequences of events are combined with qualitative information.

Mapping transformation from numeric data to qualitative description and narrative

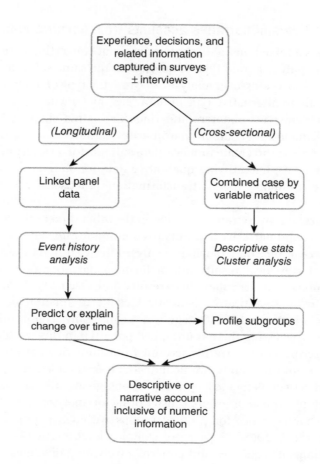

Profiling individuals, samples, and groups based on quantitative data

Individuals are profiled using descriptive demographic data and scores on scales for which group averages or normative values are available. This kind of profiling is useful in helping to situate members of a non-random sample of participants in a qualitative study by comparing their characteristics or scores with those of the broader population.

Profiled groups are usually created using cluster analysis, in which the patterns in survey responses or other variable data are used to create groups of *similar cases* such that groups are able to be differentiated from each other (between-group variation is greater than within-group variation). Groups are then labelled and described based on the quantitative characteristics that differentiate them, usually focusing on either their average characteristics or their modal (most commonly occurring) characteristic(s). Simple description may be sufficient for the study's purpose. Alternatively, the groups are used as the basis for sampling decisions, as demonstrated in Chapter 2, or as categorical subgroups in further analyses. Teddlie and Tashakkori (2009) warn that profiles can be deceptively attractive because they simplify description, but also they can obscure considerable differences within each profiled group. Members of different groups identified using cluster analysis might also share characteristics more closely than is immediately obvious from the clustered display (Bazeley & Jackson, 2013: 237–238).

Excel and SPSS were used by Katrin Niglas (2004) in a primarily quantitative content analysis of mixed methods studies. She used scales to record variation across 145 mixed methods studies on a range of design characteristics. K-means cluster analysis of the quantitative content analysis variables classified the studies into eight distinct groups, and the characteristics which best differentiated the groups were identified. Ratings for each study on these characteristics were assigned. Findings based on the statistical analysis were compared with memo-style notes taken during the initial reading of the studies to generate brief descriptions for each of the eight groups – thus qualitising the quantitative data which, in turn, had been derived from interpretive (qualitative) reading of text. These eight groups were then used to organise the articles for further statistical analyses and conceptual mapping.

Lisa Pearce (2015: 49) sees profiling of cases and related statistical strategies that cluster cases rather than variables as a way of focusing on persons in a quantitative analysis, rather than on isolated variables:

These person-based methods, in fact, try to use quantitative data to do more of what ethnographic observation or very inductive analyses of qualitative data often do, which is to consider the case as a whole and to allow for unique seemingly inconsistent beliefs and behaviors.

Pearce (2015) cited an example from her work on youth and religion. Pearce, Foster, and Hardie (2013) found their qualitative data told them that neither religiosity nor spirituality could be scaled simply from the multiple variables they had, because institutional involvement did not necessarily parallel personal religious or spiritual commitment. They had conducted a latent class analysis using relevant variables, resulting in a model with five classes (clusters) of youth, described as the Abiders, the Adapters, the Assenters, the Avoiders, and the Atheists. Those in the middle three groups expressed complex mixtures of beliefs, experiences, and practices. The authors supplemented these analyses with inductive qualitative analyses of transcripts from those who best represented each of these five classes. The narratives the young people told confirmed the usefulness of their five classes and added to the understanding they had gained from their quantitative analyses.

A complex form of profiling was used by Singer et al. (1998) in an attempt to differentiate the life stories of four pre-existing subgroups of women with different mental health outcomes who were part of a longitudinal panel study. In the first step of their process, which is relevant here, they were able to build detailed prose narratives describing the lives they were examining on the basis of the 250 multi-wave survey variables that were available to them. Further attempts to reduce and generalise the life stories to clearly differentiate the histories of the four groups of women were unsuccessful, however.

Building narrative from quantitative data

Life course researchers more generally focus on transitions in people's lives, and assume a relationship between earlier life experiences and later life events, between different domains within the life course, and between the life course and events occurring for significant others (Wu, 2003). Longitudinal panel or cohort studies in which quantitative data are gathered on multiple occasions over *time* provide *sequenced* data about events in the lives of individuals, groups, places, or conditions, and places those events within a historical and cultural *context*, thus giving them essential narrative qualities (Elliott, 2005, 2011). Examples of such studies include the British Birth Cohort studies of 1958, 1970, and 2000 (www. cls.ioe.ac.uk); the Wisconsin Longitudinal Study (www.ssc.wisc.edu/wlsresearch/); the Panel Study of Income Dynamics (https://psidonline.isr.umich. edu/), and the Australian Longitudinal Study on Women's Health (www.alswh. org.au/). As Elliott notes, the detail of data about individuals gathered in some panel studies rivals that available through qualitative research; what tends to be missing is the participant's evaluation of their life experiences. Several waves of the British studies have been supplemented, therefore, by qualitative interview data covering life course events and related topics for large subsamples ($N = 100+$) of the full cohort.

Social researchers also study other social and historical events occurring over time, not necessarily tied to the life course of individuals, such as the interval between race riots in US cities (Myers, 1997) and the passage of legislation (McCammon, 1999). These statistical analyses are usually accompanied by qualitative contextual information, but the events themselves are not necessarily treated or presented as narrative in these studies.

Observations of events might take a number of forms, as shown in Figure 9.10. Data of the first two types, (a) and (b), will be strongly influenced by the natural history of the event, its predictors, and by other factors operating at the time, such as whether each is steady or fluctuating. Type (b) will be affected also by the time elapsed between points of data observation. Event history data (type c) provides the most complete record possible (Blossfeld, Glosch & Rohwer, 2007), but can suffer from problems associated with recall if collected retrospectively through interviews (as is common). Interviews therefore typically focus on events that involve a change in status such as divorce, employment, relocation, or perhaps imprisonment or illness, as interviewees are likely to more accurately recall those.

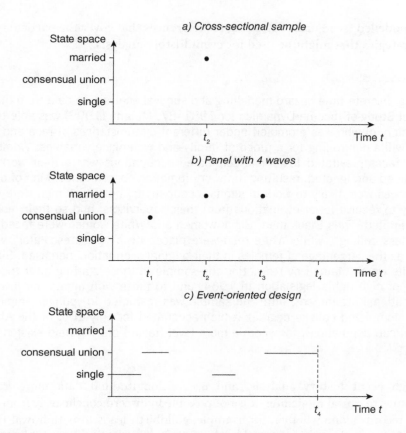

Figure 9.10 Observation of an individual's family career on the basis of a cross-sectional survey, a panel study, and an event-history-oriented design

Source: Blossfeld et al., 2007: 5, Figure 1.1.1

Drawing on longitudinal data for a cohort, event history analysis uses regression-based statistical procedures to model the likely occurrence (the "hazard" or risk) and timing of events, along with the relative importance of predictors of those events, considering also the duration between an initiating event and an outcome. For example, Cox regression (proportional hazards model), which is used extensively in epidemiological studies, models the time to an event based on predictive covariates, allowing for problems of "censored" cases (those who haven't experienced the outcome at the end point of data collection) and missing data. More advanced discrete-time techniques allow for inclusion of both time-constant and time-varying covariates, by using person-months or person-years as units of analysis, rather than person. Further statistical adjustments are made to deal with the lack of independence of these units while not losing the perspective of the whole person (Elliott, 2002). The added detail regarding the passage of time and the interactive influences occurring over time add to the narrative quality of the data. Choice of design and analytic strategy, therefore, is governed primarily by the kind of social process being modelled (see Further Reading for references that cover the particular statistical strategies that might be used for event history analysis.)

Using discrete-time hazard modelling and survival analysis on data from the US Panel Study of Income Dynamics for 1981–87, Maume (1999) was able to tell the story of who was promoted under different circumstances of race and gender, while controlling for a range of family and workplace variables. Women of both races gravitated to female-dominated occupations where their work was devalued and ignored, resulting in fewer promotion opportunities. Men of different races were likely to work in similar occupations, but Black men were more likely to receive lower evaluations from their supervisors, and so their mobility was limited. Thus Black men, Black women and White women were faced with a "glass ceiling", while White men were placed on a "glass escalator" which rose as the percentage of females in their original occupation increased. Similar results were obtained by restricting the sample to those starting after the passage of civil rights legislation in 1964, and to those with increasing levels of educational attainment, until the sample was restricted to younger employees with completed college degrees (which accounted for only 10% of the African American population), for whom a more level (racial) playing field existed.

Although event history analysis, and use of longitudinal data more generally, contributes to causal modelling, it is not possible to discern conclusively from the statistical records alone whether, for example, childbirth leads to withdrawal from the labour force, or departure from the labour force prompts having children (Elliott, 2011). Qualitative interviews are needed therefore in association with the statistical data to fill out the detail of the events and to understand the motives and mechanisms involved in their occurrence. Event history modelling, which reveals overall patterns and points to specific questions to follow up qualitatively, provides just one necessary but not sufficient link in the chain of causal evidence.

Retrospective life history data, collected through a structured narrative interview, similarly places significant events in people's lives into a temporal sequence to allow event history analysis and/or construction of a narrative account (Edmeades et al., 2010; Elliott, 2011). These too are placed within their historical and cultural contexts through cross-case (within sample) and cross-cohort analyses. Events researched in this way are generally restricted to those that mark a change of status in people's lives (to enhance accurate recall), and the highly structured accounts typically lack details of how people were affected by these events, and the meaning that they make of them (the study by Edmeades et al., which was described in the previous chapter, is an exception in this regard). When used in association with event history analysis, life history interviews provide scope for filling out the narrative quality of the statistical data with explanations, case studies, and vignettes. Alternatively, structuring a life story by means of a timeline co-constructed by participant and researcher assists in providing "factual" data regarding status changes and contextual influences while also providing qualitative material to facilitate interpretation of those events and the life as it was lived (Adriansen, 2012; Kolar et al., 2015; Sheridan et al., 2011). The addition of this more evaluative data adds to the narrative quality of the analyses.

Finocchiaro and Lin (2000) used event history analysis to show that the risk of a congressional career ending is time dependent. Previous research looking at incumbency had found a steadily declining improvement in continuing electoral success for those who survived beyond their first term, but with incumbent or voter fatigue possibly setting in after "a good number" of terms. What led to termination of tenure overall was not determined by earlier research. Most studies had used a linear measure of time, but Finocchiaro and Lin used a discrete-time hazard function to explore the varying likelihood of electoral termination for each term that a member was in office, considering also a range of time-dependent contextual factors. In doing so, they found that it was not until the fourth term that incumbents (in general) were "safe", remaining stable then until the tenth term when "the fatigue effect" became apparent. The authors then developed dynamic and contrasting narratives for two individual members, based on their individual time and context dependent histories. Their findings challenge "the conventional understanding of the advantages enjoyed by congressional incumbents in seeking reelection" (2000: 23). They also suggest that risk function is more completely understood when individual careers are considered, rather than aggregate vote margins.

An alternative approach to life history analysis that takes into account the *sequenced* nature of longitudinal data has been explored by Andrew Abbott and his colleagues (Abbott & Tsay, 2000 provide a review). Abbott "borrowed" from studies of genetic sequencing in molecular biology the technique of optimal matching to identify sequential patterns. It is considered to have particular relevance for the study of careers (e.g., Bienmann & Datta, 2014), and is seen as more holistic in its approach than event history analysis. A limitation of the approach is the restricted amount of information that can be incorporated into the sequential chains that are analysed, and so it is yet to gain acceptance among a wider circle of users.

Most readily available statistical programs cater for event history (survival) analysis, for example, using Cox proportional hazards model. Some (STATA is one example) have more facility than others for dealing with issues of independence raised by use of discrete time data.

Blended analyses and consolidated databases: coding, conversion, and combination working together

Creation of a consolidated database often involves the transformation of quantitative variables to more qualitatively described categories, as does also the creation of blended variables that draw together information from diverse sources. Each contributes to analysis of patterns and resolution of puzzles.

Mapping blended and consolidated approaches

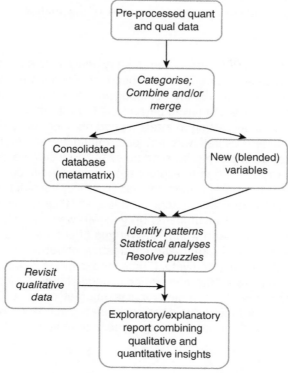

Categorising data to create a consolidated database

Researchers steeped in qualitative traditions typically regard any kind of number as quantitative data. Statisticians, however, regard nominal (categorical) data as qualitative because it has no inherent numeric properties, even though numbers are often used to label values of a variable (e.g., in surveys) and nominal data are routinely used as variables in statistical testing. Indeed, it is more natural to use text labels to describe specific examples of such data, such as red, yellow, and blue for colour categories, than to assign a number to each. Many would also class ordinal data as being essentially qualitative because its numeric properties are limited to specifying order (2nd comes before 3rd; large, medium, small are sequenced) rather than being functionally relative (where 4 would mean twice as much as 2).

The process of combining continuous numeric data with text-based (or similar) descriptive data in a consolidated database is facilitated by categorising the numeric data to create an ordinal scale on which the values are typically described using words, while still retaining the capacity to analyse the original continuous data statistically. For example, Weiss et al. (2005) report using factor analysis as a data reduction strategy to combine a number of variables into a continuous measure of school involvement that was able to be used for statistical analyses with other data from the mothers in their transition to school study. They then categorised this measure by dividing it into quartiles reflecting low, modest, moderate, and high levels of involvement to facilitate its combination with qualitative data for further descriptive analyses. Categorisation is beneficial, also, when using numeric (variable or attribute data) for comparative analyses with qualitative data using QDAS (to reduce the number of columns in the resulting comparative table).

The categorisation and combination of both qualitative and quantitative sources to construct a consolidated database allows for a form of visual pattern analysis. The database, in the form of a tabular layout, is usually referred to as either a matrix or metamatrix (Happ et al., 2006; Miles et al., 2014). Reduction of different data to a similar form and scale for presentation clarifies and simplifies joint analyses of the data. As with any data reduction process, however, categorisation of data is a "trade off" between retaining detail and managing a complex dataset (Louis, 1982b). When data are categorised, qualitative description and comparison are facilitated, but nuances within those data are lost.

Happ et al. (2006) combined categorised numeric scale data with "scaled" concepts derived from qualitative data in an individual case-based metamatrix (Table 9.1) to assist in revealing patterns of medication-taking behaviour in their sample of community dwelling patients who had dementia. Doing so helped them to refine their analysis by identifying dimensions within their key qualitative concepts.

Table 9.1 Simple metamatrix – case comparison (partial table)

Case	Mini Mental Status Exam	Caregiver Vigilance (hours on duty)	Cooperation	Trust
Jerry	8 (Low)	24 hrs (High)	Moderate *directable, doesn't resist, requires repeat cues*	Low *hides or loses pills, forgets what he is doing*
Claire	28 (High)	3 hrs (Low)	High *reminds caregiver to refill*	High *can take responsibility*

Source: Happ et al., 2006: S46, adapted from Table 2

Spreadsheets, such as Excel, are ideal for handling categorised data and data that are a mixture of numbers and text.

Creating and using blended variables

Blending or merging of diverse data sources to create new composite variables to feed back into the analysis is a generative strategy which, while often designed to resolve puzzles raised by the data, can serve also to initiate new questions. This process is best demonstrated by examples.

In a study by Kaplan and Duchon, reported by Maxwell et al. (2015), researchers from different disciplines who were using the same closed and open question survey to answer different research questions developed completely different conclusions about technicians' responses to the introduction of a computerised reporting system. The open-ended data (and Kaplan's observations) suggested there were marked differences between laboratories, but no differences between laboratories nor any based on age or experience were identified through the statistical analysis of the scaled data. With further analysis of the data, Kaplan developed an explanatory theory based on technicians' definitions of what their job entailed. To test her theory, she created blended variables to differentiate process-oriented from product-oriented technicians, variables that supported the qualitative data in clearly differentiating the response pattern in different laboratories.

Two earlier examples of studies in which analysis was enhanced by the construction of a new blended variable were described by Caracelli and Greene (1993). (1) Talmage and Rasher (1981, cited in Caracelli & Greene, 1993) were using a quasi-experimental approach to evaluate the effect of introducing an arts-in-the-schools programme, but their quantitative results were not showing the benefits their observations suggested were present. They undertook a series of mini-case studies, adding new data to the quantitative database and also creating a new variable for support from the school's principal using both sources of data. This was found to be highly correlated with the extent to which the programme was implemented. (2) Schermermhorn, Williams, and Dickison (1982, cited in Caracelli & Greene, 1993) similarly found, through "weaving together" their data sources, that they needed to consider the level of immersion of the students in the programme they were evaluating, and so constructed a new variable from a blend of quantitative and qualitative data. Having found that immersion contributed to or moderated programme outcomes, they developed a more refined way of measuring it, to include in future projects.

Lynn Kemp (1999) provided detail about the process she went through in iteratively exchanging data to create and use a blended variable in her doctoral study of the community service needs of spinal injured people. Quantitative data indicating that there was a desperate shortage of community service provision conflicted with qualitative data that suggested ambivalence in the spinal injured population about whether they would want to access services they had most complained about not having. She transferred codes reflecting this ambivalence from the qualitative to the statistical database and constructed a variable that reflected both current use of services and desire for services. Ambivalence was found to occur in response to community services that appeared to be distributed arbitrarily rather than on the basis of any mandated or perceived definition of need. When she returned the blended variable to the qualitative database, using it in combination with service satisfaction scales to compare qualitative responses about the beneficial and detrimental effects of services, she found the reason for the apparent arbitrariness of service provision. To receive services, spinal injured people had to demonstrate the "right" level of dependence–independence, gratitude, and humility – to have life plans and patterns of behaviour that met the expectations of service providers (Bazeley & Kemp, 2012).

Talmage and Rasher "summarize[d] their dialectic approach to integrating both types of data in terms of a 'spiral effect' … [in which] each type of information, when combined, displayed a dynamic interconnectedness" (Caracelli & Greene, 1993: 200–201). The term "spiralling" was used also by Mendlinger and Cwikel (2008) to describe the iterative cycling of quantitative and qualitative information through multiple complementary, developmental, and initiating phases of a programme of studies on women's health in Israel. These authors likened this process to the exchange of information through the double helix of DNA – an analogy that Kemp (2001) had identified also in another paper that reflected on her doctoral "journey through words and numbers". "The double helix of DNA comprises a sense and an antisense strand that twist around each other, unwind, reorganize, or mutate through a process of protein transfer between the strands, and rewind to reform, in an iterative process of reconstruction … both undoing and rebuilding as the different strands come together to create a cohesive organism" (Bazeley & Kemp, 2012: 68). As a metaphor for Doing iNtegrated Analysis, DNA captures the iterative processes of reconciliation and progression that occur in a mixed methods study when results diverge or new structures are needed to resolve puzzles.

Concluding remarks

Chapter 9 has continued the "story" of using transformed qualitative data for statistical analysis, but with a focus on exploratory multivariate analyses. These analyses were seen as being particularly useful for data that are extracted from a qualitative database, in part because of their exploratory nature, because also they manage multivariate data, but also because they don't require that the same assumptions are met regarding sampling and the normality of distributions. Indeed, they can make use of data that are obtainable only from a qualitative database, where direct intersections of codes within *segments* of source data are able to be identified and counted. These analyses, through their visual displays, were seen as assisting in revealing underlying dimensions or clusters within the data, and in helping to bring structure to the qualitative database.

Attention was then turned to transformation of a different kind, where profile or panel data are analysed statistically, but then interpreted in order to build a descriptive or narrative account of individual cases, groups, or processes in the lives of the participants in the research. Transformation (in either direction) was shown to be useful also for the creation of blended variables or a consolidated database, both strategies with special value for resolving puzzling issues in data.

In these methods, mixed methods are advanced through greater depth of understanding of the dimensional structure of the data, the identification and description of clusters of people or variables within the data, and the accounting of lives lived or changes in society. Again, in all procedures involving transformation of data, but especially those where the original data were qualitative, results from transformed data must be considered and written about in the light of the original data sources.

Further reading

Exploratory multivariate statistics

Bartholomew et al. (2002) present a detailed, readable overview of all exploratory multivariate statistical methods.

Dymnicki and Henry (2012) explain the application of multiple types of cluster analysis in community research, with details about when and how to use cluster analysis that groups cases (but which is also applicable to grouping variables).

Guest and McLellan (2003) recommend cluster analysis applied to qualitative data as a way of gaining a quick visual understanding of the structure of the data, to gain some distance from the data as a supplement to the closer thematic perspectives obtained through coding and through coding co-occurrences.

Borgatti provides a straightforward description of multidimensional analysis using the classic distance between cities data at www.analytictech.com/borgatti/mds.htm

Michael Greenacre (2016) is the acknowledged expert on correspondence analysis – a comprehensive, foundational text.

My Easy Statistics at www.youtube.com/watch?v=42Ts6JoG12A provides a very easy to follow explanation of the non-intuitive process of using SPSS for correspondence analysis to relate two sets of variables (published 14 January 2017).

Kienstra and van der Heuhden (2015) suggest using correspondence analysis as an alternative approach to visually comparing patterns in the case by theme matrix, where the themes are converted into variable data (e.g., counts or categories).

Phillips and Phillips (2009) provide a formula-free explanation of correspondence analysis, with examples of its use in social science for identifying types of cases.

Narrative from numbers and event history analysis

Blossfeld and Rohwer (1997, 2002) explain different models for undertaking event history analysis, with a focus on the concepts involved as much as on the mathematics.

Elliott (2002) compares results from different statistical modelling procedures, using data on return to work after childbearing, from British Birth Cohort data. See also other references to Elliott's work, from the chapter text, based on her extensive experience with the various British longitudinal cohort datasets.

Mills (2011) has written a beginner's introduction to survival and event history analysis using a range of different statistical methods, and instructions for using R.

Steele (2005) details methods and computer software for event history analysis in an open source paper, available from the National Centre for Research Methods.

10
INHERENTLY MIXED, HYBRID METHODS

CHAPTER OVERVIEW

One of the difficulties of presenting a range of analysis strategies is that it can give the false impression that each of these strategies is applied in relative isolation. Working with data in an integrative mixed methods project is actually much messier than that, and is likely to involve a mix of strategies that defies easy classification. In the collection of strategies described in this chapter, both qualitative (text or visual) and quantitative approaches are inextricably intertwined in the production and analysis of data. In one sense, almost all integrative methods can be viewed as hybrid, as numbers always have qualitative features and words are readily (and regularly) counted, sorted, and connected. The difference, here, is that deliberate attention is given to the integral nature of these elements in the data being gathered and analysed. Giampietro Gobo (2015: 331) referred to the development of "merged" methods "which could combine both qualitative and quantitative approaches in a single instrument, squeezing the advantages of both in a single technique" as the next challenge facing sociology. My response (Bazeley, 2016) was that methods and methodologies such as those outlined in this chapter have already achieved that goal (indeed, some time ago for many of them).

The strategies covered in this chapter could all be described as being inherently mixed or hybrid, although they do fall into two broad groups:

(1) *inherently mixed strategies* in which the methodology "demands" a combination of quantitative and qualitative data
(2) *hybrid strategies* that generally begin with the collection of qualitative data, but then necessarily use (usually exploratory) mathematical techniques to sort, summarise, and bring order to that data.

In both types, interpretations and conclusions will iteratively incorporate information from all sources and both types of data.

Inherently mixed strategies

Strategies that "naturally" embrace a combination of quantitative and qualitative data include case study, ethnography, and discourse analysis. While each of these might be viewed as purely qualitative approaches in other settings, mixed methods researchers will be sure to take advantage of their inherently mixed qualities, enriching their analyses as a consequence. Ethnography and case study could, alternately, be considered as applications of complementary approaches to integration, in which qualitative and quantitative data and approaches are used side by side to build a unified picture, model, or theory.

What each of these deliberations and decisions reinforces is the inherent complexity in any attempt to classify the multiplicity of strategies, methods, and methodologies embraced within the "family" of mixed methods. With that goes the importance of always describing the methods used, rather than relying on the use of labels that are dependent on a particular classification system and which are therefore subject to misinterpretation.

Mapping inherently mixed strategies

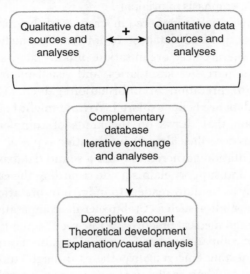

Case study as an inherently interwoven, mixed methods strategy

Case studies employ multiple methods involving a large number of "data points" or variables while maintaining a holistic perspective on the more or less bounded entity being studied. "The all-encompassing feature of a case study is its intense focus on a single phenomenon within its real-life context" (Yin, 1999: 1211). Although bounded, the boundary between a case and its context might become clouded, and both the case and its context can change over time, necessitating review of the design of the study. Cases as foci of study, and the analysis of data from their multiple, intersecting data sources, tends to be complex. Indeed, it is the complexity of a particular phenomenon that invites the use of case study as a method of investigation (Yin, 2014).

Studies of particular cases can be descriptive or explanatory in purpose. They might be of intrinsic interest only; alternatively they are designed to provide an understanding of a wider phenomenon through comprehensive description and analysis of a particular instance, or of a small number of instances, of that phenomenon. They have particular value in evaluating neighbourhood or community level intervention studies where establishing a control group is simply not feasible (as occurred in Flecha's [2014] mixed method evaluative case study, reported in Chapter 5). Case study is often considered useful only for pilot studies, but both Yin (2014) and Flyvbjerg (2006) strongly dispute this claim, presenting evidence to show that case studies using systematic data collection and analysis procedures provide practical, situated knowledge, capable of generalisation, and essential for building expertise. Analytic generalisation is further supported by theoretically based replication (Yin, 2014). Flyvbjerg, who approaches case study from a different epistemological position, presents the image of a musician building virtuosity one practice session at a time, suggesting that "rules are characteristic of expert *systems* but not of real human *experts*" and that case researchers "tend to be sceptical about erasing phenomenological detail in favour of conceptual closure" (2006: 239, emphasis in original).

Analysis of the diverse data gathered in a case study begins with the development of a systematically organised database of information including both words and numbers. Coding, hierarchical organisation, linking across sources, comparative tables, chronologies, narrative summaries, and visual maps are all used to assist exploration and interpretation of information gained. Memos record interim insights while the data are being explored. Writing might begin with a comprehensive case description that draws on the kinds of complementary analyses and integrative processes described already. Information is pieced together, sources compared, and documentation garnered to build a sound database of evidence that can be called on to test and support claims made regarding the case. Data are then presented in such a way as to allow readers to judge interpretations reported from it.

Comparative case studies, such as Crabtree et al.'s comparative study of the delivery of preventive services in medical practices (2005; see Chapter 6) are undertaken either to gain the benefit of comparative data for analysing patterns and refining understanding, or to facilitate testing emergent hypotheses through study replication. For case studies with a theory-building or theory-testing purpose, as with an evaluative study, a theory of change or logic model is useful in guiding analysis as well as design. Propositions relating to rival explanations can be developed, then evidence of various kinds gathered and reviewed in relation to these. If necessary, additional data can be sought to resolve any discrepancies and sources of scepticism. Finally, the results are built into a detailed and richly illustrated narrative.

Ashforth and Reingen (2014) undertook a mixed ethnographic case study of a food cooperative. They integrated multiple methods and sources of information to show how apparently opposing forces of idealism and pragmatism within the organisation operated as a duality and yet contributed in a complementary way to building a coordinated whole. Archival information and field notes provided historical and contextual understanding. Social network analysis differentiated and confirmed the existence of two groups among members by identifying cliques, clusters, and member embeddedness in each group. Ratings of value sets and selection of group members who were regarded as prototypes for each group further supported the differentiation of the groups, while demographic comparisons showed the actual members of each group to be demographically similar. Grounded theory and comparative displays built from multiple sources provided insight into the dynamics of conflict and cooperation between groups and over time; these also provided insight into the mechanisms that sustained the organisation.

The authors used text drawn from documents, group meetings, and interviews; insights from literature; and social network and survey data to weave a narrative explaining what made both sides of the duality salient and to present arguments for three mechanisms identified as ensuring continuity of both conflict and the organisation. This primary account was occasionally supported by simple statistical analyses. Thus, for example, the way in which the conflict between the groups was institutionalised in the founding documents and frequently expressed in meetings was counterbalanced with results of the values-rating exercise showing that both groups valued social justice, peace, and equality before competition and profit, despite idealists and pragmatists differing significantly in their respective endorsement of these value clusters. An integrated display juxtaposing trends in finances with observations of changes in management over a period of time (Figure 10.1) showed how the rise in dominance of one group or the other was related to current economic circumstances. Finally, the researchers summarised their research-based theoretical understanding of the dynamics of organisational duality in a detailed visual model (shown in Chapter 12).

Year	Gross Sales	Current ratio (i.e., Current assets/ Current liabilities)	Total cash reserve	Net profit or loss	Salient aspects of strategy/tactics
1	74	87	72	Positive	More authority for store manager Focus on operational efficiency
2	81	83	100	Positive	Investment in store technology and equipment Proposals to reduce member discount
3 (Formal study begins)	97	100	96	Positive	Managerial authority limited Move to management team
4 (Formal study continues)	93	100	85	Positive	Greater investment in member services Member discount preserved
5 (Formal study ends)	100	83	49	Negative	Member discount reduced Spending on member services curtailed
6 (Participation continues)	78	70	32	Negative	Move back to single general manager

Figure 10.1 Natura financial performance and strategy before, during, and after the ethnography period

Source: Ashforth and Reingen, 2014: 500, Table 1

Mixed data and complementary analyses within ethnography

Ethnography, as a methodology, has its roots in anthropology, with a focus on the study of society and culture. Although it is generally classed as a qualitative method, within that tradition it employs mixed methods, as illustrated by Ashforth and Reingen's (2014) ethnographic case study, shown above, and in the ethnographic study described below. Observation (both structured and unstructured) comprises a major component of ethnographic data, but this is routinely supplemented by interviews, census, and other administrative data, document analysis, collection of artefacts, and visual elicitation techniques (e.g., decision modelling, the development of folk taxonomies), "in fact, gathering whatever data are available to throw light on the issues that are the emerging focus of inquiry" (Hammersley & Atkinson, 2007: 3). Drawing together what has been learned from those diverse sources is, in itself, drawing on the strategies described earlier under complementary mixed methods. Social network analysis, in which relationships within a group are analysed both visually and mathematically, was developed to where it is today from and within anthropology and ethnography. In addition, ethnographers frequently make use of surveys, and in the area of cultural domain analysis, apply a range of exploratory statistical analyses (cluster analysis, multidimensional scaling, factor analysis) to both individual and group data collected through free listing, pile sorts, triad tests, and consensus analysis (Bernard, 2006; Borgatti, 2016). While the strategies for integrating analyses are those that have been discussed already in earlier chapters, what I am proposing here is a shift of focus from seeing ethnography as a qualitative method (where it is often positioned) to seeing it as an inherently hybrid mixed method, in which it is routinely expected that a mix of data sources and analysis strategies will be interdependently integrated.

To explore issues related to "making research visible" across seven Schools in a College of Arts, Humanities and Social Sciences within an Australian University, I employed an ethnographic approach. This involved an extended period of mixing and talking with academic staff ($N = 300$), interviews with research leaders and managers, attending research meetings, reviews and coding of research grant and publication records, media releases and web materials, a brief survey of staff members ($N = 127$), and a review of relevant literature on fostering research and measuring research performance. Data from all sources were managed within an NVivo database, where they were also sorted for each School and each member of academic staff. Evidence from the study demonstrated a significant amount of research activity and impact from research being carried out by staff that was not recognised by the standard performance assessment tools used by the university system, and consequently, neither was it always recognised or supported by the management within the Schools being studied. Results from the combined sources suggested that research activity and performance by staff could be encouraged, for example, through changing methods of allocating research funding within the University (Bazeley, 2006). Additional means of fostering greater visibility were detailed in a report. These included strategies for improving recognition of staff members' research activities, and for creating links between specific academics from different Schools based on particular areas of common interest that had been identified (using codes for topic and methods) through the study.

Anthropac is free software by Steve Borgatti to assist cultural domain analysis using free lists, pile sorts, and related analysis strategies: www.analytictech.com/anthropac/anthropac.htm

Discourse analysis as a basis for unification of methods

Discourse analysis, in its various forms, is another of those methods usually classified as belonging to the qualitative family of methods. This overlooks the variety of approaches that are included under the general discourse banner, and the detail of methods used in many of those approaches. Discursive practices are often counted in the search for patterns; conversation analysts look for regularities in turn taking sequences; social discourse analysis relates spoken words to cultural circumstances and events recorded in both words and numbers.

Numbers are a form of discourse, a language with which to communicate. Before the world adopted a common Arabic system of numbers, different cultural groups had their own ways of communicating quantities and volumes and lengths and distances just as they had different languages for communicating about day to day life, their actions, emotions, and experiences. Our universal system of numbers, and the mathematics that build on that, have evolved over time; for example, originally there was no concept of zero and no symbol for it. As social scientists we often ask people to respond to questions expressed in words by using a number that has little or no mathematical meaning to symbolise their thoughts and answers – their stance – in response to a question.

From the viewpoint of the mixed methods researcher, seeing discourse as the fundamental form of all data allows researchers to view quantitative and qualitative data as having an elemental unity. Interviews and surveys both use some of the same conversational dynamics of performing and position taking as the respondent/participant interacts with the researcher, whether that is directly or through another medium (Schrauf, 2016: 65). Schrauf's approach to survey data is to use consensus analysis – a form of factor analysis that describes intragroup patterns of agreement in a given domain – to find structure among participants rather than items. Thus "surveys make possible a bird's-eye view of the sharing and distribution of discourse at the level of the group – a synoptic view that perhaps no one speaker can ever have" (2016: 45). He also suggests that using multiple correspondence analysis or social network analysis is useful as a way of visually identifying groups that is particularly useful for cross-cultural comparisons (his area of research) because they allow a view of individuals within their social field. Within groups, the displays thus created identify key individuals, the "culture experts" who might then be selected for interviews. Interviews also are analysed as a cultural *event*, rather than as offering information *about* culture. Thus, a common framework is applied to the analysis of both forms of data in ways that direct the analysis strategies used. Although Schrauf's focus was on cross-cultural comparison, the principle of analysing discourse as a unifying strategy is applicable across other areas of investigation. For example, his strategies for analysing patterns across people rather than variables reflect those reported by Pearce (2015) in her study of youth and religion, described in Chapter 9.

Hybrid strategies

In the natural world, a hybrid is the result of combining the genetic material of two different species or varieties of plants or animals. We refer to hybrid cars as those that use both diesel or petrol and electric power. Similarly, I am adopting the term hybrid to refer to strategies that inherently combine both qualitative and quantitative elements to create a single source or set of data that is then, typically, further examined using iterative quantitative and qualitative strategies. Many of the hybrid methods involve specialised strategies for data gathering that are integrated with particular forms of data analysis. The actual data analysis strategies, however, often comprise or include methods already described, although they might now appear in slightly different forms. For example, social network analysis and geographic methods rely on linking of qualitative and quantitative data sources. They have been included here as hybrid methods because location is an inherent part of almost any data, and methods used to gather, display, and interpret social networks are largely qualitative in nature, yet they rely on statistical analyses that are then reported in combination with visual displays and interpretive comments. The remaining six methods included in this section – covering qualitative comparative analysis, Kane and Trochim's (2007) form of concept analysis, repertory grid technique, Q methodology, systematic microanalysis of observational data, and the imitation game – each apply a form of transformation from qualitative data to quantitative or "qualiquant" analyses. They nevertheless vary in important ways from those described in earlier chapters in that the quantification of qualitative data is integral to these methods rather than an add-on possibility, and both forms of the data are integral to analytic interpretation and reporting.

Mapping hybrid strategies

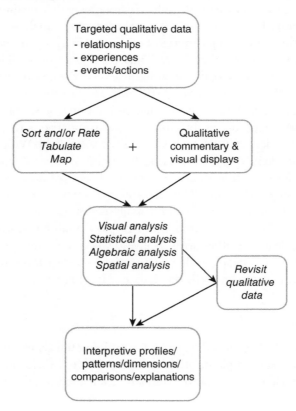

Geospatial referencing as a hybrid mixed methods tool

All data are located in time and space. Geographic referencing, therefore, provides a unique opportunity to intersect different forms of data within a hybrid analysis by connecting them through their locations. Maps convey both quantitative and qualitative data: physical distances and topography, but also houses, parks, shops, and other features which convey information about the social uses of the land. Additional statistical and textual data can be overlaid, using spatial coordinates. Geographers increasingly see their discipline as "inherently mixed", while sociologists see that adding a spatial dimension to sociology helps to build cumulative knowledge in that discipline. Adding "contextualized generalizations" show the settings in which features of social phenomena do and don't vary, adding an additional dimension to causal analyses (Fielding & Fielding, 2015: 562). The importance of having an analytic purpose that fully integrates geographical data into a project in order to further knowledge is emphasised, however, so that it is not done just to provide a "pretty" illustration.

A variety of software is available to support mixed methods analyses in situations either where cases are locations, or where case information (e.g., events, stories, history, statistics) is connected to physical locations or environments. Maps or grids emphasising different features are overlaid to explore the links between features for particular sites. Hyperlinks can be established between georeferenced locations and various forms of qualitative and quantitative data, so that all can be interpreted together. This can extend to include, for example, the geographic tracking of a "go-along" interview, recorded as the interviewee is walking through the area he or she is talking about, or observation of historical data stored in Google Earth, allowing analysis of change over time.

Different Geographic Information Systems (GIS) and QDAS options follow the same hyperlinking principles and have many basic features in common, but for more complex forms of data and analyses they work in different ways and so choices need to be governed by research purposes as well as available technology and researcher skills. Adapted and extended GIS software and Global Positioning System (GPS) technology provide tools for integrating qualitative, quantitative, and visual data through hyperlinking to the qualitative material from the GIS, recording it as additional layers directly within the GIS database, and/or by using GIS in parallel with QDAS (Jung & Elwood, 2010).

Christensen, Mickelsen, Nielsen, and Harder (2011) explored the everyday mobility of 10–13-year-old Danish children (an age when children are presumed to be becoming more independent) using a combination of GPS tracking, mobile phone technology, and ethnographic methods. GPS technology, linked to ArcGIS, recorded children's location every 30 seconds (with interruptions from various sources). Parallel responses from a subsample of children to a brief

(Continued)

(Continued)

survey about current activity were obtained through mobile phone prompts and texting. Ethnographic methods included observations of children's routine activities throughout the day, guided tour interviews with children, parent interviews, peer group discussions, and informal chats with children, parents, and teachers. The authors found that patterns of mobility varied for suburban and rural children, and for boys compared to girls. Overall, they found that mobility of children at this age is primarily social, being interdependent rather than independent.

Alternatively, most QDAS programs allow researchers to geotag sources or parts of sources, with the embedded links then opening the location in Google Earth (or in some cases, optionally in Arc-GIS), to add contextual information to those sources. Google Earth images imported as QDAS sources can be given embedded links in the same way, as well as being coded, annotated, and given quantitative attributes as occurs for other picture files and text. How this is done, and what additional features are available (e.g., linking to timelines), vary for different QDAS.

In a study focusing on community safety and the perception of risk in neighbourhoods within an English city, Jane and Nigel Fielding (2013) used geospatial software to help combine and integrate layers of emic and etic information to understand connections between community, crime, and place. Quantitative data from surveys, the census, and other sources were linked to census blocks, producing an etic-level picture of a neighbourhood that was, relative to surrounding areas, a deprived area housing a higher proportion of poor and/or sick people and a crime "hot spot" with a bad reputation among outsiders. Mobile interviews and environmental scans to observe visible indicators of risk and reassurance were synchronised with GPS tracking and reviewed using Open Street Map. These captured the emic or lived experience of individual residents at a fine-grained level, while interview data were coded in (and linked to location from) MAXQDA. Data were "coalesced" (rather than converged) in relation to times and spaces to produce related and linked information (Figure 10.2). Through their analyses, Fielding and Fielding were able to question the assumption that neighbourhood crime and disorder are major stressors or concerns for the general public. They suggested instead that public agencies are often ignorant of the resilience and resources existing within a community's networks.

Again, as with several other hybrid methods covered in this section, the actual integrative analysis processes employed when using these additional data sources and data management tools are largely those that have been described in earlier chapters.

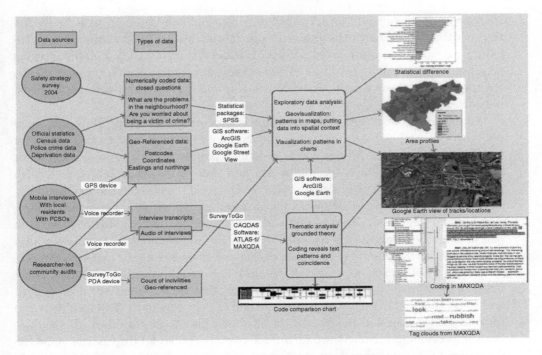

Figure 10.2 Data sources and technology and software tools for collection and analysis of georeferenced data

Source: Fielding and Fielding, 2013: 3, Figure 1

These include complementing, comparing, and relating data in order to produce holistic description and to better detect relationships, patterns, and pathways that will inform the particular topic of investigation.

> Detailed information about the geographic capabilities of different software products are provided by Fielding and Fielding (2015), including information about tools that are freely available for use in research. Information is available also on the CAQDAS networking site: www.surrey.ac.uk/sociology/research/researchcentres/caqdas/support

Social network analysis

The foundation of social network analysis (SNA) lies in mathematical graph theory on the one hand, and ethnographic studies of kinship and interpersonal relations on the other (Edwards, 2010). SNA allows the complexity of extended social relations to be reduced and summarised in a way that both facilitates comprehension and offers a new vantage point on the social world (Crossley, 2010; Hogan, 2017). The major focus of the development of SNA in the 1980s and 1990s was as a quantitative strategy for studying social relations, focusing on measuring characteristics of ties between units (i.e., cases, usually but not necessarily people) in a defined population.

Increasing worldwide and local connectivity of people and human institutions and the growth of social networks fostered by social media sites on the internet are providing a fertile ground for social network research (Hogan, 2017). Rapidly growing adoption of SNA among business and social researchers has been prompted also by the continuous improvement of readily available and user-friendly software for social network analysis.

Data about network ties comes from interviews, observations, or from analysis of relevant lists, archival documents, secondary sources such as diaries and letters, or social networking sites. All ties within a defined population might be considered, or alternatively just ties for a specific person and their connections (an egonet). Ties showing connections between organisations (or "blocks") based on common memberships between those organisations can be assessed, or ties between two types of cases, such as actors and events (2-mode networks). Presence or absence of ties between each pair of cases in the network is recorded in a matrix, often supplemented by attributes associated with the cases being considered. Ties might be directional (where A consults B but B does not consult A), or non-directional. The matrix is transformed into a visual network accompanied by graph-based measures that include the centrality, density, and connectivity of the network as a whole and of members in it. "Distance" between members is measured as the number of links that have to be traversed; cliques, isolates, and bridging members are identified as well. The visual display can show the direction of ties, weighting them for strength or frequency, and/or as signed (+ or -) to reflect the type of relationship, features that are also taken into account in the mathematical indices that are calculated. Attributes of individual cases are shown through variations in the size, colour, or shape of nodes in the network. The visual display aids considerably in interpreting the mathematical indices generated by the analysis. Overall, networks might be described as open or closed, dense or sparse, centralised or decentralised, with opportunities available to members depending on the kind of network and their position within it (e.g., Figure 10.3 and Table 10.1).

Scott et al. (2005) used social network analysis to describe and compare communication patterns in two contrasting primary care practices. Observations were made and interviews conducted over a two-week period during which an intervention was being trialled. Based on these qualitative sources, directional adjacency matrices were constructed and then represented in two visual network diagrams using NetDraw (Figure 10.3). UCINET was used to calculate measures for: "density (a measure of the relative number of connections), clustering coefficient (the tendency of the network to aggregate in subgroups), centralization, (the degree to which a network approaches a perfectly symmetric or 'star' network), and hierarchy (the extent to which network relations are ordered)" (2005: 445). The resulting measures, shown in Table 10.1, demonstrate a higher degree of collaboration generally and within subgroups for Practice 2 than for Practice 1, while relationships in Practice 1 were very hierarchical. Both practices were quite centralised, but Practice 1 is very asymmetrical, suggesting most connections are unidirectional. These measures confirm the patterns that are evidenced in Figure 10.3, and demonstrate the utility of SNA for structural analysis of a network or organisation.

Practice 1

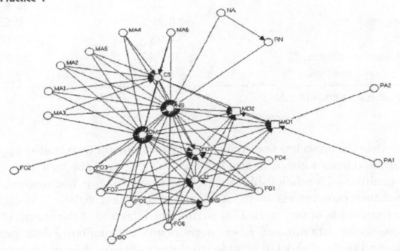

Practice 2

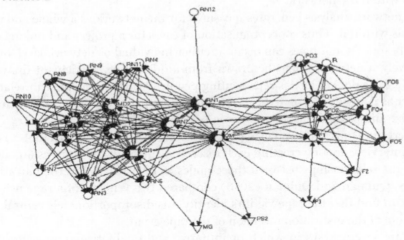

Figure 10.3 Contrasting networks in two medical practices

Source: Scott et al., 2005: 446, Figure 2

Note: Circles – Females, Squares – Males, Triangles – Outside organisations

(Continued)

(Continued)

Table 10.1 Contrasting network measures in two medical practices

Measure	Practice 1	Practice 2
Network density (SD)	0.1570 (0.3638)	0.3398 (0.4136)
Clustering coefficient	0.223	0.590
Hierarchy	0.93	0.00
Centralization – indegree, %	73.440	57.889
Centralization – outdegree, %	6.880	64.778

Source: Scott et al., 2005: 447, Table 1

Social network analysis has been criticised for its dominant quantitative approach. Numbers derived from a matrix or graph are seen as not being adequate to reflect the historical qualities of a relationship, its evolution over time, it fluctuations, or the impact of future expectations of its continuance (Crossley, 2010). Hence there is increasing recognition of the "storied" nature of social ties and of the benefit of incorporating qualitative data into analyses of networks. When qualitative data, providing explanatory and contextual detail, is added to the mix of visual displays and statistical indices, the linking of structure, process, and meaning enhances interpretation of relationships within the network.

Social network analysis generates measures for the network as a whole and for the individuals within it. Thus conceptualisation of cases for a project and linking of different data sources and types can occur at either individual or network level, or both. Alternatively, a network might be drawn from a qualitative, participant-drawn perspective (e.g., as dots or circles representing people placed on one page in relation to each other as if all had reason to be in the same room together). Measures, such as the relative size and physical distance between people, can then be applied to it.

An interesting new approach using network analysis is to apply SNA tools to narrative and interview data by creating each discrete element in the story as a node, and mapping the relationships between those nodes as revealed within the narratives or interviews. Quinlan and Quinlan (2010) compared two versions of a rape using this approach, to find that the rape victim's identity was disproportionately central to the construction of the institutional version of the rape event.

There are several ways in which quantitative and qualitative approaches can be combined in social network analysis in a mutually informative way (Crossley, 2010; Edwards, 2010):

- Use qualitative approaches to understand a cultural and linguistic context to design appropriate ways of gathering data on ties.
- Use different methods to create network maps of the same phenomenon.

- Gather associated qualitative data to contribute understanding of idiosyncratic aspects of particular ties within a network, including who initiated the tie.
- Use a mapped network to prompt conversations about the network that has been created or the interviewee's structural position within the network.
- Use a network map to prompt conversations about related topics, such as the meaning of friendship.
- Use mixed methods to contribute to understanding processes that explain change over time in networks.

Some would argue that all network data should be collected using qualitative approaches, to ensure a multidimensional perspective is obtained, with the data being transformed for statistical network analysis while also being available for content analysis to explore meanings and context. The network is then viewed in association with the qualitative data, in a complementary style of analysis.

Binz-Scharf, Kalish, and Paik (2015) explore the tension in science between specialisation within laboratories and the need to collaborate across organisations, and the role of new digital technologies in collaborative production of scientific knowledge. They combined three ethnographic studies of laboratory culture with social network analysis (SNA) of their larger scientific community based on co-authorship patterns at conferences. They analysed bivariate and multivariate matrices built on a variety of relationship factors between 219 scientists to test hypotheses developed from their ethnographic data. They found scientists collaborate primarily with others from the same geographic region and lab; face to face interactions at conferences between those who make similar contributions lead to collaboration; but also, high impact scientists attract collaborators. Quantitative analyses were both guided and supported by qualitative data.

The most commonly used programs for social network analysis are UCINET (www.analytictech.com) and Pajek (http://pajek.imfm.si/doku.php?id=pajek). Pajek is freeware and especially suitable for large networks; UCINET is somewhat easier to learn to use, and is supported by extensive documentation. NetDraw, which is packaged with UCINET is used to produce visualisations for both of these programs, and data are exchangeable between them. Add-on modules for specialist analyses have been developed by researchers, for example, to analyse aspects of social capital using triads (Prell & Skvoretz, 2008).

An added module for the NVivo software is designed to facilitate the linking process between qualitative and quantitative analysis using social network analysis. Qualitative data are coded in the usual way to capture content, but also coded for relationships between cases, as revealed within the texts (or other sources). These relationships

(Continued)

(Continued)

can then be shown in a network diagram, with basic network statistics calculated and used to adjust the display.[1] Any item in a sociogram links directly to source data for the case, including all qualitative materials and a list of attributes associated with that case, while relationships are linked to data specific to that relationship. The network (relationship) data can be exported and opened in Pajek for more sophisticated mathematical analysis. Alternatively, a matrix constructed from coding links between cases and/or thematic nodes in any QDAS can be exported as an Excel file and imported as a data matrix into UCINET.

Case-oriented quantification with qualitative comparative analysis

Qualitative comparative analysis (QCA), developed by Charles Ragin (1987), builds on the deep understanding of complex processes gained through intensive case studies by using a systematic approach to (associative) causal analysis based on the cross-case patterning of critical variables drawn from the case studies. This combination of both inductive and deductive processes is appropriate for analyses involving small to medium sized samples as well as larger samples (Rihoux & Ragin, 2009). Close case-level knowledge is combined with good theoretical understanding to identify relevant cases and a limited set of variables to include in the cross-case analysis (up to seven, quantitatively or qualitatively derived). These are arranged in a *truth table* that lists all the found configurations of variables, along with their positive, negative, or contradictory outcomes (e.g., Table 10.2).

For *crisp set* data (csQCA – the original, basic model), all variables are dichotomised, but this can cloud results where a condition or an outcome can vary in potency (Cress & Snow, 2000). This basic method has since been extended, therefore, to deal also with multivalue data (mvQCA), while fuzzy set methods (fsQCA) allow for degrees of membership in a category. Then, unlike linear statistical models that focus on the additive contribution of individual variables entered into a single model, QCA draws on the logic of set theory and uses Boolean algebra to reveal one or more possible configurations of causal and contextual variables that are necessary and/or sufficient to produce the outcome (the "complex" solution). In so doing, it is claimed, it supports the diversity and complexity reflective of the situation being studied (Berg-Schlosser et al., 2009). From this, a minimum set of interrelated *prime implicants* necessary for a given outcome (the "parsimonious" solution) is derived – this being considered the more reliable solution (Vaisey, 2014). The detailed case knowledge that assisted in the selection of variables for inclusion in the cross-case analysis then comes into play again, in assisting with interpretation of the obtained results. Ragin et al. (2003) claim the results and consequent understanding is usually achieved with greater sensitivity and reliability than can be

---

[1] Relationships between concepts can also be mapped by temporarily copying the relevant nodes into a folder under Cases.

achieved through using more traditional qualitative or quantitative techniques alone, particularly for the small to moderate sample sizes that are common for case studies and in qualitative approaches.

Based on their ethnographic studies of 15 homeless social movement organisations (SMOs) from eight US cities, Cress and Snow (2000) identified four direct outcomes achieved by the organisations and six theoretically and practically important conditions influencing those outcomes. While it was clear that the presence of more of the conditions was associated with the number of outcomes achieved, Cress and Snow were more interested in the relative importance of each of the different conditions for each of the outcomes, separately and overall (Table 10.2). For example, the pathway to achieving representation of homeless people on relevant organisations was $V*DT*SA*DF*PF + V*dt*CS*DF*PF \rightarrow Z$.[2] This can be read as showing that:

> Organizational viability, diagnostic frames and prognostic frames were necessary conditions for obtaining representation. These conditions were sufficient in combination with either disruptive tactics, where allies were present, or nondisruptive tactics in the context of responsive city bureaucracies. (Cress & Snow, 2000: 1082)

Overall, Cress and Snow found that the combination of organisational viability with diagnostic interaction with varied tactics and political contexts, were common in a successful pathway for each outcome. SMOs with contradictory combinations in their analyses were not excluded from the analysis as the authors wanted to show that while the outcomes were possible, they were not certain, thus avoiding the accusation that QCA is overly deterministic in its approach. Further examination of the conditions operating in organisations with discrepant results revealed, for example, that the more radical PUEJ competed with a more viable and less disruptive SMO in a city responsive to the needs of the homeless and was consequently unsuccessful in gaining representation for its members. Combinations of conditions and outcomes were further elaborated in relation to the available ethnographic case study data and their significance was discussed in relation to previous research. In particular, the authors noted a neglect in previous literature of the role of articulate and focused framing processes, conditions that they found were most reliably associated with a positive outcome.

(Continued)

---

[2] Labels written in lower case represent the 0 condition (i.e., absence) for those variables. In set theory, * represents AND (i.e., both together) and + represents OR (i.e., alternatives).

(Continued)

Table 10.2 Truth table of presence or absence of causal conditions and outcomes for homeless SMOs

| | Causal conditions | | | | | | Outcomes | | | |
| | V | DT | SA | CS | DF | PF | | | | |
SMO	SMO viability	Disruptive tactics	Sympathetic allies	City support	Diagnostic frame	Prognostic frame	Represen-tation	Resources	Rights	Relief
PUH, PUEJ	1	1	1	1	1	1	C	C	1	1
AOS	1	0	1	1	1	1	1	1	1	1
OUH, TUH, DtUH	1	1	1	0	1	1	1	C	C	C
HCRP	1	0	0	1	1	1	1	0	1	0
BUH	0	1	0	1	0	1	0	0	0	1
DnUH	0	1	0	0	0	1	0	0	0	1
HF	0	0	1	1	0	0	0	1	0	0
HUH, HU	0	0	0	0	0	1	0	0	0	1
MUH	0	1	0	1	0	0	0	0	0	0
HPU, MC	0	0	0	0	0	0	0	0	0	0

Source: Built from data supplied by Cress and Snow, 2000: 1081, Table 3

Note: 1 indicates presence of the condition or outcome, 0 indicates absence, C contradictory outcomes

Pathways to achieving representation: $V*DT*SA*DF*PF + V*dt*CS*DF*PF \rightarrow Z$.

Increasing enthusiasm for and use of QCA methods has prompted several critiques of the method, including by Lucas and Szatrowski (2014) who challenged the accuracy of its conclusions. More broadly, QCA has been widely criticised for its deterministic ontology. Wolf (2010: 148), for example, writes that as the number of cases increase, so does the risk of "slipping toward" deterministic logic and conclusions built on associations, as used in quantitative regression models. This is disputed by its developers and by Olsen (2014), who suggests that QCA is more closely aligned with realist assumptions. Collier (2014) is one of several who express scepticism regarding the complex algorithms that have been developed from simpler beginnings in QCA, suggesting they are ill-suited to QCA's goals. He recommends other approaches, such as process tracing (described in Chapter 12), as being more appropriate to achieving the goal of causal analysis through comparative analysis of qualitative case data.

Analyses of crisp set (dichotomised) QCA data are supported by TOSMANA and FSQCA, also by a module in R; TOSMANA also supports mvQCA, and FSQCA supports fsQCA. Access to software is free and further information is available at www.compasss.org

Participant-driven "concept analysis"

Kane and Trochim (2007) proposed a method of participant-driven concept analysis for undertaking a multidimensional needs assessment or designing an evaluation framework. This approach shares a common emphasis on participant input with nominal group technique and the Delphi method, but offers a relatively rapid approach to processing that input, using (transformational) mixed methods strategies.

Participants in the target area develop a series of statements about the topic of interest. A refined set of the statements is re-presented for them to (individually) sort into groups and rate, often for importance and feasibility but potentially for any concepts of relevance to the project or population being studied. Multidimensional scaling is applied to the sorted statements to create a clustered concept map – as in the example shown in Figure 10.4, from Trochim et al.'s (2004) study to develop a health service plan in Hawai'i. Clusters are sometimes layered to show their relative importance. The ratings attached to each cluster are used to create additional visual displays showing, for example, the relative importance versus feasibility of strategies suggested by each cluster to act as a further guide for action. These various displays are then used to effectively communicate back to the participants the key areas they saw as needing to be developed or evaluated, and the feasibility of doing so, as a stimulus for further discussion.

In describing their approach to concept analysis as an integrative mixed method, Kane and Trochim (2007: 177) suggested:

Rather than simply combining qualitative and quantitative methods, [concept analysis] challenges the distinction between these two and suggests that they may indeed be more deeply intertwined. In some sense [concept analysis] is a method that supports the notion that qualitative information can be well represented quantitatively and that quantitative information rests upon qualitative judgment.

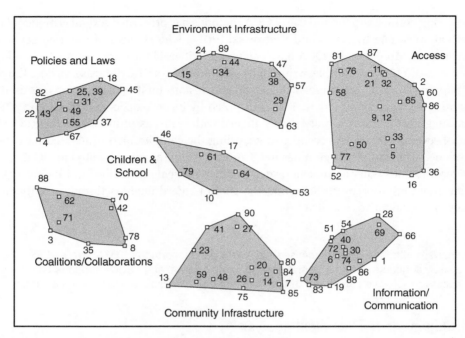

Figure 10.4 Clustered concept map showing MDS arrangement of 90 items

Source: Trochim et al., 2004: 13, Figure 1

Note: Figures refer to item numbers

Liliane Cambraia Windsor (2013) used concept mapping as a tool in her community based participatory project to investigate (and build capacity for action on) the personal and community-level dynamics of substance abuse in "distressed" areas of Newark, New Jersey – areas that were predominantly populated by people of colour. Participants included service providers, community residents, and substance users, all selected for their ability to contribute relevant information. Community brainstorming resulted in 209 statements being generated; these were refined down to a pool of 100 statements for sorting by three new sets of community-based participants. The map produced from the sorting exercise was interpreted by a further three groups who suggested modifications and assigned titles for the eight clusters identified in the map. Based on these discussions, the clusters were further grouped into three overarching themes:

1. impact of specific substance use on individuals and communities

2. impact of the drug trade and its players

3. impact of substance use and drug trade on the community.

A Community Collaborative Board reflecting the diversity of the area was then established to develop action plans, facilitated by the rapport with community members that had been developed through the research activity.

Windsor suggested that a statistical procedure to assist in reducing the original list of (209) statements would have been helpful for her study, although her goal was more to involve the community than to produce a reliable measure. Qualitative methods used to gather data and especially to assess results were useful in increasing validity for that group. Of more importance was the loss of in-depth information through the use of the very structured technique for gathering and recording the initial statements. Again, she recommended gathering additional qualitative data through less structured focus groups to supplement these.

There are two (related) statistical limitations to note with this form of concept mapping:

- Cluster analysis using usual Euclidian distances does not produce the neat solutions found in concept mapping literature when clusters are overlaid on MDS plots (see, for example, Figure 9.8). Kane and Trochim's concept mapping software uses distances calculated from the coordinates on the 2-dimensional plot (the X–Y coordinate matrix) for clustering, rather than counts in the similarity matrix, in order to ensure non-overlapping clusters in the visual map, as seen in Figure 10.4. The consequence is that the item groupings generated do not necessarily have as much conceptual coherence as they would if the original similarity matrix had been used.
- The MDS stress levels obtained are generally higher than the 0.1 usually recommended as acceptable (see previous chapter). Kane and Trochim (2007) report an average of 0.285 with a standard deviation of 0.04 from other studies (Windsor's was 0.33).

Software to facilitate rapid processing of concept mapping data is sold on a per-project or annual subscription basis by Concept Systems Inc. Website: www.conceptsystems.com/software/

Repertory grid technique

Repertory grid technique, based on the personal construct theory of George Kelly (1955), is employed as a flexible cognitive mapping tool in clinical practice. It is used also in social psychological research to ascertain how people construe a phenomenon in their world, such as an object, an event, an experience, an idea, or a set of people. Repertory grid technique is valued for the insight it provides, rather than because it tests hypotheses with traditional tests of significance.

Participants are presented with 7–10 random selections of three non-evaluative elements (people, objects, events, activities) related to the phenomenon of interest. These are drawn from theory, prior qualitative work, or the participant him- or herself. For each triad, each participant identifies ways two elements are alike but different from the third. Each comparison elicits one or more bipolar dimensions, or constructs, reflecting the way in which the participant interprets the topic of interest. Particular constructs are located and gather meaning within an entire network in which some constructs are more important than others, evolving into a form of "idiographic cartography" (Fransella, Bell & Bannister, 2003). These might then be reported as frequencies. A sample size of 15–25 participants from a similar population is considered adequate to generate constructs (dimensions) covering the universe of meaning for a particular research focus for that particular population (Tan & Hunter, 2002). Shared dimensions can be developed by having a group work on the task together.

In a further analytic step, a grid is created with the elements now being used to identify columns, while the dimensions provided by the participant identify rows. Each participant rates each element on each dimension using either dichotomous (0/1) scoring or a 5- or 7-point rating scale (Fransella et al., 2003). Alternatively, a group can rate all the dimensions from group or individual responses.

The original frequencies are used to compare relative importance of the dimensions (e.g., Moynihan, 1996), or grids are decomposed using cluster, principal components, or factor analysis to identify a more fundamental dimensional structure (Simpson & Wilson, 1999). Clusters or factors are reviewed semantically, to ensure that they really do share a fundamental aspect, and are not coincidental (Olsson, 2015). As with pile sorting, participant commentary recorded during and after the task helps to elucidate the phenomenon and its dimensions.

After providing a detailed explanation of Kelly's original repertory grid technique and variations of it, Antonina Bauman (2015) employed a simplified version of the technique to evaluate factors affecting 16 students' trust in online book sellers. Students compared and contrasted any two websites out of a selection of six, to develop lists of constructs that do and don't signal trust. All sites were evaluated against each trust signal as it was identified, using scaled measures. Comments made during the process were also recorded. Ninety-three constructs developed by the students were categorised by the researcher and two independent reviewers. Layout, ease of use, and sales (price and range of products available) were identified as most frequently used of the 15 resulting categories. Constructs in these same three categories, along with offers of guarantees and provision of reviews were nominated as first choice items and were therefore assumed to be most important. These three key (repeated) elements contrast with traditional views that rate privacy and security as more important cues for eliciting trust.

Fassin et al. (2015), in contrast, describe in detail a range of multivariate techniques used to analyse the grids developed using more traditional forms of the repertory grid technique in their relatively complex comparative study of corporate social responsibility (CSR) for SMEs in six European countries. Qualitative data about common and contrasting cultural patterns were used also in evaluating results, for example, to explain low ratings for safety (viewed as a legal compliance issue rather than a voluntary CSR issue). Philanthropy also had low ratings except in the UK; in Italy it was seen as a personal activity and in Norway it was seen as being covered by government welfare rather than being a business initiative. For most countries (especially France), business ethics were not part of CSR, whereas they were closely related in others (e.g., Italy). The authors point to the usefulness of the repertory grid technique for analysing participants' mental models concerning this type of business concept.

Computer applications to facilitate grid analysis are available (free of charge) from http://webgrid.typed.com/

Q methodology

Q methodology uses factor analysis in the study of human subjectivity. Participants (the *P-set*) sort a representative sample of qualitatively derived statements, a "concourse of communication", into 7–13 (usually 9) categories to express their views on a topic along a "most like" to "most unlike" dimension, with more to the centre and less to each side (approximating the bell shape of a normal distribution). The sorting distributions of the statements, not the participants, become the sample (the cases) to which factor analysis is applied in order to group the *people* who gave similar responses. Typical responses for each group are then examined to reveal the gestalt of their different views (McKeown & Thomas, 2013; Watts & Stenner, 2005). This strategy has a long history as an "alternative" method in psychology to capture people's subjectivities. It was popular for a time then fell into relative disuse; it is currently attracting renewed attention and use (Watts & Stenner, 2005).

All university staff will be familiar with acrimonious debates about performance and quality assessment of institutions and their teaching staff. The argument, essentially, is characterised as being about accountability versus lack of faculty input and ownership, and questions about the validity of measures. Baas, Rhoads, and Thomas (2016), working in the US environment, wondered how accurate this characterisation is, and how close to a consensual "culture of assessment" university academics have come. They chose to use Q methodology "to examine the subjective structure of the

(Continued)

(Continued)

discourse regarding assessment in higher education" (2016: 4). They selected 50 statements from a pool of 300 derived from online and print sources and interviews as representing the diversity of views expressed. Forty demographically and role diverse participants who had participated in the online debates or who had some other involvement with the assessment process ranked statements from +5 to -5 to indicate how characteristic they were of their personal beliefs about assessment. Analysis of the resulting 40 by 40 correlation matrix was resolved in a two-factor solution which identified two groups of participants, and eight who sat with neither group. The 17 "anti-assessment stalwarts" who were cynical about assessment were mostly social science or humanities faculty, while 15 mixed discipline, mixed role (administrators and faculty) "defenders of the faith" believed locally managed assessment could be helpful. Although these results were not unexpected, the authors were surprised that the results were not more nuanced. They do not expect an "all-in" consensus to occur anytime soon.

Specialised software for conducting Q sorts and the statistical (factor) analyses are available free of charge from http://qmethod.org (under Resources).

Systematic pattern identification in observations

Structured recording of observations allows the quantification of perceptible behaviours in natural contexts over a period of time. This allows for analysis of the sequential and associative relationships between those behaviours, including those that are inaudible. Such research has application, for example, in communication studies where gesturing is of interest, and in studies of movement in dance, or sport (e.g., Camerino et al., 2012; Torrents et al., 2010). A recorded behavioural session is segmented into elements (based on the purpose of the study) that become the movement units recorded for coding and analysis. The frequency, order, and duration of each unit within a behavioural episode is coded and then graphed to reveal the temporal patterning (T-patterns) of those units. These patterns are then analysed statistically to reveal the structural relations between the behaviours that were recorded, leading to an inductive process of theory construction (Anguera & Izquierdo, 2006; Sánchez-Algarra & Anguera, 2013).

OSMOS (Observational System of Motor Skills) and Theme Coder are programs designed specifically for the recording of movement and the coding of those recordings.

The imitation game

The imitation game has been recently developed as an inherently integrated (hybrid) strategy for comparative cultural analysis (Collins & Evans, 2014; Collins,

Evans et al., in press). It is included here as just one example of the kind of innovative data collection and analysis strategies that can arise when researchers combine deep theoretical understanding with what are often chance experiences, to think creatively about new ways of generating knowledge.

The imitation game is based on a parlour game in which a Judge poses written questions to a man and a woman who are both hidden from his or her sight, in order to determine who is recording geniune answers. The catch is that one (e.g., the woman) would answer naturally, while the other would pretend to be of that gender (the man would pretend to be a woman). This strategy has been adapted for sociological research covering a range of situations, particularly those concerning membership of minority groups, on the basis that the Pretender has to be culturally literate and have "interactional expertise"[3] in respect of those in the alternative group in order to answer the questions appropriately. Such interactional expertise allows a person to understand others' worldviews, even though they do not engage in practices pertaining to that world. Collins and Evans found, for example, that the blind were much more able to pass as sighted than the sighted were able to pass as blind (86% to 13%). The blind experience life-long immersion in the cultural world and discourse of sighted people, whereas sighted people rarely encounter the culture and discourse of blind people. One of the advantages of the imitation game strategy is that the players become the "proxy researchers" as it is they, rather than the researchers, who provide the cultural expertise for the game to work, at least at the operational and basic analyses levels.

Several types of data are generated from the game, including the Judge's questions and participant responses, the Judge's decision as to who is Real and who is a Pretender, with a rating of their level of confidence in that decision, and the reason each provides for their response or decision. Judges' decisions over several rounds are combined in a formula that calculates right guesses less wrong guesses over total guesses (including "don't know" to allow for variations in the tendency some people have to make don't know choices). These provide a basis for a range of comparative analyses. Qualitative data are content coded both statistically and as discourse. This mix of qualitative and quantitative data can be combined with pre-existing demographic or other quantitative information for additional analyses. Sampling can be extended by having further Judges make decisions based on transcripts of questions and answers from the live sessions. Alternatively, the game can be played with small groups taking each of the roles, thus generating a series of discussions that can be recorded for further analysis, along with their formal responses. Questions generated by groups usually are more discerning than those generated by individuals, resulting in lower pass rates for the Pretenders.

Universally, across topics, Collins and Evans have found that Judges' questions ask for information of five general types covering biographical, preference, opinion, knowledge, or situational knowledge. Topic coding, which may interact with the

---

[3] Interactional expertise: fluency in a language acquired through prolonged and deep socialisation within the spoken discourse of a specialist community that may or may not include any practical experience.

information type, is specific to the area being investigated and usually also to the country in which the data are collected. For example, UK games on sexuality have more questions about sexual behaviour, while parallel games in Poland have more on disclosure. Collins uses the imitation game format to build theoretical understanding of the nature of expertise and, through analysing the sensitivity and content of the questions that are asked, of cultural identity across groups and across nations.

> *Masquerade* is an app available from http://blogs.cardiff.ac.uk/imgame/ that enables a simple version of the game to be played on a smartphone or tablet, for demonstration purposes. For more extensive research purposes contact the originators to get access to their more elaborate computer programs.

Concluding remarks

Not all methods can be neatly categorised as qualitative or quantitative. Inherently mixed or hybrid methodologies that merge elements of both qualitative and quantitative approaches, that are neither one nor the other, have been and are continuing to be developed. Two broad types of mixed approaches have been reviewed in this chapter. The first includes well-known "qualitative" methodologies that are inherently broadly based in the actual methods that traditionally have been and continue to be used within them. Then, there were a group of much more focused hybrid methodologies involving use of specific mixed strategies to achieve often quite specific methodological purposes. A few of these have been in use now for some decades, most others are more recently developed. Advances in digital technology have often been central to these developments, making possible the complex computations needed to determine outcomes from complex sources within functional time limits. This is an exciting area in which innovative strategies for integrating both traditional and non-traditional methods have been, and still are being developed in order to answer both age-old and new questions, often with a focus on culture.

Further reading

For many of these topics, a web search can be especially rewarding.

Ethnography, case study, and discursive analysis as inherently mixed methods

Becker et al. ([1961] 1977) is a classic ethnographic study of medical students in training that used simple tables to complement their narrative reporting.

Mercer (1973) used community surveys, official records of several kinds, and unstructured interviews, combining qualitative and quantitative data in another classic ethnographic study exploring the social character and definition of "mental retardation" in children.

Bernard (2006) and Borgatti (2016) describe methods of cultural domain analysis including free listing, pile sorts, triad tests, and consensus analysis.

Hammersley and Atkinson (2007) detail a primarily qualitative approach to the practice of ethnography, including analysis and writing.

Several illuminating chapters in Weisner (2005) are based on mixed ethnographic methods.

Articles on aspects of (mixed methods) analysis in ethnographic and cultural anthropology are often published in *Field Methods* (http://journals.sagepub.com/home/fmx).

In his text, articles, and several anthologies of case studies, Robert Yin (2004, 2006, 2012, 2014) refers repeatedly to the use of multiple methods of data collection in the development and execution of case studies.

Habashi and Worley (2009) use sequential interview and survey methods in their case study of the geopolitical agency of Palestinian children. Results from both are presented together as integrated themes.

Schrauf (2016) provides rationale and context for discursive analysis of both interview and survey/questionnaire data, including detailed guides on methods of application.

Hybrid methods

Rihoux and Ragin (2009) is a basic text covering all types of QCA.

Cress and Snow (2000) provide full detail of the QCA example used earlier, demonstrating a practical application of the method.

Cragun et al. (2016) review the use of QCA in health and mixed methods research. They then demonstrate its use by providing a detailed stepwise account of their use of QCA in reviewing the effectiveness of hereditary colorectal cancer screening programmes, as indicated by patient follow-through.

Edwards (2010) has written a comprehensive working paper reviewing mixed methods applications of social network analysis.

Scott (2013) and Prell (2012) are basic texts on SNA. Prell includes instruction on using UCINET.

Hogan (2017) explores the structures of simple and complex social networks, and ways of working with multiple types of social networking data from the internet.

Bolíbar (2016) combines the quantitative methods of SNA for describing relational structures with narrative data describing the relationships that underlie and contextualise those structures.

Weishaar, Amos, and Collin (2015) use plagiarism software with policy-related sources to investigate the policy network surrounding the development of European smoke-free policy. Quantitative network analyses are supported with further qualitative analysis of the sources and 35 interviews with network members.

Christensen et al. (2011) and Skinner et al. (2005) each demonstrate different ways of linking spatial components to ethnography.

Cope and Elwood (2009) and Steinberg and Steinberg (2006) are texts covering the inclusion of social factors in geographical research and of using geospatial research as a component within social research.

As well as reporting a mixed methods study undertaken within the field of human geography, Crooks et al. (2011) provide an extensive review of other mixed methods work undertaken within that discipline.

Fielding and Fielding (2015), Knigge and Cope (2006), and Steinberg and Steinberg (2011) are chapters or articles that address the issue of "grounding" social research by incorporating locational data.

Fielding and Cisneros-Puebla (2009) describe the methodology of a mixed methods study using geographic data as a major component in the analysis.

Lee and Kang (2015) explore the opportunities and challenges afforded by geospatial big data, such as is available through mobile phone records.

Fransella et al. (2003) explain the basis for and methods of using and interpreting repertory grids.

Tan and Hunter (2002) describe the use of repertory grid for studying cognition in information systems.

Denicolo, Long, and Bradley-Cole (2016) place the repertory grid technique within its larger context of personal construct psychology.

An article and a book by Watts & Stenner (2005, 2012) give a very clear exposition of the history, theory, and practice of Q methodology, supported by many examples from the authors' research.

Torrents et al. (2010) provide a clear and comprehensive example of analysing temporal patterns to study improvised dance movements.

Collins, Evans et al. (in press), Collins and Evans (2014), and Evans and Crocker (2013) describe the theory behind and implementation of the imitation game as a tool for social and cultural research. A video describing the game and showing it being played is available at http://blogs.cardiff.ac.uk/imgame/2014/06/03/the-imitation-game-demonstration-video/

11

EXPLORING DISSONANCE AND DIVERGENCE

CHAPTER OVERVIEW

Dissonance and divergence occur in mixed methods research as different methods generate different perspectives, or particular cases reveal data at odds with those of others. Dissonance or divergence is quite frequently mentioned in research reports, but rarely does either become a focus of analysis (Pluye et al., 2009). Rather than being seen as a problem to be avoided or explained away, "dissonance, doubt, and ambiguity" can be welcomed by mixed methods researchers for their capacity to initiate creative insights (Rossman & Wilson, 1994: 323–324). Initiation, the deliberate seeking after paradox and contradiction, is described as "the analytic function that turns ideas around. It initiates new interpretations, suggests areas for further exploration, or recasts the entire research question. Initiation brings with it fresh insight and a feeling of the creative leap" (Rossman & Wilson, 1985: 637).

The experience of dissonance or divergence has been evident in some examples outlined in earlier chapters. Dissonance is encountered particularly in the context of working with complementary methods and methods seeking convergence in results. Divergent, exceptional, and negative cases generally become more apparent in comparative analyses involving linked or transformed data. This chapter will explore the sources of dissonance and divergence in mixed method analyses. It will draw from examples available to generate suggestions about ways to respond to the occurrence of dissonance and divergence as an analytic challenge.

Mapping dissonance and divergence

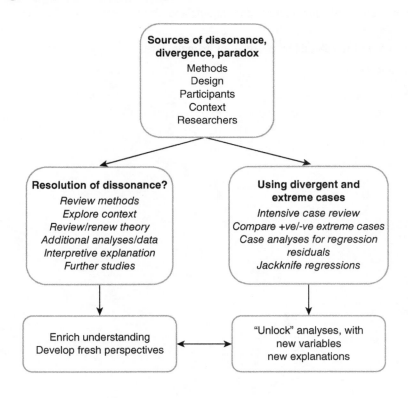

Methodological purposes

Integration of different sources and of results from different approaches to analysis is a general goal of mixed methods analyses, with the understanding that this will result in an enriched view and a deeper understanding of the phenomenon being studied. Inevitably, however, there will be times when different sources of information conflict, or particular cases do not follow a more general pattern. Researchers work with dissonant results and divergent cases to explain or resolve differences, especially where these detract from the integrative purposes to be served in the study or the overall results being obtained. They use instances of dissonance and divergence, also, as a point of initiation for further exploration, investigation, and/or interpretation that will enhance understanding of the phenomenon of interest.

Dissonance and its resolution in mixed methods studies

Dissonance is a general term referring to differences that range in intensity from inconsistency and points of disagreement through discord to conflict and contradiction. Mixed methods researchers will generally look for some resolution of dissonance, although some value the tension generated by differences between multiple views and the cross-fertilisation between them, rather than the satisfaction of achieving a tidy congruence.

> Explanations do not have to be internally consensual and neatly consistent to have meaning and to have the capacity to explain. Indeed, if the social world is multidimensional, then surely our explanations need to be likewise? I want to suggest that we should develop "dialogic" explanations which are "multi-nodal". By "multi-nodal" I mean that the explaining that is done involves different axes and dimensions of social experience. By "dialogic" I mean that the ways in which these axes and dimensions are conceptualized and seen to relate or intersect can be explained in more than one way, depending upon the questions that are being asked and the theoretical orientations underlying those questions. (Mason, 2006a: 20)

One writer in particular has championed the positive value of dissonance – or at least, of allowing for the potential of it. Throughout her mixed methods career, Jennifer Greene has encouraged researchers to take a dialectical perspective when working with data, to promote the likelihood of initiating fresh insights and understanding of the subject being studied (e.g., Greene, 2007, 2008, 2012a). She advises: "Convergence, consistency, and corroboration are overrated in social inquiry. The interactive mixed methods analyst looks just as keenly for instances of divergence and dissonance, as these may represent important nodes for further and highly generative analytic work" (Greene, 2007: 144).

While Greene sees dialectical (initiating) designs as being based on a multiparadigm stance, Burke Johnson (2017) has developed dialectical pluralism as a metaparadigm designed specifically to encapsulate a dialectical approach to mixed methods research. He suggests:

> Dialectical pluralism provides a way for researchers, practitioners, clients, policy makers, and other stakeholders to work together and produce new workable "wholes" while, concurrently, thriving on differences and intellectual tensions.

Johnson emphasises the importance of bringing the multiple mental models of different participant groups to research, in order to democratically produce collaborative knowledge that will be widely accepted and utilised. He suggests that when critical and transformative reflexivity are added and the tensions instigated by the different perspectives are worked through, the working knowledge created will be based on multiple sources of evidence and will satisfy multiple standards for validity. Such knowledge will incorporate not only new ways of thinking, but also practical theory derived from a combination of abstract theory with local values and contexts.

Dissonance in results can trigger a need to find a resolution or explanation in order to move forward, providing useful pointers to more and better evidence for meaningful propositions as a result. In some settings unresolved dissonance can be damaging, however. It can affect the credibility of results, and it is especially concerning when results of a study are to be used as the basis for clinical decision making or for design, funding, or evaluation of community services or other interventions (Slonim-Nevo & Nevo, 2009).

Methodological-participant interaction as a locus for dissonance

Researchers might deliberately choose to take a dialectical approach in designing a mixed methods study but, more often, finding dissonance is unintentional and not especially welcome. It is when researchers are specifically seeking corroboration or convergence in the results from their different sources and/or methods that dissonance is most likely to be encountered (Bazeley, unpublished data).

> In practice, triangulation as a strategy provides a rich and complex picture of some social phenomenon being studied, but rarely does it provide a clear path to a singular view of what is the case. I suggest that triangulation as a strategy provides evidence for the *researcher* to make sense of some social phenomenon, but that the triangulation *strategy* does not, in and of itself, do this ... [its value] is as a technique which provides more and better evidence from which researchers can *construct meaningful propositions* about the social world. (Mathison, 1988: 15, emphasis in original)

Dissonance as disagreement or discord might also be expected in initial results in studies with a complementary purpose, but in these the differences are likely to be viewed as revealing different aspects of a phenomenon. As different facets of an overall picture, they contribute further to an understanding of a hermeneutic whole. The researcher searches for patterns, rather like creating a bricolage or piecing together the different elements of a puzzle or creating a mosaic, as described earlier (Chapter 5).

Perhaps the aim is not to produce a tidy picture, but to allow for the messiness and tensions that exist in social reality:

In a large-scale study of Scientists in Organizations conducted many years ago, Pelz and Andrews (1976) concluded by suggesting that productive scientific environments were those that allowed for a series of "tensions" that balanced security with challenge, without specific points of resolution. These tensions included: ensuring scientists engaged in a diversity of both (pure) scientific and translational (applied) activity; fostering intellectual independence but also vigorous interaction with colleagues; focused activity but also multi-skilling; both specialisation and breadth of skills; deep-probing on an established area but also exploration into new areas; an open environment but with joint goal setting; individual autonomy within a coordinated environment; and, personal support and established collaborations despite different, combatively defended strategies.

Methods, participants, and contexts intersect to create dissonance in results. A combination of scaled with open-ended questions in a survey or interview will often generate dissonant responses. Sometimes the different methods serve different purposes and tap into different aspects of knowledge, for example, by capturing global versus specific experiences, or public versus private viewpoints (Goodwin, Polek, & Goodwin, 2013). Alternatively, the elicitation and potential disclosure of responses might affect participants in different ways that are method related. Typically survey responses are more positive, while interviews provide an opportunity to express negativity and/or report problems. In some situations, however, the apparent anonymity of a survey or questionnaire allows for expression of more negative responses.

In a study of satisfaction and quality of life in care homes, Kelle (2006) found satisfaction appeared to be much higher when assessed using a survey than through interviews. People in this situation, where they were dependent on the staff for care, were unwilling to give negative ratings, but in interviews with the researchers, especially once a level of rapport or trust was developed, they would cautiously express some negative experiences or take a more critical stance, while also making excuses for staff.

A particularly interesting analysis of the differences between scaled and open responses collected in parallel in a survey-interview assessed the satisfaction of prospective parents with genetic counselling services following diagnosis of a foetal abnormality. Green, Statham, and Solomou (2008) identified discrepancies occurring when the participant's focus differed between methods, for example, on the practical and technical aspects of care versus the emotional impact of the diagnosis; on individual factors (capacity to act or care received) compared with systemic issues; care offered versus care received; or actual care against what might ideally or even realistically be expected. There were also discrepancies when care was good but it was initiated by the parent; when care was absent or unwanted, which made rating difficult for the participant; and when there was ambiguity in questions in which the scope of care was non-specific. Because both forms of data were being collected at the same time for each question, the interviewers were able to immediately explore and obtain explanations for the discrepancies, thus enriching the data available for analysis.

Sources of discrepancy between surveys and interviews were explored also by Dunning et al. (2008). Some of the methodological problems they revealed were quite obvious; for example, questions being asked in different forms in each method, with interviews more likely to focus on "how" and "why" rather than "what". Others were more critical, especially when participants conceptualised key concepts differently from the researchers' ideas that had informed the design of the surveys, for example, with respect to the meaning of terms like "neighbourhood".

Different methods of data collection and analysis can selectively highlight or obscure variation between participants and/or between sites, as demonstrated in Trend's (1978) classic study of the implementation of a US Federal housing subsidy programme, where observation revealed differences between sites within a region that were obscured by averaged statistical measures (described in Maxwell & Loomis, 2003). Differences in sources and methods of collection of data impacted Slonim-Nevo and Nevo's (2009) evaluation of an educational programme with immigrant youth in Israel: measures varied depending on whether they were derived from standardised scales, teacher reports, parent reports, or youths' self-reports.

Methodological explanations look first at the sources used and any problems or differences in the way in which one or both methods were conducted. A determination is made of how these might have affected the results and whether an interpretive adjustment can be made or further investigation is required. Alternatively the discrepancies might point to the differential sensitivity of different methods (e.g., surveys and interviews), and so results from both are incorporated within the explanation given. Reconciliation might then take place through "plausible interpretation", application of a new conceptual framework, or through data reanalysis (Pluye et al., 2009: 60–61).

In evaluating methodological reasons for dissonance, attention should be paid (a) to differences in sampling, including the potential for a biased subgroup to provide comments in surveys, and (b) to the comparability of questions across different formats, such as whether they tap into global or specific views and experiences. Or perhaps (c) a theoretical framing imposed on the data is inappropriate, or (d) the topic was handled differently by different interviewers? Methodological, contextual, and design-related sources of dissonance, once diagnosed, often point to their own solution.

Moffatt, White, Mackintosh, and Howel (2006) evaluated a project in which specific welfare rights advice was offered to a sample of 126 older people, 60 per cent of whom received additional benefits as a consequence.

The project resulted in no measurable improvement to the lives of those receiving advice or consequent benefits compared to a comparison group without advice, and yet qualitative evidence from a subsample of partici-pants suggested wide-ranging benefits. The investigators' response was to look first for methodological explanations for this discrepancy, resulting in the following insights:

- They carried out a brief interview with the wider sample, and confirmed that demographic and baseline characteristics of the samples did not explain any differences.

- They found measurable impacts of the programme were "diluted" by par-ticipants who were not eligible for additional welfare benefits, and by implementation delays for those who were eligible. Additionally, 59 per cent of those given advice had already received benefits from other sources prior to the study.

- Many participants had chronic illnesses and did not expect an improve-ment in their physical health, but interviews with the qualitative sample suggested the intervention did result in their feeling less stressed, more secure financially, and consequently better able to maintain independence and quality of life. The SF-36, which was used as an outcome measure, had not captured these dimensions.

The problems Moffatt et al. (2006) experienced with the SF-36 are common but not exclusive to that measure. Mallinson identified multiple problems of interpre-tation in the SF-36 questions in her older-age sample that challenged claims of precision in measurement, despite its extensive use for evaluation of interventions and in multinational clinical trials. Once they have undergone the initial develop-ment phase, widely used standardised survey- or questionnaire-based scales designed to "measure" some aspect of human functioning are often treated as if their validity in reflecting the concept of interest is beyond question. Thus researchers can "fall into the trap of using questionnaires like a form of laboratory equipment (a kind of calibrated dipstick of health)" (Mallinson, 2002: 19). Attention must be given to how the concept was originally defined and operation-alised, the context in which the measure was developed, and how that compares with where it is now being applied.

Developing explanations for conflicting evidence between two datasets often leads the researchers to construct new or additional hypotheses. They might then return to their data and conduct further analyses, although Erzberger and Kelle (2003) argue that any new hypotheses or explanations should be tested in a new study with new data. While this is sometimes suggested in discussions by those reporting studies in which dissonance was experienced, actually doing so is rarely reported.

When Weiss, Kreider, Mayer, Hencke, and Vaughan (2005) interviewed parents and teachers about family involvement in school they were "repeatedly confronted with the importance of parents' work" (2005: 48). Returning to their earlier survey responses, they found working mothers talked about involvement in their child's schooling that occurred either despite their working or even because they were working. Surveyed teachers and principals, however, cited mothers' work schedules as more problematic than anything else in limiting family involvement in the school. The limited research literature that was available also focused on negative associations between parental work and school involvement. Because the numbers and the text told different stories about an issue that would not go away, Weiss et al. developed two research questions to focus the issue and then set about "dredging up" any available evidence from their qualitative case study data and open-ended survey data, to investigate these. They found, for example, that categories used in their early analyses to code survey responses had obscured the workplace as a possible site for parental involvement in their child's education. Informed by qualitative analyses, they created new composite and transformed variables for use in multivariate analyses, the statistician drew on the knowledge of those familiar with the case study material to verify her interpretation of factors, and they redesigned their later surveys to include questions that addressed this emergent issue of the impact of mothers' work and working on involvement in their children's education and learning.

With their combined data, Weiss et al. discovered and then demonstrated how parents were more involved than teachers gave them credit for, in ways that were not anticipated by teachers. They clarified the conditions that best facilitated or inhibited involvement in school, including the unexpected and inventive ways in which working parents saw their work as facilitating their children's education. Parents spoke of their child's use of a computer in the workplace; of how they gained educational information from clients; and of negotiating more flexible times for parent–teacher interviews.

Through their experience, Weiss et al. "learned that mixed-methods approaches could only be rough guides and that intentional designs might have to give way to real-world problems of data availability and deadlines. Accordingly [they] developed a sense of [their] mixed-methods work as a dynamic hands-on process, guided only very generally by mixed-methods analytic models" (2005: 61). Release from predetermined design constraints fostered added creativity and flexibility in their analysis, and yielded valuable contributions for developing policies that could "support the articulation between work and school systems" (2005: 62).

Human and contextual factors: participants and researchers as the locus for dissonance

When differences within or across participants create inconsistent or conflicting responses, there might be no solution as such, but rather a need to identify the source of the differences, and to see these as contributing to a richer understanding of the topic. Context plays a critical role, as participants in different circumstances or in different personal or professional positions will vary or will have different interpretations of a problem (the topic of investigation). Indeed, such differences might be deliberately sought by a researcher who seeks information from different stakeholders or sources about the same issue. Researchers also need to understand what motivations might give rise to different answers within a participant's reports, and how those can play out depending on the mode of data collection – as was evident in Kelle's study, described above.

Meetoo and Temple (2003) found people report lapses of self-care differently in different contexts. Some people with diabetes in their study found an interview confrontational and so reported compliance with dietary requirements while also recording instances of non-adherence in their diaries; others who admitted dietary lapses in their interviews had reported expected choices in their diaries because this was seen as the more permanent record.

Context and motivation of those responding to questions were important also in Teye's (2012) study of protection of forest resources in Ghana, reported earlier (Chapter 5). Understanding personal conflicts around issues of formal and informal social support also assisted Berger and Paul (2014) to integrate results from different methods in their study of women experiencing infertility (reported in the same chapter). Indeed, these kinds of situations appear to arise most commonly in studies where different participants are contributing data through similar or different means to a study with a complementary purpose.

More troubling are instances where researcher differences in paradigmatic and conceptual understanding are a source of dissonance. Deeply held philosophical views and disparities in disciplinary training can intersect with issues of power and control to create irresolvable conflict (Lunde et al., 2013). Similarly, a lack of common understanding of the purpose of the research can render a project less fruitful (Wall et al., 2013). Alternatively, when better managed (see guidelines for working in teams, Chapter 2), the tension arising from the intersections of team members' different views can contribute to an enriching dialogic construction of the phenomenon (Mason, 2006a; Seltzer-Kelly et al., 2012).

Wall et al. (2013) had different researchers apply deductive and inductive approaches to an analysis of the same set of visual data derived from a learning to learn project conducted in 12 schools in the United Kingdom. They described the different "story" told by each method, and concluded that, given findings from each method were "neither ... confirmed nor triangulated by the other analysis" that, "if either process were asked to stand alone then it leaves the

(Continued)

(Continued)

uneasy conclusion that [alternative] implications from the data would have remained unknown. This means that choice of analysis technique can be a risky business" (2013: 36). They further note that "without strategic integration of the quantitative and qualitative processes the findings can be contradictory rather than providing a coherent representation of the data" (2013: 37). Strategic integration, in this case, would have included ensuring that the analyses were serving a common purpose, as understood by all analysts.

Learning from the analysis of divergent or extreme cases

Cases appearing as outliers to general trends in the pattern of relationships are variously referred to as divergent cases, extreme cases, or outliers. Outliers are treated very differently in statistical and qualitative analyses. In the former, cases with extreme values – usually defined as more than three standard deviations from the mean – are potentially seen as disconfirming hypotheses, but more often are simply omitted from the main analyses. In regression-based analyses in particular, they skew the results and therefore distort the analysis of trends in relationships between variables. In contrast, divergent cases in qualitative research are valued for what they can reveal about underlying processes as further data are gathered and/or an attempt is made to understand why that case or those cases differ from the more general pattern of observations.

In mixed methods studies, when linked qualitative data are compared across different demographic groups or groups based on scaled scores, instances where individual cases go against a trend can be readily identified and then explored using the additional data that are available.

When I compared scientists' and social scientists' experiences of gaining satisfaction from engaging in research, scientists were seen to be expressing agency – valuing the experience of making things happen, of controlling processes, while social scientists gained satisfaction from what their research achieved, with two exceptions (one male, one female). Because the data were linked on an individual basis, these divergent cases could be identified, revealing that each worked in experimental cognitive psychology, a sub-discipline that has more in common with science than social science. It could be argued, then, that rather than contradicting the observed trend, these apparently discrepant cases "proved the rule".

Exploring divergent cases can "unlock" an analysis, providing insight into processes only partially (or not at all) understood.

In 2006, I worked with a doctoral student (long since graduated) who was studying responses to amalgamations of administrative regions within government health services in low-density, rural areas (Bazeley, 2009). The lack of communication with employees throughout the process of amalgamation had assumed central focus in the student's analysis, as it appeared to be a critical source of discontent. Just two of her 20 interviewees held positive views about the amalgamations, some were neutral, others negative. Exploration of these two positive cases revealed each had personally benefited from the amalgamations. This raised the question of whether the majority were less than positive because they were now worse off in a personal sense, rather than because aspects of the service had deteriorated – as some had suggested. This sparked a new line of investigation, with the student checking for evidence on self versus service orientation among participants in her interview and questionnaire data, and it challenged her generalisation about the centrality of the communication issue alone in explaining interviewees' responses. Eventually it pointed to a much richer picture in which communication issues, specifically lack of engagement and transparency by the hierarchy, created a sense of uncertainty that fostered in employees a focus on their own interests.

Several authors have pointed to the value of deliberately choosing to sample from or otherwise focus on divergent or extreme cases (Brickson, 2005; Caracelli & Greene, 1993; Patton, 2002; Rossman & Wilson, 1994) as one of several approaches to purposive sampling. Cases at the two ends of a statistical distribution might be chosen to maximise the opportunity for comparative analysis, or an extreme case might be selected for special attention on the basis of being a statistical outlier. Similarly, cases that appear as anomalous in the qualitative corpus might be selected for detailed study.

The effectiveness of primary schools in Thailand in graduating students was compared with what could be expected, given regional characteristics and school characteristics (Fry, Chantavanich, & Chantavanich, 1981: 146). Those performing at a much higher or lower level than would be expected (based on regression modelling) were then explored using ethnographic methods. This approach yielded a critical additional variable concerning affectively expressed parental aspirations that, when introduced into discriminant analyses, meant the level of continuation into secondary schooling could be predicted with much improved accuracy.

Exploration of divergent cases might be planned or unplanned. When observations or calculations unexpectedly reveal cases that stand out in some way, these too must be understood and explained. Having alternative data sources available to provide confirming or disconfirming evidence or an explanation is a particular resource favouring mixed methods researchers.

> You should constantly have conversations between the qualitative and quantitative components of the research ... [In my current study] I designed the study with the conversation built into it. I'm using ethnographic or qualitative residual analysis. You do a regression to try to explain variation in something and then you look at the cases where you've got large residuals, where really the predicted value is very different from the actual value. And then you go in and do some in-depth qualitative research to find out why that might be. And then return to your quantitative analysis to see if you can explain more of the variation in your variable based on the in-depth understanding you got from the qualitative research. (Alicia O'Cathain, quoted in Curry & Nunez-Smith, 2015: 230, Box 8.1)

Residual case analysis is a strategy for identifying divergence that builds on econometric methods. Methods of employing data from regression analyses for selection of cases for intensive case study include use of tabular and graphical displays, and the identification of turning points in time series analyses (Wolf, 2010). A danger of focusing too much on residual analysis and prediction errors is possible distortion of the overall picture, built on the more generally agreed responses of the majority. Nevertheless, even where multiple regression produces a satisfactory result, additional examination of selected cases, especially those that deviate, can be of interest. Reasons for deviation indicate limits to the generalisability of the multiple regression model, with deviations most commonly occurring at one or other end of the distribution of scores.

Frieder Wolf (2010: 159) analysed determinants of education spending in German Länder (states). Plots of residuals versus fitted values showed much less accurate predictions for two Länder at the beginning of the period studied. Follow-up qualitative interviews with officials in those two were supplemented by four "on the line" cases, so as to not skew the analyses. One of the exceptions, with a strong political leader, had been the only Land to maintain free day nurseries attached to schools. Another, with a weak political leader, was adjacent to the capital and so higher education spending was lower as it was assumed students would travel. The overall qualitative analyses contributed a further variable for the regression analyses (the number of teachers with lifelong contracts), which improved their predictive power. Each Land was then removed, in turn, from the regression model (jackknifing). Results were compared to identify which variables each Land was contributing to the overall model and conclusions drawn from it, and to what degree each identified variable was contributing. This revealed, for example, that Berlin's financial situation, alone, was the source for inclusion of the negative effect of public indebtedness as a variable in the model.

Whatever the source of divergence, further analysing divergent cases has "the potential for recasting or elaborating the theory that directs the initial analyses" (Caracelli & Greene, 1993: 200), leading to refinement of initial hypotheses and questions. This indeed was what Kerrigan (2014) found, in her study of the role of human, social, and physical resources in driving data-driven design to inform operational processes in four community colleges. In her initial approach she separately analysed survey and interview data, the latter using a theoretically informed coding system, transformed the qualitative coding, then merged the two sets of data into a combined database to allow for within-case and cross-case analyses. These analyses produced inconsistent results, and so she returned to the qualitative data and reanalysed it using an inductive approach. As a result, she identified new aspects of collaborative culture, faculty perceptions, and a practical limitation on using data, which together caused her, as Caracelli and Greene noted, to recast and elaborate her theory.

Concluding remarks

Whenever different data are integrated, there is the ever-present risk of finding discrepancies and even conflict in the results from those different sources. Different sources of dissonance were identified and strategies for managing dissonance and divergence in results from different sources and between participants have been canvassed. At the same time, dissonance, divergence, and ambiguity have been reframed as something that might be welcomed, insofar as they serve to initiate further investigation and new thinking about the topic at hand. Often, once a reason for the dissonance has been found, a solution, if needed, becomes evident. Methodological concerns associated with different data sources, differences in expectations across groups or between researchers and participants, issues in theoretical framing, or other contextual factors are all matters that might be considered when dealing with dissonant sources.

Analysis of divergent cases, encouraged in qualitative and mixed methods approaches but all too often neglected in statistical analyses, similarly can result in fresh understanding that leads to a reframing of the overall analysis and results. This is an area where the availability of both statistical and qualitative data is a definite advantage, as one can assist with the interpretation of discrepancies and divergences in the other.

Kerrigan's study, with which the chapter ended, is an exemplar in terms of providing detail and transparency in methodological explanation – an important observation on which to finish this chapter and this Part Two review of integrative strategies. It is one of several themes that will be taken up in Part 3, as we look at bringing an integrative mixed methods study to a conclusion.

Further reading

Pluye et al. (2009) analyse how researchers dealt with divergence (used as a global term to also include dissonance) in the literature and in a sample of nine reported empirical studies that specifically addressed the issue. They also provide details of dealing with dissonance in a study of their own, and suggest how to use this as a tool for mixed methods research training.

Jick's (1979) study of dissonance among employees in relation to a company merger has become a classic on dissonance in a project employing triangulation.

Maxwell and Loomis (2003) review, in detail, several more classic studies where dissonance or divergence was experienced.

Kravitz, Duan, and Braslow (2004: 662) detail the "trouble with averages" insofar as "modest average effects may reflect a mixture of substantial benefits for some, little benefit for many, and harm for a few" – always a potential source of dissonance between methods.

da Costa and Remedios (2014) propose the use of a contextually relevant Implicit Association Test, which measures reaction times to the task of pairing words, as a methodological option to consider if other methods give conflicting results when assessing implicit psychological constructs.

Vikström (2010), a historical demographer, analyses the discrepancies in three sources of information on the employment of women in a Swedish town during 1860–63, identifying issues of self-representation for women in each of those sources.

PART 3

NEGOTIATED, WARRANTED
INFERENCES

Chapters in Part 2 have provided practical, action-based strategies that help to bring together different data sources, data types, and data analyses as a step towards integration of those data and analyses. These were necessarily described as if each was a standalone strategy, but of course, each of the strategies described is often, or usually, part of a more complex design or "method in use". Whichever way they were used, the final task is to build and communicate coherent conclusions based on those integrative analyses. Effective integration doesn't suddenly happen at the end of the project; it derives from a conversation that began as initial purposes and designs were being formulated, that then continued throughout the project. Essentially, integrated and coherent inferences begin to develop in the mind of the researcher and are tested against available evidence as analysis proceeds. Eventually, these are offered as warranted assertions, supported by data.

What are you aiming for?

The analytic logic model presented in Chapter 3 (Figure 3.3) listed tertiary interpretive processes in mixed methods research as including to discover, describe, confirm, refine, explain, predict, or perhaps to resolve a puzzle or even initiate a new one. These interpretive outcomes are not a simple flow on from mechanical processing of data, but result from inferences built through higher order analysis and reflective practice. These rest, in turn, on a foundation of integrated data processing, management and interrogation. They will be evident in richly detailed, composite narratives; models of processes; and emergent or refined theories that contribute to basic knowledge, strategic goals, or practical applications.

What is a *warranted* assertion?

It is often stated that a goal of mixed methods research is to develop warranted assertions. An assertion or inference that is warranted is one that is convincingly argued and supported by research evidence. The term *warranted assertion* derives from the early pragmatists (Pierce and Dewey), who recognised that knowledge is provisional, to be judged by consequent experience. Critical realism also recognises the provisional status of knowledge, as do most epistemological approaches. Thus, while truth is fallible, one can construct assertions that are warranted by "best explanations" from empirical data, the reality of the world as we experience it. The warrant is the step in the research logic, the clear chain of reasoning that connects a research finding to a conclusion. To be convincing, the argument for the conclusion and its warrant will be comprehensible and logical to the reader or audience, and evidentially preferable to alternative conclusions.

In mixed methods research, warranted assertions are built from the integrative analyses undertaken during the course of the project. These concluding inferences are most often developed iteratively and abductively from an accumulated body of data and analyses rather than from particular bits of evidence (see example below). In Part 3 (Chapter 12) we will consider some of these strategies for negotiating, supporting, and communicating inferences from mixed methods data analyses, and for warranting the quality and validity of those inferences.

In the project in which we built a model of researcher career stages and a generic definition of what it meant to be an "early career" academic researcher, no separate source of data provided a neat answer to our question (Bazeley, 2003b; Bazeley et al., 1996). What became necessary was to consider all of the evidence from our multiple sources together. We engaged in a process involving extensive team discussions and review of that evidence, weighting and balancing different sources and evidence from across different disciplines, to arrive at common criteria that could be supported and were not contradicted by that evidence. This process was much more than a simple compilation of complementary data.

12

FROM INTEGRATIVE ANALYSES TO WARRANTED ASSERTIONS AND A COHERENT, NEGOTIATED ACCOUNT

CHAPTER OVERVIEW

> In genuinely integrated studies, the quantitative and the qualitative findings will be mutually informative. They will talk to each other, much like a conversation or debate, and the idea is then to construct a negotiated account of what they mean together. (Bryman, 2007: 21)

The problem, now, is to move from interim analyses and a bundle of ideas about what's going on in the data and what the main issues might be, to producing an evidence-based set of assertions that come together as a coherent account of what has been found on the topic being investigated. The process here is not vastly different from that used with any other kind of data. It's about asking: "What have I learned?" "What do I know?" "How do all the pieces of evidence I've gathered fit together?" "Is there a story to tell?" Essentially, developing coherence is more about reasoning than about data and methods. Data and the results that have been developed from them have to be interpreted, connected, and given meaning in relation to the purposes of the study and the context from which they were drawn. Only then can their application to other settings be considered. Strategies that might assist this process and things to take into consideration are described in this action-focused chapter. Primary among these are the particular drawing and writing skills that support coherent thinking about results and their presentation.

The negotiation starts

A period of reflexive thinking helps one approach these final stages of data analysis. In this, any assumptions that were brought into the project or that might have accumulated during the project will be reviewed and reconsidered. Reflexivity has been defined as active, ongoing, critical scrutiny of the process of knowledge generation, construction, and interpretation, with a particular focus on the relationship between the researcher and participants in the research, and on how any interpretations came about (Guilleman & Gillam, 2004: 274). Memo-writing or journaling is critical to the reflexive process.

If it hasn't been done already, structuring records of available evidence according to components of the topic will assist the negotiation process by bringing together different ways of seeing things so they can be synchronised, if not harmonised.

- All known or anticipated component parts, subunits, or debatable issues within the topic(s) being investigated need to be identified.
- Then, whatever findings are available of any type and from any source that add insights or answer questions related to each or any of those components are explored and listed in "bins" (e.g., under headings) for each.

It is likely that some of the ideas and leads emerging during the project have become sidelined and so this process of reviewing and structuring data elements and interim analyses will help to build a perspective that embraces all of the work that has been done. In reviewing what is known for each of these component parts, thought should be given also to the links between them. The strategy that is most *de*structive of coherent integration is to work through a complete analysis of each of the separate sources or data types available *before* considering how they might be integrated.

Review of aims, concepts, contexts, and processes

What were the original aims and questions established for the project? Indeed, why were mixed methods being used at all? Bryman's (2007) analyses of mixed methods articles suggests that integration problems evidenced in written reports of studies stem from losing sight of these purposes.

Beginning, therefore, with a review of both substantive and methodological purposes is a step towards confirming whether the current direction of the project is on track. The ways in which the project has developed and its questions and design have morphed will become apparent. The overall goals might remain the same, but specific questions relating to those purposes typically change and develop during the course of the project as data and analyses bring to light fresh understanding of the issues involved. Such changes should be recognised and accounted for as they reflect changed perspectives regarding aspects of the subject matter that have become important for consideration.

Similarly, emergent understanding and applications of key concepts and principles that guided the research merit consideration and elaboration. Concepts evolve as they are operationalised; new concepts come into play; models are turned on their heads. "Developing adequate conceptualizations of the phenomena and processes under investigation must remain at the heart of social analysis" (Irwin, 2008: 416). Suggested strategies to help in developing this emergent understanding are:

- Define how key concepts were understood and used for this project, keeping in mind that concepts are multidimensional and multilayered (Bazeley, 2013: Chapter 8; Goertz, 2006). Defining concepts is worthwhile in itself, but it is relevant for any study to clarify the phenomena that the project is about, and how they are being understood in the context of this project (Merton, 1968; Sayer, 2000). Interpret abstract concepts in a way that relates to concrete research processes. Show how statistical measures or other forms of assessment reflect the meaning of the concepts or the nature of the phenomena they purport to measure.

- Draw out, and summarise if necessary, key points and processes developed in earlier analyses that will directly contribute to drawing conclusions.
- Review different contexts and conditions encountered and how these have varied throughout the course of the project. Do these change how concepts and processes being considered are understood?
- Look for stories and accounts that will illuminate or illustrate key events or findings in the data, and numbers that will help to place key events in context.
- If a team is involved, have team members share stories about their experience of the project and then review these for patterns and themes. These, along with your own assumptions and experience, will sensitise you to possibilities in the data and to questions to ask of the data as you work towards drawing conclusions from the project as a whole.

If key concepts and critical processes were well developed in earlier phases of the project, it is possible at this stage that a provisional model showing links between them, based on earlier analyses, can be developed. This then would be subject to further testing and elaboration using the available data, or it could point to the need for further data to be gathered in a subsequent stage of the project.

In my own mixed methods, action research doctoral project (Bazeley, 1977), I concluded each primary literature and data-based chapter with a clarification of my understanding of key points relating to the concept or specific topic addressed in that chapter. This was based on what I had learned from the literature and/or any analyses covered in that chapter on topics including mental health, social disadvantage, and community development. Then, having defined the way in which I had come to understand and dimensionalise each of these for this project, it became relatively straightforward to "see" and then to map out and demonstrate the links between them, based on the data I had gathered. Part of this "seeing", for example, was to realise that if community development included establishing, through group-based participant action, some sense of personal competence and power, this could be directly related to the idea of self-direction, which was one of the dimensions I had specified as characterising mental health.

Synthesising, consolidating, and comparing

Cross-case synthesis builds context-dependent knowledge through bringing together results from multiple cases or individual substudies into an overall metasynthesis. Results from each case or substudy are treated as a replication of the study, with each perhaps varying in contextual details. When the available data and findings appear incomplete or lacking in coherence, it could be beneficial to build a consolidated cross-case/cross-study database of the type discussed earlier, in Chapter 9. Data elements might remain in their text or numeric form, alternatively variable data can be categorised or qualitative data transformed into numeric codes or ratings. With cases ordered according to a contextual variable, cross-case comparative techniques then assist in revealing patterns across a spread of data. The goal in doing this is to express local findings in more abstract, general terms while retaining a view of how the overall picture or processes were influenced by local context or some other factor. Or, the database might point instead to where the gaps are and what is needed to fill them.

Generating a descriptive (interim) report

Description is a first step in analysis and reporting, and in some situations description might be all that is needed (Sandelowski, 2000). As an interim step at least, it is necessary to clarify (i.e., define) how terms are being used in the current study, to situate the results in their particular context, and to provide a structured description of what has been discovered or confirmed as a result of this study. The approach to and style of writing will depend on the nature of the results and how focused they are. If the study was designed as a relatively straightforward test of hypotheses, then writing a description of what was found is likely also to be a relatively straightforward exercise – unless, of course, the mixed methods data threw up some conundrums that needed to be resolved.

If a big picture or broad canvas is sought but has not become so clearly evident, working out what to present as a conclusion to the study and how to present it will be more difficult. A start can be made by identifying some of the building blocks wherever key insights have been gained or patterns of association are evident, going back to original sources if necessary to seek out further information. Individual links will gradually build into an extended network of ideas. Determining what needs to be known by the reader before he or she can understand what is currently being described helps with sequencing.

Alternatively, a practical strategy to overcome writer's block and to start to generate a focused and coherent description from what can be overwhelming detail is to first walk away from intensely working at it. After walking, find a friend and tell that person three things that have been learned through doing the analyses. These thoughts should then be listed in simple sentences as three short, clear propositions. Each is then developed with evidence for the proposition, the conditions under which it applies, any evidence against it, and the significance of the proposition in terms of previous literature and its relevance to practice. In a mixed methods study, the evidence for each proposition will be drawn from across the methods used in the study.

Progressing the conversation

Description provides a good starting point in writing results from analyses, but unless the goal is simply to provide information to meet an immediate practical need, then it is time to move on, to continue the negotiation process with and between evidence of different kinds. It is likely that writing a descriptive piece will point to further puzzles to be resolved or questions to be answered, particularly when mixed methods are involved. The next step will be to abstract sufficiently from that to build a model or to develop some more general outcomes that can contribute to broader theoretical understanding. The ideas and strategies that follow are oriented to theory development, but even if that is not on the agenda some of the strategies described will still be of value in prompting more richly developed conclusions from a mixed methods study.

Ask questions

Patton (2011) sees persistent questioning as the ultimate method, and questions leading to credible answers as "quintessential" tools. Many of Becker's (1998) "tricks" for prompting deeper insight were simple ways of questioning routine patterns of thought or speech. Data and interim findings are subjected to interrogation and challenge. For example, when comparing or contrasting data, it is necessary to ask why any revealed similarities or differences might exist, and what else might be contributing to those similarities or differences. Dissonance provides a useful prompt to further exploration. To a significant extent, data analysis is a process of critical thinking that happens to be focused on research data. Thoughtful interrogation of the data is part of that.

Confirming, challenging, or building on preliminary theory

It was proposed earlier (in Chapter 2) that a concept model, process model, and/or a logic model be developed to guide data collection and analysis. Alternatively (or as well), the project will have been informed by a conceptual framework, or based on an existing theory. This is a good time to review preliminary models and theoretically based frameworks in relation to the data and analyses that have been conducted, to compare what was expected with what was found. Do the patterns in the data support, modify, or contradict what was predicted? Does the theory need to be reformulated? A "problem" may be that the data can be explained by more than one theory (Kelle, 2015) and so evidence will need to be weighed for each alternative.

Follow up hunches

One of the distinct strategic advantages of starting to write early (in a research journal or memos) is that this provides an opportunity to record ideas or "hunches" about what is going on, while working with the data. Hunches are naïve theories or intuitions developed during the course of the project, that now become available to test. This is a time for creative ideas and imaginative thinking, to be "undertaken with a spirit of adventure" (Greene, 2007: 144), but with the awareness that some hunches will turn out to be "dead ends".

Theory "emerges" for those who have thoroughly worked the data, *who are steeped in it*, and who, at a particular time (often when waking up, in the shower, cooking dinner, out walking, or talking to a colleague), have that flash of insight, an "Aha!" moment, where they see how things might come together. Not only does this require thorough preparation, *it also requires follow-up work* where the flashy, insightful idea is pursued back through the data, to check that it really does have some meaning and significance (it often doesn't). The idea or theory, then, emerges through your working to achieve comprehensive knowledge and deep understanding of the data; ... no magical emergence, just hard work occasionally brightened by fresh understanding or awareness of a new connection that "makes sense" [and which stands up when tested]. (Bazeley, 2013: 385, emphasis in original)

Mary Lee Smith (1997) undertook a large-scale, longitudinal evaluation of a student assessment programme, looking at how it influenced curriculum, pedagogy, school organisation, and the way teachers understood and enacted their role. Evaluation methods included case studies, focus groups, and a survey. Having begun with a set of "crude mental models", she read and re-read the entire dataset to "intuitively" develop a set of assertions that could be made, based on her emergent understanding of the whole body of data. She then sought evidence for each assertion from different components of the data. Confirming and disconfirming evidence for each was weighed, unwarranted assertions were dropped, and others were modified in accordance with the data. Through this, for example, one of her conclusions was that: "State inattention to the technical and administrative adequacy of the assessment and accountability system impeded coherent responses to the testing program's intentions" (1997: 83).

Developing causal inferences

David Hume, a key figure in the development of causal theory, proposed three conditions that had to be met to have a sufficient basis to ascribe causation: observation of a constant conjunction of events (A and B) such that when A changes, so does B; the change in A always precedes the change in B; and alternative factors that might be responsible for both A and B are eliminated. Under these conditions, however, explanation of *why* the events might be causally associated had to be derived from theory, it could not be observed.

While finding a pattern or regular association between phenomena in data can give a hint as to a coherent explanation of what is going on, on its own it is insufficient as evidence of a causal pattern (Gorard, 2013; Maxwell, 2012b). Regularity of association between items, events, or variables cannot allow for the dismissal of an alternative explanation. Associations do not guarantee an explanation for an outcome, even if accompanied by consistent sequencing or based on structural equation modelling or path analysis. For example, an unobserved variable might be influencing the patterns of association, or indeed, be an underlying cause. Additional criteria for strengthening arguments for causation were set out by Bradford Hill (1965: see https://en.wikipedia.org/wiki/Bradford_Hill_criteria) when he (with others) established the case for smoking as a cause of lung cancer. The most essential of these criteria was the desirability of being able to propose a plausible mechanism between cause and effect. Thus, for example, it was the identification of carcinogens in cigarette smoke and evidence from diseased lungs that eventually provided vital evidence of a mechanism that could be used to convict cigarette manufacturers.

Researchers seeking to develop causal inferences choose to employ a mixed methods approach in anticipation of gaining a better understanding of mechanisms underpinning associations and processes supporting outcomes. They seek answers to the *how* and *why* questions, more than to the *to what extent* questions, to give them the warrant for their conclusions and to render them of more value in other situations (Yin, 2013). Establishing such a warrant is not something that is restricted to the analysis phase of a project: preliminary research design makes a critical contribution to capacity for demonstrating causality and excluding rival explanations (Gorard, 2013; Shadish, Cook, & Campbell, 2002), as does thorough documentation of the processes engaged in during the course of the project.

The search for mechanisms underlying causation is a primary focus for researchers who have a critical realist perspective, who see causal powers as existing within objects or agents or structures (Pawson, 2006). While not denying the need for evidence of regularity of association (causal description), the critical realist also seeks causal explanation. Because mental processes are real, meaning and intention can explain individual and social phenomena, and so one source of understanding of the mechanism by which something is caused can be derived from an insider perspective of the relationship between intentions and actions (Maxwell, 2012b). It is not sufficient to simply identify a mechanism, however; *how* it brings about an effect and how that is moderated by local conditions has to be understood (Sayer, 2000). Because they are contingent on context, causal processes are not always regular and so it is outcome patterns that are sought, rather than outcome regularities (Pawson, 2006).

Complications occur when applying theory to practice. Relationships between entities can be reciprocal; causes may only intermittently result in effects, yet they still become strongly associated with those effects in the mind of the observer; multiple causes are often necessary to create an effect; the same combination of causes might create more than one in effect, with any one of those causes just raising the probability of an effect; and, of course, people can continue to believe they are creating an effect, even if they are not actually responsible for its occurrence.

Counterfactual causation, in which consideration is given to the possibility of what would happen if the cause had not been there, also contributes to causal theory development. A no-treatment control group, where this can be arranged, provides such an approach, allowing the effect of the treatment to be estimated (Johnson, Russo, & Schoonenboom, in press). Removal of a variable in a sequence might also be considered a counterfactual test of a causal process (Bennett & George, 1997). These are examples of a more general (retroductive) approach of working backward from the effect to the cause. Another is event sequence analysis, a mapping strategy that builds from narrative using counterfactual logic to model causal pathways (Heise, 1989, 2007).

Having and integrating mixed methods data facilitates the process of developing a causal explanation because it enhances the likelihood of showing both association *and* mechanism for a causal proposition. Statistical associations between variables describe regularities that hint at causal relations, but cannot confirm them. Similarly, the counterfactual experiment demonstrates an effect, but not a mechanism. When qualitative data are added to the mix, explanations supporting statistical associations can become apparent, possibly revealing causal mechanisms. For example, in the study of rural nurses by McKeon et al. (2006) described earlier in Chapter 5, the qualitative comments did more than illustrate variables used in the path analysis of medication administration in rural Australia, they also suggested an explanation as to why nurses were violating the rules. Similarly, in the study by Teye (2012), also described in Chapter 5, qualitative data provided explanations of patterns of behaviour among forest guards that had been revealed through statistical analyses. Indeed complex causal processes focusing on events and the human agents that connect them, often too difficult to demonstrate through statistical interactions, can be explored using qualitative techniques that have the advantage of operating and observing at the local level (Johnson et al., in press; Maxwell, 2012b). Inferences developed can then be "redescribed" (rendered more abstract) and further assessed by other means. Mixed methods researchers, therefore, have the advantage of being able to rely on both local and general approaches in developing a coherent, integrated approach to causal explanation.

Exploring rival explanations

More than one explanation might appear to fit the available data. These might be based on standard threats to validity arising from methodological decisions (Campbell & Stanley, 1963), the possibility of other intervening events, unplanned "third forces", or alternative theories. Rival explanations should be developed and evaluated against the available evidence, with more evidence sought if necessary. Exploring rival explanations is one of several key strategies contributing to a claim of validity for inferences (Yin, 2013).

At the design stage of the project, use of "thought experiments" will help create a design to either eliminate the possibility of alternative explanations, or to plan for and incorporate tests for the kinds of explanations that would be offered by more than one conceptual framework or theory (Maxwell, 2013). At the analysis phase, results found are evaluated against the perspectives of different theories or explanations. In a process Gorard (2013: 49) describes as involving a combination of "great creativity" and "pedantic logical analysis", predictions and theoretical pathways to outcomes based on each theory are set out, with criteria or indicators for each component. This then guides a sifting process as data and results obtained so far are reviewed, with an open mind. Support for some possibilities will be found, others will be excluded. It may be of benefit to view data and findings from an alternative epistemological stance. For example, would the data and results obtained be viewed and interpreted differently by a feminist, or someone from a less powerful minority group?

The "modus operandi" (MO) approach, drawn from forensic rather than evaluative science, uses retroductive logic and evidence to test rival explanations and identify the most likely cause for an effect (Scriven, 1976). The idea is that causes and effects follow patterns: particular causes, like criminals, have a modus operandi, a regular way of behaving. The effect and any other available clues are examined to identify any patterns that are evident. These are checked against known (potential) causes, and causes that don't fit are eliminated. Drawing on the explanatory power of background theory can assist this process. Within any remaining possibilities, there may be "signature traces" in the effect which are markers of specific causal mechanisms. These also allow for the dismissal of non-conforming explanations, until all that remains is the "best" explanation (Douglas & Douglas, 2006; Farrell, Tseloni, & Tilley, 2016).

Process tracing

Process tracing is used to build a logical chain of evidence that demonstrates a cause to effect pathway (Bennett & George, 1997; George & Bennett, 2005; Miles et al., 2014). The method usually begins with inductively developing hypotheses for testing from initial observations or theory, and proposing causal mechanisms that describe an uninterrupted path from the cause to the effect (as suggested in Chapter 2, as part of the design process for mixed methods research). Complexity is embraced. These propositions, with all their intervening variables, are then assessed for congruence with data and results obtained from interviews, observations, documentary, and/or historical evidence, typically using longitudinal data capable of showing pathways and temporal sequence.

Process tracing has been used deductively to test a hypothesis relating to causal mechanisms using multiple sources of evidence in a single case study (Ulrikson & Dadalauri, 2016). The method requires first that carefully identified hypotheses are specified, to map out the intervening causal pathway along with some possible alternative explanations. Having determined that the theoretical propositions are sound and reasonable and that their specification appropriately fits the characteristics of the case, then analysis can take place. Analysis becomes something like detective work, where the quality rather than the quantity of the "bits and pieces" of evidence gathered is important. A case is built for each of the theoretical propositions that together support the overriding hypothesis – or contrary evidence is found and the hypothesis is not supported. The fit of the evidence with established theory strengthens the value of the conclusions and the potential for wider application of the theory.

Inference to best explanation

Without being able to prove a social science proposition, what remains for the analyst is to provide provisional causal explanations, using whatever evidence can be mustered (including through any or all of the methods outlined above). Ultimately, the result will be an "inference to best explanation" – a *warranted* assertion. Inference to best explanation draws on background knowledge along with logic-based reasoning to find the best explanation of available evidence, while recognising the potential fallibility of those conclusions. This explanation is that which is best at accounting for all the facts and explaining all the data, is the most plausible, and can be expressed simply enough to be understood and accepted. It stands until there is a competing explanation that is more plausible (Harman, 1965).

Negotiating coherence through writing and visualising

Writing and drawing are overriding analytic and integrative processes that guide the researcher towards ever more refined understanding, to result in coherent, strong conclusions and well-supported theory. Writing provides an avenue for deep reflection; for putting down and thus "seeing" what is known. Writing is a method of inquiry, a way of knowing, and of discovery and analysis – all three: "By writing in different ways, we discover new aspects of our topic and our relationship to it. ... I write because I want to find something out. I write in order to learn something I didn't know before I wrote it" (Richardson, 1994: 516, 517). Both writing and creating visualisations demand articulation and organisation of thoughts. Gaps in knowledge are detected, links become apparent. Ideas, some yet to be tested, are recorded and reviewed.

For those using mixed methods, the way in which the written report is structured is closely linked to how well analysis and the findings from them are integrated. The tendency to write up results separately and defer discussion of integration until the end of a report is a major impediment to integration of the results (Bryman, 2007). Integration of both analysis and writing will benefit if, as soon as ideas are being gathered from any source, they are recorded and reflected upon in a research diary or journal that is organised on the basis of elements of the substantive topic, rather than being organised according to the source of data or the method used to gather or analyse it.

Preparing a coherent report

It has often been said that writing is a craft. Writing mixed methods is a particularly high-level form of this craft in that it involves negotiating the combination of results established in very different writing traditions, and then representing that combination in written publications. Whereas there are standard forms of reporting for results of experiments and some other kinds of studies, there is no established protocol for writing up a mixed methods study.

Mixed methods studies often generate more than one form of output. These could include one or more articles, a dissertation (thesis), a report to a stakeholder such as a funding body, a book, or perhaps some form of multimedia presentation. In view of that, it is useful to engage in some strategic planning to determine the shape of those outputs and where various elements of the study fit into them. Similarly, within any particular form of output, decisions are made about the way a longer report, such as a dissertation or book, is broken up into chapters and even how sections and subsections are arranged within an article. The ways in which that division within and between articles and between chapters is accomplished has major implications, as noted earlier, for the integrity of the study and the level of integration demonstrated for the methods and results. Further decisions then follow, with respect to the content and style of each particular item of output.

My central thesis regarding coherent writing is: if research into the topic being investigated benefited from an integration of methods, then so also the dissemination of the results from it will benefit from an integrated approach to writing. If the focus of the study was on a substantive issue, then it is logical that the writing of the results from it should be similarly focused and organised around elements of that substantive issue.

> Effective mixed methods writing is also marbled, like good pastrami. The different perspectives, voices, understandings, representational forms that are mixed in the writing are not layered or offered separately or sequentially; rather, they are mixed together, interwoven, interconnected. They collectively tell the story to be told from a given mixed methods study, not so much taking turns as joining in one chorus, likely both harmonious and discordant. (Greene, 2007: 188)

In practice this means that decisions made about how the study is presented are made on the basis of the substantive message to be communicated, and not on the basis of the investigative methods used. An integrated mixed methods report will *not* present "results from the quantitative data" followed by "results from the qualitative data" and ignore integration of those results until a discussion, as is so commonly found. Nor can entirely separate quantitative and qualitative articles effectively tell the story of a mixed methods project. Even in a sequential design, as noted in Chapter 4, if one phase of the study was designed to inform or expand on another, then it makes sense that data from both phases should mutually inform the results presented, with the potential for statistical data and comparable insights from qualitative text being reported together in a more or less complementary style, albeit dominated by one or other form of reporting. If understanding has been gained progressively through several waves of a study, with alternating methods used for each, then it might be desirable to tell the story of that progressive revelation. There must, however, have been a final understanding that was reached, warranting presentation of that as the overall result of the study and the context in which interim results are presented. The progressive revelation is really more about methods than the topic itself, and so might best be published as a separate methods paper to complement one dealing with the substantive issues of the topic.

If the study is sufficiently complex that it needs to be broken up in some way or another for presentation, then separate subtopics within the study, different aspects of the topic, or specific issues investigated as part of it need to be identified. Thus the substantive foci of the study will provide an organising rationale for the structure within any article(s) written, and for the (sub)topics covered by different chapters, different publications, or different media. Some of these might focus more on what was learned from one form of data than another, but the form of the data is not the determining factor for making these structural decisions. Within each subsection, data from different sources or analyses might be juxtaposed, as in the study by Classen et al. (2007), reported in Chapter 5, or they might be merged or blended to create a narrative in which results based on different underlying data are interwoven, as in the studies by Castro et al. (2010), also reported in Chapter 5, and by Youngs and Piggot-Irvine (2012). Different contributing components within an article or report will usually retain aspects of writing style appropriate to the methods used to generate them, for example use of third or first person for quantitative and qualitative components respectively (Sandelowski, 2003), and in a style respecting the voices of those providing the data (Greene, 2007). Greene recommends also considering non-traditional forms of representation to cover results from alternative approaches within a mixed methods study. These might include use of stories, drama, and poetry, perhaps even art, music, and dance, to communicate the dimensions of human experience often missed in "scientific" forms of reporting.

How best to write, how best to write research, and how best to write mixed methods research raises issues beyond the scope of integration of analyses, which is the focus of this book. These, and issues dealing with negotiating journal restrictions, disciplinary differences, and so on are covered by articles and chapters listed under Further Reading, and often by editorials within journals targeted by mixed methods researchers, such as in the *Journal of Mixed Methods Research*.

Visual display as a tool for analysis and communication

The use of visual models and tables to demonstrate both the methods used for a study and the thinking behind them was set out in Chapter 2. It was suggested there that visualising what was planned for a study in these ways was valuable for its capacity to clarify the methods being used for both researcher and readers. Similarly, at the analysis and writing up phase of conducting a study, a visual display that helps the researcher make sense of their data and results will also help the reader better understand the impact and report of those results. The way the information is organised in the display will shape how readers interpret it through, for example, whether it is time sequenced, role focused, or relating conditions to consequences (Sandelowski, 2003). The result gives material form and credibility to ideas, brings order to chaos, reduces complexity to simplicity. For example, a simple visual display by Crooks et al. (2011) clearly demonstrated the way in which qualitative insights about *community readiness* added to an existing quantitatively based model for deciding the siting of palliative care services in rural British Columbia, Canada (Figure 12.1). Robyn Holder (in press) used concentric circles to show the outward unfolding of victims' reflections on the meaning of justice in her longitudinal study of responses to violence, described earlier in Chapter 6 (Figure 12.2). These simpler types of models are especially of benefit in conference presentations where the visual image not only conveys a large amount of information in a small space, but also attracts and holds the attention of listeners more effectively than text.

Creating visual displays assists analytic thinking all the way through a project. As a supervisor, I find it is helpful for both the student and myself if I start to draw what

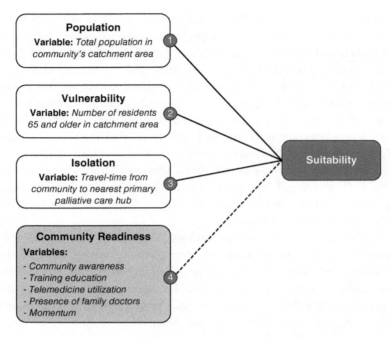

Figure 12.1   Revised mixed methods siting model for rural palliative care services

Source: Crooks et al., 2011: 89, Figure 2

Figure 12.2   Victims' unfolding thinking about preferred justice outcomes

Source: Holder, in press: 13, Figure 1

I'm hearing and understanding as we talk through some aspect of the student's project, perhaps in a rough model showing relations between entities, perhaps in a list or table. As a researcher, mapping even simple ideas helps to focus the idea in my mind, keeping it available for further development. Diagramming what one is thinking about is a skill that can be learned through practice; sophistication in itself is not important, though that too will grow with practice.

Visual displays of information might first be thought of as basic models with lines connecting shapes, but the possibilities are much wider than this. Tables, maps, and network diagrams all help to convey research results. Thus Crooks et al. (2011) effectively used an annotated map to demonstrate that the priority ranking of locations *furthest* from the heavily populated south of British Columbia had changed most (up or down) as a result of their revised siting model (Figure 12.3).

Displays might show the juxtaposition of data, usually in table format as was seen in Chapter 5. Numerically based displays and graphs are a means of rapidly revealing patterns and prompting interpretation of those patterns by the viewer. They are therefore critical to effective comprehension and communication of statistical information, as shown for example in path analyses based on regression modelling (Figure 12.4) or in

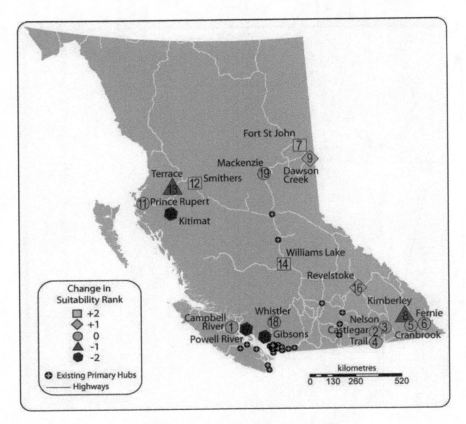

Figure 12.3 Changes in priority ranking for palliative care services

Source: Crooks et al., 2011: 88, Figure 1

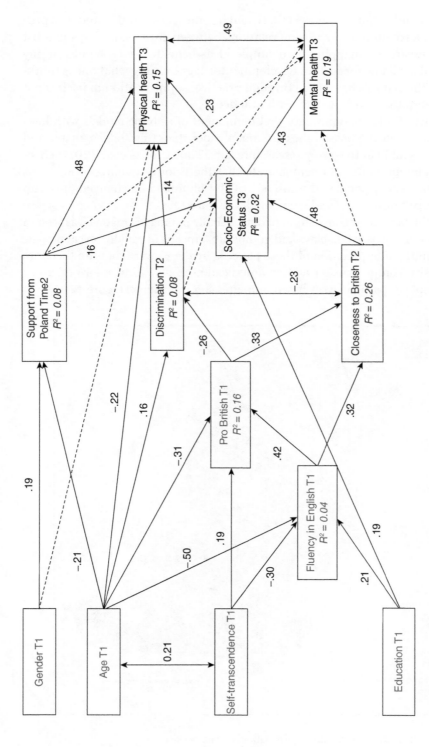

Figure 12.4 Pathways to perceptions of mental and physical health among Polish migrants to the UK

Source: Goodwin et al., 2013: 156, Figure 2

Note: numbers indicate regression beta values

the visual displays from multivariate analyses shown in Chapter 9. They "reduce cognitive load, organize information into a coherent representation, provide novel information that text alone cannot communicate, and activate prior knowledge" (Pastor & Finney, 2013: 388). Both traditional and newer exploratory forms of visual displays generated more or less automatically through spreadsheet, statistical, and qualitative software are helpful to varying degrees in revealing and displaying patterns in data – sometimes more for the researcher during the analysis process than for the reader of a report.

Visual displays in reports attract attention and can communicate a large amount of information in a restricted space (as in Figure 12.5), making them especially useful in journal articles where tight word limits often apply, or perhaps useful as a one-page summary of the project. The process of reducing and condensing information during preparation of a visual model, chart, or table forces the researcher to identify the most important aspects of what has been learned, and to discern the relationships between those things. Necessary selectivity in choosing the items and linkages shown challenges analytic thinking and focuses attention on the central argument the visual is to convey while non-essential information is discarded.

Visuals in a report – like quotes – should support, but not replace, the argument(s) being presented. At the same time, a visual, with its legend, should be able to stand alone, conveying necessary information to understand and interpret it. Although detailed information contained in the visual display does not need to be repeated in the text, the key inferences from it might be concisely stated, reflected upon, or expanded upon. The no-repeat rule applies especially if the display is a table presenting straightforward information such as demographic details or summary results.

Ensuring the warrant for mixed methods inferences

It was stated earlier that an assertion or inference that is warranted is one that is convincingly argued and is supported by research evidence. The quality of inferences from a mixed methods study builds primarily on the way in which its component parts are brought together to produce overall conclusions from the study and to a lesser extent on the quality of those separate components. In developing warranted assertions, one is building an argument rather than simply amassing information.

Authors writing about criteria for quality in mixed methods projects and their inferences have included guidelines on planning, design, data and analyses, interpretation, inference transferability, reporting, synthesisability, and utility. O'Cathain (2010: 552) synthesised all that had been written at the time about these eight domains and their multiple sub-domains to develop a very comprehensive and detailed list of criteria. From this exercise, including testing them on one of her own studies, she concluded that there were just too many criteria for widespread practical implementation. She proposed that a researcher might use the criteria as guidelines to ensure quality over the life of a project, but suggested also that a user of research really just wants to know if a study is "good enough", that it meets a minimum set of criteria. This minimum set was yet to be determined – and still is. Contributions since from other authors appear to have added to the list of criteria, rather than reducing it to its more essential components.

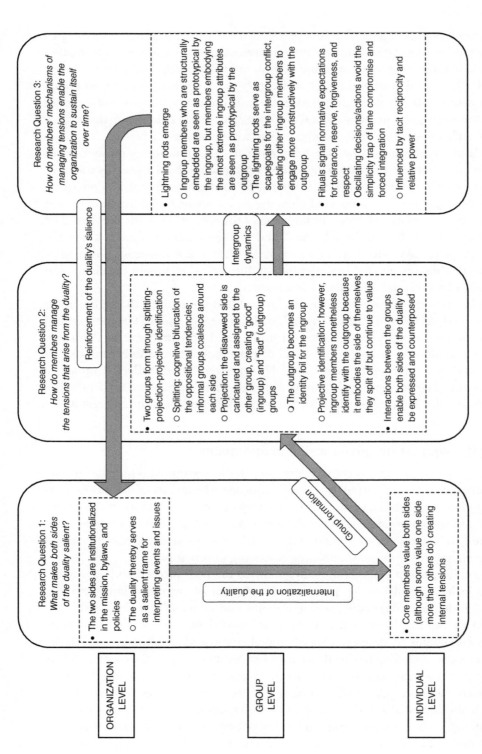

Figure 12.5 The dynamics of an organisational duality: How seeming dysfunctionality at the group level fostered functionality at the organisation level

Source: Ashforth and Reingen, 2014: 503, Figure 1

What, essentially, is needed to ensure that assertions from a mixed methods study are warranted? Three items are suggested here as a minimum set for a mixed methods study: the quality of the underlying data, and of the manner in which those data are managed; the study and its results have been enriched by integration of methods and analyses; and inferences from the study are "valid" insofar as they are consistent with the data on which they are based.

Quality of the underlying data

To draw valid inferences from a study assumes quality in the data that supports those inferences, for example in the appropriateness of the design, in the conduct of sampling, data gathering, and recording strategies for each component method, and in the thoroughness with which those procedures were carried out.

Quality criteria will be appropriate to the particular methods used, and yet there are often times in a mixed methods study where criteria applying to specific methods are "abused", especially when it comes to implementation. For example, circumstances might dictate that ethnographic components are based on immersion that is all too brief, grounded theory's constant comparative strategies are applied after a full sample has been interviewed, surveys are conducted with non-random or too-small samples, and so on. Data gathered under these conditions are compromised, yet not without value. The analyst will be very aware of the limitations the "methods in use" impose on the resulting data, and of how these might affect the conclusions being drawn from them. When inferences are based on the body of evidence as a whole, however, it means that weaknesses associated with particular components of that evidence can be balanced by evidence from other sources. The goal is for the design and methods to be "practically adequate" in serving the purpose of the study (Sayer, 2000). What then becomes critical to quality is how any available data are managed, used, and interpreted. The potential fallibility of any resulting assertions will be recognised, and the strengths and weaknesses of the argument for their warrant made clear.

Effective integration?

Ensuring the quality of each component method is not sufficient to ensure the integrative sense, value, or validity of the study as a whole. Integration of methods and/or analyses is an essential defining feature of a mixed methods study. The focus of quality assessment, therefore, will be on the design and conduct of the overall project, and whether that design and its execution effectively provide a way of meeting the purpose of the study and of answering the questions raised in relation to that purpose. To have an assurance of yield beyond that which would result from separate studies assumes that inferences will directly or indirectly draw on more than one source of data and its analyses.

Validity of inferences

Validity of inferences in mixed methods research is evident in the way in which those inferences coherently reflect and convey an understanding of the subject matter they are about. Validity of inferences is often confused with quality, but the clear consensus among methodologists is that "validity is a property of inferences. It is *not* a property of designs or methods" (e.g., Mertens et al., 2016a; Shadish et al., 2002: 34). Validity is about accounts; data or methods have quality – they are not intrinsically valid or invalid, but inferences drawn from them can be. The same method might generate valid inferences in one context, but not in another. There might be more than one valid account arising from the available evidence because an account is not independent of particular perspectives or purposes; validity is not the same as absolute truth.

Adequacy of underlying data and effective integration are necessary but not sufficient conditions for drawing valid inferences from a mixed methods study. Valid inferences are consistent with evidence on which they are based and, insofar as they are drawn from the same evidence base, they are consistent with each other.

Warranted assertions

Negotiated inferences (Bryman, 2007) or knowledge claims (Greene, 2007) from a mixed methods study are best expressed as warranted assertions, in recognition of the fallibility of knowledge, especially in the social domain of investigation. Warranted assertions are those that are supported by evidence, but which also recognise the limitations of that evidence. Gorard (2013) described good research as an argument designed to convince a sceptical audience, using evidence to lead to the conclusions. He laments that at times the warrant is omitted for conclusions, when a finding is described and a conclusion drawn from it without making clear the link between data and inference.

Warranted assertions will be best explanations supported by descriptive adequacy and characterised by transparency. Critical reflection about the data, and about what part of the data was being worked with when ideas were generated, will assist in building transparency of process. For example, it was because Carcary (2009) had kept careful notes of her thinking and action processes during her qualitative study that she was able to describe in detail how she moved from initial coding to generating a grounded theory. In a mixed methods environment, providing an account of the underlying assumptions, analytic decision processes, and procedures leading to the results obtained and conclusions drawn are key elements in demonstrating to a potentially sceptical audience the rigour with which an analysis was conducted. Such an account allows audiences to see how the assertions were developed, and thus allows them to be able to judge for themselves whether they consider them to be warranted.

Concluding remarks

This final chapter outlined some very practical steps that might be taken to bring together the results and insights that have been garnered through the course of integrating analyses in a mixed methods study. While a report might begin with a descriptive outline or synthesis of what has been found, in most situations it will progress as a result of using more probing and interpretive strategies, perhaps extending to analyses seeking to identify mechanisms underlying apparently causal associations.

The goal of these final steps in integration of mixed methods analyses is to present these results and insights as a set of "warranted assertions", knowledge claims that are clearly and coherently argued, with each supported by evidence from across the different sources and analyses employed in the study.

Further reading
Causality
Bazeley (2013), in Chapter 11, provides an extensive review of the theory underlying causal inference, with multiple strategies for developing a causal argument from qualitative data. The majority of these apply also to mixed methods data.

Johnson et al. (in press) have mustered an extensive range of approaches to causal theorising, which they describe from philosophical, scientific, and practical perspectives.

Kelle (2015) examines the contribution of mixed methods in relation to theory building and theory testing.

Gorard (2013), in Chapter 4, discusses design criteria necessary for establishing a warrant for conclusions, and in Chapter 5 he examines the nature of causal claims.

Collier (2011) describes four necessary and/or sufficient tests on which causal inference depends and illustrates each of these through an analysis of a Sherlock Holmes story.

Writing and visualising
Bazeley (2015b) covers practical, technical, and stylistic issues associated with writing up a mixed methods study.

Tufte (2001) makes for some quite entertaining reading on how to communicate (or lie) with graphics, in a book well illustrated with examples. He also provides valuable hints on preparing graphical displays based on numeric data, but if you want to find some specific guidance on how to prepare a particular kind of graphic, you might not be able to go straight to it. The material is structured according to the general presentation principles Tufte is wanting to communicate, not the type of graphic involved.

Richardson (1994) – an accomplished author and social scientist – writes about writing as analysis, and about different forms of writing to present findings.

Sandelowski (2003) describes the challenges arising from different forms of representation of qualitative and quantitative data and results, and suggests ways of dealing with these. She also discusses the role of visual displays, numbers, and quotes in mixed methods writing.

Greene's (2007) chapter on writing up a mixed methods study advocates similar principles to those outlined in this chapter. It provides useful and interesting examples of innovative writing.

Youngs and Piggot-Irvine (2012: see especially pp. 192–195) provide an example of writing about emergent, confirmatory, and contradictory findings when the data supporting each is drawn from multiple sources and analyses.

Pastor and Finney (2013) support with theory and demonstrate with practical examples the ways in which provision of graphics to supplement statistical results facilitates cognitive processing of statistical information.

Fàbregues and Molina-Azorín (in press) review studies putting forward quality criteria for mixed methods research and provide a summary of the most common criteria proposed.

REFERENCES

Abbott, A. (1992). What do cases do? Some notes on activity in sociological analysis. In C. Ragin & H. Becker (Eds.), *What is a case? Exploring the foundations of social inquiry* (pp. 53–82). New York: Cambridge University Press.

Abbott, A., & Tsay, A. (2000). Sequence analysis and optimal matching techniques in sociology. *Sociological Methods & Research*, 29(1), 3–33.

Adriansen, H. K. (2012). Timeline interviews: a tool for conducting life history research. *Qualitative Studies*, 3(1), 40–55.

Amabile, T. M., Barsade, S. G., Mueller, J. S., & Staw, B. M. (2005). Affect and creativity at work. *Administrative Science Quarterly*, 50(3), 367–403.

Anderson, R. C., Nguyen-Jahiel, K., McNurlen, B., Archodidou, A., Kim, S-y., Reznitskaya, A., & Gilbert, L. (2001). The snowball phenomenon: spread of ways of talking and ways of thinking across groups of children. *Cognition and Instruction*, 19(1), 1–46.

Anguera, M. T., & Izquierdo, C. (2006). Methodological approaches in human communication: from complexity of perceived situation to data analysis. In G. Riva, M. T. Anguera, B. K. Wiederhold & F. Mantovani (Eds.), *From communication to presence: cognition, emotions and culture towards the ultimate communicative experience* (pp. 207–226). Amsterdam: IOS Press.

Arnon, S., & Reichel, N. (2009). Closed and open-ended question tools in a telephone survey about "the good teacher": an example of a mixed method study. *Journal of Mixed Methods Research*, 3(2), 172–196. doi: 10.1177/1558689808331036

Ashforth, B. E., & Reingen, P. H. (2014). Functions of dysfunction: managing the dynamics of an organizational duality in a natural food cooperative. *Administrative Science Quarterly*, 59(3), 474–516. doi: 10.1177/0001839214537811

Baas, L., Rhoads, J. C., & Thomas, D. B. (2016). Are quests for a "culture of assessment" mired in a "culture of war" over assessment? A Q-methodological inquiry. *SAGE Open*, January–March, 1–17. doi:10.1177/2158244015623591

Bail, C. A. (2015). Lost in a random forest: using Big Data to study rare events. *Big Data & Society*, 2(2), 1–3. doi: 10.1177/2053951715604333

Bamberger, M., Rao, V., & Woolcock, M. (2010). Using mixed methods in monitoring and evaluation. In A. Tashakkori & C. Teddlie (Eds.), *Handbook of mixed methods in social and behavioral research* (2nd ed., pp. 613–641). Thousand Oaks, CA: Sage.

Bartholomew, D. J., Steele, F., Moustaki, I., & Galbraith, J. I. (2002). *The analysis and interpretation of multivariate data for social scientists*. Boca Raton, FL: Chapman & Hall/CRC.

Bauman, A. (2015). The use of the repertory grid technique in online trust research. *Qualitative Market Research*, 18(3), 362–382. doi: 10.1108/QMR-08-2014-0080

Bazeley, P. (1977). Community development for mental health. PhD thesis, Macquarie University, Sydney.

Bazeley, P. (1998). Peer review and panel decisions in the assessment of Australian Research Council project grant applications: what counts in a highly competitive context? *Higher Education*, 35, 435–452.

Bazeley, P. (2003a). Computerized data analysis for mixed methods research. In A. Tashakkori & C. Teddlie (Eds.), *Handbook of mixed methods in social and behavioral research* (pp. 385–422). Thousand Oaks, CA: Sage.

Bazeley, P. (2003b). Defining 'early career' in research. *Higher Education*, 45(3), 257–280.

Bazeley, P. (2006). Research dissemination in Creative Arts, Humanities and the Social Sciences. *Higher Education Research and Development*, 25(3), 215–229.

Bazeley, P. (2009). Analysing qualitative data: more than 'identifying themes'. *Malaysian Journal of Qualitative Research*, 2(2), 6–22. Retrieved from: www.researchsupport.com.au

Bazeley, P. (2010a). Computer assisted integration of mixed methods data sources and analyses. In A. Tashakkori & C. Teddlie (Eds.), *Handbook of mixed methods in social and behavioral research* (2nd ed., pp. 431–467). Thousand Oaks, CA: Sage.

Bazeley, P. (2010b). Conceptualising research performance. *Studies in Higher Education*, 35(8), 889–904. doi: 10.1080/03075070903348404

Bazeley, P. (2012). Integrative analysis strategies for mixed data sources. *American Behavioral Scientist*, 56(6), 814–828. doi: 10.1177/0002764211426330

Bazeley, P. (2013). Qualitative data analysis: practical strategies. London: Sage.

Bazeley, P. (2015a). Mixed methods in management research: implications for the field. *Electronic Journal of Business Research Methods*, 13(1), 27–35.

Bazeley, P. (2015b). Writing up multimethod and mixed methods research for diverse audiences. In S. Hesse-Biber & B. Johnson (Eds.), *Oxford handbook of multimethod and mixed methods research inquiry* (pp. 296–313). New York: Oxford University Press.

Bazeley, P. (2016). Mixed or merged? Integration as the real challenge for mixed methods. *Qualitative Research in Organizations and Management*, 11(3), 189–194. doi: 10.1108/QROM-04-2016-1373

Bazeley, P., & Jackson, K. (2013). *Qualitative data analysis with NVivo* (2nd ed.). London: Sage.

Bazeley, P., & Kemp, L. (2012). Mosaics, triangles, and DNA: metaphors for integrated analysis in mixed methods research. *Journal of Mixed Methods Research*, 6(1), 55–72. doi: 10.1177/1558689811419514

Bazeley, P., Kemp, L., Stevens, K., Asmar, C., Grbich, C., Marsh, H., & Bhathal, R. (1996). *Waiting in the wings: a study of early career academic researchers in Australia* (National Board of Employment Education and Training Commissioned Report No. 50). Canberra: Australian Government Publishing Service.

Bearman, P. (2015). Big Data and historical social science. *Big Data & Society*, 2(2), 1–5. doi: 10.1177/2053951715612497

Becker, H., Geer, B., Hughes, E. C., & Strauss, A. ([1961] 1977). *Boys in white: student culture in the medical school*. New Brunswick, NJ: Transaction Publishers.

Becker, H. S. (1998). Tricks of the trade: how to think about your research while you're doing it. Chicago, IL: University of Chicago Press.

Bennett, A., & George, A. (1997). Process tracing in case study research. Paper presented at the MacArthur Foundation Workshop on Case Study Methods Belfer Center for Science and International Affairs, Harvard, MA.

Berelson, B. (1952). *Content analysis in communication research*. Glencoe: Free Press.

Berg-Schlosser, D., De Meur, G., Rihoux, B., & Ragin, C. (2009). Qualitative comparative analysis (QCA) as an approach. In B. Rihoux & C. Ragin (Eds.), *Configurational comparative methods* (pp. 1–18). Thousand Oaks, CA: Sage.

Bergene, A. C. (2007). Toward a critical realist comparative methodology: context sensitive theoretical comparison. *Journal of Critical Realism*, 6(1), 5–27.

Berger, R., & Paul, M. S. (2014). Plurality of methodologies to bridge the gap between research and practice: a case study in infertility research. *Forum: Qualitative Social Research*, 15(1). Retrieved from: http://nbn-resolving.de/urn:nbn:de:0114-fqs140185

Bergman, M. M. (2008a). The straw men of the qualitative–quantitative divide and their influence on mixed methods research. In M. M. Bergman (Ed.), *Advances in mixed methods research* (pp. 11–21). London: Sage.

Bergman, M. M. (Ed.) (2008b). *Advances in mixed methods research*. London: Sage.

Bergman, M. M. (2010). Hermeneutic content analysis. In A. Tashakkori & C. Teddlie (Eds.), *Handbook of mixed methods in social and behavioral research* (2nd ed., pp. 379–396). Thousand Oaks, CA: Sage.

Bergman, M. M. (2011). The good, the bad, and the ugly in mixed methods research and design [Editorial]. *Journal of Mixed Methods Research*, 5(4), 271–275. doi:10.1177/1558689811433236

Beringer, A. J., Fletcher, M. E., & Taket, A. R. (2006). Rules and resources: a structuration approach to understanding the coordination of children's inpatient health care. *Journal of Advanced Nursing*, 56(3), 325–335. doi:10.1111/j.1365-2648.2006.04023.x

Bernadi, L., Keim, S., & von der Lippe, H. (2007). Social influences on fertility: a comparative mixed methods study in Eastern and Western Germany. *Journal of Mixed Methods Research*, 1(1), 23–47. doi: 10.1177/2345678906292238

Bernard, H. R. (2006). Research methods in anthropology: qualitative and quantitative approaches (4th ed.). Walnut Creek, CA: Altamira Press.

Berth, H., & Romppel, M. (2000). Measurement of anxiety and dogmatism using computer aided content analysis. Paper P041005, presented at the 5th International Conference on Logic and Methodology for the International Sociological Association, Cologne, Germany, 3–6 October.

Biddle, C., & Schafft, K. A. (2015). Axiology and anomaly in the practice of mixed methods work: pragmatism, valuation, and the transformative paradigm. *Journal of Mixed Methods Research*, 9(4), 320–334. doi: 10.1177/1558689814533157

Bienmann, T., & Datta, D. K. (2014). Analyzing sequence data: optimal matching in business research. *Organizational Research Methods*, 17(1), 51–76. doi: 10.1177/1094428113499408

Biesta, G. (2010). Pragmatism and the philosophical foundations of mixed methods research. In A. Tashakkori & C. Teddlie (Eds.), *Handbook of mixed methods in social and behavioral research* (2nd ed., pp. 95–117). Thousand Oaks, CA: Sage.

Binz-Scharf, M. C., Kalish, Y., & Paik, L. (2015). Making science: new generations of collaborative knowledge production. *American Behavioral Scientist*, 59(5), 531–547. doi: 10.1177/0002764214556805

Blasius, J., & Thiessen, V. (1998). Exploring response structures. Paper presented at the 14th World Congress of Sociology, Montreal, Canada, July.

Blasius, J., & Thiessen, V. (2001). Methodological artifacts in measures of political efficacy and trust: a multiple correspondence analysis. *Political Analysis*, 9, 1–20.

Blossfeld, H.-P., Glosch, K., & Rohwer, G. (2007). *Event history analysis with Stata*. Mahwah, NJ: Lawrence Erlbaum Associates.

Blossfeld, H.-P., & Rohwer, G. (1997). Causal inference, time and observation plans in the social sciences. *Quality & Quantity*, 31(4), 361–383.

Blossfeld, H.-P., & Rohwer, G. (2002). *Techniques of event history modeling: new approaches to causal analysis* (2nd ed.). New Jersey: Lawrence Erlbaum Associates.

Bolíbar, M. (2016). Macro, meso, micro: broadening the 'social' of social network analysis with a mixed methods approach. *Quality & Quantity*, 50(5), 2217–2236. doi: 10.1007/s11135-015-0259-0

Bolt, R. (2009). Urban Aboriginal identity construction in Australia: an Aboriginal pespective utilising multi-method qualitative analysis. PhD thesis, University of Sydney, Sydney. Retrieved from: http://hdl.handle.net/2123/6626

Borgatti, S. (2016). Elicitation methods for cultural domain analysis. In J. J. Schensul & M. D. LeCompte (Eds.), *The ethnographer's toolkit* (Vol. 3, pp. 115–151). Walnut Creek, CA: AltaMira Press.

Bowers, B., Cohen, L. W., Elliot, A. E., Grabowski, D. C., Fishman, N. W., Sharkey, S. S., & Kemper, P. (2013). Creating and supporting a mixed methods health services research team. *Health Services Research*, 48(6), 2157–2180. doi: 10.1111/1475-6773.12118

Boyatzis, R. E. (1998). Transforming qualitative information: thematic analysis and code development. Thousand Oaks, CA: Sage.

Bradford Hill, A. (1965). The environment and disease: association or causation? *Proceedings of the Royal Society of Medicine*, 58, 295–300.

Bradley, E. H., Byam, P., Alpern, R., Thompson, J. W., Zerihun, A., Abebe, Y., & Curry, L. A. (2012). A systems approach to improving rural care in Ethiopia. *PloS ONE*, 7(4), e35042. doi: 10.1371/journal.pone.0035042

Bradley, E. H., Curry, L. A., Spatz, E. S., Herrin, J., Cherlin, E. J., Curtis, J. P., & Krumholz, H. M. (2012). Hospital strategies for reducing risk-standardized mortality rates in acute myocardial infarction. *Annals of Internal Medicine*, 156(9), 618–626.

Brady, B., & O'Regan, C. (2009). Meeting the challenge of doing an RCT evaluation of youth mentoring in Ireland: a journey in mixed methods. *Journal of Mixed Methods Research*, 3(3), 265–280. doi: 10.1177/1558689809335973

Brannen, J., & O'Connell, R. (2015). Data analysis 1: overview of data analysis strategies. In S. Hesse-Biber & B. Johnson (Eds.), *Oxford Handbook of multimethod and mixed methods research inquiry* (pp. 257–274). New York: Oxford University Press.

Braun, V., & Clarke, V. (2006). Using thematic analysis in psychology. *Qualitative Research in Psychology*, 3, 77–101.

Brewer, J., & Hunter, A. (2006). *Foundations of multimethod research: synthesizing styles.* (2nd ed.). Thousand Oaks, CA: Sage.

Brickson, S. L. (2005). Organizational identity orientation: forging a link between organizational identity and organizations' relations with stakeholders. *Administrative Science Quarterly*, 50(4), 576–609.

Brock, T. (2005). Commentary: Viewing mixed methods through an implementation research lens: a response to the New Hope and Moving to Opportunity evaluations. In T. S. Weisner (Ed.), *Discovering successful pathways in children's development* (pp. 317–325). Chicago, IL: University of Chicago Press.

Bryans, A. N. (2004). Examining health visiting expertise: combining simulation, interview and observation.*JournalofAdvancedNursing*,47(6),623–630.doi:10.1111/j.1365-2648.2004.03150.x

Bryant, P. (2008). Self-regulation and moral awareness among entrepreneurs. *Journal of Business Venturing*, 24, 505–518. doi: 10.1016/j.jbusvent.2008.04.005

Bryman, A. (2006). Integrating quantitative and qualitative research: how is it done? *Qualitative Research*, 6(1), 97–113.

Bryman, A. (2007). Barriers to integrating quantitative and qualitative research. *Journal of Mixed Methods Research*, 1(1), 8–22. doi: 10.1177/2345678906290531

Burch, P., & Heinrich, C. J. (2016). *Mixed methods for policy research and program evaluation.* Thousand Oaks, CA: Sage.

Burrows, R., & Savage, M. (2014). After the crisis? Big data and the methodological challenges of empirical sociology. *Big Data & Society*, 1(1), 1–6. doi: 10.1177/2053951714540280

Byrne, D. (2009). Using cluster analysis, qualitative comparative analysis and NVivo in relation to the establishment of causal configurations with pre-existing large-N datasets: machining hermeneutics. In D. Byrne & C. Ragin (Eds.), *Handbook of case-based methods* (pp. 260–268). London: Sage.

Camerino, O. F., Chaverri, J., Anguera, M. T., & Jonsson, G. K. (2012). Dynamics of the game in soccer: detection of T-patterns. *European Journal of Sport Science*, 12(3), 216–224. doi: 10.1080/17461391.2011.566362

Campbell, D. T. (1974). Qualitative knowing in action research. Paper presented at the Kurt Lewin Award Address, Society for the Psychological Study of Social Issues, Annual Meeting of the American Psychological Association, New Orleans, LA.

Campbell, D. T., & Fiske, D. (1959). Convergent and discriminant validation by the multitrait-multimethod matrix. *Psychological Bulletin*, 56, 81–105.

Campbell, D. T., & Stanley, J. C. (1963). Experimental and quasi-experimental designs for research on teaching. In N. L. Gage (Ed.), *Handbook of research on teaching* (pp. 171–246). Chicago, IL: Rand McNally.

Caracelli, V. J., & Greene, J. C. (1993). Data analysis strategies for mixed-method evaluation designs. *Educational Evaluation and Policy Analysis*, 15(2), 195–207.

Caracelli, V. J., & Greene, J. C. (1997). Crafting mixed-method evaluation designs. In J. C. Greene & V. J. Caracelli (Eds.), *Advances in mixed-method evaluation: the challenges and benefits of integrating diverse paradigms* (pp. 19–32). San Francisco, CA: Jossey-Bass.

Carcary, M. (2009). The research audit trail: enhancing trustworthiness in qualitative inquiry. *Electronic Journal of Business Research Methods*, 7(1), 11–24.

Casey, D., O'Hara, M. C., Meehan, B., Byrne, M., Dinneen, S. F., & Murphy, K. (2016). A mixed methods study exploring the factors and behaviors that affect glycemic control following a structured education program: the Irish DAFNE study. *Journal of Mixed Methods Research*, 10(2), 182–203. doi: 10.1177/1558689814547579

Castro, F. G., Kellison, J. G., Boyd, S. J., & Kopak, A. (2010). A methodology for conducting integrative mixed methods research and data analyses. *Journal of Mixed Methods Research*, 4(4), 342–360. doi: 10.1177/1558689810382916

Charon, J. M. (2009). Symbolic interactionism: an introduction, an interpretation, an integration (10th ed.). Boston, MA: Prentice Hall.

Chatterji, M. (2004). Evidence on "What Works": an argument for extended-term mixed-method (ETMM) evaluation designs. *Educational Researcher*, 33(9), 3–13.

Christensen, P., Mikkelsen, M. R., Nielsen, T. A. S., & Harder, H. (2011). Children, mobility, and space: using GPS and mobile phone technologies in ethnographic research. *Journal of Mixed Methods Research*, 5(3), 227–246. doi: 10.1177/1558689811406121

Classen, S., Lopez, E. D. S., Winter, S., Awadzi, K. D., Ferree, N., & Garvan, C. W. (2007). Population-based health promotion perspective for older driver safety: conceptual framework to intervention plan. *Clinical Interventions in Aging*, 2(4), 677–693.

Coast, J., Flynn, T., Natarajan, L., Sproston, K., Lewis, J., Louviere, J., & Peters, T. (2008). Valuing the ICECAP capability index for older people. *Social Science & Medicine*, 67, 874–882. doi: 10.1016/j.socscimed.2008.05.015

Cohen, J. (1968). Multiple regression as a general data analytic system. *Psychological Bulletin*, 70(6), 426–443.

Cohen, J. (1987). Statistical power analysis for behavioral sciences. Hillsdale, NJ: Erlbaum.

Cohen, J., & Cohen, P. (1975). Applied multiple regressions/correlation analysis for the behavioral sciences. Hillside, NJ: Lawrence Erlbaum Associates.

Collier, D. (2011). Understanding process tracing. *PS: Political Science and Politics*, 44(4), 823–830. doi: 10.1017/S1049096511001429

Collier, D. (2014). Comment: QCA should set aside the algorithms. *Sociological Methodology*, 44(1), 122–126. doi: 10.1177/0081175014542568

Collingridge, D. S. (2013). A primer on quantitized data analysis and permutation testing. *Journal of Mixed Methods Research*, 7(1), 81–97. doi: 10.1177/1558689812454457

Collins, C. C., & Dressler, W. W. (2008). Cultural consensus and cultural diversity: a mixed methods investigation of human service providers' models of domestic violence. *Journal of Mixed Methods Research*, 2(4), 362–387. doi: 10.1177/1558689808322766

Collins, H., & Evans, R. (2014). Quantifying the tacit: the imitation game and social fluency. *Sociology*, 48(1), 3–19. doi: 10.1177/0038038512455735

Collins, H., Evans, R., Weinel, M., Lyttleton-Smith, J., Bartlett, A., & Hall, M. (in press). The imitation game and the nature of mixed methods. *Journal of Mixed Methods Research*. doi: 10.1177/1558689815619824

Collins, K. M. T., Onwuegbuzie, A. J., & Jiao, Q. G. (2007). A mixed methods investigation of mixed methods sampling designs in social and health science research. *Journal of Mixed Methods Research*, 1(3), 267–294. doi: 10.1177/1558689807299526

Connell, J., Kubisch, A. C., Schorr, L. B., & Weiss, C. H. (Eds.) (1995). *New approaches to evaluating community initiatives: concepts, methods and contexts*. Washington, DC: The Aspen Institute.

Cooper, G. (2008). Conceptualising social life. In N. Gilbert (Ed.), *Researching social life* (3rd ed., pp. 5–20). London: Sage.

Cope, M., & Elwood, S. (2009). *Qualitative GIS: a mixed methods approach*. Thousand Oaks, CA: Sage.

Corbin, J., & Strauss, A. L. (2015). *Basics of qualitative research* (4th ed.). Thousand Oaks, CA: Sage.

Corti, L. (2012). Recent developments in archiving social research. *International Journal of Social Research Methodology*, 15(4), 281–290. doi: 10.1080/13645579.2012.688310

Crabtree, B. F., Miller, W. L., Tallia, A. F., Cohen, D. J., DiCicco-Bloom, B., McIlvain, H. E., & McDaniel Jr, R. R. (2005). Delivery of clinical preventive services in family medicine offices. *Annals of Family Medicine*, 3(5), 430–435. doi: 10.1370/afm.345

Cragun, D., Pal, T., Vadaparampil, S. T., Baldwin, J., Hampel, H., & DeBate, R. D. (2016). Qualitative comparative analysis: a hybrid method for identifying factors associated with program effectiveness. *Journal of Mixed Methods Research*, 10(3), 251–272. doi: 10.1177/1558689815572023

Crampton, J. W., Graham, M., Poorthuis, A., Shelton, T., Monica, S., Wilson, M. W., & Zook, M. (2013). Beyond the geotag? Deconstructing "big data" and leveraging the potential of the geoweb. *Cartography and Geographic Information Science*, 40(2), 130–139. doi: 10.1080/15230406.2013.777137

Cress, D. M., & Snow, D. A. (2000). The outcomes of homeless mobilization: the influence of organization, disruption, political mediation, and framing. *American Journal of Sociology*, 105(4), 1063–1104.

Creswell, J. W., & Plano Clark, V. L. (2011). *Designing and conducting mixed methods research* (2nd ed.). Thousand Oaks, CA: Sage.

Creswell, J. W., & Tashakkori, A. (2007). Differing perspectives on mixed methods research [Editorial]. *Journal of Mixed Methods Research*, 1(4), 303–308.

Crooks, V. A., Schuurman, N., Cinnamon, J., Castleden, H., & Johnston, R. (2011). Refining a location analysis model using a mixed methods approach: community readiness as a key factor in siting rural palliative care services. *Journal of Mixed Methods Research*, 5(1), 77–95. doi: 10.1177/1558689810385693

Crossley, N. (2010). The social world of the network: combining qualitative and quantitative elements in social network analysis. *Sociologica*, 1. doi: 10.2383/32049

Crotty, M. (1998). *The foundations of social research*. Sydney: Allen & Unwin.

Curry, L. A., & Nunez-Smith, M. (2015). *Mixed methods in health sciences research: a practical primer*. Thousand Oaks, CA: Sage.

Curry, L. A., O'Cathain, A., Plano Clark, V. L., Aroni, R., Fetters, M., & Berg, D. (2012). The role of group dynamics in mixed methods health sciences research teams. *Journal of Mixed Methods Research*, 6(1), 5–20. doi: 10.1177/1558689811416941

Curry, L. A., Spatz, E. S., Cherlin, E. J., Thompson, J. W., Berg, D., Ting, H. H., & Bradley, E. H. (2011). What distinguishes top-performing hospitals in acute myocardial infarction mortality rates? A qualitative study. *Annals of Internal Medicine*, 154(6), 384–390.

da Costa, L., & Remedios, R. (2014). Different methods, different results: examining the implications of methodological divergence and implicit processes for achievement goal research. *Journal of Mixed Methods Research*, 8(2), 162–179. doi: 10.1177/1558689813495977

Danermark, B., Ekström, M., Jakobsen, L., & Karlsson, J. C. (2002). *Explaining society: critical realism in the social sciences*. London: Routledge.

Danermark, B., & Gellerstedt, L. C. (2004). Social justice: redistribution and recognition—a non-reductionist perspective on disability. *Disability & Society*, 19(4), 347–352.

de Leeuw, E., Hox, J., & Huisman, M. (2003). Prevention and treatment of item nonresponse. *Journal of Official Statistics*, 19(2), 153–176.

De Vito Dabbs, A., Hoffman, L. A., Swigart, V., Happ, M. B., Iacono, A. T., & Dauber, J. H. (2004). Using conceptual triangulation to develop an integrated model of the symptom experience of acute rejection after lung transplantation. *Advances in Nursing Science*, 27(2), 138–149.

Denicolo, P., Long, T., & Bradley-Cole, K. (2016). Constructivist approaches and research methods: a practical guide to exploring personal meanings. London: Sage.

Denzin, N. K. (1978). The research act: a theoretical introduction to sociological methods (2nd ed.). New York: McGraw-Hill.

Denzin, N. K., & Lincoln, Y. S. (Eds.) (1994). *Handbook of qualitative research*. Thousand Oaks, CA: Sage Publications.

Denzin, N. K., & Lincoln, Y. S. (2011). The discipline and practice of qualitative research. In N. K. Denzin & Y. S. Lincoln (Eds.), *Handbook of qualitative research* (4th ed., pp. 1–20). Thousand Oaks, CA: Sage.

Dockett, S., & Perry, B. (2004). Starting school: perspectives of Australian children, parents and educators. *Journal of Early Childhood Research*, 2, 171–189.

Douglas, J. E., & Douglas, L. K. (2006). Modus operandi and signature aspects of violent crime. In J. E. Douglas, A. W. Burgess, A. G. Burgess & R. K. Ressler (Eds.), *Crime classification manual: a standard system for investigating and classifying violent crimes* (pp. 19–30). San Francisco, CA: Wiley.

Dowson, M., & McInerney, D. M. (2003). What do students say about their motivational goals? Towards a more complex and dynamic perspective on student motivation. *Contemporary Educational Psychology*, 28, 91–113. doi: 10.1016/S0361-476X(02)00010-3

Drabble, S. J., & O'Cathain, A. (2015). Moving from randomized controlled trials to mixed methods evaluations. In S. Hesse-Biber & B. Johnson (Eds.), *Oxford handbook of multimethod and mixed methods research inquiry* (pp. 406–425). New York: Oxford University Press.

Duncan, S. S., & Edwards, R. (1999). *Lone mothers' paid work and gendered moral rationalities*. Houndsmills, UK: Macmillan.

Dunning, H., Williams, A., Abonyi, S., & Crooks, V. (2008). A mixed method approach to quality of life research: a case study approach. *Social Indicators Research*, 85, 145–158.

Durham, J., Tan, B.-K., & White, R. (2011). Utilizing mixed research methods to develop a quantitative assessment tool: an example from explosive remnants of a war clearance program. *Journal of Mixed Methods Research*, 5(3), 212–226. doi: 10.1177/1558689811402505

Dymnicki, A. B., & Henry, D. B. (2012). Clustering and its applications in community research. In L. Jason & D. Glenwick (Eds.), *Methodological approaches to community-based research* (pp. 71–88). Washington, DC: American Psychological Association.

Dyson, A., & Todd, L. (2010). Dealing with complexity: theory of change evaluation and the full service extended schools initiative. *International Journal of Research & Method in Education*, 33(2), 119–134. doi: 10.1080/1743727X.2010.484606

Eagle, N., & Greene, K. (2014). *Reality mining: using big data to engineer a better world*. Cambridge, MA: MIT Press.

Eagle, N., Pentland, A., & Lazer, D. (2009). Inferring friendship network structure by using mobile phone data. *Proceedings of the National Academy of Sciences (PNAS)*, 106(36), 15274–15278. doi: 10.1073/pnas.0900282106

Edmeades, J., Nyblade, L., Malhotra, A., MacQuarrie, K., Parasuraman, S., & Walia, S. (2010). Methodological innovation in studying abortion in developing countries: a "narrative" quantitative survey in Madhya Pradesh, India. *Journal of Mixed Methods Research*, 4(3), 176–198. doi: 10.1177/1558689810365699

Edwards, G. (2010). Mixed-method approaches to social network analysis. NCRM Discussion Paper. Retrieved from http://eprints.ncrm.ac.uk/842/

Elliott, J. (2002). The value of event history techniques for understanding social processes: modelling women's employment behaviour after motherhood. *International Journal of Social Research Methodology*, 5(2), 107–132. doi: 10.1080/13645570110062405

Elliott, J. (2005). Using narrative in social research: qualitative and quantitative approaches. London: Sage.

Elliott, J. (2011). Exploring the narrative potential of cohort data and event history analysis. In J. Mason & A. Dale (Eds.), *Understanding social research* (pp. 210–224). London: Sage.

Elliott, J., Gale, C. R., Parsons, S., Kuh, D., & The HALCyon Study Team (2014). Neighbourhood cohesion and mental wellbeing among older adults: a mixed methods approach. *Social Science & Medicine*, 107(1), 44–51.

Erzberger, C., & Kelle, U. (2003). Making inferences in mixed methods: the rules of integration. In A. Tashakkori & C. Teddlie (Eds.), *Handbook of mixed methods in social and behavioral research* (pp. 457–488). Thousand Oaks, CA: Sage.

Erzberger, C., & Prein, G. (1997). Triangulation: validity and empirically-based hypothesis construction. *Quality & Quantity*, 31, 141–154.

Evans, B. C., Coon, D. W., & Ume, E. (2011). Use of theoretical frameworks as a pragmatic guide for mixed methods studies: a methodological necessity? *Journal of Mixed Methods Research*, 5(4), 276–292. doi: 10.1177/1558689811412972

Evans, R., & Crocker, H. (2013). The imitation game as a method for exploring knowledge(s) of chronic illness. *Methodological Innovations Online*, 8(1), 34–52. doi: 10.4256/mio.2013.003

Ezzy, D. (2002). Qualitative analysis: practice and innovation. London: Routledge.

Fàbregues, S., & Molina-Azorín, J. (in press). Addressing quality in mixed methods research: a review and recommendations for a future agenda. *Quality & Quantity*. doi: 10.1007/s11135-016-0449-4

Fakis, A., Hilliam, R., Stoneley, H., & Townend, M. (2014). Quantitative analysis of qualitative information from interviews: a systematic literature review. *Journal of Mixed Methods Research*, 8(2), 139–161. doi: 10.1177/1558689813495111

Farmer, T., Robinson, K., Elliott, S. J., & Eyles, J. (2006). Developing and implementing a triangulation protocol for qualitative health research. *Qualitative Health Research*, 16, 377–394. doi: 10.1177/1049732305285708

Farrell, G., Tseloni, A., & Tilley, N. (2016). Signature dish: triangulation from data signatures to examine the role of security in falling crime. *Methodological Innovations*, 9, 1–11. doi: 10.1177/2059799115622754

Fassin, Y., Werner, A., Van Rossem, A., Signori, S., Garriga, E., von Weltzien Hoivik, H., & Schlierer, H.-J. (2015). CSR and related terms in SME owner-managers' mental models in six European countries: national context matters. *Journal of Business Ethics*, 128(2), 433–456. doi: 10.1007/s10551-014-2098-7

Feilzer, M. Y. (2010). Doing mixed methods research pragmatically: implications for the rediscovery of pragmatism as a research paradigm. *Journal of Mixed Methods Research*, 4(1), 6–16. doi: 10.1177/1558689809349691

Festinger, L., Riecken, H. W., & Schachter, S. (1956). *When prophecy fails*. Minneapolis: University of Minnesota Press.

Fetters, M. D., Curry, L. A., & Creswell, J. W. (2013). Achieving integration in mixed methods designs: principles and practices. *Health Services Research*, 48(6, Pt 2), 2134–2156. doi: 10.1111/1475-6773.12117

Field, A. (2012). The joy of confidence intervals. Retrieved from: www.methodspace.com/the-joy-of-confidence-intervals/

Field, A. (2018). Discovering statistics using IBM SPSS Statistics (5th ed.). London: Sage.

Fielding, J., & Fielding, N. (2008). Synergy and synthesis: integrating qualitative and quantitative data. In P. Alasuutari, J. Brannen & L. Bickman (Eds.), *Handbook of social research methods* (pp. 555–571). London: Sage.

Fielding, J., & Fielding, N. (2013). Integrating information from multiple methods into the analysis of perceived risk of crime: the role of geo-referenced field data and mobile methods. *Journal of Criminology*. Retrieved from: http://dx.doi.org/10.1155/2013/284259

Fielding, J., & Fielding, N. (2015). Emergent technologies in multimethod and mixed methods research: incorporating GIS and CAQDAS. In S. Hesse-Biber & B. Johnson (Eds.), *Oxford handbook of multimethod and mixed methods research inquiry* (pp. 561–584). New York: Oxford University Press.

Fielding, N., & Cisneros-Puebla, C. A. (2009). CAQDAS-GIS convergence: toward a new integrated mixed method research practice? *Journal of Mixed Methods Research*, 3(4), 349–370. doi: 10.1177/1558689809344973

Fielding, N. G. (2012). Triangulation and mixed methods designs: data integration with new research technologies. *Journal of Mixed Methods Research*, 6(2), 124–136. doi: 10.1177/1558689812437101

Fielding, N. G., & Fielding, J. L. (1986). Linking data: the articulation of qualitative and quantitative methods in social research. Beverly Hills, CA: Sage.

Finocchiaro, C. J., & Lin, T-m. (2000). The hazards of incumbency: an event history analysis of congressional tenure. Paper presented at the 58th Annual Meeting of the Midwest Political Science Association, Chicago, IL. www.amazon.com/hazards-incumbency-history-analysis-congressional/dp/B0006RELTI

Firestone, W. A. (1993). Alternative arguments for generalising from data as applied to qualitative research. *Educational Researcher*, 22(4), 16–23.

Fitzpatrick, K. R. (2016). Points of convergence in music education: the use of data labels as a strategy for mixed methods integration. *Journal of Mixed Methods Research*, 10(3), 273–291. doi: 10.1177/1558689814560264

Flecha, R. (2014). Using mixed methods from a communicative orientation: researching with grassroots Roma. *Journal of Mixed Methods Research*, 8(3), 245–254. doi: 10.1177/1558689814527945

Flick, U. (1992). Triangulation revisited: strategy of validation or alternative? *Journal for the Theory of Social Behaviour*, 22, 175–197.

Flick, U. (2010). Triangulation of micro-perspectives on juvenile homelessness, health, and human rights. In N. K. Denzin & M. D. Giardina (Eds.), *Qualitative inquiry and human rights* (pp. 186–204). Walnut Creek, CA: Left Coast Press.

Flick, U., Garms-Homolová, V., Herrmann, W. J., Kuck, J., & Röhnsch, G. (2012). "I can't prescribe something just because someone asks for it ...": using mixed methods in the framework of triangulation. *Journal of Mixed Methods Research*, 6(2), 97–110. doi: 10.1177/1558689812437183

Floyd, S. W., Schroeder, D. M., & Finn, D. M. (1994). "Only if I'm first author": conflict over credit in management scholarship. *Academy of Management Journal*, 37(3), 734–747.

Flyvbjerg, B. (2006). Five misunderstandings about case-study research. *Qualitative Inquiry*, 219–245. doi: 10.1177/1077800405284363

Ford, H. (2014). Big data and small: collaborations between ethnographers and data scientists. *Big Data & Society*, 1(2), 1–3. doi: 10.1177/2053951714544337

Ford, R. T. (2006). Nursing attitudes and therapeutic capacity: what are the implications for nursing care of patients who use illicit drugs? Unpublished doctoral thesis, Australian National University, Canberra.

Fransella, F., Bell, R., & Bannister, D. (2003). *A manual for repertory grid technique* (2nd ed.). Chichester: Wiley.

Fricke, T. (2005). Taking culture seriously: making the social survey ethnographic. In T. A. Weisner (Ed.), *Discovering successful pathways in children's development* (pp. 185–222). Chicago, IL: University of Chicago Press.

Friese, S. (2014). *Qualitative data analysis with Atlas.ti* (2nd ed.). London: Sage.

Frost, P. J., & Stablein, R. E. (1992). *Doing exemplary research*. Newbury Park, CA: Sage.

Fry, G., Chantavanich, S., & Chantavanich, A. (1981). Merging quantitative and qualitative research techniques: toward a new research paradigm. *Anthropology and Education Quarterly*, 12(2), 145–158.

Garcia, J., Evans, J., & Reshaw, M. (2004). "Is there anything else you would like to tell us?" – methodological issues in the use of free-text comments from postal surveys. *Quality & Quantity*, 38, 113–125.

George, A., & Bennett, A. (2005). *Case studies and theory development in the social sciences*. Cambridge, MA: MIT Press.

Gibson, G., Timlin, A., Curran, S., & Wattis, J. (2004). The scope for qualitative methods in research and clinical trials in dementia. *Age and Ageing*, 33(4), 422–426.

Gobo, G. (2015). The next challenge: from mixed to merged methods. *Qualitative Research in Organizations and Management*, 10(4), 329–331. doi: 10.1108/QROM-07-2015-1309

Goertz, G. (2006). *Social science concepts: a user's guide*. Princeton, NJ: Princeton University Press.

Goodwin, R., Polek, E., & Goodwin, K. (2013). Perceived changes in health and interactions with "the paracetamol force": a multimethod study. *Journal of Mixed Methods Research*, 7(2), 152–172. doi: 10.1177/1558689812463782

Gorard, S. (2010a). All evidence is equal: the flaw in statistical reasoning. *Oxford Review of Education*, 36(1), 63–67. doi: 10.1080/03054980903518928

Gorard, S. (2010b). Research design, as independent of methods. In A. Tashakkori & C. Teddlie (Eds.), *Handbook of mixed methods in social and behavioral research* (2nd ed., pp. 237–251). Thousand Oaks, CA: Sage.

Gorard, S. (2013). *Research design*. London: Sage.

Gorard, S. (2015). Rethinking "quantitative" methods and the development of new researchers. *Review of Education*, 3(1), 72–96. doi: 10.1002/rev3.3041

Gorard, S., & Gorard, J. (2016). What to do instead of significance testing? Calculating the "number of counterfactual cases needed to disturb a finding". *International Journal of Social Research Methodology*, 19(4), 481–490. doi: 10.1080/13645579.2015.1091235

Grant, A. M., Berg, J. M., & Cable, D. M. (2014). Job titles as identity badges: how self-reflective titles can reduce emotional exhaustion. *Academy of Management Journal*, 57(4), 1201–1225. doi: org/10.5465/amj.2012.0338

Green, J., Statham, H., & Solomou, W. (2008). Assessing satisfaction: insights from a multi-methods study. NCRM Working Paper. Retrieved from: http://eprints.ncrm.ac.uk/462/

Greenacre, M. (2016). *Correspondence analysis in practice* (3rd ed.). London: Chapman & Hall/CRC.

Greene, J. C. (2007). *Mixed methods in social inquiry*. San Francisco, CA: Jossey-Bass (Wiley).

Greene, J. C. (2008). Is mixed methods social inquiry a distinctive methodology? *Journal of Mixed Methods Research*, 2(1), 7–22. doi: 10.1177/1558689807309969

Greene, J. C. (2012a). Engaging critical issues in social inquiry by mixing methods. *American Behavioral Scientist*, 56(6), 755–773. doi: 10.1177/0002764211433794

Greene, J. C. (2012b). Integrated data analysis in mixed methods evaluation [workshop notes]. Urbana-Champaign, IL: University of Illinois.

Greene, J. C., & Caracelli, V. J. (1997). Defining and describing the paradigm issues in mixed-method evaluation. In J. C. Greene & V. J. Caracelli (Eds.), *Advances in mixed-method evaluation: the challenges and benefits of integrating diverse paradigms* (pp. 5–18). San Francisco, CA: Jossey-Bass.

Greene, J. C., Caracelli, V. J., & Graham, W. F. (1989). Toward a conceptual framework for mixed-method evaluation designs. *Educational Evaluation and Policy Analysis*, 11(3), 255–274.

Greenhalgh, T., Potts, H. W. W., Wong, G., Bark, P., & Swinglehurst, D. (2009). Tensions and paradoxes in electronic patient record research: a systematic literature review using the met-anarrative method. *Milbank Quarterly*, 87(4), 729–788.

Grimmer, J., & Stewart, B. M. (2013). Text as data: the promise and pitfalls of automatic content analysis methods for political texts. *Political Analysis*, 21(3), 267–297. doi: 10.1093/pan/mps028

Guest, G. (2000). Using Guttman scaling to rank wealth: integrating quantitative and qualita-tive data. *Field Methods*, 12(4), 346–357.

Guest, G. (2013). Describing mixed methods research: an alternative to typologies. *Journal of Mixed Methods Research*, 7(2), 141–151. doi: 10.1177/1558689812461179

Guest, G., & McLellan, E. (2003). Distinguishing the trees from the forest: applying cluster analysis to thematic qualitative data. *Field Methods*, 15(2), 186–201.

Guetterman, T. C., Creswell, J. W., & Kuckartz, U. (2015). Using joint displays and MAXQDA software to represent the results of mixed methods research. In M. McCrudden, G. Schraw & C. W. Buckendahl (Eds.), *Use of visual displays in research and testing: coding, interpreting, and reporting data* (pp. 145–176). Charlotte, NC: Information Age Publishing.

Guetterman, T. C., Fetters, M. D., & Creswell, J. W. (2015). Integrating quantitative and qualita-tive results in health science mixed methods research through joint displays. *Annals of Family Medicine*, 13(6), 554–561. doi: 10.1370/afm.1865

Guilleman, M., & Gillam, L. (2004). Ethics, reflexivity, and "ethically important moments" in research. *Qualitative Inquiry*, 10(2), 261–280. doi: 10.1177/1077800403262360

Gürtler, L., & Huber, G. L. (2006). The ambiguous use of language in the paradigms of QUAN and QUAL. *Qualitative Research in Psychology*, 3(4), 313–328. doi: 10.1177/147 8088706070840

Habashi, J., & Worley, J. (2009). Child geopolitical agency: a mixed methods case study. *Journal of Mixed Methods Research*, 3(1), 42–64. doi: 10.1177/1558689808326120

Halsey, L. (2015). Goodbye P value: is it time to let go of one of science's most fundamental_ measures, *The Conversation*. Retrieved from: http://theconversation.com/goodbye-p-value-is-it-time-to-let-go-of-one-of-sciences-most-fundamental-measures-38057; also available at: www.methodspace.com/is-it-time-to-say-goodbye-to-a-fickle-friend-the-p-value/

Hammersley, M. (2008). *Questioning qualitative inquiry*. London: Sage.

Hammersley, M., & Atkinson, P. (2007). *Ethnography: principles in practice* (3rd ed.). Abingdon: Routledge.

Happ, M. B., DeVito Dabbs, A., Tate, J., Hricik, A., & Erlen, J. (2006). Exemplars of mixed meth-ods data combination and analysis. *Nursing Research*, 55(2, Supplement 1), S43–S49.

Harden, A., & Thomas, J. (2005). Methodological issues in combining diverse study types in systematic reviews. *International Journal of Social Research Methodology*, 8(3), 257–271.

Harman, G. H. (1965). The inference to best explanation. *Philosophical Review*, 74(1), 88–95.

Hayden, H. E., & Chiu, M. M. (2015). Reflective teaching via a problem exploration–teaching adaptations–resolution cycle: a mixed methods study of preservice teachers' reflective notes. *Journal of Mixed Methods Research*, 9(2), 133–153. doi: 10.1177/1558689813509027

Heise, D. (1989). Modelling event structures. *Journal of Mathematical Sociology*, 14, 139–169.

Heise, D. (2007). Event structure analysis. Retrieved from: www.indiana.edu/~socpsy/ESA/

Hemmings, A., Beckett, G., Kennerly, S., & Yap, T. (2013). Building a community of research practice: intragroup team social dynamics in interdisciplinary mixed methods. *Journal of Mixed Methods Research*, 7(3), 261–273. doi: 10.1177/1558689813478468

Hesse-Biber, S. (2010). Mixed methods research: merging theory with practice. New York: Guilford.

Hesse-Biber, S. (2017). *The practice of qualitative research* (3rd ed.). Thousand Oaks, CA: Sage.

Hildebrandt, E., & Kelber, S. T. (2005). Perceptions of health and well-being among women in a work-based welfare program. *Public Health Nursing*, 22(6), 506–514.

Hogan, B. (2017). Online social networks: concepts for data collection and analysis. In N. Fielding, R. Lee & G. Blank (Eds.), *Handbook of online research methods* (2nd ed.). London: Sage.

Hojat, M., & Xu, G. (2004). A visitor's guide to effect sizes: statistical significance versus practical (clinical) importance of research findings. *Advances in Health Sciences Education*, 9, 241–249.

Holbrook, A., & Bourke, S. (2004). An investigation of PhD examination outcome in Australia using a mixed method approach. *Australian Journal of Educational & Developmental Psychology*, 4, 153–169.

Holbrook, A., Bourke, S., Lovat, T., & Dally, K. (2004). Qualities and characteristics in the written reports of doctoral thesis examiners. *Australian Journal of Educational and Developmental Psychology*, 4, 126–145.

Holder, R. L. (in press). Untangling the meanings of justice: a longitudinal mixed methods study. *Journal of Mixed Methods Research*. doi: 10.1177/1558689816653308

Holsti, O. R. (1969). Content analysis for the social sciences and humanities. Reading, MA: Addison-Wesley.

Houghton, S., Wood, L., Marais, I., Rosenberg, M., Ferguson, R., & Pettigrew, S. (2015). Positive mental well-being: a validation of a Rasch-derived version of the Warwick-Edinburgh Mental Well-Being Scale. *Assessment*, 1–16. doi: 10.1177/1073191115609995

Howe, K. R. (1988). Against the quantitative-qualitative incompatibility thesis or dogmas die hard. *Educational Researcher*, 17(8), 10–16.

Howe, K. R., & Eisenhardt, M. (1990). Standards for qualitative (and quantitative) research: a prolegomenon. *Educational Researcher*, 19(4), 2–9.

Howell, D. C. (2014). *Fundamental statistics for the behavioral sciences* (8th ed.). Belmont, CA: Wadsworth.

Howell Smith, M. C. (2011). Factors that facilitate or inhibit interest of domestic students in the engineering PhD: a mixed methods study. PhD thesis, University of Nebraska-Lincoln. Retrieved from: http://digitalcommons.unl.edu/cgi/viewcontent.cgi?article=1123&context=cehsdiss

Hunter, A., & Brewer, J. (2015). Designing multimethod research. In S. Hesse-Biber & B. Johnson (Eds.), *Oxford handbook of multimethod and mixed methods research inquiry* (pp. 185–205). New York: Oxford University Press.

Huysmans, P., & De Bruyn, P. (2013). A mixed methods approach to combining behavioral and design research methods in information systems research. *Proceedings of the 21st European Conference on Information Systems, ECIS 2013 Completed Research*. Retrieved from: http://aisel.aisnet.org/ecis2013_cr/29

Irwin, S. (2008). Data analysis and interpretation: emergent issues in linking qualitative and quantitative evidence. In S. Hesse-Biber & P. Leavy (Eds.), *Handbook of emergent methods* (pp. 415–436). New York: Guilford.

Ivankova, N. V. (2014). Implementing quality criteria in designing and conducting a sequential QUAN → QUAL mixed methods study of student engagement with learning applied research methods online. *Journal of Mixed Methods Research*, 8(1), 25–51. doi: 10.1177/1558689813487945

Jang, E. E., McDougall, D. E., Pollon, D., Herbert, M., & Russell, P. (2008). Integrative mixed methods data analytic strategies in research on school success in challenging circumstances. *Journal of Mixed Methods Research*, 2(3), 221–247. doi: 10.1177/1558689808315323

Jick, T. D. (1979). Mixing qualitative and quantitative methods: triangulation in action. *Administrative Science Quarterly*, 24, 602–611.

Johnson, R. B. (2017). Dialectical pluralism: a metaparadigm whose time has come. *Journal of Mixed Methods Research*, 11(2), 156–173. doi: 10.1177/1558689815607692

Johnson, R. B., & Gray, R. (2010). A history of the philosophical and theoretical issues for mixed methods research. In A. Tashakkori & C. Teddlie (Eds.), *Handbook of mixed methods in social and behavioral research* (2nd ed., pp. 69–94). Thousand Oaks, CA: Sage.

Johnson, R. B., & Onwuegbuzie, A. J. (2004). Mixed methods research: a research paradigm whose time has come. *Educational Researcher*, 33(7), 14–26.

Johnson, R. B., Onwuegbuzie, A. J., & Turner, L. A. (2007). Toward a definition of mixed methods research. *Journal of Mixed Methods Research*, 1(2), 112–133. doi: 10.1177/1558689806298224

Johnson, R. B., Russo, F., & Schoonenboom, J. (in press). Toward a pluralistic theory of causation for mixed methods research: the meeting of philosophy, science, and practice. *Journal of Mixed Methods Research*. doi: 10.1177/1558689817719610

Jung, J.-K., & Elwood, S. (2010). Extending the qualitative capabilities of GIS: computer-aided qualitative GIS. *Transactions in GIS*, 14(1), 63–87. doi: 10.1111/j.1467-9671.2009.01182.x

Kane, M., & Trochim, W. M. K. (2007). *Concept mapping for planning and evaluation*. Thousand Oaks, CA: Sage.

Kanzaki, H., Makimoto, K., Takemura, T., & Ashida, N. (2004). Development of web-based qualitative and quantitative data collection systems: study on daily symptoms and coping strategies among Japanese rheumatoid arthritis patients. *Nursing & Health Sciences*, 6(3), 229–236.

Kelle, U. (2006). Combining qualitative and quantitative methods in research practice: purposes and advantages. *Qualitative Research in Psychology*, 3(4), 293–311. doi: 10.1177/1478088706070839

Kelle, U. (2015). Mixed methods and the problems of theory building and theory testing in the social sciences. In S. Hesse-Biber & B. Johnson (Eds.), *Oxford handbook of multimethod and mixed methods research inquiry* (pp. 594–605). New York: Oxford University Press.

Kelly, G. (1955). *The psychology of personal constructs*. New York: Norton.

Kemp, L. (1999). Charting a parallel course: meeting the community service needs of persons with spinal injuries. PhD thesis, University of Western Sydney, Sydney.

Kemp, L. (2001). The DNA of integrated methods. Paper presented at the Annual Conference of the Australian Association for Social Research, Wollongong, New South Wales, Australia.

Kennerly, S., Yap, T., Hemmings, A., Beckett, G., Schafer, J. C., & Borchers, A. (2012). Development and psychometric testing of the Nursing Culture Assessment Tool. *Clinical Nursing Research*, 21(4), 467–485. doi: 10.1177/1054773812440810

Kerrigan, M. R. (2014). A framework for understanding Community Colleges' organizational capacity for data use: a convergent parallel mixed methods study. *Journal of Mixed Methods Research*, 8(4), 341–362. doi: 10.1177/1558689814523518

Kienstra, N. H. H., & van der Heuhden, P. G. M. (2015). Using correspondence analysis in multiple case studies. *Bulletin de Methodologie Sociologique*, 128(4), 5–22. doi: 10.1177/0759106315596920

King, G. (2016). Preface: Big Data is not about the data. In J. M. Alvarez (Ed.), *Computational social science: discovery and prediction*. Cambridge: Cambridge University Press.

King, G., Pan, J., & Roberts, M. E. (2013). How censorship in China allows government criticism but silences collective expression. *American Political Science Review*, 107(2), 326–343. doi: 10.1017/S0003055413000014

Kingston, A., Sammons, P., Day, C., & Regan, E. (2011). Stories and statistics: describing a mixed methods study of effective classroom practice. *Journal of Mixed Methods Research*, 5(2), 103–125. doi: 10.1177/1558689810396092

Kitchin, R. (2014). Big Data, new epistemologies and paradigm shifts. *Big Data & Society*, 1(1), 1–12. doi: 10.1177/2053951714528481

Knigge, L., & Cope, M. (2006). Grounded visualization: integrating the analysis of qualitative and quantitative data through grounded theory and visualization. *Environment and Planning A*, 38, 2021–2037.

Knowlton, L. W., & Phillips, C. C. (2013). *The logic model guidebook* (2nd ed.). Thousand Oaks, CA: Sage.

Kolar, K., Ahmad, F., Chan, L., & Erickson, P. G. (2015). Timeline mapping in qualitative interviews: a study of resilience with marginalised groups. *International Journal of Qualitative Methods*, 14(3), 13–32.

Kramer, J. M. (2011). Using mixed methods to establish the social validity of a self-report assessment: an illustration using the child occupational self-assessment (COSA). *Journal of Mixed Methods Research*, 5(1), 52–76. doi: 10.1177/1558689810386376

Krantz, D. L. (1995). Sustaining versus resolving the quantitative-qualitative debate. *Evaluation and Program Planning*, 18, 89–96.

Kravitz, R. L., Duan, N., & Braslow, J. (2004). Evidence-based medicine, heterogeneity of treatment effects, and the trouble with averages. *The Milbank Quarterly*, 82(4), 661–687.

Krippendorff, K. (2004). *Content analysis: an introduction to its methodology* (2nd ed.). Thousand Oaks, CA: Sage.

Krohwinkel, A. (2015). A configurational approach to project delays: evidence from a sequential mixed methods study. *Journal of Mixed Methods Research*, 9(4), 335–361. doi: 10.1177/1558689814522709

Kruskal, J. B., & Wish, M. (1978). *Multidimensional scaling*. Beverly Hills, CA: Sage.

Kuckartz, U. (2014). *Qualitative text analysis*. London: Sage.

Kuhn, T. S. (1970). *The structure of scientific revolutions* (2nd ed.). Chicago, IL: University of Chicago Press.

Latcheva, R. (2011). Cognitive interviewing and factor-analytic techniques: a mixed method approach to validity of survey items measuring national identity. *Quality & Quantity*, 45(6), 1175–1199. doi: 10.1007/s11135-009-9285-0

Laudel, G., & Gläser, J. (2008). From apprentice to colleague: the metamorphosis of early career researchers. *Higher Education*, 55(3), 387–406.

Lawrenz, F., & Huffman, D. (2002). The archipelago approach to mixed method evaluation. *American Journal of Evaluation*, 23(3), 331–338.

Lee, J.-G., & Kang, M. (2015). Geospatial big data: challenges and opportunities. *Big Data Research*, 2(2), 74–81. doi: 10.1016/j.bdr.2015.01.003

Lincoln, Y. S., & Guba, E. G. (1985). *Naturalistic inquiry*. Beverly Hills, CA: Sage.

Lincoln, Y. S., & Guba, E. G. (2013). *The constructivist credo*. Walnut Creek, CA: Left Coast Press.

Louis, K. S. (1982a). Multisite/multimethod studies: an introduction. *American Behavioral Scientist*, 26(1), 6–22.

Louis, K. S. (1982b). Sociologist as sleuth: integrating methods in the RDU study. *American Behavioral Scientist*, 26(1), 101–120.

Lucas, S. R., & Szatrowski, A. (2014). Qualitative comparative analysis in critical perspective. *Sociological Methodology*, 44(1), 1–79. doi: 10.1177/0081175014532763

Lunde, Å., Heggen, K., & Strand, R. (2013). Knowledge and power: exploring unproductive interplay between quantitative and qualitative researchers. *Journal of Mixed Methods Research*, 7(2), 197–210. doi: 10.1177/1558689812471087

Luyt, R. (2012). A framework for mixing methods in quantitative measurement development, validation, and revision: a case study. *Journal of Mixed Methods Research*, 6(4), 294–316. doi: 10.1177/1558689811427912

Lynch, M. (1993). *Scientific practice and ordinary action*. New York: Cambridge University Press.

Mallinson, S. (2002). Listening to respondents: a qualitative assessment of the Short-Form 36 Health Status Questionnaire. *Social Science & Medicine*, 54(1), 11–21.

Maltseva, K. (2016). Using correspondence analysis of scales as part of a mixed methods design to access cultural models in ethnographic fieldwork: prosocial cooperation in Sweden. *Journal of Mixed Methods Research*, 10(1), 82–111. doi: 10.1177/1558689814525262

Mark, M. M. (2015). Mixed and multimethods in predominantly quantitative studies, especially experiments and quasi-experiments. In S. Hesse-Biber & B. Johnson (Eds.), *Oxford handbook of multimethod and mixed methods research inquiry* (pp. 21–41). New York: Oxford University Press.

Mason, J. (2006a). Mixing methods in a qualitatively-driven way. *Qualitative Research*, 6(1), 19–25.

Mason, J. (2006b). *Six strategies for mixing methods and linking data in social science research*. Real Life Methods Working Paper, ESRC National Centre for Research Methods (4/06). University of Manchester.

Mathison, S. (1988). Why triangulate? *Educational Researcher*, 17(2), 13–17.

Maume, D. J. (1999). Glass ceilings and glass escalators. *Work and Occupations*, 26(4), 483–509.

Maxwell, J. A. (2004a). Causal explanation, qualitative research, and scientific inquiry in education. *Educational Researcher*, 33(2), 3–11.

Maxwell, J. A. (2004b). Using qualitative methods for causal explanation. *Field Methods*, 16(3), 243–264.

Maxwell, J. A. (2012a). The importance of qualitative research for causal explanation in Education. *Qualitative Inquiry*, 18(8), 655–661.

Maxwell, J. A. (2012b). *A realist approach for qualitative research*. Thousand Oaks, CA: Sage.

Maxwell, J. A. (2013). *Qualitative research design* (3rd ed.). Thousand Oaks, CA: Sage.

Maxwell, J. A. (2016). Expanding the history and range of mixed methods research. *Journal of Mixed Methods Research*, 10(1), 12–27. doi: 10.1177/1558689815571132

Maxwell, J. A., Chmiel, M., & Rogers, S. (2015). Designing integration in multimethod and mixed methods research. In S. Hesse-Biber & B. Johnson (Eds.), *Oxford handbook of multimethod and mixed methods research inquiry* (pp. 223–239). New York: Oxford University Press.

Maxwell, J. A., & Loomis, D. (2003). Mixed method design: an alternative approach. In A. Tashakkori & C. Teddlie (Eds.), *Handbook of mixed methods in social and behavioral research* (pp. 241–271). Thousand Oaks, CA.: Sage.

Maxwell, J. A., & Miller, B. A. (2008). Categorizing and connecting strategies in qualitative data analysis. In S. Hesse-Biber & P. Leavy (Eds.), *Handbook of emergent methods* (pp. 461–477). New York: Guilford.

Mayring, P. (1983). Qualitative content analysis: fundamentals and techniques. Weinheim: Beltz Verlag.

Mayring, P. (2000). Combination and integration of qualitative and quantitative analysis. *Forum: Qualitative Social Research*, 2(1). Retrieved from: http://qualitative-research.net/fqs-texte/1-01/1-01mayring-e.htm

McCammon, H. J. (1999). Using event history analysis in historical research: with illustrations from a study of the passage of women's protective legislation. In L. J. Griffin & M. van der Linden (Eds.), *New methods for social history* (pp. 33–56). Cambridge: Cambridge University Press.

McFarland, D. A., & McFarland, H. R. (2015). Big Data and the danger of being precisely inaccurate. *Big Data & Society*, 2(2), 1–4. doi: 10.1177/2053951715602495

McKeon, C. M., Fogarty, G. J., & Hegney, D. G. (2006). Organizational factors: impact on administration violations in rural nursing. *Journal of Advanced Nursing*, 55(1), 115–123.

McKeown, B., & Thomas, D. B. (2013). *Q methodology* (2nd ed.). Thousand Oaks, CA: Sage.

Meetoo, D., & Temple, B. (2003). Issues in multi-method research: constructing self-care. *International Journal of Qualitative Methods*, 2(3), Article 1. Retrieved from: www.ualberta.ca/~iiqm/backissues/2_3final/html/meetootemple.html

Mendlinger, S., & Cwikel, J. (2008). Spiraling between qualitative and quantitative data on women's health behaviors: a model for mixed methods. *Qualitative Health Research*, 18(2), 280–293.

Mercer, J. R. (1973). *Labeling the mentally retarded: clinical and social system perspectives on mental retardation*. Berkeley, CA: University of California Press.

Mertens, D. M. (2007). Transformative paradigm: mixed methods and social justice. *Journal of Mixed Methods Research*, 1(3), 212–225. doi: 10.1177/1558689807302811

Mertens, D. M. (2009). *Transformative research and evaluation*. New York: Guilford.

Mertens, D. M. (2015). Research and evaluation in education and psychology: integrating diversity with quantitative, qualitative and mixed methods (4th ed.). Thousand Oaks, CA: Sage.

Mertens, D. M., Bazeley, P., Bowleg, L., Fielding, N., Maxwell, J., Molina-Azorin, J. F., & Niglas, K. (2016a). Expanding thinking through a kaleidoscopic look into the future: implications of the Mixed Methods International Research Association's Task Force Report on the Future of Mixed Methods. *Journal of Mixed Methods Research*, 10(3), 221–227. doi: 10.1177/1558689816649719

Mertens, D. M., Bazeley, P., Bowleg, L., Fielding, N., Maxwell, J., Molina-Azorín, J. F., & Niglas, K. (2016b). *The future of mixed methods: a five year projection to 2020*. Mixed Methods International Research Association. Retrieved from: www.mmira.org

Merton, R. K. (1968). *Social theory and social structure*. New York: Free Press.

Meurer, W. J., Lewis, R. J., Tagle, D., Fetters, M., Legocki, L., Berry, S., & Barson, W. G. (2012). An overview of the Adaptive Designs Accelerating Promising Trials Into Treatments (ADAPT-IT) project. *Annals of Emergency Medicine*, 20(10). doi: 10.1016/j.annemergmed.2012.01.020

Meyer, A. D. (1982). Adapting to environmental jolts. *Administrative Science Quarterly*, 27, 515–537.

Meyer, A. D. (1992). From loose coupling to environmental jolts. In P. J. Frost & R. E. Stablein (Eds.), *Doing exemplary research* (pp. 82–98). Newbury Park, CA: Sage.

Miles, M. B., & Huberman, A. M. (1984). *Qualitative data analysis: a sourcebook of new methods*. Beverly Hills, CA: Sage.

Miles, M. B., & Huberman, A. M. (1994). *Qualitative data analysis: an expanded sourcebook* (2nd ed.). Thousand Oaks, CA: Sage.

Miles, M. B., Huberman, A. M., & Saldaña, J. (2014). *Qualitative data analysis: a methods sourcebook* (3rd ed.). Thousand Oaks, CA: Sage.

Milgram, S. (1974). *Obedience to authority: an experimental view*. New York: Harper & Row.

Mills, M. (2011). Introducing survival and event history analysis. London: Sage.

Moffatt, S., White, M., Mackintosh, J., & Howel, D. (2006). Using quantitative and qualitative data in health services research – what happens when mixed method findings conflict? *BMC Health Services Research*, 6, 10. Retrieved from: www.biomedcentral.com/1472-6963/6/28 doi:10.1186/1472-6963-6-28

Molina-Azorín, J. F., Tarí, J. J., Pereira-Moliner, J., López-Gamero, M. D., & Pertusa-Ortega, E. M. (2015). The effects of quality and environmental management on competitive advantage: a mixed methods study in the hotel industry. *Tourism Management*, 50(1), 41–54. doi: 10.1016/j.tourman.2015.01.008

Moorkens, J. (2015). Consistency in translation memory corpora: a mixed methods case study. *Journal of Mixed Methods Research*, 9(1), 31–50. doi: 10.1177/1558689813508226

Moran-Ellis, J., Alexander, V. D., Cronin, A., Dickinson, M., Fielding, J., Sleney, J., & Thomas, H. (2006). Triangulation and integration: processes, claims and implications. *Qualitative Research*, 6(1), 45–59.

Morgan, D. L. (1998). Practical strategies for combining qualitative and quantitative methods: applications to health research. *Qualitative Health Research*, 8(3), 362–376.

Morgan, D. L. (2007). Paradigms lost and pragmatism regained: methodological implications of combining qualitative and quantitative methods. *Journal of Mixed Methods Research*, 1(1), 48–76. doi: 10.1177/2345678906292462

Morse, J. M. (1991). Approaches to qualitative-quantitative methodological triangulation. *Nursing Research*, 40, 120–123.

Morse, J. M. (2015). Issues in qualitatively-driven mixed-method designs: walking through a mixed-method project. In S. Hesse-Biber & B. Johnson (Eds.), *Oxford handbook of multimethod and mixed methods research inquiry* (pp. 206–222). New York: Oxford University Press.

Morse, J. M., & Niehaus, L. (2009). *Mixed method design: principles and procedures*. Walnut Creek, CA: Left Coast Press.

Moynihan, T. (1996). An inventory of personal constructs for information systems project risk researchers. *Journal of Information Technology*, 11(4), 359–371.

Myers, D. J. (1997). Racial rioting in the 1960s: an event history analysis of local conditions. *American Sociological Review*, 62(1), 94–112.

Nickel, B., Berger, M., Schmidt, P., & Plies, K. (1995). Qualitative sampling in a multi-method survey. *Quality and Quantity*, 29, 223–240.

Nightingale, A. (2003). A feminist in the forest: situated knowledges and mixing methods in natural resource management. *ACME: An International E-Journal for Critical Geographies*, 2(1), 77–90. Retrieved from: www.acme-journal.org

Niglas, K. (2004). The combined use of qualitative and quantitative methods in educational research. Tallinn, Estonia: Tallinn Pedagogical University.

Norman, G. R., & Streiner, D. L. (1994). *Biostatistics: the bare essentials*. St Louis, MO: Mosby.

O'Cathain, A. (2010). Assessing the quality of mixed methods research. In A. Tashakkori & C. Teddlie (Eds.), *Handbook of mixed methods in social and behavioral research* (2nd ed., pp. 531–555). Thousand Oaks, CA: Sage.

O'Cathain, A., Goode, J., Drabble, S. J., Thomas, K. J., Rudolph, A., & Hewison, J. (2014). Getting added value from using qualitative research with randomized controlled trials: a qualitative interview study. *Trials*, 15(1). Retrieved from: www.trialsjournal.com/content/15/1/215

O'Cathain, A., Murphy, E., & Nicholl, J. (2007). Integration and publications as indicators of "yield" from mixed methods studies. *Journal of Mixed Methods Research*, 1(2), 147–163. doi: 10.1177/1558689806299094

O'Cathain, A., Murphy, E., & Nicholl, J. (2008). Multidisciplinary, interdisciplinary or dysfunctional? Team working in mixed methods research. *Qualitative Health Research*, 18(11), 1574–1585. doi: 10.1177/1049732308325535

O'Cathain, A., & Thomas, K. J. (2004). "Any other comments?" Open questions on questionnaires – a bane or a bonus to research? *BMC Medical Research Methodology*, 4, 25. Retrieved from: http://bmcmedresmethodol.biomedcentral.com/articles/10.1186/1471-2288-4-25

Obstfeld, D. (2005). Social networks, the *tertius iungens* orientation, and involvement in innovation. *Administrative Science Quarterly*, 50, 100–130.

Olsen, W. (2014). Comment: The usefulness of QCA under realist assumptions. *Sociological Methodology*, 44(1), 101–107. doi: 10.1177/0081175014542080

Olsson, C. M. (2015). Systematic interviews and analysis: using the repertory grid technique. In P. Lankoski & S. Björk (Eds.), *Game research methods: an overview* (pp. 291–308). Halifax, Canada: ETC Press.

Onwuegbuzie, A. J., & Combs, J. P. (2010). Emergent data analysis techniques in mixed methods research. In A. Tashakkori & C. Teddlie (Eds.), *Handbook of mixed methods in social and behavioral research* (2nd ed., pp. 397–432). Thousand Oaks, CA: Sage.

Onwuegbuzie, A. J., & Hitchcock, J. (2015). Advanced mixed analysis approaches. In S. Hesse-Biber & B. Johnson (Eds.), *Oxford handbook of multimethod and mixed methods research inquiry* (pp. 275–295). New York: Oxford University Press.

Onwuegbuzie, A. J., & Teddlie, C. (2003). A framework for analyzing data in mixed methods research. In A. Tashakkori & C. Teddlie (Eds.), *Handbook of mixed methods in social and behavioral research* (pp. 351–384). Thousand Oaks, CA: Sage.

Pager, D., & Quillian, L. (2005). Walking the talk? What employers say versus what they do. *American Sociological Review*, 70(3), 355–380.

Panda, S., Das, R. S., Maruf, S. K. A., & Pahari, S. (2015). Exploring stigma in low HIV prevalence settings in rural West Bengal, India: identification of intervention considerations. *Journal of Mixed Methods Research*, 9(4), 362–385. doi: 10.1177/1558689814535843

Park, P., & Macy, M. (2015). The paradox of active users. *Big Data & Society*, 2(2), 1–4. doi: 10.1177/2053951715606164

Pastor, D. A., & Finney, S. J. (2013). Using visual displays to enhance understanding of quantitative research. In G. Schraw, M. McCrudden & D. Robinson (Eds.), *Learning through visual displays* (pp. 387–415). Charlotte, NC: Information Age Publishing.

Patton, M. Q. (2002). *Qualitative evaluation and research methods* (3rd ed.). Thousand Oaks, CA: Sage.

Patton, M. Q. (2011). Developmental evaluation: applying complexity concepts to enhance innovation and use. New York: Guilford.

Pawson, R. (2006). *Evidence-based policy*. London: Sage.

Pearce, L. D. (2015). Thinking outside the Q boxes: further motivating a mixed research perspective. In S. Hesse-Biber & B. Johnson (Eds.), *Oxford handbook of multimethod and mixed methods research inquiry* (pp. 42–56). New York: Oxford University Press.

Pearce, L. D., Foster, E. M., & Hardie, J. H. (2013). A person-centred examination of adolescent religiosity using latent class analysis. *Journal for the Scientific Study of Religion*, 52(1), 57–79.

Pelz, D. C., & Andrews, F. M. (1976). *Scientists in organisations*. Ann Arbor, MI: Institute for Social Research, University of Michigan.

Phillips, D., & Phillips, J. (2009). Visualising types: the potential of correspondence analysis. In D. Byrne & C. Ragin (Eds.), *Sage handbook of case-based methods* (pp. 148–168). London: Sage.

Plano Clark, V. L., Anderson, N., Wertz, J. A., Zhou, Y., Schumacher, K., & Miaskowski, C. (2015). Conceptualizing longitudinal mixed methods designs: a methodological review of health sciences research. *Journal of Mixed Methods Research*, 9(4), 297–319. doi: 10.1177/1558689814543563

Plano Clark, V. L., Garrett, A. L., & Leslie-Pelecky, D. L. (2010). Applying three strategies for integrating quantitative and qualitative databases in a mixed methods study of a nontraditional graduate education program. *Field Methods*, 22(2), 154–174.

Plano Clark, V. L., & Sanders, K. (2015). The use of visual displays in mixed methods research. In M. McCrudden, G. Schraw & C. W. Buckendahl (Eds.), *Use of visual displays in research and testing: coding, interpreting, and reporting data* (pp. 177–206). Charlotte, NC: Information Age Publishing.

Plano Clark, V. L., Schumacher, K., West, C., Edrington, J., Dunn, L. B., Harzstark, A., & Miaskowski, C. (2013). Practices for embedding an interpretive qualitative approach within a randomized clinical trial. *Journal of Mixed Methods Research*, 7(3), 219–242. doi: 10.1177/1558689812474372

Pluye, P., Grad, R. M., Levine, A., & Nicolau, B. (2009). Understanding divergence of quantitative and qualitative data (or results) in mixed methods studies. *International Journal of Multiple Research Approaches*, 3(1), 58–72.

Popper, K. ([1963] 2002). *Conjectures and refutations: the growth of scientific knowledge* (2nd ed.). London: Routledge Classics.

Popping, R. (2015). Analyzing open-ended questions by means of text analysis procedures. *Bulletin de Methodologie Sociologique*, 128, 23–39. doi: 10.1177/0759106315597389

Prell, C. (2012). *Social network analysis*. London: Sage.

Prell, C., & Skvoretz, J. (2008). Looking at social capital through triad structures. *Connections*, 28(2), 1–13.

Quinlan, E., & Quinlan, A. (2010). Representations of rape: transcending methodological divides. *Journal of Mixed Methods Research*, 4(2), 127–143. doi: 10.1177/1558689809359000

Ragin, C. (1987). The comparative method: moving beyond qualitative and quantitative strategies. Berkeley, CA: University of California Press.

Ragin, C., & Becker, H. (Eds.) (1992). *What is a case? Exploring the foundations of social inquiry*. New York: Cambridge University Press.

Ragin, C. C., Shulman, D., Weinberg, A., & Gran, B. (2003). Complexity, generality, and qualitative comparative analysis. *Field Methods*, 15(4), 323–340.

Rallis, S. F., & Rossman, G. B. (2003). Mixed methods in evaluation contexts: a pragmatic framework. In A. Tashakkori & C. Teddlie (Eds.), *Handbook of mixed methods in social and behavioral research* (pp. 491–512). Thousand Oaks, CA: Sage.

Reznitskaya, A., Anderson, R. C., McNurlen, B., Nguyen-Jahiel, K., Archodidou, A., & Kim, S-y. (2001). Influence of oral discussion on written argument. *Discourse Processes*, 32(2&3), 155–175.

Richards, L. (2014). *Handling qualitative data* (3rd ed.). London: Sage.

Richardson, L. (1994). Writing: a method of inquiry. In N. K. Denzin & Y. S. Lincoln (Eds.), *Handbook of qualitative research* (pp. 516–529). Thousand Oaks, CA: Sage.

Richardson, L. (2000). Writing: a method of inquiry. In N. K. Denzin & Y. S. Lincoln (Eds.), *Handbook of qualitative research* (2nd ed., pp. 923–948). Thousand Oaks, CA: Sage.

Rihoux, B., & Ragin, C. (Eds.) (2009). *Configurational comparative methods*. Thousand Oaks, CA: Sage.

Roller, E., Mathes, R., & Eckert, T. (1995). Hermeneutic-classificatory content analysis: a technique combining principles of quantitative and qualitative research. In U. Kelle (Ed.), *Computer-aided qualitative data analysis: theory, methods and practice* (pp. 167–176). Thousand Oaks, CA: Sage.

Rosenberg, B. D., Lewandowski, J. A., & Siegel, J. T. (2015). Goal disruption theory, military personnel, and the creation of merged profiles: a mixed methods investigation. *Journal of Mixed Methods Research*, 9(1), 51–69. doi: 10.1177/1558689813508006

Rossman, G. B., & Wilson, B. L. (1985). Numbers and words: combining quantitative and qualitative methods in a single large-scale evaluation study. *Evaluation Review*, 9(5), 627–643.

Rossman, G. B., & Wilson, B. L. (1994). Numbers and words revisited: being "shamelessly eclectic". *Quality and Quantity*, 28, 315–327.

Saint Arnault, D., & Fetters, M. D. (2011). RO1 funding for mixed methods research: lessons learned from the "Mixed-method analysis of Japanese depression" project. *Journal of Mixed Methods Research*, 5(4), 309–329. doi: 10.1177/1558689811416481

Saldaña, J. (2015a). *The coding manual for qualitative researchers* (3rd ed.). London: Sage.

Saldaña, J. (2015b). *Thinking qualitatively*. Thousand Oaks, CA: Sage.

Sale, J. E. M., Lohfield, L., & Brazil, K. (2002). Revisiting the quantitative–qualitative debate: implications for mixed-methods research. *Quality and Quantity*, 36, 43–53.

Sampson, F. C., O'Cathain, A., & Goodacre, S. (2010). Is primary angioplasty an acceptable alternative to thrombolysis? Quantitative and qualitative study of patient and carer satisfaction. *Health Expectations*, 9 pp. doi: 10.1111/j.1369-7625.2009.00589.x

Sánchez-Algarra, P., & Anguera, M. T. (2013). Qualitative/quantitative integration in the inductive observational study of interactive behaviour: impact of recording and coding among predominating perspectives. *Quality & Quantity*, 47, 1237–1257. doi: 10.1007/s11135-012-9764-6

Sandelowski, M. (1995). Triangles and crystals: on the geometry of qualitative research. *Research in Nursing & Health*, 18, 569–574.

Sandelowski, M. (2000). Whatever happened to qualitative description? *Research in Nursing & Health*, 23(4), 334–340.

Sandelowski, M. (2001). Real qualitative researchers do not count: the use of numbers in qualitative research. *Research in Nursing & Health*, 24(3), 230–240.

Sandelowski, M. (2003). Tables or tableaux? The challenges of writing and reading mixed methods studies. In A. Tashakkori & C. Teddlie (Eds.), *Handbook of mixed methods in social and behavioral research* (pp. 321–350). Thousand Oaks, CA: Sage.

Sandelowski, M., Voils, C. I., & Knafl, G. (2009). On quantitizing. *Journal of Mixed Methods Research*, 3(3), 208–222. doi: 10.1177/1558689809334210

Sanford, N. (1970). Whatever happened to action research? *Journal of Social Issues*, 26(4), 3–23.

Sayer, A. (2000). *Realism and social science*. London: Sage.

Schoonenboom, J., & Johnson, B. (in press). How to construct a mixed methods research design. Kölner Zeitschrift für Soziologie und Sozialpsychologie [Cologne Journal for Sociology and Social Psychology]. doi: 10.1007/s11577-017-0454-1

Schrauf, R. W. (2016). *Mixed methods: interviews, surveys, and cross-cultural comparisons*. Cambridge: Cambridge University Press.

Schrodt, P. A. (2000). Automated coding of international event data using sparse parsing techniques. Paper presented at the 5th International Conference on Logic and Methodology for the International Sociological Association, Cologne, 3–6 October.

Schrodt, P. A. (2011). Automated production of high-volume, near-real-time political event data. Paper presented at the New methodologies and their applications in comparative politics and international relations, Princeton University. Retrieved from: www.princeton.edu/~pcglobal/conferences/methods/papers/schrodt.pdf

Schulenberg, J. L. (2007). Analyzing police decision-making: assessing the application of a mixed-method/mixed-model research design. *International Journal of Social Research Methodology*, 10, 99–119. doi: 10.1080/13645570701334050

Schultz, M., & Hatch, M. J. (1996). Living with multiple paradigms: the case of paradigm interplay in organizational culture studies *Academy of Management Review*, 21(2), 529–557.

Schumacher, K. L., Koresawa, S., West, C., Dodd, M., Paul, S. M., Tripathy, D., & Miaskowski, C. (2005). Qualitative research contribution to a randomized clinical trial. *Research in Nursing & Health*, 28(3), 268–280. doi: 10.1002/nur.20080

Schwandt, T. A. (2000). Three epistemological stances for qualitative inquiry: interpretivism, hermeneutics, and social constructionism. In N. Denzin & Y. Lincoln (Eds.), *Handbook of qualitative research* (2nd ed., pp. 189–214). Thousand Oaks, CA: Sage.

Scott, J. (2013). *Social network analysis* (3rd ed.). London: Sage.

Scott, J., Tallia, A. F., Crosson, J. C., Orzano, A. J., Strobel, C., DiCicco-Bloom, B., & Crabtree, B. F. (2005). Social network analysis as an analytic tool for interaction patterns in primary care practices. *Annals of Family Medicine*, 3(5), 443–448. doi: 10.1370/afm.344

Scriven, M. (1976). Maximising the power of causal investigation: the modus operandi method. In G. V. Glass (Ed.), *Evaluation studies annual review* (Vol. 1, pp. 120–139). Beverly Hills, CA: Sage.

Seale, C. (2004). Quality in qualitative research. In C. Seale, G. Gobo, J. F. Gubrium & D. Silverman (Eds.), *Qualitative research practice* (pp. 409–419). London: Sage.

Sedgwick, P. (2013). What is a patient preference trial? *British Medical Journal*, 347. doi: 10.1136/bmj.f5970

Seltzer-Kelly, D., Westwood, S. J., & Peña-Guzman, D. M. (2012). A methodological self-study of quantitizing: negotiating meaning and revealing multiplicity. *Journal of Mixed Methods Research*, 6(4), 258–274. doi: 10.1177/1558689811425798

Shadish, W. R., Cook, T. D., & Campbell, D. T. (2002). *Experimental and quasi-experimental designs for generalized causal inference*. Boston: Houghton Mifflin.

Shaffer, D. W., & Serlin, R. C. (2004). What good are statistics that don't generalize? *Educational Researcher*, 33(9), 14–25.

Sharp, J. L., Mobley, C., Hammond, C., Withington, C., Drew, S., Stringfield, S., & Stipanovic, N. (2012). A mixed methods sampling methodology for a multisite case study. *Journal of Mixed Methods Research*, 6(1), 34–54. doi: 10.1177/1558689811417133

Shaw, J. (2014). Why "Big Data" is a big deal. Information science promises to change the world. *Harvard Magazine*, March–April.

Sheridan, J., Chamberlain, K., & Dupuis, A. (2011). Timelining: visualizing experience. *Qualitative Research*, 11(5), 552–569. doi: 10.1177/1468794111413235

Silver, C. (2015). QDA Miner (With WordStat and Simstat). *Journal of Mixed Methods Research*, 9(4), 386–387. doi: 10.1177/1558689814538833

Silver, C., & Lewins, A. (2014). Using software in qualitative research: a step by step guide (2nd ed.). London: Sage.

Silver, C., & Woolf, N. (2015). From guided-instruction to facilitation of learning: the development of Five-level QDA as a CAQDAS pedagogy that explicates the practices of expert users. *International Journal of Social Research Methodology*, 18(5), 527–543.

Simons, L. (2007). Moving from collision to integration: reflecting on the experience of mixed methods. *Journal of Research in Nursing*, 12(1), 73–83. doi: 10.1177/1744987106069514

Simpson, B., & Wilson, M. (1999). Shared cognition: mapping commonality and individuality. In J. A. Wagner (Ed.), *Advances in qualitative organization research* (Vol. 2, pp. 73–96). Stamford, CT: JAI-Emerald.

Sine, W. D., Haveman, H. A., & Tolbert, P. S. (2005). Risky business? Entrepreneurship in the new independent-power sector. *Administrative Science Quarterly*, 50(2), 200–232.

Singer, B., Ryff, C. D., Carr, D., & Magee, W. J. (1998). Linking life histories and mental health: a person centred strategy. *Sociological Methodology*, 28, 1–51.

Sivesind, K. H. (1999). Structured, qualitative comparison: between singularity and single-dimensionality. *Quality and Quantity*, 33, 361–380.

Skinner, D., Matthews, S., & Burton, L. (2005). Combining ethnography and GIS technology. In T. A. Weisner (Ed.), *Discovering successful pathways in children's development* (pp. 223–239). Chicago, IL: Chicago University Press.

Slonim-Nevo, V., & Nevo, I. (2009). Conflicting findings in mixed methods research: an illustration from an Israeli study on immigration. *Journal of Mixed Methods Research*, 3(2), 109–128. doi: 10.1177/1558689808330621

Small, M. L. (2009). "How many cases do I need?" On science and the logic of case selection in field-based research. *Ethnography*, 10(1), 5–38. doi: 10.1177/1466138108099586

Small, M. L. (2011). How to conduct a mixed methods study: recent trends in a rapidly growing literature. *Annual Review of Sociology*, 37, 57–86. doi: 10.1146/annurev.soc.012809.102657

Smith, J. K., & Heshusius, L. (1986). Closing down the conversation: the end of the quantitative-qualitative debate among educational researchers. *Educational Researcher*, 15(4), 4–12.

Smith, M. L. (1997). Mixing and matching: methods and models. In J. C. Greene & V. J. Caracelli (Eds.), *Advances in mixed-method evaluation: the challenges and benefits of integrating diverse paradigms* (pp. 73–86). San Francisco, CA: Jossey-Bass.

Smithson, M., & Verkuilen, J. (2006). *Fuzzy set theory: applications in the social sciences*. London: Sage.

Song, M.-K., Sandelowski, M., & Happ, M. B. (2010). Current practices and emerging trends in conducting mixed methods intervention studies in the health sciences. In A. Tashakkori & C. Teddlie (Eds.), *Handbook of mixed methods in social and behavioral research* (2nd ed., pp. 725–747). Thousand Oaks, CA: Sage.

Spillane, J. P. (2010). Mixing methods in randomized controlled trials (RCTs): validation, contextualization, triangulation, and control. *Educational Assessment, Evaluation and Accountability*, 22(1), 5–28. doi: 10.1007/s11092-009-9089-8

Srnka, K. J., & Köszegi, S. T. (2007). From words to numbers – how to transform rich qualitative data into meaningful quantitative results: guidelines and exemplary study. *Schmalenbach Business Review*, 59(1), 29–57.

Steele, F. (2005). Event history analysis. NCRM Methods Review Papers (NCRM/004), 1–37. Retrieved from: eprints.ncrm.ac.uk/88/1/MethodsReviewPaperNCRM-004.pdf

Steinberg, S. J., & Steinberg, S. L. (2006). Geographic information systems for the social sciences: investigating space and place. Thousand Oaks, CA: Sage.

Steinberg, S. J., & Steinberg, S. L. (2011). Geospatial analysis technology and social science research. In S. N. Hesse-Biber (Ed.), *Handbook of emergent technologies* (pp. 563–591). Oxford: Oxford University Press.

Stevens, S. S. (1946). On the theory of scales of measurement. *Science (New Series)*, 103(2684), 677–680.

Stewart-Brown, S., Tennant, A., Tennant, R., Platt, S., Parkinson, J., & Weich, S. (2009). Internal construct validity of the Warwick-Edinburgh Mental Well-being Scale (WEMWBS): a Rasch analysis using data from the Scottish Health Education Population Survey. *Health Quality of Life Outcomes*, 7(15). Retrieved from: http://hqlo.biomedcentral.com/articles/10.1186/1477-7525-7-15

Sutton, R. I., & Rafaeli, A. (1988). Untangling the relationship between displayed emotions and organizational sales: the case of convenience stores. *Academy of Management Journal*, 31(3), 461–487.

Szostak, R. (2015). Interdisciplinary and transdisciplinary mulitmethod and mixed methods research. In S. Hesse-Biber & B. Johnson (Eds.), *Oxford handbook of multimethod and mixed methods research inquiry* (pp. 128–143). New York: Oxford University Press.

Tabachnick, B. G., & Fidell, L. S. (2013). *Using multivariate statistics* (6th ed.). Boston: Pearson.

Tan, F. B., & Hunter, M. G. (2002). The repertory grid technique: a method for the study of cognition in information systems. *MIS Quarterly*, 26(1), 39–57.

Tashakkori, A., & Teddlie, C. (1998). Mixed methodology: combining qualitative and quantitative approaches. Thousand Oaks, CA: Sage.

Tashakkori, A., & Teddlie, C. (Eds.) (2010). *Handbook of mixed methods in social and behavioral research* (2nd ed.). Thousand Oaks, CA: Sage.

Teddlie, C., & Tashakkori, A. (2009). *Foundations of mixed methods research*. Thousand Oaks, CA: Sage.

Teddlie, C., & Tashakkori, A. (2010). Overview of contemporary issues in mixed methods research. In A. Tashakkori & C. Teddlie (Eds.), *Handbook of mixed methods in social and behavioral research* (2nd ed., pp. 1–41). Thousand Oaks, CA: Sage.

Teddlie, C., & Tashakkori, A. (2012). Common "core" characteristics of mixed methods research: a review of critical issues and call for greater convergence. *American Behavioral Scientist*, 56(6), 774–788. doi: 10.1177/0002764211433795

Teddlie, C., & Yu, F. (2007). Mixed methods sampling: a typology with examples. *Journal of Mixed Methods Research*, 1(1), 77–100. doi: 10.1177/2345678906292430

Teye, J. K. (2012). Benefits, challenges, and dynamism of positionalities associated with mixed methods research in developing countries: evidence from Ghana. *Journal of Mixed Methods Research*, 6(4), 379–391. doi: 10.1177/1558689812453332

Tonkin-Crine, S., Anthierens, S., Hood, K., Yardley, L., Cals, J. W. L., Francis, N. A., & Little, P. (2016). Discrepancies between qualitative and quantitative evaluation of randomised controlled trial results: achieving clarity through mixed methods triangulation. *Implementation Science*, 11(66), 1–8. doi: 10.1186/s13012-016-0436-0

Torgerson, D. J., & Sibbald, B. (1998). What is a patient preference trial? *British Medical Journal*, 316, 360.

Torrents, C., Castañer, M., Dinušová, M., & Anguera, M. T. (2010). Discovering new ways of moving: observational analysis of motor creativity while dancing contact improvisation and the influence of the partner. *Journal of Creative Behaviour*, 44(1), 53–69.

Tracy, S. J. (2013). Qualitative research methods: collecting evidence, crafting analysis, communicating impact. Chichester: Wiley-Blackwell.

Trend, M. G. (1978). On the reconciliation of qualitative and quantitative analyses: a case study. *Human Organization*, 37(4), 345–354.

Trochim, W. M. K., Milstein, B., Wood, B. J., Jackson, S., & Pressler, V. (2004). Setting objectives for community and systems change: an application of concept mapping for planning a statewide health improvement initiative. *Health Promotion Practice*, 5(1), 8–19. doi: 10.1177/1524839903258020

Tufte, E. R. (2001). *The visual display of quantitative information* (2nd ed.). Cheshire, CT: Graphics Press.

Ulrikson, M. S., & Dadalauri, N. (2016). Single case studies and theory-testing: the knots and dots of the process-tracing method. *International Journal of Social Research Methodology*, 19(2), 223–239. doi: 10.1080/13645579.2014.979718

Uprichard, E. (2009). Introducing cluster analysis: what can it teach us about the case? In D. Byrne & C. Ragin (Eds.), *Sage handbook of case-based methods* (pp. 132–147). London: Sage.

Vaisey, S. (2014). Comment: QCA works—when used with care. *Sociological Methodology*, 44(1), 108–112. doi: 10.1177/0081175014542083

Van Ness, P. H., Fried, T. R., & Gill, T. M. (2011). Mixed methods for the interpretation of longitudinal gerontologic data: insights from philosophical hermeneutics. *Journal of Mixed Methods Research*, 5(4), 293–308. doi: 10.1177/1558689811412973

Vaughan, D. (1992). Theory elaboration: the heuristics of case analysis. In C. Ragin & H. Becker (Eds.), *What is a case? Exploring the foundations of social inquiry* (pp. 173–202). New York: Cambridge University Press.

Verkuilen, J. (2005). Assigning membership in a fuzzy set analysis. *Sociological Methods & Research*, 33(4), 462–496. doi: 10.1177/0049124105274498

Vikström, L. (2010). Identifying dissonant and complementary data on women through the triangulation of historical sources. *International Journal of Social Research Methodology*, 13, 211–221. doi: 10.1080/13645579.2010.482257

Vogt, W. P. (2008). Quantitative versus qualitative is a distraction: variations on a theme by Brewer & Hunter (2006). *Methodological Innovations Online*, 3(1), 18–24. Retrieved from: http://journals.sagepub.com/doi/pdf/10.4256/mio.2008.0007

von der Lippe, H. (2010). Motivation and selection processes in a biographical transition: a psychological mixed methods study on the transition into fatherhood. *Journal of Mixed Methods Research*, 4(3), 199–221. doi: 10.1177/1558689810365149

Wagner-Pacifici, R., Mohr, J. W., & Breiger, R. L. (2015). Ontologies, methodologies, and new uses of Big Data in the social and cultural sciences [Editorial]. *Big Data & Society*, 2(2), 1–11. doi: 10.1177/2053951715613810

Wall, K., Higgins, S., Remedios, R., Rafferty, V., & Tiplady, L. (2013). Comparing analysis frames for visual data sets: using pupil views templates to explore perspectives of learning. *Journal of Mixed Methods Research*, 7(1), 22–42. doi: 10.1177/1558689812450211

Watts, S., & Stenner, P. (2005). Doing Q methodology: theory, method and interpretation. *Qualitative Research in Psychology*, 2(1), 67–91. doi: 10.1191/1478088705qp022oa

Watts, S., & Stenner, P. (2012). Doing Q methodological research: theory, method & interpretation. London: Sage.

Weaver-Hightower, M. B. (2014). A mixed methods approach for identifying influence on public policy. *Journal of Mixed Methods Research*, 8(2), 115–138. doi: 10.1177/1558689813490996

Webb, E. J., Campbell, D. T., Schwartz, R. D., & Sechrest, L. (1966). *Unobtrusive measures: nonreactive research in the social sciences*. Chicago, IL: Rand McNally.

Weine, S. (2015). Applying multimethod and mixed methods to prevention research in global health. In S. Hesse-Biber & B. Johnson (Eds.), *Oxford handbook of multimethod and mixed methods research inquiry* (pp. 447–465). New York: Oxford University Press.

Weinstein, E. A., & Tamur, J. M. (1978). Meanings, purposes, and structural resources in social interaction. In J. G. Manis & B. N. Meltzer (Eds.), *Symbolic interaction* (3rd ed., pp. 138–140). Boston: Allyn & Bacon.

Weishaar, H., Amos, A., & Collin, J. (2015). Capturing complexity: mixing methods in the analysis of a European tobacco control policy network. *International Journal of Social Research Methodology*, 18(2), 175–192. doi: 10.1080/13645579.2014.897851

Weisner, T. S. (Ed.) (2005). *Discovering successful pathways in children's development: mixed methods in the study of childhood and family life*. Chicago, IL: University of Chicago Press.

Weiss, H. B., Kreider, H., Mayer, E., Hencke, R., & Vaughan, M. A. (2005). Working it out: the chronicle of a mixed-methods analysis. In T. S. Weisner (Ed.), *Discovering successful pathways in children's development: mixed methods in the study of childhood and family life* (pp. 47–64). Chicago, IL: University of Chicago Press.

Wendler, M. C. (2001). Triangulation using a meta-matrix. *Journal of Advanced Nursing*, 35(4), 521–525. doi:10.1046/j.1365-2648.2001.01869.x

Wertz, F. J., Charmaz, K., McMullen, L. M., Josselson, R., Anderson, R., & McSpadden, E. (2011). *Five ways of doing qualitative analysis: phenomenological psychology, grounded theory, discourse analysis, narrative research, and intuitive inquiry*. New York: Guilford.

Wesely, P. M. (2010). Language learning motivation in early adolescents: using mixed methods research to explore contradiction. *Journal of Mixed Methods Research*, 4(4), 295–312. doi: 10.1177/1558689810375816

Williams, D., Ducheneaut, N., Xiong, L., Zhang, Y., Yee, N., & Nickell, E. (2006). From tree house to barracks: the social life of guilds in World of Warcraft. *Games and Culture*, 1(4), 338–361. doi: 10.1177/1555412006292616

Windsor, L. C. (2013). Using concept mapping in community-based participatory research: a mixed methods approach. *Journal of Mixed Methods Research*, 7(3), 274–293. doi: 10.1177/1558689813479175

Wisdom, J. P., & Fetters, M. (2015). Funding for mixed methods research: sources and strategies. In S. Hesse-Biber & B. Johnson (Eds.), *Oxford handbook of multimethod and mixed methods research inquiry* (pp. 314–332). New York: Oxford University Press.

Wolf, F. (2010). Enlightened eclecticism or hazardous hotchpotch? Mixed methods and triangulation strategies in comparative public policy research. *Journal of Mixed Methods Research*, 4(2), 144–167. doi: 10.1177/1558689810364987

Woods, M., Macklin, R., & Lewis, G. K. (2016). Researcher reflexivity: exploring the impacts of CAQDAS use. *International Journal of Social Research Methodology*, 19(4), 385–403. doi: 10.1080/13645579.2015.1023964

Woolley, C. M. (2009). Meeting the mixed methods challenge of integration in a sociological study of structure and agency. *Journal of Mixed Methods Research*, 3(1), 7–25. doi: 10.1177/1558689808325774

Wu, L. L. (2003). Event history models for life course analysis. In J. T. Mortimer & M. J. Shanahan (Eds.), *Handbook of the life course* (pp. 477–502). New York: Kluwer Academic/Plenum Publishers.

Yin, R. K. (1999). Enhancing the quality of case studies in health services research. *Health Services Research*, 34(5, Pt. 2), 1209–1224.

Yin, R. K. (2004). *The case study anthology*. Thousand Oaks, CA: Sage.

Yin, R. K. (2006). Mixed methods research: are the methods genuinely integrated or merely parallel? *Research in the Schools*, 13(1), 41–47.

Yin, R. K. (2012). *Applications of case study research* (3rd ed.). Thousand Oaks, CA: Sage.

Yin, R. K. (2013). Validity and generalization in future case study evaluations. *Evaluation*, 19(3), 321–332. doi: 10.1177/1356389013497081

Yin, R. K. (2014). *Case study research: design and methods* (5th ed.). Thousand Oaks, CA: Sage.

Youngs, H., & Piggot-Irvine, E. (2012). The application of a multiphase triangulation approach to mixed methods: the research of an aspiring school principal development program. *Journal of Mixed Methods Research*, 6(3), 184–198. doi: 10.1177/1558689811420696

Znaniecki, F. (1934). Analytic induction. In F. Znaniecki (Ed.), *The method of sociology* (pp. 249–331). New York: Farrar & Rinehart.

INDEX